From Cosmopolitanism to Human Rights

This collection of essays charts the question of how we might develop a democratic theory of international law. Characterised by a back-and-forth between theory and practice, it operates at two levels: a theoretical level which reflects on and criticises the categories, words and concepts through which international law is understood, and a more applied level which focuses on 'cosmopolitan building sites'. The first part of the book presents elements of a democratic theory of international law, if not a complete theory: it addresses the meaning of legal cosmopolitanism, the theory of the international constitution, questions the interpretation of humanitarian intervention and the responsibility to protect. It also engages in a more defensive path to counter recent attacks on international law, cosmopolitanism and human rights. The second part bridges theory and practice. Here the collection takes a closer look at 'cosmopolitan building sites' like the status of civil society in international organisations, the reform of the Security Council or the project of a World Court of Human Rights. It shows that international law is already embarked on a cosmopolitan process and locates these developments within the appropriate theoretical framework.

Volume 8 in the series French Studies in International Law

French Studies in International Law

General Editor: Emmanuelle Jouannet (Sorbonne Law School)

French Studies in International Law is a unique new series which aims to bring to the attention of an English-speaking audience the most important modern works by leading French and French-speaking scholars of international law. The books which appear in this series were selected by Professor Emmanuelle Jouannet of the University of Paris 1 (Sorbonne Law School). French Studies in International Law is a books collection of the IREDIES Paris 1 Sorbonne Law School (The Center of Studies and Research on International Law). The IREDIES is the largest French research Center in international law comprising 11 professors, 3 lecturers, 21 research professors and researchers, and 188 PhD students. IREDIES follows an active policy of collective work around several fields of key research, including: general international law, law of the United Nations, international dispute, international economic and finance law (in particular WTO), international human rights law, theory, philosophy and history of international law and foreign doctrines, international air space law, and the law of the sea.

Volume 1: *Ordering Pluralism: A Conceptual Framework for Understanding the Transnational Legal World* Mireille Delmas-Marty translated by Naomi Norberg

Volume 2: *International Law, Power, Security and Justice: Essays on International Law and Relations* Serge Sur

Volume 3: *The Advancement of International Law* Charles Leben

Volume 4: *The Law against War: The Prohibition on the Use of Force in Contemporary International Law* Olivier Corten

Volume 5: *What is a Fair International Society?: International Law Between Development and Recognition* Emmanuelle Tourme-Jouannet

Volume 6: *Humiliation in International Relations: A Pathology of Contemporary International Systems* Bertrand Badie

Volume 7: *The Law Against War: The Prohibition on the Use of Force in Contemporary International Law, Second Edition* Olivier Corten

Volume 8: *From Cosmopolitanism to Human Rights* Olivier de Frouville

From Cosmopolitanism to Human Rights

Olivier de Frouville

•HART•
OXFORD • LONDON • NEW YORK • NEW DELHI • SYDNEY

HART PUBLISHING

Bloomsbury Publishing Plc

Kemp House, Chawley Park, Cumnor Hill, Oxford, OX2 9PH, UK

1385 Broadway, New York, NY 10018, USA

29 Earlsfort Terrace, Dublin 2, Ireland

HART PUBLISHING, the Hart/Stag logo, BLOOMSBURY and the Diana logo are trademarks of Bloomsbury Publishing Plc

First published in Great Britain 2021

A catalogue record for this book is available from the British Library.

Library of Congress Cataloging-in-Publication data

Names: Frouville, Olivier de, author.

Title: From cosmopolitanism to human rights / Olivier de Frouville.

Description: Oxford ; New York : Hart, 2021. | Series: French studies in international law ; volume 8 | "Some of the chapters contained in this volume were originally published in English, but most of them were published in French and translated into English"—ECIP acknowledgements. | Includes bibliographical references and index.

Identifiers: LCCN 2021042751 (print) | LCCN 2021042752 (ebook) | ISBN 9781509938520 (hardback) | ISBN 9781509955510 (paperback) | ISBN 9781509938544 (pdf) | ISBN 9781509938537 (Epub)

Subjects: LCSH: International law. | Human rights. | Cosmopolitanism—Political aspects.

Classification: LCC KZ3410 .F7595 2021 (print) | LCC KZ3410 (ebook) | DDC 341—dc23/eng/20211004

LC record available at https://lccn.loc.gov/2021042751

LC ebook record available at https://lccn.loc.gov/2021042752

ISBN: HB: 978-1-50993-852-0
ePDF: 978-1-50993-854-4
ePub: 978-1-50993-853-7

Typeset by Compuscript Ltd, Shannon
Printed and bound in Great Britain

Series Editor's Preface

This Series aims to contribute to the dissemination in English of the works of the most eminent international law scholars writing in French. Because these works have not yet been published in English, this scholarship is inaccessible to a great number of potential readers who, due to the language barrier, cannot become acquainted with or discuss it. This is highly regrettable, as it limits the debate on international law to works in English – the *lingua franca* of our contemporary world – and thus primarily to Anglophone scholars.

The publication of these works in English therefore seeks to create the conditions for genuine debate among Francophone and Anglophone international law scholars across the globe, a debate that should ideally be based on the work of both. *Learning* of the others' theories through translation is in fact the first essential step towards *acknowledging* the contributions and differences of each. Knowledge and acknowledgement lead to understanding the core of irreducibility, as well as truth, in each legal culture's international law doctrine, its traditions and distinct ideas, as well as each author's way of thinking. They should make it possible to avoid the all-too-frequent misunderstanding of each other's position on international law that results from simple ignorance of each other's work. Between the Francophone and Anglophone worlds, the rule is still too often mutual, even courteous indifference or ignorance, dialogue the exception.

Emmanuelle Jouannet
Professor, University of Paris I *(Sorbonne Law School))*

Preface

There is a fascinating relationship between the history of social forms and the history of our ideas about social forms. They are separate histories but they interact permanently and vigorously. Old ideas can hinder social progress. New ideas can encourage social progress. Ideas can sponsor both revolution and reaction.

In an excellent phrase Jules Michelet described the history of France as *le travail de soi sur soi*. He had rediscovered Giambattista Vico, eccentric philosopher of history, whose work had been largely forgotten. In his *Scienza Nova* (1725) Vico had explored the influence of social ideas on social reality in a strikingly original way. The human species has humanised and civilised itself through the creative use of language. Vico's central metaphor is that of poetry. But it is much more than a metaphor. Society is a work of social poetry. Society tells an every-changing story about itself and about the universe. In his *Éléments d'Idéologie* (1817-18) Antoine Destutt de Tracy gave us the idea of ideology as the study of such society-forming ideas, a word which would have a troubled second life in the twentieth century.

A great debate in the French eighteenth century centred on disputes about the meaning of the long history of France. Should its past ideas about itself rule the present or did they contain the possibility of a different future? D'Alembert said that a function of public intellectuals is 'to fix the use of language'. The English example of party politics ruled by public opinion was seen by Montesquieu as a descent into anarchy. The problem of involving the people in the politics of government was resolved in the grandiose social poem that is written in the French Constitution of 1795, so different from the US Constitution of 1787.

The problem is that words may become things with great social force in the real world, things that people may live and die for. The American revolutionaries might suppose that they were creating a new nation on a blank sheet of paper, but it was paper covered with nine centuries of English constitutional history. In defence of their rebellion they themselves invoked 'the rights and liberties of the English people' from Anglo-Saxon times.

The French revolutionaries, in the *Jeu de Paume* oath, undertook 'to fix the constitution' of France knowing that they were intruding into 10 centuries of French constitutional history. They argued passionately about the right words to choose in making a new future. Revolution, constitution, nation, sovereignty, state, representation, estates, citizen, rights, duties. They produced something that did determine the future of France in the real world, something that people would live and die for.

The debate about the past and future of the international social system is now intense and urgent. It must also centre on the use of language in new ideas drawn from the past and liable to have great social force, but capable of making a better future. The human world is facing a big problem of social re-imagining.

The history of international law since the end of the fifteenth century up to the present day is a vivid example of the tortuous relationship between ideology and social reality. 1492 was a Copernican moment for the Eurocentric view of the human world. Our violent intrusion into a transatlantic New World posed a new challenge. We had always known that there was a vast and ancient human world beyond Europe, but we had not integrated it into our social and legal worldview. How should we treat these people who seemed to have complex social forms of their own and their own social histories? Europe's social cosmology which had seemed to be a rational construction revealed itself to be inadequate to explain a new and complex human social world.

Since 1945 we have gradually realised that the cosmology of the human world that we had inherited from Grotius and Vattel is wholly inadequate to explain the dramatically new and complex human world that has emerged since then. It is no longer merely a world of a number of states existing in a horizontal relationship whose social processes are diplomacy and war manipulated by the executive branches of the governments of those states.

International law now intrudes into national society in a vigorous reciprocal relationship with national law. International law has had to examine its own underlying high values, analogous to the high values that are present in all well-ordered national societies. International law has had to concern itself at last with the common good of humanity, analogous to the common good that national law serves in all well-ordered national societies. International law has had to reconsider the institutional structure required by the newly emerging international society, as national societies must constantly review and renew their constitutional structures. International lawyers have had to consider what a true international Rule of Law might be.

In his scholarly writing and in his professional activity, Olivier de Frouville is participating in the exciting development of the new international social reality and in its new self-imagining. The chapters in the present volume, in their exceptional breadth and depth, are an eloquent expression of the contribution he is making to the new human cosmology.

Philip Allott
Professor Emeritus of International Public Law,
University of Cambridge

Acknowledgements

This book would not have been possible without Emmanuelle Tourme-Jouannet, the director of this collection at Hart Publishing. Emmanuelle has been a fantastic intellectual inspiration from the time I began working on my PhD thesis. After completing this early work, she encouraged me to pursue tortuous paths, following jurisprudential orientations that were not necessarily well considered by all international lawyers. Emmanuelle's extraordinary contribution to the history of international law and to a critical theory of international law is well known. In addition, she has always been passionate about building bridges between French and English speaking international lawyers. She founded the 'Doctrine(s)' series at Pedone in France and, symmetrically, the 'French Studies in International Law' series at Hart. In addition to being such a mentor and being so friendly, Emmanuelle cares about people – and sometimes it seems hard to imagine how to reciprocate. I suppose there is no point in trying to do so, for Emmanuelle is the kind of person – like Jacques Phytilis to whom I dedicated the first piece of this volume – who gives without any particular expectations. Only deep gratitude remains to express what I owe to her.

Another person who counted greatly in the course of writing these essays is Philip Allott. I met Philip on the 'barricades of the mind'[1] somewhere around Trinity College, Cambridge, England. From that moment, I became passionate about his work and extremely fond of the man. Philip is a sort of archetypal scholar – a 'savant' and, for a Frenchman living in the UK, the very best of the British intellectual tradition and spirit – 'l'esprit anglais par excellence'. Philip Allott's *Eunomia* and his other works literally empowered me at a time when I needed a renewed confidence in the power of ideas. Not only the substance of his work, but also the style of writing and the humanity of the man convinced me that 'the only power over power is the power of ideas'.[2] I now stand on his side of the barricade. I would like to express my deepest gratitude to him for agreeing to write the preface to this book.

Some of the chapters contained in this volume were originally published in English, but most of them were published in French and translated into English. I wish to warmly thank Mr Christopher Sutcliffe for translating most

[1] P Allott, 'The Idealist's dilemma', International Law Association British Branch, Spring Conference, King's College London – Inner Temple, London, 23–24 May 2014.

[2] ibid.

of these articles, including the most difficult ones such as 'What is Legal Cosmopolitanism?' I would also like to express my deep appreciation to Rachel Forster for her translation of chapter 12 'The Universal Declaration of Human Rights is 70 Years Old: What Challenges Await the United Nations?' and for the revisions on several other articles. Also, I wish to address my many thanks for helping me with my English to Christopher Hall for his careful reading of 'On the Theory of the International Constitution', Augusta Rentenbach who, as an intern at the Paris Human Rights Center, provided very useful advice on certain linguistic issues and to Edouard Beuve-Méry for revising the introduction.

And finally, Hart publishing and its staff, especially the editorial director Sinéad Moloney, were invaluable in carrying out this project.

Many others deserve to be thanked here, in particular for inviting me to give conferences and encouraging me to deepen my reflection on certain questions, some of which I initially had not thought of. I am thinking in particular of Denis Alland, Denis Baranger, Olivier Beaud, Laurence Boisson de Chazournes, Gesa Dannenberg, Emmanuel Decaux, Edouard Dubout, Pierre-Marie Dupuy, Francesco Francioni, Antoine Garapon, Andreas Helmis, Justine Lacroix, Ludovic Hennebel, Phil Lynch, Géraldine Muhlmann, Alexandra Novosselof, Anne Peters, Vincent Ploton, Jean-Yves Pranchère, Valéry Pratt, Stéphane Rials, Marie-Clotilde Runavot, William A. Schabas, Serge Sur, Hélène Tigroudja, Sébastien Touzé, Marc Weller, and Valentine Zuber.

Contents

Introduction

This book is a collection of essays written from 2012 to 2018 as part of my research project at the French University Institute (*Institut Universitaire de France*). The project is called 'Around a Democratic Theory of International Law' and was developed while I was on research leave in 2011–12 in Cambridge (United Kingdom), benefitting from a fellowship at Clare Hall and at the Lauterpacht Center of International Law. The project was based on a factual conclusion increasingly shared amongst international lawyers: the inability of the 'classical' theory of international law, based on the principle of sovereignty, to explain most contemporary developments in international law and, above all, on a prospective level, to meet the challenges of globalisation. In the nineteenth century, the main problem for international law was to ensure peaceful coexistence between sovereign entities – that is, states that consider themselves as monads, completely autonomous both within their borders and in their external relations with other states. Today, the fundamental question is no longer that of the coexistence of states – for this coexistence is no longer a choice, it is a necessity insofar as all countries are interdependent, in a finite world. The contemporary problem of international law is now primarily the defence and survival of humanity against a number of global threats.

Continuing to consider sovereignty as the founding principle of international law in this context not only prevents us from understanding the current process of development of contemporary international law, but also, more seriously, deprives us of the means to conceptualise the conditions of possibility of its legitimacy. And it is no less dangerous to try to build an international order on the basis of the selfishness of nations and sovereign states than it is to try to develop a global law that, deprived of any guarantee of legitimacy, could well become the vehicle for a new imperialism. As Jürgen Habermas points out, the world is now caught in a risky transition:

> Halfway between the order of nation states and the cosmopolitan order, it is unclear what is the most dangerous: the declining world of the sovereign subjects of international law that have long since lost their innocence or the unclear situation of supranational institutions and conferences, which are certainly able to acquire a legitimacy of borrowing, but are still relying on the goodwill of States and alliances detaining power.[1]

[1] J Habermas, 'Le débat interculturel sur les droits de l'homme' in J Habermas, *L'intégration républicaine* (Paris, Fayard, 1996) 245–56, 246 (personal translation).

In the face of these challenges, the development of alternative theories of international law appeared to me as a necessity. I had already tried to clarify the basis of what I called a 'democratic conception of international law' in an earlier article published in 2001.[2] The question I was asking myself in 2011–12 was whether it would be possible to move from a democratic 'conception' – which is normative in its content – to a democratic 'theory' of international law, the purpose of which would be to provide the conceptual tools necessary to develop a coherent and faithful account of the evolution of contemporary international law. Central to the theory was Kant's argument that modern law should not be defined solely as a command of authority, but must be understood as the exercise of collective autonomy in order to institute the autonomy of each individual in a given society. This does not mean that law *should* or *must* preserve autonomy, but that autonomy is a necessary concept for understanding law as a phenomenon. In this sense, the theory I have begun to elaborate can be called a *cosmopolitan theory of international law* in at least two respects: it is based on a *monist* conception of law, in the sense that it recognises that international law and national laws are not separate but part of a global legal order; it seeks to describe the phenomenon of law in a world-society having engaged in a process of cosmopolitan transition.[3]

Methodologically, my research has always been characterised by a back-and-forth between theory and practice. When I started working on my thesis at the University of Paris-Nanterre in 1995, I also started to get involved in practice at the United Nations as a representative of an international NGO. From there, I continued to practice in the fields I was investigating scientifically, to the point that the two activities became interdependent.[4] This back and forth led me to conduct my research on three levels: (i) a very *practical and technical level*, considering and using law as a practicing lawyer; (ii) *an intermediate level*, between practice and theory, involving myself in institutional engineering and a reformist agenda in international law in what I call my 'cosmopolitan building sites'; (iii) and finally at the *theoretical level*, by pursuing the aim of changing the categories, words and concepts through which the phenomenon of international law as it exists today is generally understood, in order to better apprehend and understand the phenomenon of international law as it develops.

Very often, international law theorists lose sight of the technicalities and constraints of 'real' international law in 'real' social life, leading them to

[2] O de Frouville, 'Une conception démocratique du droit international' (2001) XXXIX *Revue européenne des sciences sociales (Cahiers Vilfredo Pareto)* 101–44.

[3] For a more in-depth presentation, see in particular this volume, ch 7, 'Towards a Democratic Theory of International Law'.

[4] In the period 2011–18, I held the position of member and then Chair-Rapporteur of the United Nations Working Group on Enforced or Involuntary Disappearances (from 2008 to 2014) and of member of the United Nations Human Rights Committee (from 2015 to 2018).

formulate abstract reasoning and unworkable propositions. Conversely, legal practitioners tend to ignore their own theoretical assumptions in 'doing law' and thus lose the chance to discern that things that 'have always been done' in this way could be done differently. Practitioners do not necessarily lack imagination, but their reformist proposals are driven more by opportunity than by a clear vision of the desired solution. 'Thoughts without content are empty; intuitions without concepts are blind.'[5]

The back and forth between practice and theory has allowed me, I hope, to avoid these two perils: my practice has informed my theoretical thoughts and theory has 'given sight' to my practice.

Of course, 'holding together' practice and theory has not been without its challenges – for it has led me to live a kind of 'double-life'. And this explains to some extent the detours I have sometimes made, and also that my plans have changed between the beginning of this research and the publication of this book.

The essays collected do not cover my strictly 'technical'/legal works, in particular in the fields of human rights law and international criminal law.

The first part of the book brings together a number of contributions that operate at the theoretical level. Although they do not constitute, taken as a whole, a complete 'theory', they represent parts and pieces, 'elements', as I called them, of what could be a democratic theory of international law. The chapters are not presented in chronological order. Rather, I have tried to organise them in a logical sequence. It starts with a chapter I wrote between 2011 and 2013, which, although I consider it as a 'sidestep' in my reflections on cosmopolitan law is, I think, a good starting point: 'What is Legal Cosmopolitanism?'[6] does not aim to conceptualise cosmopolitan law, but rather to answer the question: *why* does cosmopolitan law exist? To do this, I used the phenomenology of the relation to the other, as developed by several philosophers, from Husserl to Ricoeur. Specifically, I was intrigued by the basic fact that we have 'cosmopolitan emotions' for the other across borders, but that most of the time these emotions are nipped in the bud, and that international law actually participates in the 'nipping' by asserting that *there is nothing we can do* to help the suffering other. I then realised that law itself participates in framing our own feelings to give rise to 'sentiments': classical international law favoured patriotism, but increasingly international law – subject to a process of cosmopolitisation – gives right to our

[5] I Kant, *The Critique of Pure Reason* [1781], tr M Weigelt based on M Müller, 2nd edn (London, Penguin Books, 2007) 86.

[6] Originally published in French as 'Qu'est-ce que le cosmopolitisme juridique ?' in O de Frouville (ed), *Le cosmopolitisme juridique. Actes du colloque international des 21–23 novembre 2013 à l'Université Panthéon-Assas* (Paris, Pedone, 2015) 11–54. This article is dedicated to the memory of Jacques Phytilis, who happened to be both a close family member and also my Professor of History of Law in my early years at the faculty of law.

cosmopolitan feelings: under the Universal Declaration of Human Rights, not only do we have a right, but we also have an obligation to care about how the remote other is treated in a world of sovereign states. The question of the relation to others is no different, whether it applies to the near or remote other. Only the structuring of the world into sovereign states has led us to believe that the problem of my relation to the remote other might be different from my relation to the nearby other.

The two following chapters do not explain but apply a democratic theory of international law to two distinct theoretical problems: the concept of 'international constitution' and the justification of humanitarian intervention. 'On the Theory of the International Constitution' was originally published in English in a volume dedicated to one of my masters, Professor Pierre-Marie Dupuy.[7] It deliberately breaks with the dominant approach to 'constitutionalism' in international law and instead assumes *there is* indeed a constitution of international law. Georges Scelle is a starting point in this perspective. But I am led to formulate a critique of a theory of Scelle, in the light of a democratic definition of law, which rearticulates a systematic link between facticity, legitimacy and validity. This is the opportunity to introduce the tenets of a democratic theory of international law, from which I can deduce a proposal for a theory of the international constitution, combining two sets of concepts: autocracy/democracy and anarchy/federal state – reflecting the entire diversity of constitutional experiences, and allowing a kind of 'mapping out' of the evolution of the international constitution over time.

'A Cosmopolitan Perspective on the Responsibility to Protect' was developed during my visiting fellowship at Cambridge, and the main ideas were presented at a lecture at the Lauterpacht Center for International Law at the University of Cambridge on 11 May 2012.[8] The final version was the object of a communication at the University Paris II in the same year, before being originally published in French in *Droits*,[9] thanks to professors Denis Alland and Stéphane Rials. In this chapter, I wanted to focus on what I consider to be the central problem of all theories of law, namely the use of 'legitimate' violence. At the same time, I was interested in the so-called

[7] 'On the Theory of the International Constitution' in D Alland, V Chetail, O de Frouville and J Viñuales (eds), *Unité et diversité du droit international. Ecrits en l'honneur du professeur Pierre-Marie Dupuy* (Leiden/Boston, Brill/Nijhoff, 2014) 77–103. On the same topic, see also, in French, 'Le paradigme de la constitutionnalisation vu du droit international' in S Hennette-Vauchez and JM Sorel (eds), *Les droits de l'Homme ont-ils 'constitutionnalisé le monde'? Retour sur la construction savante du droit européen des droits de l'homme, à l'occasion du 60ème anniversaire de la Convention européenne des droits de l'homme* (Brussels, Bruylant, 2011) 193–216; 'Une théorie non-constitutionnaliste de la constitution internationale' (2018) 19 *Jus Politicum. Revue de droit politique, Institut Michel Villey* 95–103.

[8] The text of the conference given in Cambridge is unpublished, but the video is available online.

[9] 'Perspectives du droit cosmopolitique sur la responsabilité de protéger' (2014) 57 *Droits* 95–118.

'humanitarian intervention', which I saw as an attempt to give right to a cosmopolitan feeling, *despite* the structure of international law based on the equality of sovereign states. The world of sovereign states is governed by the principle of non-intervention, which also applies, in principle, when citizens of a state are subjected to mass persecution by their governments. Cosmopolitan feelings imply intervention to rescue these human beings from their persecutors, but international law strictly prohibits such action for good reasons based on the need to preserve the independence of peoples. This has led to the intervention conundrum, as expressed clearly after the NATO intervention in Kosovo by the UN Secretary General, Kofi Annan, opposing 'two sovereignties', that of the state, and that of the individual.[10] An attempt to answer the conundrum emerged as the 'Responsibility to protect' (R2P), which, at the time of writing the article, still seemed to be a way out. As some have been tempted to see the R2P as a cosmopolitan doctrine, I argue that this is not the case and that, rather, the R2P can be analysed as a poorly fitting patchwork of doctrines. Instead, I propose a reconstruction of what I believe can be considered as a 'truly' cosmopolitan theory of humanitarian intervention, based on the tenets of a democratic theory of international law.

The following three chapters offer a different standpoint. They were written in the same period, between 2014 and 2018, which has seen a rise in criticism of modernity and human rights, not only in intellectual and academic circles, but also at the political level. Populist and nationalist parties have emerged in the wake of the 2008 economic crisis and austerity policies, promising to regain control of the destiny of nations against 'cosmopolitan elites'. As I recall, on 2 October 2016, the Conservative British Prime Minister Theresa May famously declared: '[I]f you believe you're a citizen of the world, you're a citizen of nowhere'. In a brief and striking mode, it encapsulated the spirit of the times, which seemed to eerily echo that of the inter-war period, when fascists and stalinists cried 'rootless cosmopolitans'. It became clear to me (and to many others) that the time when we could be satisfied with positively constructing theoretical schemes was over. We could not limit ourselves to 'internal' debates among cosmopolitans or even international lawyers. We had to take a defensive stance and justify our assumptions in the face of critics who have gained growing popular support – otherwise supporters of democracy, human rights, multilateralism and international law would soon be submerged by the populist wave. 'Justifying International Law, Defending Cosmopolitanism' was written to honour another master, Professor Emmanuel Decaux, who also was my PhD supervisor.[11] It is a defence against what I understood as the three main ideas underlying most

[10] See K Annan, 'Two concepts of sovereignty', *The Economist* (18 September 1999).

[11] 'Justifier le droit international, défendre le cosmopolitisme' in *Réciprocité et universalité. Sources et régimes du droit international des droits de l'Homme. Mélanges en l'honneur d'Emmanuel Decaux* (Paris, Pedone, 2017) 1159–78.

criticisms of international law and cosmopolitanism, generally expressed by philosophers: cosmopolitanism is allegedly nothing but the other face of neoliberalism; cosmopolitanism supposedly contributes to the formation of rootless individuals driven by self-interests alone; and any world politics is supposedly impossible both in theory and in practice.

'A Critical Defence of Human Rights' was written on the occasion of a conference organised by my colleagues Sébastien Touzé and Edouard Dubout in Paris in 2017.[12] It focuses on the critiques of human rights by lawyers themselves. I distinguish between an 'internal' critical approach, purporting to pertain to legal positivism, which developed in the 1990s, and an 'external' critical approach which seeks input from judgement criteria outside positive law, particularly in philosophy. In this second category, I oppose a critical approach that generally challenges 'rights', to a critical approach, that I support, that defends human rights.

The next chapter could also be considered in some way defensive, although it does not have the same structure of reasoning, but rather takes the shape of critical approach to 'natural law'. Written on the occasion of a conference organised at the University of Aix-Marseille in 2014 where I was invited to speak about the 'topicality of natural law in international law',[13] it was first of all an opportunity for me to come back on the discourse of sovereignty and voluntarism, as a basis for modern international law, and to repeat that these belonged to 'natural law', as it had already been established in the 1930s by Georges Scelle and Hans Kelsen. It is this natural law dimension that human rights helped to unveil after 1945, by refocusing on the individual as a subject of international law, behind or beyond the state. But then the critic had to go further and recognise that human rights were also, in themselves, a discourse belonging to natural law: it too, told a fable of the world, and could be accused of being anthropocentric and of 'naturalising' the domination of the human race over the rest of the living on earth. It was a way for me to introduce the questioning on 'nature' that I think must be part of any cosmopolitan theory, if it is to pretend to be a genuine cosmopolitics. Some at that time were already drawing conclusions that there was an unsurpassable contradiction between human rights as belonging to the general framework of modernity, and the reconciliation of humans with the rest of the living on earth. My conclusion is different and is based on the idea of the acknowledgement of two distinct though non-equivalent 'autonomies': that of humans, and that of 'nature' considered in its diversity. This is a way, I think, to take leave of natural law, without falling into *hubris*. As Kelsen

[12] 'L'état des critiques dans le champ juridique: un déni?' in E Dubout and S Touzé (eds), *Refonder les droits de l'Homme. Des critiques aux pratiques* (Paris, Pedone, 2019) 77–97.

[13] 'L'actualité du droit naturel en droit international' out of series (March 2016) *Revue Québecoise de droit international* 43–55.

taught us, relinquishing the mirage of absolute knowledge is the beginning of positivist thinking.[14]

Finally, this first part ends up with an overview of the foundations and of the main tenets of a democratic theory of international law. Presented in the context of two conferences given in 2017,[15] 'towards a democratic theory of international law' is a way of summing up the main conclusions of my research from 2011 onwards, and at the same time of explaining to myself and to readers why there is a need for such a theory and what are the main conceptual and legal tools I have used to analyse various issues in contemporary international law.

The pieces gathered in the second part of the book correspond to the second or intermediate level as defined above: between theory and practice, or what I often call my 'cosmopolitan building sites'. Cosmopolitan law and world citizenship are often said to be 'projects' for the future, generally considered to be largely utopian. My main point is that this is wrong and that cosmopolitan law and world citizenship already exist, although not in the systematic way that most lawyers expect. Lawyers – even international lawyers – cannot generally help thinking of law as state law and judging legal phenomena by taking an ideal image of state law as a model. That is: state law as a complete 'legal order' – the supposedly Kelsenian ideational pyramid, growing from the fundamental norm to the individual norms, with the organs and institutions necessary to create, adjudicate and apply these norms. But law can present itself in a much less 'ordered' and systematic or systemic manner. In particular, international law is more of a patchwork than as a system: it is composed of various layers of normativity, some of which have universal reach, others of which are simply relative, and is an assemblage of norms expressing various interests, ideologies, beliefs, or moral tenets. The multiplication of legal orders within the international legal order – with hundreds of international organisations producing their own laws – and the growing expansion of regional or sub-regional orders add to the complexity.

[14] H Kelsen, 'Natural Law Doctrine and Legal Positivism' in *General Theory of Law and State*, tr A Wedberg (Cambridge, MA, Harvard University Press, 1945) Appendix, 433–34: 'Even a philosophy which is free of metaphysics and based only on scientific experience must remain conscious of the eternal secret which surrounds the world of experience on all sides. Only blindness or delusion could presume to deny the riddle of the universe, or declare it scientifically soluble. It is the attitude of the philosophical ideal type under discussion, which alone deserves to be called "scientific", that it stops before the ultimate enigma which it freely recognise, because it is conscious of the limitations of human knowledge. It is a self-discipline of the human mind which is as conscious of its vigor as of its unsurpassable limitations.'

[15] Global public law lecture, at the invitation of Ludovic Hennebel and Hélène Tigroudja, Aix-Marseille University, 27 April 2017. And a conference at the University of Cergy-Pontoise, organised by Marie-Clotilde Runavot on 9 June 2017 on 'Democracy as applied to international law: what are we speaking about?' The article published here in English is unpublished. A first and shorter version was published previously in French: 'Vers une théorie démocratique du droit international ?' in MC Runavot (ed), *La démocratie appliquée au droit international : de quoi parle-t-on?* (Paris, Pedone, 2018) 143–52.

As a result, international law can be said to be, in parts, classical interstate law, but in other parts, cosmopolitan law. International human rights law, for instance, is clearly cosmopolitan in its inspiration and foundations, but institutionally partly cosmopolitan (the independent experts and the UN secretariat components of the system) and partly interstate (the intergovernmental components of the system), the two parts being closely intertwined and interdependent. In this context, it is also not accurate to present world citizenship as a mere project, let alone a utopia. As I write this, I am already a citizen of my own state, a European citizen, but also a citizen of the world. Different rights and prerogatives belong to all three levels, and I certainly have more rights as a French citizen than I do as a European citizen and even more so as a world citizen. But having the right, for instance, to complain before the United Nations Human Rights Committee or before the Special Rapporteur on Freedom of Association and Assembly, makes me a citizen, just as my fellow-citizen, in this respect, from Belarus, Cameroon, Colombia or Nepal. Building cosmopolitan law and world citizenship, therefore, in this perspective, is not necessarily about creating *ex nihilo* new state-like institutions (such as a World Parliament, a World Government etc) but rather considering existing international institutions in their cosmopolitan aspects, and reforming these institutions so as to value and maximise these aspects. This is my purpose when writing about specific institutions while often being practically involved in institutional engineering at the United Nations.

For this publication, I have chosen three 'cosmopolitan building sites': the status of civil society in international organisations; the reform of the universal system for the protection of human rights; and the reform of the working methods of the Security Council and the right of veto of permanent members. In this selection, I have chosen to include two types of articles: typical 'academic' pieces and shorter articles published in newspapers or online. These combined formats illustrate the strong connection between academic research and concrete proposals made in the public debate. The three chosen themes, taken together, could be a significant part of a cosmopolitan reformist agenda in international law. With the possible exception of the proposal to abolish the right of veto at the Security Council, all ideas developed in this part do not imply radical change, but rather mere 'improvements' to existing institutions.

Civil society organisations are already present and actively involved in all stages of the work of international organisations. In a piece that was originally presented for the European Society of International Law conference at the University of Geneva at the invitation of Professor Laurence Boisson de Chazournes,[16] I argue that despite this reality, the participation

[16] 'Le rôle de la société civile dans les organisations internationales : théorie(s) et pratique(s)' ESIL Lecture Series, Geneva, 31 October 2017, at the invitation of Laurence Boisson de Chazournes. The English version presented here is a revised version of the original conference

of civil society in international organisations remains an unthought-of point. Better conceptualising this reality would allow for better regulation of the activities of non-state actors internationally and would improve the system overall. More substantively, it would contribute to the promotion and realisation of the right to participate in public affairs at the global level, and thus democratise international organisations.[17]

The second piece concerns the universal system of human rights protection. This system not only already exists, but is strong and well entrenched in international law. However, it still needs to be vigorously defended, as a number of states and other actors are constantly trying to weaken it in order to, they believe, protect their short-term interests. And it is far from optimal, and still needs to be improved and also better funded. The article was written for a collective book at the invitation of William A Schabas and Cherif Bassiouni.[18] They were themselves trying to provide inputs to the then High Commissioner for Human Rights, Navi Pillay, who had called on academics and civil society organisations to come up with new ideas to reform in particular the treaty body system, but also to give a new impulse to the Human Rights Council – created in 2006 but to be reviewed in 2011. My contribution focused on the Council and attempted to assess the added value of the Council to the protection of human rights worldwide. It also supported the idea of the creation of a World Court of Human Rights – as originally proposed by Julia Kozma, Manfred Nowak and Martin Scheinin in 2010 – and introduced the proposal for the creation of a 'World Commission of Human Rights', which would be composed of independent experts. Unfortunately the proposal of a 'World Court' was not well understood by states and even by civil society organisations. It was even subject to rebuttal, including by United Nations experts or academics who could

presented in French. The French version is unpublished but the video of the conference is available online.

[17] On the status of civil society in international organisation, see also O de Frouville, 'Domesticating Civil Society in the United Nations' in PM Dupuy and L Vierucci (eds), *NGOs in International Law. Efficiency in Flexibility?* (Cheltenham, Edward Elgar, 2008) 71–115; and 'La place de la société civile dans les organisations internationales: quelle stratégie pour la France au XXIème siècle?' in G Cahin, S Szurek and F Poirat (eds), *La France et les organisations internationales au XXIème siècle* (Paris, Pedone, 2014) 295–325. And on the broader issue of the right to participation in international organisations, O de Frouville, 'Vers une démocratie continue à l'échelle globale? Nouvelles perspectives sur le droit de participer aux affaires publiques' *in Mélanges en l'honneur du Professeur Dominique Rousseau. Constitution, justice, démocratie*, (Paris, LGDJ, 2020) 395–407.

[18] 'Building a Universal System for the Protection of Human Rights: The Way Forward' in C Bassiouni and WA Schabas (eds), *New Challenges for the UN Human Rights Machinery* (Cambridge, Intersentia, 2011) 229–53. See also on the same topic 'Strengthening the Rule of Law. The Right to an Effective Remedy for Victims of Human Rights Violations. Contribution to the Vienna+20 Event' in J Kozma, M Nowak and A Müller-Funk (eds), *Vienna+20. Advancing the Protection of Human Rights – Achievements, Challenges and Perspectives 20 Years after the World Conference* (Vienna, Neuer Wissenschaftlicher Verlag, 2013) 125–35.

not be suspected of being hostile to human rights, quite the contrary.[19] At a certain point – and being a member of the Human Rights Committee at the time and thus having to deal with individual complaints before a 'universal' expert body – I felt it necessary to revisit the concept of a World Court and to respond to the reasonable objections that had been raised. In the piece which is translated[20] here – and the first version of which was presented in French at a conference held in Strasbourg at the European Court of Human Rights in March 2018 – I speak rather of a 'United Nations Human Rights Court', so as to underscore that the idea – far from utopian – is inscribed in the somehow 'natural' becoming of individual complaint mechanisms as already existing before the nine committees created under the nine 'core conventions' of the United Nations. The project to create a United Nations Human Rights Court in this perspective should not be seen as a revolution, but rather as a further refinement of an already existing procedural framework. To complement these two chapters, I have added two brief contributions. The first is a blog post about the human rights treaty body system (the 'committees') in 2020 and beyond.[21] 2020 was supposed to be a key date for the treaty bodies, as it officially marked the end of a 'strengthening' process for the system initiated by General Assembly resolution 68/268 in 2014.[22] In this post, I advocate for short-term measures, but also for longer-term reforms, including the project of a Court, as detailed in the previous chapter. The second short piece was originally published online in *The Conversation* on the occasion of the 70th anniversary of the Universal Declaration for Human Rights, on 10 December 2018. I am taking a broader view on the future of international human rights law and the challenges it is expected to face in the next 10 years, which are not only institutional (the procedures and institutions), normative (new topics such as surveillance or climate change) but also intellectual (the rise of the anti-Enlightenment school of thought and their success in politics).

Last but not least, the Security Council is the central element of the post-World War II international constitutional order. Not only is it charged with 'maintaining peace and security', but it has grown over time as a world oligarchic power governing all matters related to international peace and security.

[19] See in particular P Alston, 'Against a World Court for Human Rights' (2004) 28(2) *Ethics and International Affairs* 197–212.

[20] 'Pourquoi nous avons besoin d'une Cour des droits de l'Homme des Nations Unies ?' in N Aloupi, DP Fernandez Arroyo, C Kleiner, LA Sicilianos and S Touzé (eds), *Les droits humains comparés. A la recherche de l'universalité des droits humains. Actes du colloque à la Cour européenne des droits de l'homme des 8 et 9 mars 2018* (Paris, Pedone, 2019) 129–61.

[21] Originally published on 21 November 2019 on openglobalrights.org, in three languages, French, Spanish and English.

[22] For an update on the '2020 process' in times of pandemia, see O de Frouville, 'The United Nations Treaty Bodies in a Transition Period – Progress Review March-December 2020 Chronicle', Working Paper, Geneva Academy/Paris Human Rights Center, June 2021 at www.geneva-academy.ch/geneva-humanrights-platform/ressources.

Its quasi-legislative power, its power to decide on sanctions against states or individuals and even to authorise or decide to resort to the use of armed force by states has turned it into a de facto cosmopolitan institution – a global legal actor. This chapter is an updated translation of an article originally written at the invitation of Alexandra Novosseloff and the *Centre Thucydide* of the *Université Panthéon-Assas* for a book on the Security Council.[23] More specifically, I was asked to think about reforming the Council 'without amending the UN Charter'. I was able to show that the reform was already underway and that, in fact, much progress had been made in providing more transparency, participation and accountability to the procedures of the Security Council. These changes are analysed through the lens of a democratic theory of international law. Despite the progress, I conclude that two issues remain unaddressed for the moment. One is the submission of the Security Council to the Rule of law. Article 24(2) provides for the Council to act in accordance with the purposes and principles of the United Nations – but practically lacks a legal mechanism to exercise control over the Council's decision. The second issue is the 'elephant in the room', that is the veto of the five permanent members. On this issue, I have added a short chapter originally published as an op-ed in the French newspaper *Le Monde*, in which I advocated the abolition of the veto, based on the factual conclusion that the veto does not bring more stability to the world, quite the contrary. I also argue that the only realistic way to address this issue is not to leave it to the states. States and the interstate system are, by their very nature, incapable of bringing this reform to fruition and the only way forward is for civil societies across the world and through transnational networks to advocate strongly for such reform.

Such 'cosmopolitan building sites' are not only important because if the planned reforms are achieved, they may change the face of international law; their importance is drawn from the fact that they valorise the concept of world citizenship. Being a citizen of the world does not mean having the right to vote for representative seats in an international parliament. It means being aware that international law – having to deal with global challenges – affects the daily lives of all humans and indeed all living things on earth; and as a consequence being willing and ready to participate in decision-making procedures at all levels of decisions so as to have a say in the drafting and implementation of rules affecting global issues. Forming transnational civil society coalitions is not only the expression of an awareness that international law can change our future; it also participates in creating new practices of participation and, in turn, strengthens the conscience of all people belonging to an interdependent humanity. In other words,

[23] 'Réforme du fonctionnement du Conseil de sécurité: que peut-on faire sans modifier la Charte ?' in S Sur (ed), *La réforme du Conseil de sécurité* (Paris, CNRS, 2016) 297–314; 2nd edn to be published in autumn 2021.

cosmopolitan building sites are not only important because of the change they can bring about in the structure of international law, their importance also lies in the processes themselves.

A democratic theory of international law is a theory of the cosmopolitan transition process affecting contemporary international law. The chapters collected in this book do not propose a new utopia for international law – or if it can be called utopia, it would be a 'realistic utopia' as Antonio Cassese so elegantly put it.[24] We know that ideas and facts are closely intertwined, and as Philip Allott reminds us in the fine preface he so generously offered to open this collection of essays: 'Old ideas can hinder social progress. New ideas can encourage social progress. Ideas can sponsor both revolution and reaction'. This book aims to forge new ideas for designing, better framing, planning and regulating the cosmopolitan transition that is taking place before our eyes today.

[24] See in particular his introduction A Cassese (ed), *Realizing Utopia. The Future of International Law* (Oxford, Oxford University Press, 2012).

Part I

Elements for a Democratic Theory of International Law

1

What is Legal Cosmopolitanism?

To Jacques Phytilis[1]

I owe an immense debt to Jacques Phytilis: he taught me, in no particular order, Socratic dialogue in the course of long talks – that often turned into shouting matches – over Sunday lunches, on rue Crillon; poetry, the solar (and not just Saturnian) dimension of which I only came to understand by perusing Récitatifs du temps; he taught me that law has more to do with the word and poetry than with science; that law has nothing to do with science; that we can do law by philosophising and vice versa – and that when we think we are judging, we are philosophising still. He taught me that law is not just a game of wits, but a game of life and death. He taught me maieutics and practised it on me, in having me give birth to my PhD thesis, which – naughty offspring that it was – was turning this way and that inside me but not wanting to come out. He taught me excess and ascesis; concern with passing things on, devotion to passing things on.

All of these things – to which must be added, among so many others, that slightly held-back affection from someone so affectionate and so discreet – I owe him. And yet, it is a debt I shall never repay. For the good reason that, pitiable student that I am, I have mistaken its legal characterisation: it was a gift and a gift does not give rise to a debt for the recipient but a moral duty of recognition and recollection, a duty to make a counter-gift, that is alleviated, if Ricœur is to be believed, by the gratitude felt by the recipient.[2] *Jacques expected nothing in return for what he gave, other than the give and take: he gave out of friendship, for the pleasure of the encounter with the other, for the pleasure of seeing life, of contemplating 'that unfathomable, revolting wandering that has been ours from the origins of the species and that we seek to mark out, tie down, and make human through the absolute rigour of style'.*[3]

[1] This contribution originated in a communication for the meeting in memory of Jacques Phytilis, organised by Professor Andreas Helmis in Athens on 3 June 2013 on the topic of 'Friendship and Law'. It has been reworked and revised in particular in light of discussion in Athens to serve as an introductory report to the symposium organised as part of my research programme at the Institut Universitaire de France on 'legal cosmopolitism'.

[2] P Ricœur, *The Course of Recognition*, tr D Pellauer (Cambridge, MA, Harvard University Press, 2005).

[3] '[C]ette errance incompréhensible, révoltante, qui depuis les origines de l'espèce est la nôtre, et que nous cherchons à borner, amarrer, rendre humaine enfin par l'absolue rigueur du style.' J Phytilis, *Les récitatifs du temps* (Marseille, Sud, 1988) 5.

'What is cosmopolitanism?' Now there is a question that might have interested Jacques on several accounts. Of course, there is his attachment to Greece and Athens, and he would have remembered in this respect that cosmopolitanism is rooted in the philosophy of the Cynics, authors he does not quote as far as I know, but to whom one cannot help thinking he was close, both in the way he was and his ethics of life. Then there is the point that the question is neither strictly legal nor strictly philosophical and lies at the intersection of the two.[4] *He would probably also have been interested by a consideration on the particular status of human rights in the construction of contemporary international law – a theme that following Michel Villey, Jacques thought eminently suspicious, until at the end of his career he joined the law faculty of Limoges and then discovered that human rights, well, they were law too! Lastly, there is the Aristotelian theme of friendship, which as we shall see is at the heart of our questioning on 'cosmopolitan sentiment'. Andreas Helmis clearly could not have found a better theme for the days in memory of Jacques Phytilis in June 2013, because for Jacques friendship was not only a human quality but an existential feature. Friendship as mutual love,*[5] *friendship that is living together, as in these two days spent together remembering all those days spent with Jacques and his friends. How true it is, as Aristotle wrote in conclusion to his meditation on friendship, that 'whatever existence means for each class of men, whatever it is for whose sake they value life, in that they wish to occupy themselves with their friends; and so some drink together, others dice together, others join in athletic exercises and hunting, or in the study of philosophy, each class spending their days together in whatever they love most in life'.*[6] *Thank you, Jacques, for enabling your friends to indulge together, during these two days, in what it is they love most in life.*

My aim in this essay is not to come up with some sort of necessarily contended and contentious definition of legal cosmopolitanism, nor even to review *theories* of legal cosmopolitanism. What I would like to do here is, in a sense, to move upstream and return to the sources of legal cosmopolitanism: to answer the question 'What is legal cosmopolitanism?' by pondering *the whys and wherefores* of legal cosmopolitanism. In other words, why did we not

[4] J Phytilis, *Espaces grecs, espaces méditerranéens. Variations sur le thème de l'Antiquité* (Nanterre, Editions européennes Erasme, 1990) 9: '[I]t is time, it seems to me, for academic knowledge to become again moral – or ethical as one likes – knowledge *too*, for academic work to become moral work, academic teaching moral teaching. For – I ask sincerely – by what right should a teacher lay claim to his titles, what social or even metasocial justification could he give for himself, other than the fact that he is called upon in the City to shape citizens, and over the long term of the human adventure to perfect Humankind?'

[5] Aristotle, *Nichomachean Ethics*, tr WD Ross, revised with an introduction and notes by Lesley Brown (Oxford, Oxford University Press, 2009), bk VIII, 1155 b 25–35: 'Now there are three grounds on which people love: of the love of lifeless objects we do not use the word "friendship"; for it is not mutual love, nor is there a wishing of good to the other (for it would surely be ridiculous to wish wine well; if one wishes anything for it, it is that it may keep, so that one may have it oneself); but to a friend we say we ought to wish what is good for his sake. But to those who thus wish good we ascribe only goodwill, if the wish is not reciprocated; goodwill when it is reciprocal being friendship.'

[6] Aristotle, *Nichomachean Ethics* (n 5) bk IX, 1172 a 1–10.

stick with moral cosmopolitanism? Why has it been thought helpful, or even necessary, to extend cosmopolitanism to the sphere of law?

Answering this question involves recourse to a phenomenology of the relationship with others, which at the same time touches upon the phenomenology of law in the sense that it sheds light on the transition from the interpersonal relationship to *living together*, that is, life in society, under what are not just moral rules but also, and necessarily, legal rules.

By way of introduction I would like to recall the important philosophical controversy prompted by an article in the *Boston Review* in 1994 by Martha Nussbaum, professor of law and ethics at the University of Chicago. The article spawned no fewer than 29 critical commentaries – the number alone revealing the impact of what Nussbaum had to say in the US context.[7] Nussbaum's article, soberly entitled 'Patriotism and Cosmopolitanism' was itself a reaction to an article by communitarian philosopher Richard Rorty in the *New York Times*, emphasising the importance of national pride and calling on Americans to rally around their shared identity.

Nussbaum expounds from the outset her suspicion of such patriotism that seems to lead to nationalism tinged with ethnicism. The quest for a 'national identity' and the pride attached to that identity would supposedly promote inwardness, intolerance, or at least incomprehension of other peoples, and above all it would lead to the adoption of behaviours contrary to the moral values, such as justice and equality, that are supposed to bond the national community together. Asserting the primacy of the particular over the universal would lead individuals to turn increasingly in on themselves, defining themselves by reference to ever more particular communities (national of such-and-such a country, inhabitant of such-and-such a city or district, member of such-and-such an ethnic, religious, or linguistic community, and so on) and ultimately losing the universal perspective.

Nussbaum then sets against patriotism the cosmopolitanism of the Ancients, which alone is able to overcome such divisions and lead individuals to pledge allegiance to what is morally right rather than the 'colourful idol' that is the Nation.

She draws on Cynic and Stoic philosophers to develop her own conception of cosmopolitanism beginning with Diogenes Laertius telling of Diogenes of Sinope who, when anyone asked him where he came from, replied he was a 'citizen of the world'.[8] This world citizenship, Nussbaum tells us, forces us to think of ourselves as being both part of a particular community, which is the

[7] This debate was published in 1996 in a book including Nussbaum's text, 11 of the original contributions published in the *Boston Review*, plus five new contributions. The work was published again in 2002, with a new introduction by Nussbaum, in the context of the debate further to 11 September 2001. References here are to this 2002 edition: J Cohen (ed), *For Love of Country? Martha C. Nussbaum* (Boston, MA, Beacon Press, 2002).

[8] D Laërce in M-O Goulet-Cazé (ed), *Vies et doctrines des philosophes illustres*, 2nd edn (Paris, Le Livre de Poche, 'La pochothèque', 1999) 733.

one we were born into, and part of a universal human community that knows no borders. It also forces us to find the source of our moral obligations in that human community rather than in the local community. Nussbaum calls for a 'cosmopolitan education' for young Americans: rather than teaching children they are first Americans and possibly that all people are equal – that is, basically a number of abstract principles of a legal and constitutional kind – it would be better to teach them they are first citizens of the world and that, if by chance they happen to have been born in the United States, they still share the world with the other citizens of the world born elsewhere.[9] In other words, she invites us to develop a 'cosmopolitan outlook' among young Americans, which she defines as a love of humanity.[10]

The criticisms levelled at Nussbaum can be schematically grouped into two main arguments that are interrelated for that matter:

- The first critique is that the 'cosmopolitan outlook' is actually inaccessible for mere mortals: it is a sentiment constructed by philosophers at the end of a considerable effort of work on themselves. It is an ascesis rather than a spontaneous sentiment. Spontaneity prompts us to grant our affection and care primarily to those close to us and only afterwards to those who are more remote. It even leads us more generally to dismiss those who are remote and different, and different because remote. And those commentators do not fail to observe that Nussbaum herself points out the ascetic character of cosmopolitanism of a Diogenes or a Marcus Aurelius: to proclaim oneself a citizen of the world and in so doing to claim to obey only the moral law of humanity is to discard local conventions from the outset and to stand apart from others. If Diogenes slept in a barrel and rubbed shoulders with dogs, it was to demonstrate this naturalness and universality that distanced him from human society.[11] But such asceticism is obviously not within everyone's reach, and it seems to be ruled out that it can be taught to children. It must remain the privilege of the few, who beckon others towards more universality at the cost of uprooting them from their community of origin.
- The second main critique is that Nussbaum underestimates the moral value of patriotism: we have sound moral reasons, say some commentators, to grant a preference to our fellow citizens rather than world citizens. Just as we have cause to expend more care on our children than on the

[9] Cohen, *For Love of Country?* (n 7) 6.
[10] ibid 15.
[11] ibid 7: 'Diogenes knew that the invitation to think as a world citizen was, in a sense, an invitation to be an exile from the comfort of patriotism and its easy sentiments, to see our own ways of life from the point of view of justice and the good.' See also at 15: 'In the writings of Marcus Aurelius … a reader can sometimes sense a boundless loneliness, as if the removal of the props of habit and local boundaries had left life bereft of any warmth or security. … Cosmopolitanism offers no such refuge; it offers only reason and the love of humanity, which may seem at times less colorful than other sources of belongings.'

> children of others. If we want to do good, we must begin by doing good around ourselves – any ambition to move towards some sort of universal Good means disregarding those around us.[12]

This is compounded by the fact that we cannot gain access to the universal other than in the particular: it is only through rooting in a culture, in an environment, in a group, in particular experiences and in emotions towards those with whom we share our existence that we can have access to the notion of the universal. We therefore need to experience the sentiments that develop within the family, group, and nation in order to gain an understanding of what love of humanity might be. In fact, it is by loving those close to us that we come to love humanity, since we cannot materially love humanity.

In other words, if we follow Martha Nussbaum's detractors, the sharing of a cosmopolitan sentiment – the sentiment related to world citizenship as love of humanity – by all human beings is not only impossible but even if it were possible it would not be desirable: more simply put, we can question the viability of a society in which all the members were Diogeneses, refusing all social convention, tirelessly aspiring to the universal, even if it meant neglecting those close to them and their fellow citizens in order to be constantly at the bedside of humanity in the name of abstract moral values.

It seems to me, though, that something slips through the net of the lines of argument of both Martha Nussbaum and her detractors. Ultimately, they leave us only the choice between an elevated cosmopolitan sentiment – a Cynical or Stoic asceticism – and a total absence of feeling for others beyond our borders. We are seemingly summoned either to love humanity unconditionally and embrace the ascetic life of those who decline any particular allegiance so as to blend into the Whole, or to fall back upon our communities of origin, our friends and family, refraining from any emotion towards others whose immediate presence is not experienced.

Now, if we begin with our own experience, it can readily be acknowledged that our emotions do not stop at national borders but extend to people who are not geographically close to us. We daily feel compassion for or fraternity with human beings on the other side of the world, whom we do not

[12] Martha Nussbaum does not contest this, that is, both the need for anchoring in what is local and the priority granted to those closest to us, especially our family. She justifies it as a universal value on the scale of humankind – and consequently consistent with a cosmopolitan outlook. But she fails to explain, then, how different priorities hang together and how, concretely, the cosmopolitan sentiment will be reflected when it comes to choosing among different allegiances. How do we shift from a love of humanity in principle to a love of humanity in act, that is what Martha Nussbaum fails to explain, so risking producing a feeling of frustration among cosmopolitans, who are unable to match their acts to their principles. The question is raised materially by S Bok, 'From part to whole' in Cohen, *For Love of Country?* (n 7) 42: 'I see no reason to teach children that claims to national or other identities are "morally irrelevant". Rather, the question is how, and on what grounds, to weigh these claims when they conflict, and what responsibility to acknowledge with respect to each. Educational programs that declare either a global or a more bounded perspective to be the only correct one are troubling insofar as they short circuit reflection concerning such choices.'

know, whose faces we see in photos, news reports, and whose suffering it seems to us we share, or with whom more generally we feel empathy. We have compassion for victims of remote conflicts – conflicts for which we ignore the underlying rationales but whose disastrous effects on martyrised civilian populations we do see; for the victims of famine (the famous image that invariably shocks, afflicts, and revolts us, of the undernourished child who is only skin and bone); we feel a degree of fraternity, solidarity for the oppressed behind bars whose dignity and strength we admire, and so on. While we can be sure that the subject of such emotion varies with times, places, and the political passions peculiar to each people or each group within a population, the fact that such emotion can extend beyond borders, on the other hand, does not seem peculiar to any particular epoch or region.

There is therefore an 'ordinary' compassion for the remote other, a compassion that has nothing to do with asceticism but nor does it prevent us from setting out priorities among our affections: feeling moved while watching a news report on civilians being bombarded in Syria does not preclude us from being patriotic and from loving our children or our nearest and dearest. What I would like to do here is to elucidate the nature of this compassion beyond borders, because it seems to me we cannot understand legal cosmopolitanism without first shedding light on what, in a way, is its driving force.

This implies, in the first place, casting light on the question of the relationship with others, not psychologically but analytically rather: how do we describe the different forms of relationship we have with others, and in particular those peculiar experiences of relationships with remote others, others we do not know but whose faces alone speak to us, move us?

On this point it seems helpful to resort to phenomenology in that it enables us to return to the pure forms of the relationship with others, that is, the categorical forms of that relationship (I).

What I would like to show, on that basis, is how the return of consciousness to the 'life-world' disrupts the relationship with the other and causes a sometimes sudden transition from one category to another – more specifically how the perception of the remote other may shift from absolute non-identification to cosmopolitan emotion, that is, to genuine compassion or effective solidarity for a remote being we do not know and who yet stirs such emotion within us (II).

The claim I would like to defend here is that law has the function of *stabilising*, *maintaining*, and *regulating* the shift from one category to another. In particular, the function of *cosmopolitan* law is to give meaning and continuity to our cosmopolitan emotions, which would otherwise remain forever frustrated in a world of 'sovereign' states, governed by the classical international law of the society of sovereign states. For emotion towards others beyond borders to be perpetuated and change into a genuine *cosmopolitan sentiment* – the equivalent of patriotic sentiment within a nation – the support of *cosmopolitan law* is required. That, to my mind, is what justifies cosmopolitan law, and imparts to it, in some sense, its ontological foundation (III).

I. Cosmopolitan Sentiment and Phenomenology of the Relation to Others

Phenomenology shall be called up on here in two separate stages. First, I would like to apply unquestioningly Edmund Husserl's 'phenomenological method' of his *Cartesian Meditations*.[13] The purpose is to inspire the reader to ponder the various types of pre-cognitive relation that may be established between him and the other, based on the sight of the face of an unknown other. Secondly, I shall enquire into the categories of relations with others that arise out of such an experience. In a way, in this state, we still remain faithful to Husserl's 'phenomenological method', but we relativise his conclusions about the phenomenology of the relation with others compared with other 'dialogical' interpretations. That is, the phenomenological method probably makes it possible to grasp categories of the relation to others that Husserl had not described but that others have managed to highlight (thereby relativising the value of the method itself).

The experiment proposed here to the participant (at the conference) and the readers (of the book) is to look at the faces in the photographs below (projected on a screen at the conference),[14] while putting oneself in a particular frame of mind consisting in 'bracketing the objective world', 'suspending the thesis of the natural standpoint', to use Husserl's expressions. It is a matter, in other words, of practising phenomenological *epoché* in order to get into a position to elucidate the 'giving of sense' by my consciousness to the face before me.[15] We must try particularly to suspend any value judgements, any prejudice, anything these images bring to mind through their normative, historical, or axiological content – a difficult task, I confess, for the first picture that is saturated with such content.[16]

[13] E Husserl, *Cartesian Meditations.An Introduction to Phenomenology*, tr D Cairns (The Hague, Martinus Nijhoff, 1960). See also on *Meditations*, the contributions collected in P Ricœur, *A l'école de la phénoménologie* (Paris, Vrin, 2004), esp 'Etudes sur les *Méditations cartésiennes* de Husserl', ibid 187ff; J Toussaint Desanti, *Introduction à la phénoménologie*, 2nd edn (Paris, Gallimard, Folio/essais, 1994). See also P Huneman and E Kulich, *Introduction à la phénoménologie* (Paris, Armand Colin, 1997) 10ff on Husserl's work as a whole.

[14] Other photos were shown at the conference to multiply examples, particularly the poorly-named 'Benthala Madonna' taken by Hocine Zaourar and Steve McCurry's 'Afghan girl'. For the aesthetic and political polemics surrounding the 'Madonna', see PA Delannoy, *La pietà de Bentalha. Etude du processus interprétatif d'une photo de presse* (Paris, L'Harmattan, 2005); J Hanrot, *La Madone de Bentalha. Histoire d'une photographie* (Paris, Armand Colin, 2012).

[15] Husserl, *Cartesian Meditations* (n 13) First Meditation, § 8, esp at 20–21.

[16] This picture was obviously chosen intentionally: being so laden with content, it seems to me we can better grasp the gap there may be between my intentionality towards others on the categorical level (in some sense the structure of my perceptive lived experience) and my perception of others in the existing world. I thus subscribe also to Susan Sontag's thoughts on the transformation of the relationship to others engendered by the development of photography and photo-journalism. No doubt such a development facilitated the extension in all directions of cosmopolitan emotions in the way in which I interpret the term below. See S Sontag, *Regarding*

Figure 1.1 *Napalm girl*, Nick Ut, centred on the girl's face

Figure 1.2 *Egyptian woman*, Gilles Perrin

The choice of pictures is obviously not a neutral one. It is dependent on what I was intuitively able to understand of the perception the photographers had or wanted to get across about these faces of others. Nick Ut's *Napalm girl* – centred here on the girl's face[17] – clearly shows the subject's suffering and starts from the hypothesis that the intentional relationship uniting me to these subjects will be of sympathy or compassion. Gilles Perrin's *Egyptian woman* expresses no suffering but her gaze speaks to us and creates a mysterious bond with the unknown, remote other – unknown because never encountered, but unknown too because forever unknowable. If the bond is mysterious it is precisely because of this contrast between the impossibility of knowing and the feeling of being close, which arises from the unknown other looking at me, and from me looking at her – including through the medium of a photo.

The second step in the experiment consists in moving on to the second 'phenomenological reduction', namely the 'eidetic' reduction,[18] by which we can shift from phenomena to essences. It is a question of elucidating what the giving of sense by our consciousness to the faces perceived – giving of sense perceived by *epoché* – tells us of the essence of the relationship we entertain with others.

Edmund Husserl devoted his fifth *Cartesian Meditation* to this issue. The Husserl of *Cartesian Meditations* takes to extremes subjectivism and the position of 'solipsism', namely the idea that the world is constituted *in* and *from* the thinking subject. Husserl is aware of the challenge set by such a position when he comes to the question of the relationship with others, that is, with another human being as opposed to a straightforward relation with objects:

> Transcendental reduction restricts me to the stream of my pure conscious processes and the unities constituted by their actualities and potentialities. And indeed it seems obvious that such unities are inseparable from my ego and therefore belong to this concreteness itself.

the Pain of Others (New York, Picador, 2003). She claims (at 12) 'Being a spectator of calamities taking place in another country is a quintessential modern experience, the cumulative offering by more than a century and a half's worth of those professional specialized tourists known as journalists.'

[17] Another centring will be commented upon below. Another example in the same register is the 'Benthala Madonna'; see especially Hanrot, *La Madone de Bentalha* (n 14) 111, comparing this photo with Christian representations of the Virgin weeping for Christ: 'Artworks should help souls feel more deeply the tie between the sacrament and the Saviour's body. The objective of the Benthala Madonna thus comes close to religious art. It seeks to procure emotion, to entail *empathy*. Yet more, it makes it possible to feel the suffering of others. Through it, we *penetrate* the wound, we *gain access* to the victims. The photographic theme of the Mater dolorosa thus proves a relevant choice when it comes to accounting for extreme violence that is literally *incomprehensible*, that cannot be perceived either by the senses or by thought.'

[18] From the Greek *eidos*, form, idea, essence. Husserl speaks of 'eidetic' reduction for example in the *Fourth Cartesian Meditation* to designate a truth 'with absolute "*essential universality*", and with "*essential necessity*" for every particular case selected, hence for every de facto perception, since every *fact can be thought of merely as exemplifying a pure possibility*'. Husserl, *Cartesian Meditations* (n 13) § 34 at 71.

> But what about other egos, who surely are not a mere intending and intended in me, merely synthetic unities of possible verification in me, but, according to their sense, precisely others?[19]

Unlike the object that can be apprehended directly in its appearance – the table in front of me is just one 'variation' of the idea of table – the other human being is another *ego* for whom the mere perception of their body is not sufficient to account. There is no *presentation* of the other, but just 'appresentation' says Husserl, that is, mediate presentation: the body alone is presented but perception of the body only indirectly accounts for the other, whose interiority and intentionalities remain hidden.[20] Hence, if we refuse to grasp him as a mere object, the other invariably escapes us as an other in that the perceiving *ego* is unable to capture his essence. In order to solve this difficulty of solipsism, Husserl resorts to both *analogy* and *imagination* in a 'three step' progression.[21] As the first step, the other is seized *by analogy*, as another me, an *alter ego*. As the second step, this analogy is attested, body to body, in matching the behaviours of others. Then as the third step, the other is genuinely constituted as other by the imagination which conveys the *ego here* to where the other is, that is *over there*.

Husserl's phenomenology of the relationship with others inspired all his phenomenologist successors, who in turn took an interest in the 'problem of others'. All of them, beginning with Heidegger, considered that Husserl had failed in his attempt to 'hold together' two requirements that were so difficult to reconcile: to maintain the hypothesis of solipsism and to constitute the other in his own peculiar otherness.[22] For Heidegger, '*dasein*' is thought of as being 'always already there' but also as 'being-with':

> On the basis of this like-with being-in-the-world, the world is always already the one that I share with the others. The world of Da-sein is a with-world. Being-in is being-with others. The innerworldly being-in-itself of others is Mitda-sein.[23]

[19] 'Fifth Cartesian Meditation' ibid § 42 at 89.

[20] ibid § 50 at 108–9: 'Experience is original consciousness; and in fact we generally say, in the case of experiencing a man: the other is himself there before us "in person". On the other hand, this being there in person does not keep us from admitting forthwith that, properly speaking, neither the other Ego himself, nor his subjective processes or his appearances themselves, nor anything else belonging to his own essence, becomes given in our experience originally. If it were, if what belongs to the other's own essence were directly accessible, it would be merely a moment of my own essence, and ultimately he himself and I myself would be the same. … *A certain mediacy of intentionality* must be present here … We have here, accordingly, a kind of *making "co-present"*, a kind of "*appresentation*".'

[21] I refer readers to the fifth Meditation and the illuminating analysis by Paul Ricœur in *A l'école de la phénoménologie* (n 13) 233ff.

[22] See P Ricœur, 'Sympathie et respect' in Ricœur, *A l'école de la phénoménologie* (n 13) 335ff and esp at 336: 'It is safe to say the *Fifth Meditation* is an impossible challenge …'; Toussaint Desanti *Introduction à la phénoménologie* (n 13) 121ff.

[23] M Heidegger, *Being and Time, A Translation of Sein und Zeit,* tr J Stambaugh (New York, State University of New York Press, 1996) § 26.

For Sartre, '[a]ctually if solipsism is to be rejected, this can only be because it is impossible or, if you prefer, because nobody is truly solipsistic'.[24] The other asserts himself, he imposes himself on my *ego* by his *seeing* me, which 'makes an object of me'.[25] Along the same lines, Merleau-Ponty also relativises the hypothesis of solipsism, which becomes an attitude I adopt with respect to the world in which I am already 'situated' and 'involved'.[26] Thus solipsism is a possibility, a possible state of consciousness and not its natural state.[27]

In parallel with this discourse with and against Husserl, another phenomenological strand is asserted, with as its point of departure the writings of Martin Buber and Gabriel Marcel, who influenced thinkers such as Emmanuel Levinas and Paul Ricœur.[28] Here it is quite simply the egological starting point that is contested to the benefit of a mutual formation of the *I* and the Other. Buber set the *I – It* relation against the *I – Thou* relation, the relation to objects and the relation to others. Whereas the *I – It* relation is

[24] JP Sartre, *Being and Nothingness*, tr HE Barnes (New York, Open Road Media, 1956) 337. Note however that the English translation of this particular passage is not correct, so we have substituted our own translation from the original French text.

[25] ibid 344–45: '[I]f the Other-as-object is defined in connection with the world as the object which *sees* what I see, then my fundamental connection with the Other-as-subject must be able to be referred back to my permanent possibility of being *seen* by the Other. It is in and through the revelation of my being-as-object for the Other that I must be able to apprehend the presence of his being-as-subject. For just as the Other is a probable object for me-as-subject, so I can discover myself in the process of becoming a probable object for only a certain subject.' And ibid: 'In a word, my apprehension of the Other in the world as *probably* being a man refers to my permanent possibility of *being-seen-by-him*, that is, to the permanent possibility that a subject who sees me may be substituted for the object seen by me.'

[26] M Merleau-Ponty, *Phenomenology of Perception*, tr C Smith (London, Routledge & Kegan Paul, 1962) 360: 'The central phenomenon, at the root of both my subjectivity and my transcendence towards others, consists in my being given to myself. *I am given*, that is, I find myself already situated and involved in a physical and social world – *I am given to myself*, which means that this situation is never hidden from me, it is never round about me as an alien necessity, and I am never in effect enclosed in it like an object in a box.'

[27] Thus for Sartre *indifference* is 'de facto solipsism': 'Then we are dealing with a kind of *blindness* with respect to others. ... I practice then a sort of factual solipsism; others are those forms which pass by in the street, those magic objects which are capable of acting at a distance and upon which I can act by means of determined conduct. ... Those "people" are functions: the ticket-collector is only the function of collecting tickets; the café waiter is nothing but the function of serving the patrons. In this capacity they will be most useful if I know their *keys* and those 'master-words' which can release their mechanisms.' Sartre, *Being and Nothingness* (n 24) 495. Merleau-Ponty also accepts solipsism as an attitude with respect to the world: 'Against the social world I can always avail myself of my sensible nature, close my eyes, stop up my ears, live as a stranger in society, treat others, ceremonies, and institutions as mere arrangements of colour and light, and strip them of all their human significance. ... The truth of solipsism is there.' Merleau-Ponty, *Phenomenology of Perception* (n 26) 360.

[28] M Buber, *I and Thou*, tr RG Smith (Edinburgh, T & T Clark, 1937). Levinas points out Martin Buber's influence in E Levinas, *Totality and Infinity. An Essay on Exteriority*, tr A Lingis (The Hague, Martinus Nijhoff, 1979) 68 and makes several studies of him (some of which also relate to Gabriel Marcel), collected in E Levinas, *Hors sujet* (Paris, Fata Morgana, 1987) 15ff.

characterised by utility, the *I – Thou* relation is founded on reciprocity: 'My *Thou* affects me as I affect it.'[29]

Admittedly each of these philosophies must be told apart from the others. But all of them dismiss the idea of solipsism as the 'natural' starting point of consciousness: the *I* and the Other are 'always already there', and it is from their encounter that the Self is born. That is, the Self is constructed not in a monadologic mode, as in Husserl, but a *dialogic* mode.

It seems to me, though, that *epoché*, if it is accepted to apply it as a simple phenomenological method,[30] gives access to that general category of relation with others that Husserl had overlooked, being too concerned with maintaining the stringency of his starting hypothesis, namely solipsism. Reduction applied to the remote others who are both re-presented and appresented in the photos projected suggests two forms of relation: a fundamentally *compassionate* relation in the face of the suffering of others that can be associated with imagining the fellow creature formed *in* and *from* my ego – and which is still compatible with the solipsistic attitude; a *dialogic* relation, sustained by a gaze that, in speaking to me, brings me to ponder about the other and to question the other without ever being able to circumscribe them. In other words, the fact that the other shows no signs of suffering and simply beckons me with their gaze, inviting dialogue, precludes us from seeing the analogising understanding through to its term. The other is *absolutely other* in that they cannot be restricted to their suffering: they are their history, their life, which lead me to ponder my own history and life and consequently change the perspective I have of myself.

It is therefore on the basis of these two categories of relation that I must try to understand my relation with the remote other and the existence of emotion for the remote other, whom I do not know and with whom I have no particular tie.

So far we have remained at a purely descriptive stage. But it seems that, to get to the bottom of things, we need to add some *ethical* consideration to that description. In this spirit, Michael Theunissen, by way of a post scriptum to a detailed study of doctrines of the phenomenology of the relation to the other

[29] Buber, *I and Thou* (n 28) 15.

[30] It should be observed that although *epoché* is relativised by the authors who followed Husserl, it is not entirely discredited as a method. It is simply doubted whether it can lead to a total reduction to its own proper sphere, as the person can never totally be abstracted out of the world which is pre-given to consciousness. eg Merleau-Ponty, *Phenomenology of Perception* (n 26), Preface at xiii: 'It is because we are through and through compounded of relationships with the world that for us the only way to become aware of the fact is to suspend the resultant activity, to refuse it our complicity (to look at it *ohne mitzumachen* as Husserl often says), or yet again, to put it "out of play". Not because we reject the certainties of common sense and a natural attitude to things – they are, on the contrary, the constant theme of philosophy – but because, being the presupposed basis of any thought, they are taken for granted, and go unnoticed, and because in order to arouse them and bring them to view, we have to suspend for a moment our recognition of them.'

from Husserl to Gabriel Marcel, summarises those doctrines in the form of an ethical advancement in a Hegelian type of ternary dialectic:

> To a certain extent, this movement can be grasped in a Hegelian schema. It can be presented as a history of the human spirit, which comes out of its being-for-itself into otherness and eventually wins itself back again out of alienation through mediation with the Other. The three steps are therefore presented as thesis, antithesis, and synthesis. On the first step, the I is nothing but an I, on the second, it is with the Other in such a way that it itself becomes an Other; and on the third, it is with itself in being-with-the-Other.[31]

The starting point, in ethical terms, lies therefore in *pure solipsism* or the 'egological' or, if it is preferred, subjectivist position, which is also the starting point of phenomenology in Husserl: the *I* (which is here *in itself*) is unable to get out of itself and the other is constituted *in* and *from* the *ego* (*ego*). Only, in this initial position, the *ego* fails to constitute the other *in its otherness*, as in Husserl. It confines itself to *constituting* it: that is, the other is merely an extension of the *I*, it is a pure creation of my consciousness. As the other is a part of the *I*, I am obviously unable to be com-passionate: the other's suffering is not perceptible unless it is my own suffering at the same time.

The second stage marks an *alter-ation*, a decentring relative to the self at the end of which the *I actualises* itself until it is able to perceive itself as *other*. It seems this stage can be likened to what Rousseau conceptualised as *imagining one's fellow*,[32] which is not quite the exit point from the transcendent *ego*, but the possibility of constitution of others not just in their sameness but also their otherness. At this stage, my compassion arises from an understanding beginning with the *I* of the particular plight of the other, which I can imagine as being my own: therefore the *other* whom I can *imagine as like me* (and not as the *same*), because I make an effort to shift my point of view, to step outside of myself. This is the outer bound of the domain of phenomenology of the Husserl of *Cartesian Meditations*: the body-to-body analogy is superseded by imagining one's fellow, by which the other can be constituted as other, but still *in me* and *from me*.

Lastly, the final stage, after the alter-ation, is the dialogic relation when my *I* finds itself altered by the encounter with the other, resulting in a genuine detachment of the *ego*: the *I* becomes *self-with-the-other*. When I contemplate the face of Gilles Perrin's *Egyptian woman*, I engage in a dialogue with an other who is now characterised *only* by her otherness – an appeased relation that is no longer perturbed as in the first picture by the feeling in the other of intense pain. I go outside myself to meet the other. Or at any rate the

[31] M Theunissen, *The Other. Studies in the Social Ontology of Husserl, Heidegger, Sartre and Bubber* (Cambridge, MA, The MIT Press, 1977) Postscript, 369.

[32] cf Section II. On the notion of imagining one's like, see the work of Myriam Revault d'Allonnes and especially 'A l'épreuve des camps, l'imagination du semblable' (1998) 60 *Philosophie* 63–78; 'Peut-on élaborer le terrible?' (2000) 67 *Philosophie* 33–50.

constitution of the other in me affects me in return and shifts my view of the other, enhancing it with new content.[33]

Theunissen's 'genetic' approach makes it possible to understand the various categories of the relation to others along a *continuum*, along which the ethical charge of the relation established increases progressively. We begin with a solipsistic perception centred on the *ego* and admitting the other only as an analogue of the self: in such a relation, perception of the other as otherness is necessarily limited, or even non-existent – which does not preclude the deployment of emotion, but purely solipsistic emotion, centred on the other as the same. From this initial solipsistic position, Theunissen's *continuum* describes a gradual process of decentring, during which there arises the possibility of a feeling of obligation towards others. Along with the imagining of one's fellow there arises the possibility of a reciprocal norm, based on the 'golden rule': *do not do to others what you would not like them to do to you.* Ultimately, the dialogic relation opens the way to the universal norm, the general reconciliation of *egos*, as so many othernesses that cannot be reduced to self and others.

This 'ethical' dimension of the dialogic relation is heavily marked, although differently, in Buber, Levinas, and Ricœur. Buber distinguishes between the 'I–Thou' and 'I–It' relation, that is, between the relation between people and the relation between a person and an object.[34] The 'I–Thou' relation is characterised both by its reciprocity in equality and by its transcendence of the 'Thou' which cannot be reduced to the same or to 'It'.

Levinas begins with Heidegger and his break with the transcendental egology of both Husserl and Buber. He calls into question, though, the idea of reciprocity in Buber: the relation of the *I* to the transcendent 'Other' cannot be a mutual one.[35] It is a relation with the outside, the *I* being radically

[33] A category of relation to others that can be likened to the maxim of 'enlarged thought' conceptualised by Kant in para 40 of his *Critique of Judgement*: save that we are not here in the register of phenomenological description but rather, as Myriam Revault d'Allonnes shows, in an attempt to think out 'the conditions under which universal communicability is possible' based on the transcendental subject (Revault d'Allonnes, 'Peut-on élaborer le terrible?' (n 32) 38). It may, however, be wondered in the light of what is to follow whether the, as it were 'pure', dialogic relation truly exists in experience. Is it not rather a question of transcendence towards which we strive without ever being able to attain it? On imagining one's fellow and the maxim of 'enlarged thought' in Kant, see ibid.

[34] Buber, *I and Thou* (n 28).

[35] Of Buber, Levinas explains in a retrospective re-reading of *Totality and Infinity*: 'My interrogation consisted in questioning that initial reciprocity. The other whom I address – is he not initially the one with whom I stand in the relationship one has with one who is weaker? … Although Buber is one of the first thinkers to put the accent on an I–You relation in conjunction with an I–That, this concept of reciprocity bothered me, because the moment one is generous in hopes of reciprocity, that relation no longer involves generosity but the commercial relation, the exchange of good behaviour. In the relation to the other, the other appears to me as one to whom I owe something, toward whom I have a responsibility. Hence the asymmetry of the I–You relation and the radical inequality between the I and the you, for all relation to the other is a relation to a being toward whom I have obligations.' E Levinas, *Alterity and Transcendence*, tr MB Smith (London, The Athlone Press, 1999). See also Levinas, *Totality and Infinity* (n 28) 68.

separate from the Other. Language alone makes a relation possible.[36] In this respect Levinas holds on to the idea of appresentation in Husserl: the Other can never be 'represented' like a thing, he is always 'appresented' because his interiority always remains hidden from us. The relation to the Other can therefore only be thought of like the 'idea of infinity' in Descartes.[37] Infinity is opposed to a totality in which the Hegelian dialectic between *I* and the Other is supposedly resolved. The Other is expressed by his 'face' which designates precisely what, in the other, goes beyond what is represented.[38] Hence any relation with the other is ethical by definition: it is always goodness, responsibility of me for the other. It is also respect, and never appropriation: in this regard, Levinas condemns a conception of unbounded liberty as arbitrary power.[39]

We find this ethical reading of the different categories of the relation to others in Paul Ricœur too. In his *Oneself as Another*, Ricœur forges the concept of *solicitude*[40] which sets the question of the relation to others back at the heart of concern about ethics on one side, understood as 'the aim of the good life', and morality on the other 'for the articulation of this aim in *norms* characterised at once by the claim to universality and by an effect of constraint …'.[41] Ricœur thus manages to show that the dialogic dimension of the relation to others – which he explains via the concept of *solicitude* – is central not just to leading a 'good life', but also to living in just (fair)

[36] Levinas, *Totality and Infinity* (n 28) 39: 'We shall try to show that the relation between the same and the other … is language. For language accomplishes a relation such that the terms are not limitrophe within this relation, such that the other, despite the relationship with the same, remains transcendent to the same.' See also, eg, ibid 209.

[37] ibid 48: 'This relation of the same with the other, where the transcendence of the relation does not cut the bonds a relation implies, yet where these bonds do not unite the same and the other into a Whole, is in fact fixed in the situation described by Descartes in which the "I think" maintains with the Infinite it can nowise contain and from which it is separated a relation called "idea of infinity".'

[38] ibid 50: 'The way in which the other presents himself, exceeding *the idea of the other in me*, we here name face.'

[39] ibid 302: 'Whether in scientific thought or in the object of science, or in history understood as a manifestation of reason, where violence reveals itself to be reason, philosophy presents itself as a realization of being, that is, as its liberation by the suppression of multiplicity. Knowledge would be the suppression of the other by the grasp, by the hold, or by the vision that grasps before the grasp. In this work metaphysics has an entirely different meaning. If its movement leads to the transcendent as such, transcendence means not appropriation of *what is*, but its respect. Truth as a respect for being is the meaning of metaphysical truth.'

[40] P Ricœur, *Oneself as Another*, tr K Blamey (Paris, University of Chicago Press, 1992): concept of solicitude laid down on the basis of a 'hermeneutics of the self' which 'is placed at an equal distance from the apology of the cogito and from its overthrow' (ibid 4) and which thereby makes it possible to found an *otherness as selfhood (ipseity)* (ibid 3): 'Oneself as … Another'. Solicitude constructs a relation based on mutuality through experience of *lack* (ibid 225) and so unearths 'the paradox of the exchange at the very place of the irreplaceable', the equivalence between 'the esteem of *the other as a oneself* and the esteem of *oneself as an other*' (ibid 193–94).

[41] ibid 170.

institutions. The 'ethical aim' that is reflected by 'self-esteem' necessarily involves a dialogic type of relation with others, termed 'solicitude':

> To self-esteem, understood as a reflexive moment of the wish for the 'good life', solicitude adds essentially the dimension of lack, the fact that we need friends; as a reaction to the effect of solicitude on self-esteem, the self perceives itself as another among others.[42]

This results in the solipsistic attitude being condemned ethically: solipsism is not in reality compatible with the 'ethical aim' or it leads the person on a search for the 'good life' that is a dead-end, because it abstracts away plurality.

With the concept of solicitude, Ricœur takes the phenomenological description of the relation to the other further by accepting the principle of asymmetry between *I* and others that is present in the phenomenology of Emmanuel Levinas. But instead of remaining in a profoundly asymmetric relation – a sort of counterproof of solipsism – in which the other summonses me to responsibility in a position of absolute exteriority, Ricœur draws on the concept of friendship in Aristotle, to come up with the idea of a 'search for equality in the midst of [the fundamental] inequality' between me and the other:

> Let us attempt, in conclusion, to take an overview of the entire range of attitudes deployed between the two extremes of the summons to responsibility, where the initiative comes from the other, and of sympathy for the suffering other, where the initiative comes from the loving self, friendship appearing as a midpoint where the self and the other share equally the same wish to live together. While equality is presupposed in friendship, in the case of the injunction coming from the other, equality is reestablished only through the recognition by the self of the superiority of the other's authority; in the case of sympathy that comes from the self and extends to the other, equality is reestablished only through the shared admission of fragility and, finally, of mortality.[43]

This brings us to a very complete description of the relation to others in a dialogic mode in which, contrary to what happens for Levinas, the asymmetry between me and the other does not preclude reciprocity, as the relation can be understood as a search for equality, with the figure of *friendship* as the balancing point.

Above all, for our focus here, Ricœur includes in his phenomenology the question of sentiments, which forms in a way the pre-cognitive crux of the relation to others, even before the question of ethics and before the question of the moral or legal norm. Levinas's injunction is already akin to the norm: the other summonses me to responsibility, he obligates me.[44] What Ricœur wants to show, it seems to me, is that the relation to the other does not stem

[42] ibid 192.
[43] ibid 192.
[44] ibid 190.

from either ethics (the search for the good life), or morality (obligation), but from something far more spontaneous, which is sentiment:

> That is why it is so important to us to give solicitude a more fundamental status than obedience to duty. Its status is that of benevolent spontaneity, intimately related to self-esteem with the framework of the 'good' life.[45]

The sentiment is consequently the 'affective flesh' of the ethical quest:

> Let us confine ourselves here to emphasizing the role played by feelings – which, in the last analysis, are affects, in solicitude. For it is indeed feelings that are revealed in the self by the other's suffering, as well as by the moral injunction coming from the other, feelings spontaneously directed toward others. This intimate union between the ethical aim of solicitude and affective flesh of feelings seems to me to justify the choice of the term 'solicitude'.[46]

But, following Martha Nussbaum,[47] Ricœur also acknowledges the fragility of feeling, the precariousness of goodness that characterises solicitude. Benevolent spontaneity may give way to the reification of the other, their negation as a person worthy of respect. It is in the face of this risk conceptualised in the figure of Evil that the requirement of the universal norm, whether moral or legal, comes in. For Ricœur, moral obligation (ethics for Levinas) therefore provides a sort of guarantee of solicitude in the face of the dangers stalking it.

But before coming to the place of the law in these considerations, and in particular cosmopolitan law, we must try to explain this precariousness of sentiment, from which it can be inferred that solipsism, far from being a category made obsolete by the discovery of the dialogic relation, retains to the contrary its actuality when, extending our attention beyond the pre-cognitive relation to the other, we take an interest in what becomes of this relation in society.

II. Relation to the Other and Society

To address the issue of the relation to the other in society, it seems there is no better starting point than Jean-Jacques Rousseau's phenomenology-before-its-time.[48] Rousseauist *pity* is the ability we have to imagine ourselves

[45] ibid.
[46] ibid 224.
[47] Ricœur cites M Nussbaum, *The Fragility of Goodness. Luck and Ethics in Greek Tragedy and Philosophy* (Cambridge, Cambridge University Press, 2001).
[48] Notice already that Tocqueville was to take up this concept of 'pity' and the idea of 'imagining one's fellow' as a consequence of the principle of equality in democratic societies: 'When the ranks in a nation are roughly equal and everyone thinks and feels in almost the same way, then each person can judge everyone else's sensations in an instant: all he has to do is cast a quick glance at himself. Hence there is no misery that he cannot readily conceive, or whose extent

in someone else's shoes, in other words 'imagining one's fellow' succeeding, in Husserl, to the analogising grasp, including from a solipsistic attitude:

> It is therefore certain that pity is a natural sentiment, which, by moderating in every individual the activity of self-love, contributes to the mutual preservation of the whole species. It is this pity which hurries us without reflection to the assistance of those we see in distress; it is this pity which, in a state of nature, takes the place of laws, manners, virtue, with this advantage, that no one is tempted to disobey her gentle voice: it is this pity which will always hinder a robust savage from plundering a feeble child, or infirm old man, of the subsistence they have acquired with pain and difficulty, if he has but the least prospect of providing for himself by any other means: it is this pity which, instead of that sublime maxim of rational justice, *Do to others as you would have others do to you*, inspires all men with that other maxim of natural goodness a great deal less perfect, but perhaps more useful, *Do good to yourself with as little prejudice as you can to others*. It is in a word, in this natural sentiment, rather than in finespun arguments, that we must look for the cause of that reluctance which every man would experience to do evil, even independently of the maxims of education.[49]

This 'innate abhorrence to see beings suffer that resemble him' is indeed a 'natural virtue' 'before all manner of reflection', in other words it is a pre-cognitive disposition, 'so natural, that the beasts themselves sometimes give evident signs of it'.[50] Now this disposition is not annihilated but the expression of it is greatly disrupted by the transition from the state of nature to the social state. Thus 'all social virtues' flow from compassion in the social state. Even so, these virtues seldom find scope to express themselves in the social state, where interests prevail and man turns in upon himself as his ability to identify with his fellow diminishes and as 'egoism' (as opposed to self-respect, the instinct of preservation) grows.

> Though it were true that commiseration is no more than a sentiment, which puts us in the place of him who suffers, a sentiment obscure but active in the savage,

is not revealed to him by a secret instinct. No matter if strangers or enemies are involved: his imagination instantly puts him in their place. His pity is thereby tinged with something personal, causing him to suffer when the body of his fellow man is torn to pieces.' A de Tocqueville, *Democracy in America*, tr A Goldhammer (New York, Literary Classics of the United States, Inc, 2004) vol II, pt III, ch I, 658. However, we shall return specifically to Tocqueville when discussing the question of law in Section III.

[49] J-J Rousseau, 'The Second Discourse: Discourse on the Origin and Foundations of Inequality Among Mankind' in *The Social Contract and The First and Second Discourses (Rethinking the Western Tradition)*, ed and with an Introduction by S Dunn (New Haven, CT, Yale University Press, 2002) 108 (English translation).

[50] ibid 106. By extending the capacity for emotion to animals, Rousseau raises the question of animal ethics: 'Not to speak of the tenderness of mothers for their young; and of the dangers they face to screen them from danger; with what reluctance are horses known to trample upon living bodies; one animal never passes unmoved by the dead carcass of another animal of the same species: there are even some who bestow a kind of sepulture upon their dead fellows; and the mournful lowings of cattle, on their entering the slaughterhouse, publish the impression made upon them by the horrible spectacle they are there struck with.'

> developed but dormant in civilized man, how could this notion affect the truth of what I advance, but to make it more evident? In fact, commiseration must be so much the more energetic, the more intimately the animal, that beholds any kind of distress, identifies himself with the animal that labors under it. Now it is evident that this identification must have been infinitely more perfect in the state of nature, than in the state of reason. It is reason that engenders self-love, and reflection that strengthens it; it is reason that makes man shrink into himself; it is reason that makes him keep aloof from everything that can trouble or afflict him; it is philosophy that destroys his connections with other men; it is in consequence of her dictates that he mutters to himself at the sight of another in distress, You may perish for aught I care, I am safe. Nothing less than those evils, which threaten the whole community, can disturb the calm sleep of the philosopher, and force him from his bed. One man may with impunity murder another under his windows; he has nothing to do but clap his hands to his ears, argue a little with himself to hinder nature, that startles within him, from identifying him with the unhappy sufferer.[51]

If any human being can imagine the other as his fellow, such imagination is made more difficult, or even impossible, when man joins society; and the spontaneous emotion may vanish completely for the benefit of a constructed sentiment that leads individuals as far as to murder their fellows. We shall return to this in speaking of international law, which Rousseau judges harshly in this respect.[52] Meanwhile, we cannot but observe with Ricœur, taking up Nussbaum in this, the 'fragility of goodness', that is, the precarious character of a feeling that, however, forms the 'flesh' of ethics. Now, this fragility can be observed daily. Of course, Rousseau's distinction between 'state of nature' and 'civil state' does not refer to any historical fact – 'Let us begin by laying aside facts'[53] – but falls in rather with the conclusions of a phenomenology of the social world, or even a 'realist' sociology, such as that of a Tönnies,[54] distinguishing between 'community' and 'society', or a Durkheim with 'organic solidarity' and 'solidarity by division of labour'.[55]

We also come back to the conclusions of post-Husserlian phenomenology: the individual is 'always-already-there' in the world, with others: there is no pre-social state and *epoché* cannot totally 'reduce' this pre-given with which consciousness is imbued. So the transition from 'pity to 'reason' occurs in the social world, in the 'ordinary' relation that we maintain with others

[51] ibid 107.

[52] See quotation below.

[53] As the clinching expression of the *Discourse* has it.

[54] F Tönnies, *Community and Society* [1887], tr CP Lommis (New York, Dover Publications, 1957).

[55] E Durkheim, *De la division du travail social* [1930], 7th edn (Puf, Paris, 2007). See Emile Durkheim's review of Tönnies' book in 'Communauté et société selon Tönnies' (1889) 27 *Revue philosophique* 416–22, reproduced in E Durkheim, *Textes I. Eléments d'une théorie sociale* (Paris, Ed de Minuit, 1975) 383–90.

who are there in front of me, but also with remote others: it suffices that because an interest arises, pre-cognitive emotion should give way to a socially constructed sentiment.

I would like to illustrate this idea using an example from current events and then take a detour through literature before proposing to the reader to look again at a photograph, but from a different viewpoint.

An example from 'real life' first from an article in *Le Monde* of 6 April 2013:

> 'At first, when Roms move in, the neighbourhood is always favourable, because no one is indifferent to human misfortune,' says Louis Souchal, who handles such matters for Nantes council. 'But after a couple of months or so, things go downhill.'
>
> ...
>
> At Choisy-le-Roi, M. Bellucci, keeps a close tally on things. Initially, he was told the situation was a temporary one. But after two and a half years, only four Rom families had been re-housed under through the insertion work.
>
> 'I'm not asking them to go back home, I just want them out of there. People say we're racists but if the council wants to do social work, then let it take them in itself!'[56]

The 'at first (...) no one is indifferent to human misfortune' connotes the population's initially sympathetic attitude. The inhabitants spontaneously put themselves into a relation in which they welcome the suffering outsider, as they are touched by 'human misfortune'. As Ricœur would put it, solicitude deploys 'sympathy for the suffering other where the initiative comes from the loving self'.[57] But the question of interest soon dissipates 'benevolent goodness'. The self folds in upon the *I*. In this example, compassion is not entirely eliminated, but it is expressed exclusively from the solipsistic point of view of the local inhabitant. He does not want them 'to go back home', which shows a remnant of compassion, but while compassion should give rise to action, its effects are neutralised by the transfer of responsibility to an *other*, and moreover an abstract other (further facilitating the transfer): 'if the council wants to do social work, then let it take them in itself!'.

A detour through literature might well make the idea easier to understand from a slightly different angle. In the opening scene of his novel *Ninety-Three*, Victor Hugo describes the encounter between the Bonnets Rouges battalion and a peasant-woman and her children who have taken refuge in the woods after the sack of their village.[58] The sergeant interrogating her seeks

[56] E Vincent, 'A Choisy-le-Roi, la difficile cohabitation entre riverains et campements roms', *Le Monde* (6 April 2013).

[57] Ricœur, *Oneself as Another* (n 40) 192.

[58] The following quotations are taken from the translation by F Lee Benedict (New York, Harper and Brothers, 1874).

immediately to find out 'which side' she is on. Hugo's immense talent is to describe a wholly non politicised subject, which first completely wrong-foots the battalion. How can anyone be of no party, no nation, no faction? How can the other escape being *situated*?

> ' (...) What are your political opinions?'
>
> The woman looked at him [the sergeant], but did not reply.
>
> 'Did you hear my question?'
>
> She stammered, —
>
> 'I was put into a convent very young – but I am married – I am not a nun. The sisters taught me to speak French. The village was set on fire. We ran away so quickly that I had not time to put on my shoes.'
>
> 'I ask you, what are your political opinions?'
>
> 'I don't know what that means.'
>
> The sergeant continued, —
>
> 'There are such things as female spies. We shoot spies. Come, speak! You are not a gipsy? Which is your side?
>
> (...)
>
> 'I don't know,' she said.
>
> 'How? You do not know your own country.'
>
> 'Ah, my country! Oh, yes, I know that.'
>
> 'Well, where is it?'
>
> The woman replied, —
>
> 'The farm of Siscoignard, in the parish of Azé.'
>
> It was the sergeant's turn to be stupefied. He remained thoughtful for a moment, then resumed: 'You say —'
>
> 'Siscoignard.'
>
> 'That is not a country.'
>
> 'It's my country' said the woman.

And further on, at the end of a long dialogue of the deaf:

> 'Get to the facts! Who are you?'
>
> 'I don't know.'
>
> 'You don't know who you are?'
>
> 'We are people who are running away.'
>
> 'What party do you belong to?'
>
> 'I don't know.'
>
> 'Are you Blues? Are you Whites? Who are you with?'
>
> 'I am with my children.'

The peasant-woman is her existence. She *is*... 'with her children'. They *are* ... 'people who are running away'. It is a dual embodiment of a pure organic community, virtually outside of any social and political world. The woman and her children are simply a body that is running to escape, pure transcendental *ego* ahead of its time. After a few minutes of bemusement (how can one be only *oneself*?), the realisation that the peasant-woman does not know how she is *situated* – despite here effective submission to the local lord and priest – leave free course to emotion, compassion, and fraternisation:

> The sergeant approached the woman, and fixed his eye on the sucking baby. The little one left the breast, turned its head gently, gazing with its beautiful blue orbs into the formidable hairy face, bristling and wild, which bent toward it, and began to smile.
>
> The sergeant raised himself and they saw a great tear roll down his cheek and cling like a pearl to the end of his moustache.
>
> He lifted his voice —
>
> 'Comrades, from all this I conclude that the regiment is going to become a father. Is it agreed? We adopt these three children?'
>
> 'Hurrah for the Republic!' chorused the grenadiers.
>
> 'It is decided!' said the sergeant.
>
> He stretched his two hands above the mother and her babes.
>
> 'Behold the children of the battalion of the Bonnet Rouge!'.
>
> The vivandière leaped for joy.
>
> 'Three heads under one bonnet!' cried she.
>
> Then she burst into sobs, embraced the poor widow wildly, and said to her, 'What a rogue the little girl looks already!'
>
> 'Vive la République!' repeated the soldiers.
>
> And the sergeant said to the mother —
>
> 'Come, citizeness!'

The reverse realisation of a politicisation of the face would have led to the conclusion that the peasant-woman was conniving with the enemy and so to her execution. For that matter, the beggar Tellmarch later finds the injured woman, left for dead, her children having been taken from her by the Vendeans, after been discovered in the ranks of the Bonnets Rouges battalion. The fact that she can potentially be the victim of all sides to the conflict, being on no side, allows Hugo to bring out her status of absolute innocence – that is, absolute depoliticisation – pure sensitivity, detachment from the social world – detachment that alone allows a direct, unmediated relation with the other – of the dialogic type.[59]

[59] A relation that only Tellmarch, the hermit beggar, can establish with everyone in this great butchery of *civil war*: the Vendean leader like the peasant-woman injured in the Bonnets-Rouges ranks. His compassion is universal and in this sense Tellmarch is an embodiment of Rousseauist

The account brings out first this toing-and-froing between the various ethical 'stages' of the relation to others, from solipsism to dialogism. The battalion and the sergeant are initially immersed in the world and address the other in a solipsistic attitude. They 'constitute' the peasant-woman *in* and *from* their *ego*, with the telling question, 'What are your political opinions?' The gradual discovery of the absolute innocence of the peasant-woman, that is, the fact that she is 'out of this world', leads them to release their pre-cognitive emotion – Rousseauist 'pity' – and establish a new relation, on a dialogic mode, through recognition that the other is their fellow creature: 'Come, citizeness!'

Next, Hugo's account confronts us with a new figure that we have not grasped so far who is the Enemy or the strange-stranger – the Alien, so to speak, because the term, since the eponymous film, has taken on a meaning of absolute strangeness, something that is completely foreign to humankind and must consequently be destroyed.

It is probably the phenomenology of Jean-Paul Sartre that will be of the greatest help to us in understanding this relation with the other. For Sartre, consciousness is always 'for itself', it is the annihilation of being, that is, 'in itself'. I am characterised therefore by non-coincidence with myself: 'I am what I am not and … I am not what I am'.[60] Being alone, I am unable to apprehend my own *situation* which 'reflects to me at once both my facticity and my freedom; on the occasion of a certain objective structure of the world which surrounds me, it [facticity] refers my freedom to me in the form of tasks to be freely done'.[61] This situation is revealed to him by the gaze of others, which seeks to bring the *for-itself* to the *in-itself*. Sartre takes the well-known example of shame, of which he says 'it is in its primary structure shame *before somebody*':

> I have just made an awkward or vulgar gesture. This gesture clings to me; I neither judge it nor blame it. I simply live it. I realize it in the mode of for-itself. But now, suddenly I raise my head. Somebody was there and has seen me. Suddenly I realize the vulgarity of my gesture, and I am ashamed. It is certain that my shame is

pity and reminds us that evil arises out of society, that power corrupts, and that consequently only the hermit is protected against corruption in these troubled times (at 96): 'Poverty, riches – that makes a terrible business. That is what brings on the catastrophes, – at least, I have that Idea. The poor want to be rich; the rich are not willing to be poor. It think that is about what it is at the bottom. I do not mix myself up with matters. The events are the events. I am neither for the creditor nor for the debtor.' This can be compared with Rousseau: 'He who has nothing desires little, he who commands no one has little ambition. But superfluity arouses greed; the more one gets, the more one desires. He who has much want to have all; and the madness for universal monarchy never tormented any but a great king's heart. Such is the march of nature, such is the development of the passions.' JJ Rousseau, *The Social Contract and Other Later Political Writings*, ed and tr V Gourevitch (Cambridge, Cambridge University Press, 1997) 164–65, 'The State of War'.

[60] Sartre, *Being and Nothingness* (n 24) 348.

[61] ibid.

> not reflective, for the presence of another in my consciousness, even as a catalyst, is incompatible with the reflective attitude; in the field of my reflection, I can never meet with anything but the consciousness which is mine. But the Other is the indispensable mediator between myself and me. I am ashamed of myself as I appear to the Other. By the mere appearance of the Other, I am put in a position of passing judgment on myself as on an object, for it is as an object that I appear to the Other.[62]

In this way, the gaze of others tends to reduce me to what I *am* (an *in-itself*), it dictates my *situation* at least in part through a constraint that redefines the possibilities of my liberty, makes a slave of me, and endangers me:

> I am a slave to the degree that my being is dependent at the center of a freedom which is not mine and which is the very condition of my being. In so far as I am the object of values which come to qualify me without my being able to act on this qualification or even to know it, I am enslaved. By the same token in so far as I am the instrument of possibilities which are not my possibilities, whose pure presence is beyond my being, I can not even glimpse, and which deny my transcendence in order to constitute me as a means to ends of which I am ignorant – I am in danger. This danger is not an accident but the permanent structure of my being-for-others.[63]

Victor Hugo's story is the fiction of an impossible *situation* through the gaze of others. The first questions have as their subject matter this transition from the *for-itself* of the unknown peasant-woman to an *in-itself*: 'What are your political opinions?' 'Which is your side?' 'Are you Blues? Are you Whites?' But this attempt to situate her proves a dead-end because the peasant-woman lost in the midst of the woods is a pure *for-itself*, she is in some sense thoroughgoing *existence* that cannot be assigned to any substance or any situation. 'We are people who are running away.' 'I am with my children.' And it is being confronted with this purity of a bare existence, so to speak, that moves the battalion and allows an outflow of feeling *in the state of nature*. Conversely, the Vendeans upon seeing the peasant-woman situate her as one of the 'reds'. This particular situation designates here as the Enemy, the strange-stranger, the Alien to be exterminated. Thus the gaze of others, by assigning to a substance, comes to negate the other as a human being deserving respect: here with this approach to massacre, we touch upon the link between ethics and norms.

The final example comes to illustrate Rousseau's idea that pity subsists in society in the form of 'social virtues': sentiment is not entirely annihilated, it is only the circumstances in which it emerges that are disrupted. I propose that readers look again at Nick Ut's *Napalm girl*, but this time with the original framing of the photo, which encompasses the context surrounding the face

[62] ibid 302.
[63] ibid 358.

of the little girl suffering. At the same time I give up on my attempt at *epoché* and look at the photo no longer setting aside what I know about it, the context it captures, its symbolic value, and the immense impact it had on US and world public opinion in the midst of the Vietnam War.[64] What I do observe is that the suffering face is full of this background that I no longer deny to my consciousness. Here again 'pity' as a pre-cognitive sentiment seems to have been exhausted.

Figure 1.3 Nick Ut, *Napalm girl*, original centring

But this disappearance of compassion does not mean the disappearance of all sentiment: it seems that the affect remains but transformed into 'social virtue', that is either into a feeling of *indignation* in the face of horror or a feeling of political solidarity with its victims, and more generally, with the Vietnamese people faced with America fighting an unjust war. It is therefore a genuine cosmo-political sentiment, that is, a feeling that is no longer of the order of 'spontaneous benevolence', but a political feeling constructed and developed in a self that is immersed in 'the world of life'.

[64] See B Stora, *Imaginaires de guerre. Les images dans les guerres d'Algérie et du Vietnam* (Paris, La Découverte, 2004).

Let us come back to our initial amazement: there is indeed 'ordinary compassion' for the remote other, the compassion we *naturally* feel for the other we do not know but who, a world away, is suffering in mind and body, a victim of injustice, being tortured to death at the tormentor's hands ... We have identified this compassion as Rousseauist 'pity', 'goodness' in Levinas, 'benevolent spontaneity' forming the 'affective flesh' of solicitude in Ricœur. It is each time a question of describing an a-social emotion, expressing itself at a stage at which consciousness is still capable of abstracting itself from the determinations of the world. These determinations are situated in the immediacy of the encounter,[65] at a pre-cognitive, *natural* stage, because they are not yet part of an 'extended-consciousness',[66] informed by memory and deformed by a plan.

We have also seen how this sentiment constitutes the 'affective flesh' of a relationship to others described categorically but also in accordance with an ethical advancement. Sentiment towards others is missing in a position of pure solipsism, in which the other becomes a product of the *I*, a function of the ego – with that constant risk of the negation of others: the other as pure volition, exposed to the risk of 'not wanting'. This feeling breaks through at a second stage of the relation, when the solipsistic consciousness manages to constitute the other as a *fellow*, that is to *imagine* as another myself, to step into the other's shoes. Compassion becomes possible: it is a form of *suffering together*, although determined by the *I*'s capacity to represent the other's suffering. But the limitations of such a relation can be understood: the other remains an *alter ego*, the other remains fundamentally 'same', meaning, for example, that their suffering can only be understood inasmuch as it refers back to my own experience of suffering.

Lastly, the ethical advancement reaches the stage of a dialogic relation, already included in Husserl's idea of 'appresentation': a reciprocal relation

[65] In terms of sociology, Tönnies' description of community suggests this immediacy of the encounter that correspond to the fictitious 'original and natural' in which it is supposed to arise: 'the theory of Gemeinschaft starts from the assumption of perfect unity of human wills as an original or natural condition ... The common root of this natural condition is the coherence of vegetative life through birth ... This close interrelation as a direct and mutual affirmation is represented in its most intense form by three types of relationships, namely: (1) the relations between a mother and her child; (2) the relations between husband and wife in its natural or general biological meaning; (3) the relation among brother and sisters, that is, at least among those who know each other as being the offspring of the same mother.' Tönnies (n 54) 37.

[66] I refer here to the distinction drawn by neurologist AR Damasio in his works – that I cannot go into more closely in the context of this contribution – between two types of consciousness: 'The simplest kind, which I call *core consciousness*, provides the organism with a sense of self about one moment – now – and about one place – here. The scope of core consciousness is the here and now. ... On the other hand, the complex kind of consciousness, which I call *extended consciousness* and of which there are many levels and grades, provides the organism with an elaborate sense of self – an identity and a person, you or me, no less – and places that person at a point in individual historical time, richly aware of the lived past and of the anticipated future, and keenly cognizant of the world beside it.' AR Damasio, *The Feeling of What Happens. Body and Emotion in the Making of Consciousness* (New York, Harcourt Brace, 1999) 16.

between the 'I' and 'Thou' that breaks away from the relation between the 'I' and 'It' in Buber; an asymmetrical relation between the *I* and the Other in Levinas, where the Other is transcendence, exteriority in the face of a radically separated *I*, with the connection being ensured by language; an unequal relation but that is constantly seeking equality in *friendship* in Ricœur, marked by the *solicitude* that arises as much from the *I* as from the Other. Feeling then appears in all its ethical dimension: it is no longer merely affect. There seems to be a difference, however, between Levinas and Ricœur: in Levinas, feeling and ethics are one, because the relation to the other is completely ethical; Ricœur, by contrast, makes a two-fold dissociation between ethics and morality on the one hand and between feeling, ethics, and morality on the other. In both instances, feeling is the flesh, the impulse, or the motive behind an obligation of the *I* towards the other. But morality takes up the running as it were from ethics when self-love threatens to change into *love of self*, under the effect of a *propensity to evil*. Fundamentally, it is the fragility of feeling, of solicitude in society that is emphasised here.

It is this fragility, this instability of feeling for others, and the slipping from one category to another of the relation to others that we have been able to explore through our three examples.

First the natural disposition of the local inhabitants to sympathise with the misfortunes of a refugee Rom population … gradually changing into exasperation and into a turning in on themselves: solipsistic consciousness, without quite forgetting the other facing it, looks to cast off its responsibility by ascribing it to some anonymous public institution. Then the fictional hypothesis of a pure existence that ushers in the transition from the solipsistic stage to the dialogic stage teeming with ethical life: confronted with the bareness of the peasant-woman's face, the battalion has 'the idea of infinity', of exteriority and speaks of goodness and justice, as in Levinas. Moreover, the phenomenology of Jean-Paul Sartre enables us to understand, perhaps more clearly still than that of Levinas, the massacre that ensues: the *situated* other, reduced to an *in-itself* Enemy is doomed to destruction. Lastly, to look at Nick Ut's photo as it was originally centred, is to understand that the pre-cognitive sentiment that supports the dialogical relation can be superseded by another sentiment, that recoups as it were the emotional substance from it, but to change it into something different: a political feeling, a cosmo-political sentiment, in the case at hand, when it takes the defence of the citizen of the world, my equal, my sister, the little girl burnt by US napalm.

'Benevolent spontaneity' flickers out in the politicisation of the other's face – the act of *situating* the other in the world – without this resulting in a return to solipsism.[67] The question of the cosmo-'political' sentiment,

[67] Here again Tönnies' formulas on the concept of society are evocative: 'The theory of the Gesellschaft deals with the artificial construction of an aggregate of human beings which superficially resembles the Gemeinschaft in so far as the individuals live and dwell together peacefully.

is therefore to find out how the feeling I have for the remote other can be maintained beyond the initial emotion and can form the substance of a dialogical relation. This is where the norm comes into play: a moral norm, initially, but also a legal norm with cosmopolitan law.

III. From Cosmopolitan Feeling to Legal Cosmopolitanism

How could passion be born between two beings despite the politicisation of their faces? Love of this kind is always miraculous in literature – and it is ultimately always an impossible love. Are not Romeo and Juliet representative in this respect of what was to be an aspiration of Modernity? Namely, the consecration of a freedom to escape from the social, economic, and political class or the family, tribal, and ethnic group into which birth assigns us. "Tis but thy name that is my enemy', says Juliet to Romeo in the garden of the Capulets, as if the spontaneity of love could separate Romeo's being, Romeo's face, from his social condition – that is from his surname, Montague:

> Thou art thyself, though not a Montague.
> What's Montague? It is nor hand, nor foot,
> Nor arm, nor face, nor any other part
> Belonging to a man. O, be some other name!
> What's in a name? That which we call a rose
> By any other name would smell as sweet;
> So Romeo would, were he not Romeo call'd,
> Retain that dear perfection which he owes
> Without that title. Romeo, doff thy name;
> And for thy name, which is not part of thee,
> Take all myself.[68]

Tragedy is inevitable because law is absent: and it is probably no chance matter if, after the death of the two lovers, it is the voice of the Prince that closes the play, blaming himself 'for winking at your discords' and announcing a 'glooming peace' and a morning on which '[t]he sun for sorrow will not show his head'.[69]

However, in the Gemeinschaft they remain essentially united in spite of all separating factors, whereas in the Gesellschaft they are essentially separated in spite of all uniting factors. … On the contrary, here [in the Gesellschaft] everybody is by himself and isolated, and there exists a condition of tension against all others. Their spheres of activity and power are sharply separated, so that everybody refuses to everyone else contact with and admittance to his sphere …' Tönnies (n 54) 65.

[68] *Romeo and Juliet*, Act 2, scene II, 38–48.

[69] ibid Act 5, scene III, 290–309.

Feeling for others is first pure spontaneity, as shown. It is situated before any social relation, before any situation of one person with respect to another. In Levinas, the third-party intervention puts an end to the face-to-face and changes the nature of the relation to others: henceforth this inter-human relation 'is a matter of justice' that is, of choice and judgment, of *situation* of the one relative to the other.[70] It is this *inter-est* that for Levinas is a source of conflict and violence[71] and calls for reflection on fair political institutions – if there can be such a thing.[72]

Paul Ricœur too discerns the perils of the inter-human relation arising from solicitude: if solicitude stems from asymmetry between the *I* and the other, it is open to 'all the maleficent offshoots of interaction, beginning with influence and culminating in murder'. It is these offshoots or excesses, this 'propensity to evil' identified by Kant,[73] that for Ricœur are behind the transition from solicitude to norm.[74] Whereas self-esteem (ethical quest for a good life) leads to solicitude, self-respect (the autonomous relation to obligation) has its dialogical counterpart in the respect due to people.[75]

Interaction in society is the opportunity to exercise '[t]he *power-over*, grafted onto the initial disymmetry between what one does and what is done

[70] Levinas, *Alterity and Transcendence* (n 35) 142–43: 'Responsibility for the other man is, in its immediacy, certainly prior to all questions. But how does it oblige, if a third party disturbs that exteriority of two people, in which my subjection qua subject is a subjection to my neighbour? The third party is other than the neighbour, and also a neighbour of the other, and not just his counterpart [*semblable*]. What am I to do? What have they already done to one another? Which one comes before the other in my responsibility? What are they, then, the other and the third party, in relation to one another? Birth of the question. The first question in the inter-human is the question of justice. Henceforth it becomes necessary, to make oneself a conscience. To my relation with the *unique* and the incomparable, comparison is superimposed, and, with a view to equity or equality, a weighing, a calculation, the comparison of incomparables, and therewith neutrality – presence or representation – of being, the thematization and visibility of the face, discountenanced [*dévisagé*] in a manner of speaking as the simple individuation of the individual; the weight of having and of exchanges; the necessity of thinking together beneath one synthetic theme the multiple and the unity of the world; and thereby the promotion of the relation and ultimate signifyingness of being to intentional and intelligible thought; and finally thereby the extreme importance in human multiplicity of the political structure of society under the rule of law, and hence institutions in which the *for-the-other* of subjectivity – in which the *I* – enters with the dignity of the citizen into the perfect reciprocity of political law that are essentially egalitarian or held to become so.' See also, E Levinas, *Otherwise than Being or Beyond Essence*, tr A Lingis (Dordrecht/Boston/London, Kluwer, 1991) ch V, 'Subjectivity and Infinity'.

[71] In *Otherwise than Being or Beyond Essence* (n 70) 4, interest is defined as *conatus of beings*, it is therefore the *esse* of being that exceeds the mere context of inter-human relations: 'Being's interest takes dramatic form in egoisms struggling with one another, each against all, in the multiplicity of allergic egoisms which are at war with one another and are thus together. War is the deed or the drama of the essence's interest.'

[72] Just institutions that are possible only if it is considered that the relation to others is one of disinterest (*dés-intér-essement*): Levinas, *Alterity and Transcendence* (n 35) 148.

[73] In his reflection on 'radical evil' in the first part of *Religion within the Boundaries of Mere Reason* (1793).

[74] Ricœur, *Oneself as Another* (n 40) 220.

[75] ibid 219.

to another – in other words, when the other suffers – can be held to be the occasion par excellence of the evil of violence'. Ricœur cites torture by which 'the tormentor seeks to reach and sometimes – alas! – succeeds in destroying the victim's self-esteem, esteem which our passage by way of the norm has elevated to the level of self-respect'.[76]

Conversely, solicitude remains present like the 'hidden soul' of the moral (and legal) norm. Solicitude 'is what, ultimately, arms our indignation, that is, our rejection of indignities inflicted on others'.[77]

The question of the relation to others is therefore a question of norms and so of law. When the force of the face-to-face has been exhausted, when solicitude gives way under the effect of social distinction that leads the one to seek to annihilate the other, the constraint of law steps in to regenerate feeling in the shape of civic feeling. Law is a regulator for the emotions: it boosts them when inadequate and curbs them when excessive.

Civic feeling is built up by the law with the material of solicitude, like Rousseau's 'social virtues' which are what is left of 'pity' in the civil state. In this way the law defines towards whom it is not only permitted but also mandatory to feel emotions. Tocqueville plainly showed this connection between sympathy and law in his patient enquiry into democratic peoples.[78] In Part Three of *Democracy in America*, he looks at the influence of democracy on mores: he shows in chapter one '[h]ow mores become milder as conditions become more equal', that is, that equal conditions and gentler manners (manifested through sympathy for others) go together.[79] In a hierarchical society such as aristocratic society, one feels sympathy for one's fellows only, that is, whoever belongs to the same 'caste' as oneself. And the services or succour rendered to someone of a different caste are rendered on the basis of mutual obligations, obligations that are not 'born of natural right but of political right',[80] because nobles cannot truly imagine the serf's suffering and vice versa 'and they scarcely even think of themselves as belonging to the same

[76] ibid 220.

[77] ibid 221. On indignation as a catalyst for political reforms see especially L Bradshaw, 'Emotions, Reasons and Judgements' in R Kingston and L Ferry (eds), *Bringing the Passions Back In. The Emotions in Political Philosophy* (Vancouver, University of British Columbia Press, 2008) 173–88, esp at 182–83. Stéphane Hessel's 'indignation' followed by the movement of the 'indignés' is not meaningless, as some have claimed. See S Hessel, *Indignez-Vous*, (*Cry Out*), revised and extended edn (Montpellier, Indigènes, 2011).

[78] I owe it to reading the work of Myriam Revault d'Allonnes to have drawn my attention to this passage of *Democracy in America*. See M Revault d'Allonnes, *L'homme compassionnel* (Paris, Seuil, 2008) 17ff. While using that work as a guide, I quote Tocqueville directly rather than using indirect quotations.

[79] de Tocqueville, *Democracy in America* (n 48) vol II, pt III, ch 1, 655ff. It would be worth citing the entire first chapter which is, as so often in Tocqueville, of rare intelligence and insight. I have to settle here for summarising and paraphrasing it with a few quotations, but I encourage readers to read it in full.

[80] ibid 656.

humanity'. Tocqueville remarks how medieval chroniclers reported with infinite pain the tragic end of a nobleman, but related 'the massacre and torture of men of the people in a single breath without batting an eye'. He cites a letter from Mme de Sévigné telling with amusement of the fierce repression of a popular revolt in Brittany, but goes on:

> It would be a mistake to assume that Mme de Sévigné, the writer of these lines, was a selfish, barbarous creature. She loved her children dearly and was quite sensitive to the sufferings of her friends. It is clear from reading what she wrote that she treated her vassals and servants with kindness and indulgence. But Mme de Sévigné had no clear notion of what it meant to suffer when one was not a nobleman.[81]

Democratic peoples probably are no more sensitive than Mme de Sévigné, but their sensitivity, says Tocqueville, bears on more objects, because of the principle of equality:

> In democratic centuries, men rarely sacrifice themselves for one another, but they do exhibit a general compassion for all members of the human species. They do not inflict useless ills, and when they can relieve another person's pain without much harm to themselves, they take pleasure in doing so. They are not disinterested, but they are mild.[82]

The conclusion is that, in the civil state, it is indeed law that directs compassion towards such and such an object, authorises it, makes it possible, prompts it:

> Thus, the same man who is full of humanity toward his fellow men when they are also his equals becomes insensitive to their sufferings once equality ceases. This man's mildness must therefore be attributed to equality more than to civilization or enlightenment.[83]

It is therefore the principle of equality that deploys Rousseauist 'pity', that is, the capacity to step into someone else's shoes: imagining being one's fellow. If one follows Tocqueville, this sympathy towards others may be deployed 'for all members of the human species'. What can this mean if not that the inclusion of the principle of equality into positive law gives rise to what we have termed a 'cosmopolitan feeling', that is, sympathy towards not just my 'fellow countryman' but towards every member of the human race who, *as of right*, by virtue of the principle of equality, is also as 'citizen of the world', that is, endowed with political and legal status?

Such a 'cosmopolitan feeling', however, runs up against three major difficulties. And it is to these three major difficulties that legal cosmopolitanism seeks to respond. In other words, legal cosmopolitanism can be conceived

[81] ibid 658.
[82] ibid 658.
[83] ibid 659.

as a legal elaboration of the principle of equality aimed at letting that principle deploy all its virtualities.

The first difficulty stands out in what Tocqueville has to say: if compassion extends to the whole *human race*, the idea of humanity itself does not designate a fixed set of members, as is shown by the example Tocqueville takes of the black slaves of Americans who are 'repeatedly subjected to very cruel punishments'. Slaves are excluded from humankind, which precludes any form of compassion towards them. It has long been known that the extension of the concept of humanity is variable: initially it is limited to the social group which stands apart from other social groups. Drawing on the work of Claude Levi-Strauss, Alain Finkielkraut observes that 'the idea that all people in the world form a single humanity is not, it is true, proper to the human species. What has for long distinguished mankind from most other animals is precisely the fact *that he does not identify with others of his kind*'.[84]

This first difficulty is compounded by a second: even if we successfully match the extensions of the concept of humanity with its real extension (all human beings on Earth), compassion for others would still run up against the problem of solipsism. Rousseauist 'pity' as 'imagining one's fellow' remains a prisoner of the limitations on constituting the other *in* and *from* my *ego*. Tocqueville saw this clearly too, comparing again aristocratic peoples to democratic peoples. Aristocratic peoples do not conceive general ideas since, because of the unequal circumstances between individuals, 'there seem to be as many distinct forms of humanity as there are classes'. On the contrary, the 'fellow' calls for a generalisation of ideas and application of his 'truths' to others:

> By contrast, a person who lives in a democratic country sees around him only people more or less like himself, so he cannot think of any segment of humanity without enlarging and expanding his thought until it embraces the whole of mankind. Any truth applicable to himself seems applicable in the same way to all his fellow citizens and fellow human beings.[85]

The relation to others remains a monadology, without moving forward to the dialogic stage: my equal is a Same, an *alter ego*, his otherness is

[84] A Finkielkraut, *In the Name of Humanity, Reflections on the Twentieth Century* (New York, Columbia University Press, 2000) 5. He cites *Structural Anthropology 2* by Claude Levi-Strauss: '[T]he concept of an all inclusive humanity, which makes no distinction between races or cultures, appeared very late in the history of mankind and did not spread very widely across the globe. … For the majority of human species, and for tens of thousands of years, the idea that humanity includes every human being on the face of the earth does not exist. The designation stops at the border of each tribe, or linguistic group, sometimes even at the edge of the village: so common is the practice that many of the people we call primitive call themselves by a name which means "men".'

[85] de Tocqueville, *Democracy in America* (n 48) vol II, pt I, ch 3, 495–96.

unthought – hence true equality is impossible, that is, *real* equality, which is not an abstract universal but which allows for differences, like part of the identity of the Same to the Other.

The final difficulty that besets the cosmopolitan feeling is related to the other two: it has to do with the structuring of the world: the 'sovereign states'. In the closed world we live in,[86] territories and populations find themselves in point of law (under international law) and usually in point of fact under the control of politico-administrative entities called states. This control is expressed legally in the form of *jurisdictions* that the state exercises exclusively over a given territory delimited by borders.

Such structuring of the world contributes to the previous two difficulties, namely the restriction of the concept of humanity and the solipsistic generalisation of 'truths'. It raises, besides, a difficulty of its own which is not to prevent the formation of a cosmopolitan feeling but to limit its effectiveness, the practical possibility that it should not be frustrated in its impetus but that this impetus might effectively be deployed in the real world. Let us look at these three points in turn, because they are the key to understanding legal cosmopolitanism.

First, the formation of a world of sovereign states is a curb on the process of matching the scope of the concept of humanity to its true extent (all human beings on Earth). Such a process was primed in Europe under Christian thought – but exclusively from a solipsistic perspective. In the famous controversy of Valladolid,[87] the point of view of Las Casas (against the Aristotelian view of Sepúlveda) was to accept that 'Indians' are part of humanity. That meant, for Las Casas, that their vocation was to become Christians, just as Europeans were. Accordingly, Christian thinking of the Second Scholasticism was universalist: Humanity is all one, composed of those who had already discovered Christ and those who were intended to discover Him. A detail of the magnificent fresco by Diego de Rivera in the National Palace in Mexico City shows Bartoloméo de Las Casas on the right using his crucifix to restrain the conquistadors who are killing the natives. But on the left, it can be seen that this protection is afforded so as to facilitate the conversion of the natives.

[86] René Jean Dupuy has so far made the most insightful analysis there is of this 'closure': RJ Dupuy, *La clôture du système international. La cité terrestre* (Paris, PUF, 1989).

[87] For an in-depth analysis of the positions of Las Casas and Sepúlveda, in the context of reflection on the relation with the other applied to the discovery of America, see T Todorov, *The Conquest of America. The Question of the Other*, tr R Howard (Norman, OK, University of Oklahoma Press, 1984) esp at 245ff. For a splendid reconstruction of the controversy worked into a novel, see JC Carrière, *La controverse de Valladolid* (Paris, Belfond, 1992).

Figure 1.4 DIEGO DE RIVERA, DETAIL, *HISTORY OF MEXICO* MURALS, 1929–30, PALACIO NACIONAL, MEXICO CITY

Religious quarrels and then wars within Christendom itself put an end to this solipsistic illusion of one Humanity. Europe itself renounced its unity, figured by the dual tutelage of Pope and Emperor: it broke up into 'sovereign states'. And with the emergence of sovereign states, it was equally many separate humanities that formed progressively under the name of 'nations'. Nations that are 'nation states', that is, the 'national' human set is determined essentially by a connection made between the identity of the state and the 'national' identity.[88] The national 'belongs' to the state, not just because of a legal tie – nationality – but because of his identity, cultural, descent, and even his 'race'.[89] This tie is exacerbated by 'nationalism', the development of which is the outcome of existential doubts related to the economic crisis and political climate, but whose origin rests upon the connection made between the modern state – as a politico-administrative organisation – and the Nation.

[88] See in this respect the insights of Gérard Mairet in his Foreword to the new edition of *Du contrat social* (Paris, Librairie générale française, Le livre de poche, 2011) 24: 'As concerns morality, democracy too is confronted with a very serious limitation: within the State, democracy is necessarily related to particularism, to national identity, and, when historical circumstances lend themselves to it, to outright nationalism. In truth, there is nothing surprising in that, since the moral characters of democracy are those of sovereignty itself: the particularism of the one, identity of the nation, citizenship thought of in reference to nationality, all of these are constituent ingredients of the sovereign that define the grammar of the modern state.'

[89] See the classical Benedict Anderson's *Imagined Communities* (London, Verso, first published 1983, 2006).

Jean-Jacques Rousseau was a spectator of this great separation that only intensified with the French Revolution. He saw in it the logical (or natural) continuation of the process that led men to unite into nations, then states, in order to try to end the perpetual state of war among them. But having (theoretically) ended *internal* war by the formation of states, men created the conditions for perpetual war among nations. So the same atrocities were committed but this time among 'nationals' of different countries and on ten times the scale:

> The civil law being thus become the common rule of citizens, the law of nature no longer obtained except between the different societies, where under the name of the law of nations, it was modified by some tacit conventions to render commerce possible, and supply the place of natural compassion, which, losing by degrees all that influence over societies which it originally had over individuals, no longer exists but in some great souls, who consider themselves as citizens of the world, force the imaginary barriers that separate people from people, after the example of the sovereign being from whom we all derive our existence, and include the whole human race in their benevolence.[90]

And Rousseau described very lucidly the consequences of such peace established by modern international law, the peace of 'graveyards' as Kant was to call it,[91] heralding the great massacres of the twentieth century:

> Political bodies, thus remaining in a state of nature among themselves, soon experienced the inconveniencies that had obliged individuals to quit it; and this state became much more fatal to these great bodies, than it had been before to the individuals who now composed them. Hence those national wars, those battles, those murders, those reprisals, which make nature shudder and shock reason; hence all those horrible prejudices, which make it a virtue and an honor to shed human blood. The worthiest men learned to consider cutting the throats of their fellows as a duty; at length men began to butcher each other by thousands without knowing for what; and more murders were committed in a single action, and more horrible disorders at the taking of a single town, than had been committed in the state of nature during ages together upon the whole face of the earth. Such are the first effects we may conceive to have arisen from the division of mankind into different societies.[92]

The second point is that the construction of the modern state and the formation of modern international law, further to the Reformation and the attempts to restore peace to Europe, themselves follow from a solipsistic attitude. International law is not based on the recognition of the other as

[90] Rousseau, 'The Second Discourse' (n 49) 125–26.

[91] I Kant, *Perpetual Peace: A Philosophical Essay* [1795], tr M Campbell Smith (London, George Allen & Unwin Ltd, 1917) Ak 8:347, 115: 'Whence it follows that a war of extermination, where the process of annihilation would strike both parties at once and all right as well, would bring about perpetual peace only in the great graveyard of the human race.'

[92] Rousseau, 'The Second Discourse' (n 49) 126.

Other, but as Same, sameness being defined narrowly by a legal status, that of equal sovereignty, from which a series of rights and duties flow. The two founding ideas of the European order of the seventeenth and eighteenth centuries – at the time the authority of the Emperor and Pope are in decline and the modern states on the rise – are *tolerance* and the *cujus regio, ejus religio* (whose realm, his religion) principle: in other words, the principle of *coexistence* at the price of mutual *indifference*. Each sovereign chooses his subjects' religion and by extension each sovereign chooses the political regime, and the economic, social, and cultural model applicable to his subjects. And each sovereign refrains from judging the choices made by any other sovereign and more so still from intervening in order to exert influence: that is called the '*domaine réservé*', or the 'principle of non-interference'. In other words, international law establishes the coexistence of states by excluding all discussion about what it is that divides them – religion, political and economic systems, etc. – and on the prohibition imposed all round on 'interfering' in the answer each state finds to those questions. The outcome is that each state refuses as a matter of principle any challenge to what it is that in its view forms its identity. On the contrary, the state is defined by its identity, by its relation to others. It is in maintaining and developing its own identity that it places its sovereignty.

The state in modern international law – the 'sovereign' state – is therefore solipsistic in its very principle: it *constitutes* the world and others *in* and *from* itself. International law itself is understood as drawing its validity from the *will* of the state (by a fiction making the state a *person* endowed with consciousness and will, like a natural person). By *dualist* reasoning that draws the consequences from the principle of sovereignty, international law can only be valid *from the state's point of view*, on the basis of a provision of municipal law, and generally a constitutional provision.[93] Likewise, the state constitutes humanity *in* and *from* its 'consciousness'. Thus it moves forward by generalisation, like Tocqueville's democratic man: all truths applicable to it are applicable to the human race. Humanity itself is constituted by analogy, then by universalising the specific case of the state that thinks it up. On the basis of this premise, some truth must be recognised in Carl Schmitt's anathema, 'Whoever invokes humanity wants to cheat'.[94] Except that the 'intent to harm' (to keep to anthropomorphic metaphors) is not

[93] Dualism that still prevails in most states, including those claiming to be monist. On the question of 'dualism' and its contradictions, see esp O de Frouville, 'Anzilotti d'hier et d'aujourd'hui' (2012) 56 *Droits* 239–53.

[94] In writing this Carl Schmitt claims to be applying 'a somewhat modified expression of Proudhon's', but fails to say which expression of Proudhon's he borrows. He also writes, 'The concept of humanity is an especially useful instrument of imperial expansion, and in its ethical-humanitarian form it is a specific vehicle of humanitarian imperialism.' C Schmitt, *The Concept of the Political*, tr G Schwab (Chicago, University of Chicago Press, 1996) 52.

necessarily established. Schmitt see malignance there where the state merely follows its natural propensity: from the moment it constitutes humanity *in* and *from* itself – without ever going through a dialogic stage of relation to the other – its action in favour of humanity necessarily has an imperialistic tendency. That is, it naturally tends to reduce the Other to the Same, to generalise its own truths and apply them to the other.

The third point is that the structuring of the world into sovereign states results in frustrating the cosmopolitan feeling that cannot find its extension in effective action, for want of any *capacity to act* and legal channels to do so. In the context of 'classical' international law, it is impossible to act for nationals of another state who, for example, are victims of arbitrary imprisonment. For one thing because the treatment reserved by the state for its nationals on its territory is an 'internal matter' covered by the principle of 'non-interference'; for another thing because individuals are not 'subjects' of international law: only states are subjects and have a capacity to act in the international arena. In light of classical international law, the state's *power over* its national (to use Ricœur's expression) is absolute; consequently, my *power-to-do*[95] is zero: I will be moved, sympathise, feel solidarity in vain because I can do strictly nothing about it, except perhaps call on my own state to intervene, knowing though that such an intervention lies ultimately within its discretionary power. Thus my feeling, because it can find no outlet, is in danger of becoming completely choked: I shall move from indignation to resignation and then indifference. The world divided by borders stifles the cosmopolitan feeling, which is ultimately reserved, as Rousseau writes, to a few 'great cosmopolitan souls'.

This brings us back to our initial question: *What is legal cosmopolitanism?* The world structured into sovereign states and international law gives rise to war, that 'state to state relation'[96] in which the 'propensity to evil' has free rein. Legal cosmopolitanism is the doctrine that seeks to grant entitlement to my cosmopolitan feeling, that is, my solicitude for the remote other in a world made up of sovereign states. More profoundly, it seeks to make an answer to the crucial question of the egalitarian relation to be maintained with every member of the human race in a world that is structured in law and in fact into sovereign states.

Legal cosmopolitanism rests on the double assertion of equality and respect, the quintessence of modernity concentrated by Kant at the double

[95] Ricœur, *Oneself as Another* (n 40) 220: 'We termed power-to-do, or power to act, the capacity possessed by an agent to constitute himself or herself as the author of action, with all the related difficulties and aporias.'

[96] Rousseau, *The Social Contract* (n 59) ch IV ('*Slavery*'), 11: 'War then is a relation, not between man and man, but between State and State, and individuals are enemies only accidentally, not as men, nor even as citizens, but as soldiers; not as members of their country, but as its defenders. Finally, each State can have for enemies only other States, and not men; for between things disparate in nature there can be no real relation.'

level of the formulation of the categorical imperative and the definition of law. Paul Ricœur has demonstrated the genius of a practical imperative that, in formulating the moral norm, combines the universalising force of the concept of humanity with the requirement to take account of the other in his otherness, with the idea of a person existing as 'end and never merely as means'.[97] The same tension can be found in the definition of law, whose 'universal principle' is:

> Every action which by itself or by its maxim enables the freedom of each individual's will to co-exist with the freedom of everyone else in accordance with a universal law is *right*.[98]

Universality comes to counter the 'propensity to evil' engendered by the asymmetry of the relation with others; but that universality must itself 'co-exist' with 'the free will of each and everyone', a will that reintroduces the person and the respect owed to them.

Whether in terms of morality or law, the task is always to cover the ethical continuum that stretches from the solipsistic attitude to the dialogic position. The task is even more to make the dialogic position both a moral and a legal duty, and moreover one of universal scope. There is in this requirement to hold together the dialogic attitude and universality, an extreme tension, a continual temptation to turn back to the *I*, to the solipsistic attitude.

In ordering interiority always to consider the person as end and never merely as means, the categorical imperative turns the 'consciousness of infinity' into a moral obligation. Pre-cognitive emotion is welcomed but kept at a remove by the respect owed to the person. Moral obligation tends to reduce the asymmetry of solicitude to bring the relation to the ultimate level of friendship. Moral obligation thus becomes the precondition for friendship, that is, the precondition for mutual consideration and reciprocity.

But this relation is clouded, as said, by the intervention of the third party, which raises the question of justice and consequently of law. There is no longer any room for either pre-cognitive emotion or morality: feeling changes into civic obligation, it is the flesh of an outside relation between myself and all others in society. No dialogic relation is possible – no possible reconciliation of freedoms – without constraint: the question of law then becomes the question of 'the possibility of universal reciprocal coercion being combined with the freedom of everyone'.[99]

[97] I Kant, *Groundwork for the Metaphysics of Morals [1785]*, Section 2, Ak 4:429, ed and tr AW Wood (New Haven, CT, and London, Yale University Press, 2002) 47: 'The practical imperative will thus be the following: *Act so that you use humanity, as much in your own person as in the person of every other, always at the same time as end and never merely as means.*' See also Paul Ricœur's commentary in *Oneself as Another* (n 40) 220ff.

[98] I Kant, 'The Metaphysics of Morals' [1797], Introduction, §C, Ak 6:230 in Kant, *Political Writings*, ed HS Reiss, tr HB Nisbet, Cambridge Texts in History of Political Thought (Cambridge, Cambridge University Press, 1970) 131–75, 133.

[99] ibid Introduction, § E, Ak 6:232, 134.

Thus the requirement of a dialogic relation is taken in charge in turn by morality and law, in a complex dialectic between the universal and the particular. And it is in this reconciliation between the universal and the particular that the formula can be found that is deployed step by step, from public law to the law of peoples, then from the law of peoples to cosmopolitan law, with each level being the guarantee for the other until it extends to all of humanity. Thus:

> It can indeed be said that this task of establishing a universal and lasting peace is not just a part of the theory of right within the limits of pure reason, but its entire ultimate purpose. For the condition of peace is the only state in which the property of a large number of people living together as neighbours under a single constitution can be guaranteed by *laws*.[100]

The first contribution of legal cosmopolitanism is therefore to put an end to a fragmented vision of the world and of law. The question of the relation to others is no different whether it is applied to the nearby other or the remote other. Only the structuring of the world into sovereign states could have given us to believe that the problem of my relation to the remote other might be different from my relation to the nearby other. By adopting a loftier point of view, that extends beyond borders, the cosmopolitan vision begins with the principle of one single humanity, within which the problem of law is itself unique, as if it were founded on the unique character of the problem of the relation to others.

Towards perpetual peace. This programme, which is at the heart of legal cosmopolitanism, does not, as is often thought, have as its sole purpose to establish peace among states. Perpetual peace refers to the problem of law in its entirety, itself defined on the basis of the relation to others. It crosses borders from the outset because it highlights the fact that war between states has no other cause than and is not different in nature from the violence among men within states:

> What is the use of working for a law-governed civil constitution among individual men, i.e. of planning a *commonwealth*? The same unsociability which forced men to do so gives rise in turn to a situation whereby each commonwealth, in its external relations (i.e. as a state in relation to other states), is in a position of unrestricted freedom. Each must accordingly expect from any other precisely the same evils which formerly oppressed individual men and forced them into a law-governed civil state.[101]

The propensity to evil that prompts one man to torture another or prompts states to wage war is invariably the same: the same moral and legal norms

[100] ibid Conclusion, Ak 6:355, 174.
[101] I Kant, 'Idea of a Universal History on a Cosmopolitical Plan' [1784], in *Kant. Political Writings* (n 98) Seventh proposition, 41–53, 47.

are necessary to try to curb that propensity and maintain friendship as a precarious balance, as the mark of both moral and civic virtue.

It is not the purpose here, as said, to expound the meaning of legal cosmopolitanism and describe in detail how it claims to achieve and maintain the ideal of a dialogic relation in plurality. The keys to such a balancing act seem however once again to have been developed by Kant in the three definitive articles for perpetual peace:

- First, all states must have a 'republican' constitution articulating freedom and equality as the regulating principles of a self-legislating practice.[102]
- Secondly, 'The law of nations shall be founded on a federation of free states',[103] an expression whose apparently contradictory character I have attempted elsewhere[104] to show actually conceals the idea of a process rather than a particular institution: a process that aims to extend the achievement of the 'republican' constitution in relations among peoples.
- Thirdly, '[t]he rights of men, as citizens of the world, [cosmopolitan law] shall be limited to the conditions of universal hospitality', each individual having *a right of visitation*, and this 'in virtue of our common right of possession on the surface of the earth on which, as it is a globe, we cannot be infinitely scattered, and must in the end reconcile ourselves to existence side by side; at the same time, originally no one individual had more right than another to live in any one particular spot'.[105]

It is hardly surprising that it is under this article that there arises the virulent denunciation not just of inhospitality but above all of colonialist practices of 'civilised nations' that 'fill us with horror'. Colonialism that is in a sense the very expression of solipsism eager to impose its truths on the other and in doing so to deny the other's existence.[106] Confronted with this solipsistic tendency that exasperates the asymmetry of the relation and leaves the propensity to evil to flourish, Kant recommends the modest *right of visitation* as the mark of respect for the infiniteness of difference of other people; this right, says Kant, 'does not amount to more than what is implied in a permission to make an attempt at intercourse with the original inhabitants'. A permission to make an attempt at intercourse and not permission to engage in intercourse: permission to make an attempt at the dialogic relation imbued with respect for the other in his own otherness – permission to make an attempt, that in its essence has no guarantee of achieving a result enabling 'far distant territories [to] enter into peaceful relations with one another.

[102] Kant, *Perpetual Peace* (n 91) Ak 8:349, 120.
[103] ibid Ak 8:354, 128.
[104] See in this volume ch 2, 'On the Theory of the International Constitution'; and ch 3, 'A Cosmopolitan Perspective on the Responsibility to Protect'.
[105] Kant, *Perpetual Peace* (n 91) Ak 8:357, 138.
[106] ibid Ak 8:358–359, 139.

These relations may at last come under the public control of law, and thus the human race may be brought nearer the realisation of a cosmopolitan constitution'.

It is at the end of this patient quest to strike a balance in a dialogic relation with others that a cosmopolitan law forms, that provides a basis for the interest and right of action of each of us for the other:

> The intercourse, more or less close, which has been everywhere steadily increasing between the nations of the earth, has now extended so enormously that a violation of right in one part of the world is felt all over it.[107]

So it is that cosmopolitan law grants entitlement to cosmopolitan sentiment, released by the dual assertion – insane in its reason and humble in its hubris – of equality and humanity.

[107] ibid Ak 8:360, 142.

2

On the Theory of the International Constitution

Pierre-Marie Dupuy is an inspired and inspiring mind. He invites young students and academics like myself to open their minds to new and different ways of thinking, to overcome strict formalism, while remaining lawyers and academics. His enlightened positivism underscores the necessity of situating law in its sociological and political context: law is a tool for regulating social relations, not a set of rules without consequences in real life:

> Les normes juridiques ne sont pas des expressions de la seule logique formelle. Ce sont aussi des instruments empiriques destinés à la régulation sociale. Elles ont elles-mêmes une histoire; elles sont l'expression de choix politiques et idéologiques qui ont des implications sur leur dynamique propre.[1]

Professor Dupuy constantly reminds us that our theories should be mainly descriptive, and only marginally prescriptive, if we want to remain in the spheres of science. However, he also recognises that academic discourse could and in fact should, at times, be prospective and attempt to devise new schemes more in line with present day sociological conditions.[2]

Among all of the issues Professor Dupuy addresses with his concern for opening minds and highlighting new perspectives, he gives particular attention to the concept of an international constitution.[3] This concept generally generates a lot of scepticism among international lawyers, especially French international lawyers. Pierre-Marie Dupuy has examined this concept very closely, and in particular the argument according to which the UN Charter is

[1] PM Dupuy, 'L'unité de l'ordre juridique international. Cours général de droit international public' (2002) 297 *Collected Courses of the Academy of International Law* (hereinafter '*Cours général*') 9–489, 209.

[2] *Cours général*, 211: 'Descriptive, non prescriptive, l'analyse juridique du droit international ne doit pas forcément s'effrayer d'être à l'occasion prospective, dans la mesure où elle est contrainte par l'accélération de l'histoire comme par l'affirmation ostensible d'une volonté collective de "moralisation du droit" à intégrer la composante idéologique et la variable temporelle dans l'analyse de la dynamique inhérente à la norme qu'elle a pour objet d'examiner.'

[3] PM Dupuy, 'The Constitution Dimension of the Charter of the United Nations Revisited' (1997) 1 *Max Planck Yearbook of United Nations* 1–33; *Cours général*, 215ff; PM Dupuy, 'Ultimes remarques sur la "constitutionnalité" de la Charte des Nations Unies' in R Chemain and A Pellet (eds), *La Charte des Nations Unies, Constitution mondiale?* (Paris, Pedone, 2006) 219–32.

seen as the 'Constitution of the International Community'.[4] While acknowledging the constitutional dimensions or the constitutional flavour of the UN Charter, Pierre-Marie Dupuy also develops a critical perspective based on the difficulties in terms of interpretation raised by this position. Difficulties arise, in particular, from the vagueness of the concept of a constitution. A constitution means different things in different legal traditions with the result that applying an indeterminate concept of a constitution to the UN Charter may not help in clarifying its content and its meaning.[5] Professor Dupuy recognises that viewing the UN Charter as a constitution may have an impact on providing a substantial unity to the international legal order. At the same time, he remains sceptical about what fundamentally appears to be an analogy with a concept generally used in relation to a state. Thus his cautiousness in handling the concept: at a certain level, it is quite certain that the UN Charter gives organic unity to the international community, as well as substantial common principles, but that does not clearly mean that it is appropriate to call it a 'constitution'.

I fully agree with this critical view on what has also been called the doctrine of the 'constitutionalisation' of international law. What is disturbing here is the failure to come to an agreement on the concept of a constitution. The movement described as constitutionalisation is not premised on a clear understanding of what its result is supposed to be.

Another question is whether we need the concept of a constitution in the first place to describe international law? I tend to think that under certain conditions such a concept would be very useful in understanding contemporary international law. International law is not what it used to be anymore, as Pierre-Marie Dupuy has taught us. The concepts which were forged by Vattel and his successors – sovereignty, consent, *non-interference* – clearly fall short of what we need to describe the changing structure of international law. We need new types of concepts – which does not mean that we need to reinvent law altogether. This chapter is based on the idea that legal theory offers a limited range of concepts to describe a limited phenomenon. Law is not everything and it is not an indeterminate phenomenon. It is a phenomenon which is immanent in any society (*ubi societas, ibi jus*) and that cannot be conflated with other types of phenomenon – for instance habits, courtesy, or certain types of moral rules the sanction of which is not socially organised. On this basis, I would like to argue that the concept of a constitution is useful in depicting the reality of any legal order. And the time may have come when the concept of a constitution should be put at the forefront again, not because there was no constitution before – in fact I will argue that there has always been a constitution in international law – but because this concept is now more useful than ever in understanding and describing international

[4] *Cours général*, 227.
[5] *Cours général*, 229.

law as it is today, that is a legal order which has become more complex, fragmented, and difficult to conceptualise with such elementary concepts such as sovereignty and consent.

In this attempt to make the concept of a constitution useful, I will come back to the thinking of the author who took the concept of 'Constitution' more seriously: Georges Scelle. Pierre-Marie Dupuy gives credence to Georges Scelle mostly for his 'dédoublement fonctionnel' – the role splitting theory,[6] but is quite reluctant when it comes to his constitutional thinking, and in particular his attempt to have recourse to the concept of social functions when reflecting upon the implementation of international law.[7] My belief is that there might be more to take from Georges Scelle than the *dédoublement fonctionnel*. At the same time, I also recognise the limits of his sociological position, and am particularly critical of the fact that this theory is obviously unable to explain how the facticity of power may take into account the 'social fact' in order to produce rules that claim to be both valid and legitimate.

In other words, Georges Scelle's theory reveals itself incoherent when it tries to explain how ethics meets power in order to produce law. I propose to try to remedy this defect by applying a democratic definition of law, that is a Kantian definition of law closely linked with the concept of freedom, albeit revised in light of discourse theory as developed by Jürgen Habermas.

I. Georges Scelle's Concept of the International Constitution

It seems quite natural to try to find support in Georges Scelle's work when reflecting upon the theory of the International Constitution. After all, Georges Scelle's second volume of the *Précis de droit des gens*, is simply called: 'Droit constitutionnel international'.[8] However, it is a fact (and maybe an injustice) that not much attention has been given to his views on international constitutional law.

This may be explained by, among other reasons, the fact that Scelle is often considered with sympathy by academics today, but also viewed as 'old fashioned'.[9] His sociological perspective based on Durkheim's work on the

[6] PM Dupuy, 'Humanité, Communauté et efficacité du droit' in *Humanité et droit international. Mélanges René-Jean Dupuy* (Paris, Pedone, 1991) 133–48, 138ff.

[7] *Cours général*, 79.

[8] G Scelle, *Précis de droit des gens. Principes et systématique*, vol 2: *Droit constitutionnel international* (Paris, Recueil Sirey, 1934) (hereinafter '*Précis de droit des gens*, vol 2').

[9] See Martti Koskenniemi's thorough analysis of Scelle's doctrine in M Koskenniemi, *The Gentle Civilizer of Nations. The Rise and Fall of International Law 1870–1960* (Cambridge, Cambridge University Press, 2002) esp at 338: 'By the onset of the Cold War such a view had lost political force. Its combination of realism and utopia seemed insufficient under both headings, too abstract to ground a realistic program for renewal and far from independent of the political struggles that it hoped to overcome. ... That he was sidelined from the preparation of

social division of labour seems too systemic in the eyes of post-Nietzschean thinkers, who reject the very idea of a general theory as applied to law or society. Also, the way Scelle sometimes opposes 'objective' and 'positive' law, and tends to judge positive law in the light of objective law is too evocative of a natural law framework which may lead some authors to the paradoxical conclusion that Scelle is not even a 'positivist' lawyer.

It would be a shame though, on the basis of these general ideas, not to read Scelle thoroughly, as we continue, for instance, to read Kelsen 80 years after he gave his course at the Hague Academy on the general theory of international law (1932). In particular, Scelle's writings on the concept of the International Constitution deserve at least to be studied carefully, even if one may, in the end, reject them in their entirety.

My aim is to take a closer look at this particular way of thinking and in particular to see how it develops an alternative theory to what could be considered as a more communitarian version of international constitutional theory, which supports the idea of the progressive 'constitutionalisation' of the international legal order.[10] Georges Scelle's thinking can be distinguished from

the Schuman Declaration of May 9, 1950, the century's most significant federalist move, betrays the sense in which his *Droit des gens*, must have seemed to the cultivators of the new pragmatism as old wine in yesterday's bottles.' In France, too, Georges Scelle is often seen as 'old wine in yesterday's bottles': see Carlo Santulli's Preface to the reprint edition of G Scelle, *Précis de droit des gens. Principes et systématique*, vol 1 (Paris, Dalloz, 2008) (hereinafter '*Précis de droit des gens*, vol 1'). See, however, the contributions included in the first volume of the *European Journal of International Law*, and in particular those of Hubert Thierry, René-Jean Dupuy and Antonio Cassese, who all demonstrate the actuality of Scelle's doctrine relating to a number of aspects of present international and European law.

[10] Almost all writings on the International Constitution or on the 'constitutionalisation of international law' adopt a communitarian perspective, insisting on 'community interests' and on the formation of an international community which would explain the development of an international constitution. This tradition may find its origins in the work of Alfred Verdross (see A Verdross, *Die Verfassung der Völkerrechtsgemeinschat* (Vienna and Berlin, Springer, 1926)), quoted by B Simma in his general course referenced below. See also A Verdross, 'Règles générales du droit international de la paix' (1929) 30 *RCADI*, esp at 354: 'En effet, le droit des gens contient des règles coutumières bien établies qui forment une véritable *constitution internationale* obligeant toutes les autorités. La primauté du droit des gens, ou mieux de la constitution internationale, n'est donc pas un postulat, mais une réalité'. Professor Bruno Simma co-authored the 1976 edition of Verdross, *Universelles Völkerrecht*, (Berlin, Duncker & Humblot, 1976, 2010) describing the UN Charter as the constitution of the international community. His general course in The Hague maintains this position: B Simma, 'From Bilateralism to Community Interest in International Law' (1994) 250 *RCADI*, esp at 258ff. On similar lines are, among the most important authors: C Tomuschat, 'Obligations Arising for States without or against Their Will' (1993) 241 *RCADI* 195; J Frowein, 'Reactions by not directly affected States to breaches of public international law' (1994) 248 *RCADI* 345; J Klabbers, A Peters and G Ulfstein, *The Constitutionalization of International Law* (Oxford, Oxford University Press, 2009); E De Wet, 'The International Constitutional Order' (2006) 55 *ICLQ* 51–76. The same type of approach can be found in the analysis of European Law: see in particular A von Bogdandy and J Bast, *Principles of European Constitutional Law*, 2nd edn (Oxford, Hart Publishing, 2009). Bardo Fassbender distinguishes three currents in the doctrine of the International Constitution: Verdross and his School, the New Haven School, and the Doctrine of International Community (starting with Hermann Mosler and continued by Christian Tomuschat). See B Fassbender,

this discourse on the constitutionalisation of the international community in three ways: the constitution is immanent in any society and not transcendent of a given community; the constitution is a phenomenon and not an idea of reason; and the constitution is a process and cannot be contained exclusively in a single written document.

A. Community and Society

Let us start with what is probably the most crucial issue, as it is the one that best reveals the differing positions of Scelle and what we could call the communitarian position. For the latter, the concept of a constitution is closely linked to the idea of community. On the contrary, for Georges Scelle, a constitution is inherent to law and law is inherent to society. Central to the communitarian conception is the distinction between community and society, originally crafted by Ferdinand Tönnies in one of the seminal pieces that gave birth to sociology as a science.[11]

Georges Scelle relies on another distinction, contemporary of Tönnies' and which is partly but not totally overlapping, namely Durkheim's distinction between two types of solidarities: solidarity by similarities (or 'mechanical solidarity'), and solidarity arising from the division of social labour (or 'organic solidarity').[12] To a certain extent, solidarity by similarities is consonant with Tönnies's concept of community existing in even 'primitive' human groups, whereas solidarity through division of social labour only takes place in more evolved social groupings, called societies by Tönnies. Tönnies' and Durkheim's descriptions and theories of the evolution of any human groupings are more or less the same: 'primitive' human groups are unified by strong beliefs in common values, as well as by traditions, which are habits turned into rules. In such communities, individuals are tied by similarities. As social and economic activities develop, a social division of labour takes place, differentiating between individuals who become more aware of their

'The United Nations Charter as the Constitution of the International Community' (1988) 36 *Columbia Journal of Transnational Law*, 529 and 'Rediscovering a Forgotten Constitution: Notes on the Place of the UN Charter in the International Legal Order' in JL Dunoff and JP Trachtman (eds), *Ruling the World? Constitutionalism, International Law and Global Governance* (Cambridge, Cambridge University Press, 2009) 133.

[11] F Tönnies, *Community and Society* [1887], tr CP Lommis (New York, Dover Publications, 1957). The distinction was also foundational in René-Jean Dupuy's reflection on the 'international community'. See for instance, RJ Dupuy, *L'Humanité dans l'imaginaire des Nations* (Paris, Julliard, 1991) 98: '"Communauté" et "société internationale", ces deux expressions, couramment utilisées indifféremment comme des synonymes, recouvrent des notions distinctes. Toute société suppose une communauté de base. En revanche, la communauté n'est pas nécessairement organisée en société. … La vieille distinction de Toennis entre communauté et société (*Gemeinschaft und Gesellschaft*) est ici parfaitement applicable.'

[12] E Durkheim, *De la division du travail social* [1930], 7th edn (Paris, PUF, 2007).

particularities and thus less inclined to unquestionably abide to the common rules as dictated by 'the conscience of community'. Society is primarily driven by interests, including common interests, whereas community is driven by values. The main difference between Tönnies and Durkheim is that Tönnies remains within the ambit of an idealistic view of history, inherited from Marx: he sees the evolution from community to society as a linear and inevitable movement of modern history, progressively leading to fragmented and conflicting societies. By contrast, Durkheim's views tend to be much more realistic and do not rely on a teleological view of history: the evolution towards society does not preclude the survival of community values, even though their influence tends to diminish. Society remains a natural but not mechanical phenomenon.[13] Any evolved human grouping is characterised by a tension between the two types of solidarities. Society and community coexist at each time in different ways and at different levels and in the end it is a mixture of interests and values that keeps the society tied together.

One implicit point of agreement between the communitarian school and Scelle, is that at the international level, the evolution takes exactly the reverse path: in other words, society precedes community.[14] Those human groupings that emerge as sovereign states in the beginning of the sixteenth century were precisely born on the rejection of common values, and in particular of common religion. *Cujus regio, ejus religio* was the key to peace among European nations. Tolerance, in international law, meant the right to non-interference in domestic affairs. Thus the society of states that takes its rise from that moment is not and cannot be a community: its rules are based on the idea of minimum relations to regulate their coexistence in war and peace. It is only in its most recent history from the end of the nineteenth century that the idea that *values* should innerve the content of international law took a second breath. This was concretised progressively through the hardships of the two world wars and based on the experience of globalisation which gave a growing sense of interdependence and of common destiny. Thus international society was first a society based on the division of social labour, and it was only at a certain stage of its evolution that a solidarity based on similarities emerged. One clear symptom of this can be seen through the evolution of the concept of a crime in international law. Durkheim's point of departure

[13] See E Durkheim's note on Tönnies' book, 'Communauté et société selon Tönnies' (1889) 27 *Revue philosophique* 416–22, reproduced in E Durkheim, *Textes I. Eléments d'une théorie sociale* (Paris, Ed de Minuit, 1975) 383–90. On this debate, see S Paugam, 'Durkheim et le lien social' in E Durkheim, *De la division du travail social* [1930] (Paris, PUF, 1990) 8–10, also mentioning the position taken by Raymond Aron.

[14] See however René-Jean Dupuy's interpretation who tends to associate the concept of Society with institutionalisation: Dupuy, *L'Humanité dans l'imaginaire des Nations* (n 11) 98–99: 'La société est non plus un fait spontané, mais le fruit d'un vouloir délibéré, rationalisé et définissant un ordre légal. Elle se concrétise dans l'organisation internationale. Cette société organisée pourra, à son tour, agir sur la communauté de base et la consolider.'

in the analysis of the two types of solidarity is to show that criminal law is the *first type of legal norm* to appear in any human grouping, as the most immediate and basic expression of a solidarity within the group based on similarities. Conversely, the weight of criminal law tends to diminish in more evolved social settings, and other branches of law, like civil law and commercial law tend to develop in order to regulate the phenomenon associated with the division of labour. As far as international law is concerned, criminal law only emerged as a legal category in positive law in recent times – starting with the trials of Nuremberg and Tokyo after World War II. This late appearance of criminal law as a branch of international law clearly demonstrates that there was an international society before an international community finally took shape.[15]

The fundamental divergence between Scelle and the communitarian school lies in the fact that the latter associates the concept of a constitution with the idea of community. In other words, in the perspective of Verdross and his successors, a constitution can only come into force with the formation of the international community, understood as a human grouping which is tied together not only by common interests, but also by common values. For the neo-Verdrossian authors like Simma or Tomuschat, a constitution means universal legal values and sufficiently developed institutions that are able to implement those legal values.

Conversely, Georges Scelle sees the constitution as an inherent feature of any legal order, which itself is the natural consequence of the coming into being of a society. According to Scelle, solidarity decreases in intensity as its range expands and similarities become less obvious. But still, world solidarity does exist in international society, and like in every society social functions have to be fulfilled. Rules relating to the fulfilment of social functions form the essential part of constitutional law and, says Scelle, no society can persist without them.[16]

[15] Pierre-Marie Dupuy follows this line of reasoning when he shows that the 'International Community' as integrated in positive international law is essentially a fiction which has a dynamic effect on the development of the International Society and of International Law. The fiction works as a Pure Idea of Reason in Kant's philosophy, *Cours général*, 268: 'Qu'est-ce, en droit, que la "communauté internationale dans son ensemble"? C'est la fiction juridique d'une solidarité universelle affirmée a priori, pour inciter les Etats à agir comme s'il était avéré qu'elle existe vraiment: le droit, et la technique de la fiction dont il a la maîtrise, comme instrument de formalisation du projet philosophique proposé aux nations, ainsi unies.'

[16] See *Précis de droit des gens*, vol I, 51: 'Il est aujourd'hui indiscutable que le fait juridique intersocial est mondial: que des relations sociales existent en puissance entre tous les habitants de la terre, et que les échanges de produits, de services et d'idées s'entrecroisent comme un réseau sur l'ensemble de la planète. Cette solidarité mondiale est nécessairement la plus diffuse et la plus lâche, car cette solidarité diminue d'intensité à mesure que son aire s'élargit, par l'affaiblissement des similitudes. Mais dans toutes ces sociétés interétatiques, les fonctions sociales doivent être et *sont remplies*: la règle de droit est exprimée; les compétences conférées; les situations juridiques réalisées; leur régularité constatée, leur effectivité assurée …' And *Précis de droit des gens*, vol 2, 7: 'Toute collectivité intersociale, y compris la communauté universelle

In other words, Scelle's constitution does not come at the end of a process of evolution for international society when states tend to form an international community based on common values and institutions.[17] It is there right from the beginning, from the moment a minimal society is formed and exchanges take place between nationals of different countries. The constitution is not a project, it is a reality. And this leads us to the second important distinction.

B. The Constitution as a Phenomenon

Depending on the definition one gives to the concept of a constitution, the International Constitution can be understood either as a phenomenon or as an idea of reason. Its content can be very demanding, corresponding to what one might call a 'thick' concept of a constitution, described as follows by Samantha Besson:

> a superior legal norm that is usually but not always laid down in written document and adopted according to a specific procedure (1) that constitutes and defines the powers of the main organs of the different branches of government (2) and that is in principle protected through specific revision rules against modification by ulterior legislation, over which it therefore has priority (3).[18]

In other words, this concept of a constitution is one of 'constitutionalism' as a political and legal doctrine, reflecting the ideal of a democratic constitution and of the rule of law, as these ideas were developed from the end of the eighteenth century in the western world.

The International Constitution, in this regard, appears much more as a distant goal than as a reality. In this vein, the concept of a constitution fulfils two functions: heuristic, in the sense that it allows us to build a different understanding of international law from the more classical one; but also dynamic,

du Droit des Gens repose, comme les collectivités mieux intégrées et notamment les collectivités étatiques, sur un ensemble de règles constitutives essentielles à leur existence, à leur durée, à leur progrès. Là même où ces collectivités paraissent avoir l'organisation la plus rudimentaire, où les normes fondamentales semblent les plus indécises et où les institutions paraissent inexistantes, une *constitution* au sens large, mais au sens juridique, ne s'en révèle pas moins. Elle est apparente dans les systèmes super-étatiques ou fédératifs et dans les systèmes extra-étatiques. Elle l'est moins dans les systèmes interétatiques où le droit classique voyait les phénomènes internationaux typiques; – elle ne peut pas cependant ne pas s'y rencontrer.'

[17] One can trace a parallel with the debate – in the context of the European Union – on the 'no demos' thesis, ie the thesis according to which there can be no Federal Democracy at the level of the EU – and thus no Constitution – because there is nothing such as a 'European People'. This thesis is brilliantly deconstructed by R Schütze, *European Constitutional Law* (Cambridge, Cambridge University Press, 2012) 71–74, who shows it is based on 'three constitutional denials' which are all 'false problems' created by a 'wrong constitutional theory', ie the 'Europe's statist tradition'. See also, L Lourme, *Qu'est-ce que le cosmopolitisme?* (Paris, Vrin, 2012) 57.

[18] S Besson, 'Whose Constitution(s)? International Law, Constitutionalism, and Democracy' in JL Dunoff and JP Trachtman (eds), *Ruling the World? Constitutionalism, International Law and Global Governance* (Cambridge, Cambridge University Press, 2009) 381–407, 386.

as it identifies an aim of the evolution of the interstate society, an aim which, once declared, is to be pursued by social actors. The more recent discourse on the constitutionalisation of international law follows the same logic. In his introductory chapter to a book on the *Constitutionalization of International Law*, Jan Klabbers defines the intent of the authors as follows: '... our aim is to see what a constitutional international legal order could look like'. This approach thus situates itself 'somewhere in between the strictly normative ... and the strictly descriptive'.[19] In this context, the concept of a constitution is often used as a benchmark to evaluate the degree of evolution of a legal order. Authors would *compare* the current state of international law with the Idea of Constitution as understood by constitutionalist thinking.

Partly normative, partly heuristic, the concept of a constitution thus appears as a regulatory idea, a project to be pursued but never reached.

As we have already seen, Scelle's position is totally different: he does not conceive of the constitution as an idea, but as a reality, as a phenomenon that can be known through the analysis of positive law – and thus present since international law came into existence.[20] In other words, the concept of a constitution is inherent in the phenomenon of law – it is immanent and not transcendent. If a constitution exists as soon as legal norms emerge in a society, it can only be the 'thin' concept of a constitution. Again, following Samantha Besson:

> The thin constitution is an ensemble of secondary rules that organize the law-making institutions and processes in a given legal order. Any autonomous legal order entail a thin constitution.[21]

This perfectly matches Georges Scelle's definition of the constitution as a legal instrument that contain rules and principles having primacy over other rules, regulating the devolution and the exercise of power and organising the implementation of social functions in a given society. There is no mention of such sophisticated ideas, such as the separation of powers or the rule of law. In other words, Scelle's constitution is not constitutionalist. It gives up all the complex apparatus developed to make the constitution a tool for the preservation and the development of human freedom. Does this mean that Scelle's

[19] J Klabbers, 'Setting the Scene' in Klabbers, Peters and Ulfstein, *The Constitutionalization of International Law* (n 10) 1–44, 4.

[20] It should be noticed that Verdross, while closely linking the notion of an international constitution to the idea of an international community, also asserts that the constitution is a *reality* (in 1929). See the quotation from Verdross, 'Règles générales du droit international de la paix' (n 10).

[21] Besson, 'Whose Constitution(s)?' (n 18) 385. See also, Fassbender, 'Rediscovering a Forgotten Constitution' (n 10) 139, describing his ideal type of the constitution: 'A constitution is a set of fundamental norms about the organization and performance of governmental functions in a community, and the relationship between the government and those who are governed. It shall, in principle, for an indefinite period of time, provide a legal frame, as well as guiding principles for the political life of a community.'

conception totally omits the question of freedom? Certainly not. But freedom is not central to Scelle's construction, something that we will discuss later on, as it is, in my opinion, the main difficulty of Scelle's conception.

C. The International Constitution as a Process

A third issue is to know whether the constitution can be localised in a written document, or whether it is mainly composed of unwritten rules which may, or may not, be codified in a written document. Most of the constitutionalist authors would follow Verdross' proposal that the UN Charter has become the constitution of the international community. They would tend to perceive it as a 'constitutional moment' in the history of humanity. This is not to deny that there have ever been any 'constitutional principles' before the UN Charter. But broadly speaking, the relationship between international constitutional principles and the International Constitution is thought of in the same way the French revolutionnaire thought of the relationship between the Kingdom Laws (*Lois du Royaume*) and the 1791 Constitution. The *Ancien Régime* certainly had constitutional laws, but not a constitution, because those laws were conceived as having their source in nature, or God's command rather than in History. Those laws were a legacy, not a novation.

According to this position, a constitution is the result of an act of will, and not of a spontaneous and continuous process. The legal constitution is the expression of the values of a community, but it also represents a particular moment in history: there is a *before* and an *after*. The constitution also has an institutional dimension. It is not merely normative. The constitution means new international organs and a reasoned and voluntary distribution of competences between them, in order to try to manage a certain balance of powers.

One comes back to the idea of a constitution as an idea of reason and the *thick* concept of the constitution, but also a constitution as a political technology, rather than as a legal technique.

The second position sees the constitution essentially as an unwritten body of rules. This does not exclude that certain constitutional rules are established by treaty. But the core constitution is of a customary nature. Two elements should be underscored.

First, the constitution is the result of a process and not of a decision. There may be a text, adopted at a certain moment in time, that would integrate a number of constitutional rules in a single document. But such a text does not prevent the constitution from evolving. Philip Allott's theory of the 'three constitutions of society' is consonant to this approach. According to Allott, 'the constitution is three constitutions in one – the legal, the real, the ideal':

> The *legal constitution* is the constitution as law, a structure and a system of retained acts of will. Retained acts of will which are concerned with the distribution and

> use of social power are carried in the legal constitution … The *real constitution* is the constitution as it is actualized in the current social progress, a structure and a system of power. It is the constitution as it takes effect in the present-here-and-now, as actual persons exercise the social power made available by the legal constitution to realize the possibilities of the ideal constitution … The *ideal constitution* is the constitution as it presents to society an idea of what society might be. … In the ideal constitution, society conceives of its other selves, possible selves which conform to the idea of itself as society. In willing, society chooses to make an actual self out of one of its possible selves. Its possible selves are possibilities inherent in the legal constitution and the real constitution.[22]

A second important dimension of this position is that the constitution does not necessarily include an institutional dimension: there may be a constitution without any specific bodies to implement it. The constitution may simply distribute the competences between individuals or pre-existing collective bodies. There is no need for separation of powers or even a balance of powers so that 'power stops power'. Once again, this conception brings with it a *thin* definition of a constitution.

Of course, the solution to that problem is the best known part of Georges Scelle's work: the *dédoublement fonctionnel*. Scelle shows that a legal order may prosper without any specific organs of its own. The social functions are nonetheless implemented because the 'inorganic society' 'borrows' its governing personnel from the 'organic societies' – that is, in the case of international law, from national societies.[23] The legislative, judicial and executive functions *are effectively* implemented, but this does not mean that one can identify any specific legislative, judicial or executive organs.

D. A Critique of Georges Scelle's Theory

Georges Scelle leads us to an alternative concept of the International Constitution which is, in my view, potentially very fruitful. It allows us to conceive of a constitution not as the expression of a community – as opposed to a society – but as a mere legal technique. From this point of view, the constitution needs not be seen as an idea of reason – a kind of sophisticated ideal when applied to international law – but as a phenomenon inherent in any society. Any society, as elementary and loose as it may be, generates legal norms; and any legal order includes a constitution. And finally, Scelles' concept of the constitution allows us to better situate the phenomenon of a constitution in time, as it shows that a constitution is not a single

[22] P Allott, *Eunomia, New Order for a New World* (Oxford, Oxford University Press, 1990) 134–36.

[23] *Précis de droit des gens*, vol 2, 12.

written document adopted at a certain moment in time (Philip Allott's *legal constitution*), but a constant process which is being actualised at every moment (the *real constitution*) as a result of the evolution of society and the evolution of how society sees itself (the *ideal constitution*).

However, Georges Scelle's conception of the constitution is also, in other aspects, problematic. This is what I would like to focus on here with a view to finding ways to cure these problems so as to be able to reconstruct the concept of the International Constitution starting from Scelle's theory. The main problem with the theory is that it fails to explain properly the link between freedom and constraint.

According to Scelle, positive law is the product of the encounter between social fact and power. In other words, power does not create law, it only 'takes note' of a rule which is already established at the level of society – what Scelle calls 'objective law'.

Such a conception meets two obstacles. The first is that Scelle admits that power has a will of its own and may at times, far from 'taking note' of objective law, deviate from it. He comes to the conclusion that in these cases, positive law reveals itself to be 'anti-legal' (*anti-juridique*). This is often perceived as one of the main weaknesses of Scelle's theory: a new dualism at the very heart of monist theory, between 'positive law' and 'objective law', with the latter being used as a benchmark to judge the former.

The second obstacle lies in the fact that Scelle does not explain practically how power is supposed to take note of social fact and even why power should take note of social fact in the first place. Power is itself a product of the division of labour: the individuals who fulfil governmental functions are the most powerful.[24] It is thus difficult to understand why the most powerful individuals, being in office, could be incited or even forced to take into account the social fact. According to Scelle, this is precisely the function of the constitution to organise this coincidence.[25] But at the same time he demonstrates the priority of facticity against both legitimacy and validity: a legitimate power, Scelle argues, ceases to be a legal power, from the moment that it is not a factual power anymore.[26] Finally, Scelle's construction lies on an unstable foundation: the rulers' morals.[27] The rulers have to be wise enough not

[24] *Précis de droit des gens*, vol 1, at 23: 'Les gouvernants qui exercent ou contrôlent l'exercice des fonctions publiques sont en fait les individus qui détiennent les forces matérielles: les armes, la richesse ou le nombre.'

[25] ibid: 'Les constitutions ont pour but, qu'elles soient écrites ou coutumières, de constater et d'organiser cette concordance.'

[26] ibid 23–24: '[L]e pouvoir dit *légitime* ne le demeure, ne reste un gouvernement de *droit*, que tant qu'il dispose de la force nécessaire à accomplir les fonctions sociales. *Lorsque son efficacité disparaît, il ne possède plus de titres juridiques. Il cesse d'être gouvernement de droit dès l'instant qu'il n'est plus gouvernement de fait.* Il est alors du devoir de ceux qui détiennent la force de prendre en main l'exercice des fonctions publiques. *Leurs titres juridiques sont dans l'efficacité de leur action*, dans sa conformité avec la solidarité sociale.'

to use their power in contravention of objective law. It is easy to see that there is no guarantee at all that they would do so. To the contrary, following Montesquieu's wise remark – '*tout homme qui a du pouvoir est porté à en abuser*' – it seems quite obvious that the rulers, once in place, will tend to try to find ways to stay in power and to impose their own will, even if at some point it runs counter to the solidarity needs of society. There is a strong chance that the government will enact 'anti-legal' laws. And what then is the remedy against such a situation? Scelle admits that there is only one: revolution.[28]

The difficulties of Scelle's doctrine can be traced to the dual systematic link that he establishes between *validity and legitimacy* on the one hand, and *facticity and validity* on the other hand. Scelle insists on their convergence, on the necessary '*concordance*' between force, law and legitimacy. But he does not explain how exactly this *concordance* can happen. On the contrary, by recognising the priority of power over law and social fact, he seems to admit that divergence will be the rule, rather than the exception. Divergence between validity and legitimacy: this is what Scelle calls 'anti-legal law' – a piece of legislation that is formally law, but which is in fact the product of an arbitrary exercise of power. Divergence between facticity and validity: that happens when the rulers use illegal means (contrary to positive, valid law) to govern in the name of solidarity needs which provide a source of legitimacy for power against law.

It is thus clear that the problem that needs to be solved lies in the relationship between these three components of power: facticity, legitimacy and validity. A model must be found that keeps their relative autonomy, instead of insisting on their necessary convergence and of denouncing as contrary to 'objective law' situations where this convergence does not happen – a position which in fact brings us back to a natural law type of reasoning. A concept of the constitution should be found that allows us to cover all the types of relations between those three components without excluding any in an aprioristic manner, while making it possible to figure out how convergence can be achieved. My submission is that a democratic theory of international law allows us to find the solution.

II. A Theory of the International Constitution Based on a Democratic Theory of International Law

The missing element in Scelle's theory is freedom. This is not to say that Scelle ignores *freedoms*, as part of the International Constitution. He dedicates

[27] ibid 24: 'Arrivés à ce point limite, il faut bien constater que dans une société déterminée la soumission du pouvoir à la règle de droit est une question d'équilibre de forces et de moralité gouvernementale.'

[28] ibid 5: 'La discordance entre le droit objectif ou naturel et le droit positif peut alors engendrer des ruptures de solidarité qui se traduisent par des révolutions.'

a whole chapter to the question of freedoms and clearly makes them an integral part of international constitutional law. But he doesn't see *freedom* as a founding principle of the Constitution, only as an object of the Constitution. The clear reason for this, of course, is that he does not believe that an abstract freedom exists as such. Scelle's sociological conception generally rejects all abstracts ideas and transcendental concepts. Freedom, like sovereignty, is one of those transcendental concepts. My intention is not to bring back freedom as an idea of pure reason to the foundation of law. I totally adhere to Scelle's belief that scientific knowledge should be rooted in social fact. To this regard, I have argued in an earlier article that Jürgen Habermas' theory of communicative action has made it possible to reconstruct Kant's theory of morals and law while taking into account the objectivist turn of the social sciences.[29] Kant's central concept of freedom as autonomy is kept, but autonomy is no longer understood as a legislative activity of the self through practical reason, but as the product of the social practice of communication.[30]

Autonomy does not mean that each subject should consent to the rules so that they acquire legal validity and become enforceable including through the use of force, but instead that each one should be able to think of herself *as if she was* the author of the rule and not only the subject of the rule.[31] Such a conception brings us very near to Georges Scelle, except on one crucial point: it puts itself in the position of reconciling normativist and objectivist theories, by finding a correct balance between facticity, validity and legitimacy.[32] The practice of discussion becomes the social medium through which constraint and social fact can be reconciled. In other words, a proper use of discussion in society leads to the enactment of legal rules enforceable by public

[29] O de Frouville, 'Une conception démocratique du droit international' (2001) XXXIX *Revue européenne de Sciences Sociales (Cahiers Vilfredo Pareto)* 101–04, available at ress.revues.org/659.

[30] Thus, from now on, when I use freedom, I mean by this word not the transcendental Idea of Pure Reason, but autonomy as realised *through the social practice of discussion.*

[31] This principle of autonomy as self-legislation was originally crafted by Rousseau. Kelsen acutely summarises the idea as follows: 'The problem of political freedom is: How is it possible to be subject to a social order and still be free? Thus, Rousseau has formulated the question to which democracy is the answer. A subject is politically free insofar as his individual will is in harmony with the "collective" (or "general") will expressed in the social order. Such harmony of the "collective" and the individual will is guaranteed only if the social order is created by the individuals whose behaviour it regulates. Social order means determination of the will of the individual. Political freedom, that is, freedom under social order, is self-determination of the individual by participating in the creation of the social order. Political freedom is Freedom, and Freedom is autonomy.' H Kelsen, *General Theory of Law and State* (Cambridge, MA, Harvard University Press, 1945) 285.

[32] See J Habermas, *Between Facts and Norms* (Cambridge, Polity Press, 1996) 6–7: 'Tossed to and fro between facticity and validity, political theory and legal theory today are disintegrating into camps that hardly have anything more to say to one another. The tension between normative approaches, which are constantly in danger of losing contact with social reality, and objectivistic approaches, which screen out all normative aspects, can be taken as a caveat against fixating on one disciplinary point of view. […] Here my concern is to work out a reconstructive approach that encompasses two perspectives: the sociology of law and the philosophy of justice.'

constraint which, at the same time, may claim to be legitimate because they reflect social fact.

Following that path, I have identified a 'democratic conception of international law' which is normative in its content, in the sense that it prescribes a certain type of evolution of the international legal order, from the international law of the society of sovereign states to the cosmopolitan law of the universal human society.[33] In contrast, I have tried to build a democratic theory of international law which is non-normative in nature. Its goal is not to *prescribe* a particular evolution of the international legal order, but rather to *describe* that evolution. It does so through a lens which is not the one still widely used today, namely the Westphalian theory of international law. It does so on the assumption that law cannot be separated in its very essence from freedom. Central to the theory is Kant's argument that law is based on autonomy and aims at the preservation and reconciliation of the freedom of each individual with the freedom of all. It does not mean that law *should* or *must* preserve freedom, but that freedom is a necessary concept to understanding law as a phenomenon.

Starting from this conception, a constitution, like any legal phenomenon, must be understood as being closely related to freedom. A constitution is, as we have said above, fundamentally a group of norms organising the attribution and exercise of power within society, in particular by setting rules on how basic social functions are fulfilled. Seen from the other side, a constitution aims at determining how and how far individuals in a given society can exercise their freedoms. In other words, every constitution is a constitution of freedom, not in the sense that it *institutes freedom*, but in the sense that all constitutional rules fundamentally aim at regulating freedoms in a society. Freedom, understood as a social practice, is the key to understanding how a constitution balances facticity, validity and legitimacy. Freedom refers us to two sets of concepts which, when combined together, reflect the entire diversity of constitutional experiences. Those two sets of concepts are autocracy and democracy at the level of constitutional theory; and anarchy and the federal state at the level of international legal theory. Kant's cosmopolitanism will give us the key to relate the two sets of concept and thus establish the concept of an international constitution under a democratic theory of international law.

A. Between Autocracy and Democracy

The first set of concepts relate to constitutional theory. Hans Kelsen is certainly the author who best characterised the concept of the constitution in

[33] de Frouville, 'Une conception démocratique du droit international' (n 29).

relation to the idea of freedom. Kelsen rightly saw that '[t]he central problem of a political theory is the classification of governments. From a juristic point of view, it is the distinction between different archetypes of constitutions'.[34] The classification of forms of state has indeed been one of the main tasks of political philosophy since Plato. Kelsen recalled that 'the political theory of Antiquity distinguished three forms of state: monarchy, aristocracy, and democracy'. To this trichotomy, Kelsen substitutes a dichotomy differentiating between 'two types of constitutions: democracy and autocracy'. And he adds that '[t]his distinction is based on the idea of political freedom'.[35] Kelsen's theory of the constitution based on political freedom constitutes the missing part of Scelle's doctrine:

> Politically free is he who is subject to a legal order in the creation of which he participates. An individual is free if what he 'ought to' do according to the social order coincides with what he 'wills to' do. Democracy means that the 'will' which is represented in the legal order of the state is identical with the wills of the subjects. Its opposite is the bondage of autocracy. There the subjects are excluded from the creation of the legal order, and harmony between the order and their wills is in no way guaranteed.[36]

Here the relationship between facticity, validity and legitimacy is well explained. In a democracy, the three components are perfectly in line, in the sense that the legal (valid) rule is legitimate (because in harmony with the will of the subjects), and not only binding but enforceable (facticity). By contrast, in an autocracy facticity prevails over validity (the government can act in an illegal manner) and the link between validity and legitimacy is broken (valid laws are not legitimate, because they are not in harmony with the wills of the subjects). Translated into more Habermassian terms it means that the democratic constitution guarantees and permits the full exercise of communicative freedoms, so that subjects can also think of themselves as if they were the authors of the rules, thus making legal constraint legitimate. The autocratic constitution is characterised by the limitation or the suppression of communicative freedoms, reducing as far as possible the public space for discussion, and thus preventing the process of the legitimisation of legal rules and transforming constraint into an arbitrary use of violence by those possessing force.

Autocracy and democracy are schemata under the pure idea of the constitution or, as Kelsen puts it in a more Weberian fashion, ideal types:

> In political reality, there is no State conforming completely with one or the other ideal type. Every State represents a mixture of elements of both types, so that some communities are closer to the one, some closer to the other pole. Between

[34] Kelsen, *General Theory of Law and State* (n 31) 283.
[35] ibid 284.
[36] ibid.

> the two extremes, there is a multitude of intermediate stages, most of which have no specific designation. According to the usual terminology, a State is called a democracy if the democratic principle prevails in its organization; and a State is called an autocracy if the autocratic principle prevails.[37]

All constitutions that exist can be characterised using this set of concepts – autocracy and democracy.[38] The International Constitution is no exception to that rule. When we look at the International Constitution and try to understand its nature we can refer to these concepts and try to determine whether it is rather an autocratic constitution or a democratic constitution.

But this alone is not enough because the International Constitution is not only a constitution; it is also an *international* constitution. This is where the second set of concepts comes in.

B. Between Anarchy and the Federal State

The second set of concepts comes from international legal theory and more specifically from the Kantian/cosmopolitan theory of international law. Freedom, at the level of states, is not only about the freedoms of individuals but also the freedom of states as collective entities. And it is clear – from the very beginnings of modern international law – that the former is closely linked to the latter, that is: the freedom of states has always been understood as being the condition for the freedom of individuals. In other words, there can be no freedom of individuals subject to foreign domination. Thus, for the state as considered in the society of sovereign states, the road from absolute freedom to the deprivation of freedom is not the one that goes from democracy to autocracy, but instead the one that goes from anarchy to the federal state. The state of anarchy in the society of sovereign states is a state of absolute freedom for states: there is no superior authority and states are perfectly autonomous. In the federal state, by contrast, states lose their 'sovereignty', that is their autonomy, and submit themselves to a bond.

In Kant's philosophy, the road from anarchy to the federal state is considered from a normative perspective: it is a duty imposed by reason that states should leave the state of nature so as to put an end to *all wars* and establish peace. As is well known, Kant contemplates the possibility of a world

[37] ibid.

[38] I would tend however to follow Hannah Arendt by saying that the only exception would be the constitution of the totalitarian state. Arendt shows that the constitutions of totalitarian states cannot be assimilated into what we understand as autocracy or what she calls 'tyranny': it is of a different 'essence'. See H Arendt, *The Origins of Totalitarism* (Cleveland/New York, Meridian Books. The World Publishing Company, 1958) 464: 'If lawfulness is the essence of non-tyrannical government and lawlessness is the essence of tyranny, then terror is the essence of totalitarian domination.'

federal state,[39] but ultimately resists the idea, apparently convinced by a realist argument. Of course the world federal state remains an idea of pure reason and one should work tirelessly to achieve it *as if* it were possible, although it may not be. The only thing that can be achieved for certain is not anarchy or the world federal state, but, submits Kant, a 'federation of free states'.[40] This expression takes the form of an antinomy: there can be no institution that is at the same time both a federal state (abolishing the sovereignties of the states to the benefit of the federal state) and what is usually called a *confederation* (in which states keep their sovereignty but transfer a number of competences to common organs). It must be one or the other. What Kant must mean by that is that the institution to be created is something in between the federal state and the confederation. It is, in fact, a *process* rather than a fixed institution. It is a process that starts from the society of sovereign states (a state of anarchy) and tends to the model of the world federal state without ever reaching it. The European Union is, of course, the example which is most commonly cited to illustrate this Kantian idea of the 'federation of free states' – being neither a classic 'international organisation' nor a federal state, but which combines characteristics of the two types to form an original and constantly evolving institution.[41] Theories of the Federation have been elaborated on this basis following two distinct traditions: the objectivist tradition on the one hand, with Hans Kelsen and Georges Scelle;[42]

[39] I Kant, 'Idea for a Universal History with a Cosmopolitan Purpose' in *Kant. Political Writings*, ed HS Reiss, tr HB Nisbet, Cambridge Texts in History of Political Thought (Cambridge, Cambridge University Press, 1970) Seventh Proposition, 41–53, 47.

[40] See I Kant, 'On the Common Saying: "This May be True in Theory, but it does not Apply in Practice"' in *Kant. Political Writings* (n 39) 61–92, 90, 92; and the Second Definitive Article of a Perpetual Peace: 'The Rights of Nations shall be based on a Federation of Free States' in I Kant, 'Perpetual Peace. A Philosophical Sketch' in *Kant. Political Writings* (n 39) 93–130, 102–05.

[41] See for instance the thorough analysis by S Oeter, 'Federalism and Democracy' in von Bogdandy and Bast (eds), *Principles of European Constitutional Law* (n 10) 55, esp at 80: 'The united Europe of the European Union will not be a federal state in the classical sense for quite some time, but will remain a treaty-based hybrid – a mixed system that will gradually develop more federal characteristics and at the same time keep some traits of an arrangement of international co-operation.' See also, on the classification of the European Union as a Federal Union, Schütze, *European Constitutional Law* (n 17) 47ff.

[42] Kelsen, *General Theory of Law and State* (n 31), 316: 'Only the degree of decentralization distinguishes a unitary State divided into autonomous provinces from a federal State. And as the federal State is distinguished from a unitary State, so is an international confederacy of States distinguished from a federal State by a higher degree of decentralization only. On the scale of decentralisation, the federal State stands between the unitary State and an international union of States.' G Scelle, *Précis de droit des gens*, vol 1, ch III, esp at 200: 'Il n'y a pas une, mais plusieurs formes d'Etat fédéral: aucune ne peut être considérée comme la forme type exclusive. L'Etat fédéral n'est lui-même que l'intégration la plus poussée du fédéralisme, mais en étudiant le droit positif, on s'aperçoit que ce n'est pas toujours dans l'Etat fédéral que le génie du fédéralisme est le mieux respecté, ni l'indépendance des collectivités fédéralisées la mieux assurée.' See also ibid ch III, section IV, 'League of Nations as a Federal Organization'. On similar lines is Hersch Lauterpacht in his brilliant conference 'Sovereignty and Federation in International Law' in E Lauterpacht, *International Law. Being the Collected Papers of Hersch Lauterpacht*, vol III (Cambridge, Cambridge University Press, 1977) 5–25, esp the conclusions at 25: 'The ultimate

and the organicist Schmittian tradition.[43] Despite their radical differences, both come to the conclusion that the traditional dichotomy between the federal state and the confederation is not satisfactory, as the reality of constitutional experiences offers no examples of such types. What separates the federal state from the confederation is only a difference of degree, not of nature. And most of the constitutional arrangements which aim at conciliating the freedom of component states with a strong centralised power can be subsumed under the unique concept of *federation*, a concept which corresponds to Kant's 'federation of free states'.

C. Synthesis: The Definition of the Constitution

Kant's cosmopolitan perspective not only allows us to understand the nature of the constitution as perceived from the point of view of the society of sovereign states, it is also the key to joining the states' perspective with that of the individuals. Kant's Second Definitive Article of a Perpetual Peace – which prescribes a federation of free states – is inseparable from the First Definitive Article – according to which 'the Civil Constitution of Every State shall be Republican'.[44] The state of peace inside the states is conditioned by those states having a republican constitution (that is what we would call today a 'democratic' constitution). But this state of peace is unstable and uncertain whilst the society of states is still in a state of anarchy. Only by submitting themselves to a republican constitution can states establish a lasting state of peace.[45] There can be no democracy without peace, and no peace without democracy. In other words, the harmony between facticity, validity and legitimacy inside a state is precarious until this harmony is also established between the states.

Kant's doctrine is, as we said, normative in the sense that the establishment of a democratic federation of free states is a requirement of reason. But we

rational solution of the problem of international organization will be hastened – and this may be submitted as a summary of the conclusions of this lecture – by the acceptance of the view that the differences between the typical forms of unions of States are to a large extent a matter of degree [...]'.

[43] Schmitt's theory of the Federation can be found in C Schmitt, *Théorie de la Constitution* (Paris, PUF, 1993). This aspect of Schmitt's theory is the subject of Olivier Beaud's thorough analysis in *Théorie de la Fédération* (Paris, PUF, 2007).

[44] See Kant, 'Perpetual Peace' (n 40) 99.

[45] See I Kant, 'The Metaphysics of Morals' [1797], *The Theory of Right*, pt II, § 61 in *Kant. Political Writings*, ed HS Reiss, tr HB Nisbet, Cambridge Texts in History of Political Thought (Cambridge, Cambridge University Press, 1970) 131–175, 171: 'Since the state of nature among nations (as among individual human beings) is a state which one ought to abandon in order to enter a state governed by law, all international rights, as well as all the external property of states such as can be acquired or preserved by war, are purely provisional until the state of nature has been abandoned. Only within the universal *union of states* (analogous to the union through which a nation becomes a state) can such rights and property acquire *peremptory* validity and a *true state of peace* be attained.'

can still use this model in a non-normative, purely descriptive way. Under anarchy, states maintain their full autonomy. The society of sovereign states is a 'democratic' society of states – in that they are all equally sovereign. Conversely, in the federal state, the states lose their freedom: it is a state of heteronomy/autocracy, as the law of each state is subject to federal law. The only autonomy that states retain is by virtue of federal law which determines the competencies left to the components. But at the domestic level, this heteronomy (from the states' point of view) can lead the individuals to be submitted either to a state of autonomy/democracy or to a state of heteronomy/autocracy, depending on the nature of the federal constitution. If the constitution of the federal state is democratic, then the individuals will find themselves in a state of autonomy; if it is autocratic, they will find themselves in a state of heteronomy. In other words, there is no synchrony between the two sets of concepts. The democracy of states (the society of sovereign states) may go with either an autocratic or a democratic rule on individuals. Similarly, a federal state does not automatically mean that individuals will live in democracy, as the federal constitution may be of an autocratic type.

Georges Scelle does not say anything else, when he notes that the evolution of international law will inevitably lead to a growing institutionalisation of the international order and will finally result either in a universal empire, or a world federation.[46]

III. An Overview of the Evolution of the International Constitution

We now have a concept of the International Constitution that we can apply to positive international law. The aim of this theory – like any theory – is to create a system made up of concepts that helps us to understand reality. I think that the concept of the International Constitution and the argument that there is and has always been an international constitution are useful when trying to understand international law. Of course, it is not possible in the limited framework of this chapter to examine thoroughly the present state of international law in the light of the theory of the International Constitution.

[46] G Scelle, 'Quelques reflexions sur l'abolition de la compétence de guerre' (1954) LVIII *RGDIP* 5, 22: 'Dans une époque d'anarchie comme celle que nous vivons, le pouvoir n'est pas encore parvenu à s'intégrer au sein du féodalisme inter-étatique. Il est à la recherche d'un centre unique et faute de son établissement les règles éthiques les plus indispensables à la réalisation de l'ordre juridique international demeurent inefficaces. On sait qu'il n'est que deux remèdes possibles à cet état de choses dont nous n'avons effleuré qu'un aspect: l'Empire universel ou le Fédéralisme œcuménique. Nous assistons à la gestation de l'un ou de l'autre. Les époques révolutionnaires ne comportent aucune sécurité, même si les principes qu'elles dégagent sont une préfiguration de l'ordre juridique à venir.'

But we can at least try to draw some very broad conclusions on the evolution of international law.[47]

Clearly, the 'Westphalian' or classical constitution of international law was the constitution of an anarchic and democratic society of sovereign states. The main constitutional principle from which all others derived was equal sovereignty. Among the major corollaries were the constitutional principles of exclusive territorial jurisdiction and of non-intervention. The aim was to preserve the states' sovereign autonomy within their frontiers. The ultimate goal was the promotion of peoples' freedom through the medium of sovereignty. This Constitution was simple and remarkably stable. It remained almost untouched for nearly two centuries (between the middle of the eighteenth century and 1919). Today's International Constitution, by contrast, is complex and unstable. The Charter of the United Nations has certainly become the main building block of the Constitution. It brings a number of important innovations, sometimes in continuity with the Covenant of the League of Nations, sometimes in rupture.[48] All of these should be studied thoroughly, but let me here present a very brief overview of these innovations:

- The shift from a concept of negative peace to a concept of positive peace: international law and international organisations are now entrusted with the task of creating the necessary conditions for a lasting peace, thus provoking a tremendous extension of the field of international law which rapidly overcomes the domain of the relations between states and progressively extends to all types of human activities.
- New rules conditioning the formation of states and government: whereas this field was left totally unregulated under the 'Westphalian' Constitution, the principles of self-determination and respect for human rights tend to bring new conditions to the creation of a state and to the establishment of an effective government.
- Prohibition of the use of force for the settlement of disputes and creation of the Security Council invested with the right to use legitimate violence in order to maintain peace and security. This is of course a major shift in the allocation of power at the international level: the use of legitimate violence becomes a residual competence of states and is partly institutionalised.
- Proclamation of universal human rights, meaning first the guarantee of fundamental rights for individuals at the level of the federation and second the recognition of a democratic principle at all levels, including

[47] For a complementary – awaiting a more complete – account, see O de Frouville, 'Le paradigme de la constitutionnalisation vu du droit international' in S Hennette-Vauchez and JM Sorel, *Les droits de l'homme ont-ils constitutionnalisé le monde?* (Bruxelles, Bruylant, 2011) 193–215, esp at 201–11.

[48] See J Crawford, 'The Charter of the United Nations as a Constitution' in J Crawford, *International Law as an Open System. Selected Essays* (London, Cameron & May, 2002) 123.

at the level of international organisations (the first Kantian Definitive Article: the Constitution of every state shall be Republican).

- Growing centralisation of the fulfilment of social functions, whereas decentralisation was the rule under the Westphalian Constitution.
- Establishment of a hierarchy of norms, with the Charter prevailing over all obligations of states under any other treaty (article 103).
- Constitutional regulation of the relations with regional organisations (articles 53–54).

This attempt to establish a global constitutional order through a written constitution is, however, facing major obstacles because no effective mechanism has been put in place to enforce the hierarchic principle set forth in the Charter. In fact, the International Constitution is fragmented. There is a *geographic fragmentation* due to the fact that regional constitutional orders maintain a certain degree of autonomy. Each of the supposedly lower levels in the hierarchy have their own dynamic and no specific mechanism is provided for to ensure that the law and practices produced are in conformity with the constitutional and legislative principles at the universal level. It is clear that there is an effort made by judges to ensure complementarity and harmony, rather than multiply cases of duplication and conflict. However, in some extreme cases, the regional level may affirm its own principles in contradiction with the obligations set at the superior level – like in the *Kadi* case, where the Court of the European Union reproduced the 'Solange' type of argumentation, putting the federal level in check.

Sectorial fragmentation is also apparent as sites of production of constitutional norms multiply outside the effective reach of the United Nations. Even within the UN System, there are a range of international organisations each with their own 'constitution' (their constitutive treaty) and each developing constitutional principles in a more or less autonomous manner. It is true that coherence here is more or less maintained through self-regulatory mechanisms – a general sense of the communities of lawyers, diplomats and civil servants working with or in relation to those organisations that there should be a certain degree of coherence at the level of principles and rules and that the UN Charter is the ultimate reference when devising new rules or interpreting existing rules. Lack of coherence is more visible outside the UN system, particularly within organisations that developed separately or parallel to the UN like the economic organisations. The constitutions of those organisations do not even formally take into account the principles of the United Nations and may develop their own principles in isolation. Again, judges would try to minimise this 'clinical isolation', but with obvious limits as long as they continue to consider themselves organs of the constitution of their partial legal order rather than organs of the federation.

The contemporary Constitution thus appears relatively stable as far as its fundamental principles are concerned, but at the same time subject to a degree of instability because of its relative fragmentation. These difficulties are not exclusive to the International Constitution. Specific procedures aimed at ensuring the conformity of enacted rules to the constitution are a recent innovation in many countries. It is difficult to systematically ensure that principles and rules developed by all institutions within a state are in strict conformity with the constitution and it is even more so at the decentralised level or at the level of the states in a federal system. To those who would argue that there can be no international constitution because of these difficulties, we would answer by recalling that until very recently in France it was not possible to effectively sanction the non-conformity of an already adopted legislation with the Constitution. The only available remedy was the invocation of international legal principles having the same content as constitutional norms … since the system of the *question prioritaire de constitutionnalité* (*Priority Preliminary Rulings on the issue of constitutionality*, best known as the 'QPC') has been set up in 2010, its growing success has shown at least the uncertain state of conformity of many laws with the Constitution.[49]

It is also a fact that some geographic fragmentation may be permitted in certain cases to accommodate local peculiarities. Acting on a QPC, the Conseil constitutionnel has recently recognised the conformity to the French Constitution of the specific regime applied in Alsace-Moselle providing for the payment by the state of pastors, in clear contradiction with the general principle of secularism, provided by the first article of the Constitution. The Conseil has admitted that in declaring the principle of secularism, the authors of the Constitution had no intention of bringing into question this regime which dated back to the period of the French Consultate.[50]

The final question is where to situate the International Constitution in the light of the two sets of concepts we identified earlier? The principle of self-determination and the principle of respect for human rights, clearly confer on the International Constitution a federal and a democratic character. The system of collective security and the ability of the Security Council to decide on the use of force against a state also have a clear federal dimension. But at least two other elements tend to moderate this characterisation.

First, the principle according to which all states must obey and implement the decisions of the Security Council gives an autocratic flavour to the Constitution. The Security Council appears to be an oligarchic type of organ. By reason of its discretionary power and in absence of any judicial control of its decisions, it may also intervene in fields and fulfil functions which do

[49] See the figures dated March 2013 on the Conseil Constitutionnel's website; since the entry into force of the QPC in 2010, the Conseil has registered 1,520 applications. It has taken 255 decisions on 297 applications, among which 137 decisions reached a conclusion of conformity, while the others concluded on the at least partial non conformity of the law to the Constitution.

[50] Decision 2012-297, QPC, 21 February 2013, note by A Macaya and M Verpeaux, 15 *La Semaine Juridique*, 15, 8 April 2013, 426.

not fall in the purview of its initial attribution. Being initially entrusted with the exercise of certain executive powers within the field of the maintenance of international peace and security, the Security Council may overstep its mandate at will and act as a legislative or judicial body in all fields which are more or less loosely connected with the issue of peace and security. The Constitution does not realise democracy, but records the social fact of domination by a limited number of states. At the same time, this autocracy is not a tyranny and it may not even be a dictatorship. The Council is based on the idea of creating a balance between the most powerful states, in this sense it generally prevents unilateral power automatically prevailing and integrates 10 additional states on a rotating basis to the deliberation. The main problem remains the veto power, which compromises the Council's efficiency and relative legitimacy. As long as the veto power is seen by the five permanent members of the Council (the 'P5') as a necessary condition for the balance of power, the influence of the Council will remain limited. Another factor which reduces the autocratic nature of the Council's power is that it does not intervene in all fields of social life, but mainly in fields which have, as we said, a more or less loose link with issues of security. In other words, the Council will never play the role of a world dictator who would monopolise the three functions of government. The Council is comparable to a Minister of Interior who would have superior powers compared to the other ministers of the government and who would be able to derogate at times to statutes in order to deal with specific cases or situations. But he will, for instance, rarely be directly involved in issues related to culture, health or economy … thus granting the 'ministers' in charge of these areas a large degree of autonomy.

The second element which tends to moderate against the characterisation of the Constitution as democratic and federal is, more generally, the weakness of existing international institutions. Certainly, it is not possible to say anymore that the international society is inorganic. There are today a great number of international institutions which play a fundamental role in the fulfilment of social functions at all levels. However, these institutions can rarely be said to be democratic. It is clear that the idea of representative democracy (like a world parliament or deliberative assemblies elected by citizens of the world) is clearly out of reach at this stage of the development of international law. The only options to be explored are deliberative democracy types of institutional arrangements allowing the effective participation in the processes of deliberation by a maximum number of stakeholders.[51]

[51] On the role of NGOs in coping with the democratic deficit in international organisations, see PM Dupuy, 'Sur les rapports entre sujets et "acteurs" en droit international contemporain' in LC Vohrah et al (eds), *Man's Inhumanity to Man: Essays on International Law in Honour of Antonio Cassese* (The Hague, Kluwer Law International, 2003) 261–78; 'Le concept de société civile internationale. Identification et genèse' in H Gherari and S Szurek, *L'émergence de la société civile internationale. Vers la privatisation du droit international?* (Paris, Pedone, 2003) 5–18.

Another weakness of international institutions lies in their fragmentation and their limited powers. For instance, in the field of human rights, the galaxy of mechanisms and procedure at the universal and regional levels have at least the virtuous effect of obliging states to justify themselves, but their effectiveness still ultimately depends on the cooperation of states.

IV. Conclusion

The International Constitution as it appears today reflects the reality of an international society caught between the search for efficiency and the quest for legitimacy.

The *search for efficiency* is an incentive towards federalisation and autocracy. It reflects the project of the survival of humanity: efficient global governance seems imperative in the face of global risks like the shortage of natural resources, demographic growth, mass migration or global warming. If such efficient governance is to take place, states will have to renounce their national egoisms and waive short term national interests. Such a waiver cannot be granted – at least not in the proportions needed to attain the desired efficiency – by governments subject to periodic election or facing strong oppositions ready to take advantage of nationalist passions, at the risk of compromising the fulfilment of cosmopolitan obligations. Such waivers should be imposed from the federal level through binding legislation. In the present state of the Constitution, however, it is hard to conceive how such a bond could be imposed democratically – that is how to reconcile constraint with freedom. There is no procedure that would enable the implementation of the principle of autonomy and that would guarantee that all individuals would understand themselves as having authored such legislation. The only body which would have the capacity to overcome national interests in the field of, say, global warming, and impose an efficient plan of reducing carbon emissions through a binding unilateral legislation, would be the Security Council. But it is quite obvious that this oligarchic body would not respect the minimum conditions of democracy. It is even hard to believe that it would respect the principle of equality, as the P5 would be in a position to except themselves from the restrictions. In fact, it is more likely that they would resist taking such a decision in the first place. And there exists no counter power to prevent this from happening, or to substitute itself in cases where the Council should be found to be deficient.[52] Paralysis or refusal of the Council to act

See also the broad and thorough analysis by A Peters, 'Dual Democracy' in Klabbers, Peters and Ulfstein, *The Constitutionalization of International Law* (n 10) 263–341.

[52] See S Szurek, 'La Charte des Nations Unies. Constitution mondiale ?' in JP Cot, M Forteau and A Pellet (eds), *La Charte des Nations Unies. Commentaire article par article*, 3rd edn (Paris, Economica, 2005) 23–68, 53. On the 'democratisation' of the UN Security Council, see esp

when it should act is obviously one of the main constitutional defects of the Charter: as long as this remains unchanged, the Constitution will retain a strong autocratic dimension and will constantly be at risk of being ineffective.

This search for efficiency is supported by global economic actors promoting a neo-liberal agenda: a certain unification of the world would facilitate trade and lead to the maximisation of profits and of general wealth. Citizens would become mainly consumers and this de-politisation of the world would bring peace. The undesirable effects of such a process – the increase of social inequalities, with 'winners' and 'losers' of world trade liberalization – would be dealt with by insisting that states should concentrate on their core functions and in particular on ensuring security and stability in societies within their borders and keeping their borders safe to prevent mass migration. A minimum oligarchic federal state under the control of major economic trusts would ensure global security and see to the progressive dismantlement of barriers to trade and economic exchanges. This is roughly what a world liberal empire could look like.

On the other hand, the *quest for legitimacy* aims at implementing the principle of autonomy and is thus led by the idea of freedom. Globalisation has seen the loss by states and their peoples of their autonomy. As globalisation is mainly an economic phenomenon – and only world economic actors are able to establish efficient executive strategies at the global level – the economic order dominates the political order. Political life has lost its meaning within the states' borders, as choices are dictated 'from above' by the rules of the global economy under the guise of a neutral science.

This quest for legitimacy should rationally lead to the federalisation and democratisation of the International Constitution. The only way for the political order to recover its primacy over the economic order is to reconstitute the tools it disposed of at the domestic level before the economy became globalised. But it seems difficult to conceive and build a federal system which ensures the sufficient degree of constraint on its components and which would at the same time be fully democratic. Either the system is reactive and efficient and risks being accused of being non democratic; or the system gives sufficient space for discussion and deliberations, and risks being accused of maintaining the status quo at great (and unjustified) costs.[53] In both cases, people may draw on their communitarian passions in the desperate hope of finding in the nation or in any other type of community a way of regaining some pieces of their lost autonomy.

I Johnstone, 'Legislation and Adjudication in the UN Security Council: Bringing Down the Deliberative Deficit' (2008) 102 *AJIL* 275–308.

[53] Habermas has recently noticed that the economic crisis has led the European leaders to develop a kind of 'executive federalism' – supposedly efficient, but purely autocratic. J Habermas, 'The Crisis of the European Union in the light of a constitutionalization of International law' (2012) 23 *EJIL* 335–48.

Finally, it seems that we end up with what was René-Jean Dupuy's conclusion: the 'International Community', in the process of realising itself, is constantly at risk of returning to the state of nature. Between anarchy and the federal state, autocracy and democracy, there is no certainty as to what the future brings, no certain destiny for humanity and no end of history that would flow from a rational dialectic. The dialectic remains 'open'. It is subject to history and its hazards, to the irrational decisions of rulers heading superpowers … Nothing has ever been promised to us …

3

A Cosmopolitan Perspective on the Responsibility to Protect

'Though Italy and King's are far way,
And Truth a subject only bombs discuss ...'

WH Auden, *Sonnets from China*, XXI.

This chapter endeavours to answer the question: what are the connections between responsibility to protect (R2P) and cosmopolitan theory? Can a line of descent or at any rate a family likeness be established between R2P 'doctrine'[1] and cosmopolitan theory?

The question calls into play terms that are not necessarily clear. This compels me to provide a few brief definitions from the outset, first for R2P and its related concepts and then for cosmopolitan theory.

By R2P, I mean primarily the doctrine ratified in paragraphs 138 and 139 of the outcome document adopted by the United Nations General Assembly at its 2005 World Summit.[2] Secondarily I shall refer also to the report by the ad hoc commission set up by Canada with the approval of the former UN Secretary General, Kofi Annan, and known as the 'International Commission on Intervention and State Sovereignty' (ICISS), which led to the first formulation of R2P in a report published and submitted to the Secretary General in 2001.[3]

As for its content, I consider that R2P is essentially a doctrine of humanitarian intervention.[4] It defines the conditions by which the

[1] The question of how to characterise R2P has been much discussed. Is it a 'concept', a 'principle' or a 'norm'? See eg AJ Bellamy, *Responsibility to Protect. The Global Effort to End Mass Atrocities* (Cambridge, Polity, 2009) 4–7. I shall use the term 'doctrine' in the sense of a set of principles and ideas reflecting a certain conception of a given problem, meant to apply to concrete experiences. One speaks for instance of a state's 'security doctrine'. R2P is a particular doctrine of the problem or dilemma of humanitarian intervention.

[2] '2005 World Summit Outcome', United Nations General Assembly Resolution 60/1, 16 September 2005.

[3] On the process leading to the formulation of R2P doctrine, see Bellamy, *Responsibility to Protect* (n 1) 35ff.

[4] English does not have the expression *intervention for humanity* or *humanity intervention* ('intervention d'humanité', in French), which is unfortunate because 'humanitarian intervention' evokes international humanitarian law, pertaining to the rules applicable in armed conflicts,

'international community' is called upon to intervene to protect civilian populations against four types of serious crime: genocide, crimes against humanity, war crimes and ethnic cleansing. It begins with the principle that states have a responsibility to protect, but when they fail in their responsibility, then it passes on to the international community, who may exercise it in several ways, including by armed intervention, although such intervention cannot be decided on other than in compliance with the UN Charter, that is, and this is crucial, with Security Council authorisation. In this respect, the R2P 'doctrine' is a form of interpretation of the Charter but it does not amend the Charter and in particular it does not alter the circumstances under which an action involving the use of force may be decided on by the Security Council. In legal terms, R2P has not given new powers to the Security Council. What the Council decides on in mentioning R2P could have been decided on without any such mention. Vice versa, several experiences show that R2P does not compel the Security Council to react. The interests of the powers still prevail within this organ, especially through the right of veto.[5]

In what follows I shall only use the term R2P to refer to this particular doctrine of humanitarian intervention adopted in 2005. I shall use the expression 'humanitarian interventions' to refer to the *practice* of

especially with a view to the protection of civilians but also humanitarian action on the ground to provide emergency aid to endangered populations. The proponents of R2P tend to baulk at assimilating R2P and humanitarian intervention. They emphasise first that R2P is not limited to setting out criteria by which the international community is called upon to make an armed intervention. The ICISS report identified 'responsibility to warn, responsibility to react and responsibility to rebuild'. The UN Secretary General established a 'three pillar' typology that has been largely taken up since. The first pillar focuses on the protective responsibilities of the state, the second pillar deals with international assistance and capacity building and the third pillar concerns the 'timely and decisive response' of the international community including armed intervention but not only that. The third pillar also includes 'peaceful' measures such as investigations or fact-finding missions, judicial settlement, including international criminal justice or missions to negotiate and mediate under Chapter VI of the Charter. (For the establishment of the typology see the report 'Implementing the responsibility to protect', A/63/677. On the third pillar, see the 2012 report on the same theme, A/66/875-S/2012/578.) Moreover, the proponents of R2P consider there is a 'conceptual' difference between R2P and 'humanitarian intervention'. See, eg, S Adams, *Libya and the Responsibility to Protect*, Occasional Paper Series, Global Center for the Responsibility to Protect, 2012, 11. *Humanitarian intervention* is supposedly characterised as being unilateral and unlawful with respect to the UN Charter. Besides, R2P supposedly does not establish a 'right' of intervention but emphasises the 'responsibility' of the state and the international community.

However, these two sets of arguments are hardly convincing. The central question R2P seeks to answer is that asked by Kofi Annan further to the 1999 Kosovo intervention: How can we reconcile the principle of Sovereignty underpinning international law with the imperative necessity to react to massacres of civilian populations? (See 'Two concepts of sovereignty', *The Economist* (16 September 1999).) Obviously it can always be argued that prevention is better than cure and R2P can be included in all manner of 'preventive' questions, that already existed before R2P, such as observance of human rights, the fight against poverty, transitional justice, and so on. But one always comes back to the ultimate question which is the true subject: When, on what conditions and under what circumstances should one intervene by force?.

[5] This is obviously the case of Syria recently.

armed interventions for which the official objective is to protect civilian populations with or without Security Council authorisation and whether unilateral or multilateral interventions.

Lastly I shall also speak of the 'theory of humanitarian intervention'. This time it shall be to refer to the systematisation by Antoine Rougier in a paper published in the *Revue générale de droit international public* in 1910. In that article, Antoine Rougier sought to set out a theoretical framework for the practice of intervention by European states in the Ottoman Empire and colonial countries.[6]

By 'cosmopolitan theory' I mean the theory that seeks to conceptualise institutional and legal *states of transition* that are impelled by a cosmopolitan philosophy.

And 'cosmopolitan philosophy' is the philosophy that recommends states advance out of the state of nature in order to put an end to the permanent state of war that reigns among them, in order to establish a *perpetual peace*. When I refer to cosmopolitan philosophy, I refer not to the ancient version of this philosophy (Diogenes of Sinope, Cicero, and so on) but to its modern formulation and more specifically Kant's formulation of cosmopolitanism particularly in his *Essay on Perpetual Peace* and *Doctrine of Right*.[7]

The international legal order after World War I was determined at least in part by the principles of *cosmopolitan philosophy* and the purpose of perpetual peace as formulated by Kant as an Idea of Reason. Accordingly, analysis of that legal order requires the implementation of the instruments of a *cosmopolitan theory*. These instruments fall into two main categories: those relating to the *theory of federation* and those relating to the *theory of democracy*. The work towards the Idea of perpetual peace in cosmopolitan philosophy is related to the establishment of a *World Federation of Democratic States* (implying homogenising regimes, etc). These are the two poles of thinking currently part of my research project at the Institut Universitaire de France. Here I shall simply outline a few lines of enquiry taking into consideration the instruments resulting from the theory of federation.

If we look into the origins of cosmopolitan theory, we do indeed find that Kant theorises about intervention or at any rate what might rather be identified as a specifically Kantian formulation of the theory of just war.

In his *Theory of Right*, Kant devotes a number of developments to international law, in the course of which he addresses the definition of the unjust enemy, in other words the determination of the just cause of a war. What is the unjust enemy? Kant asks. 'It must mean someone whose publicly

[6] A Rougier, 'La théorie de l'intervention d'humanité' (1910) *RGDIP* 468–526.

[7] On the growing relevance of this version of cosmopolitanism in debates on developments in international law and international relations see, eg R Chung and G Nootens (eds), *Le cosmopolitisme. Enjeux et débats contemporains* (Montréal, Les presses de l'Université de Montréal, 2010).

expressed will, whether expressed in word or in deed, displays a maxim which would make peace among nations impossible and would lead to a perpetual state of nature if it were made into a general rule.'[8]

And Kant identifies the very type of violation that is of a nature to constitute a just cause of war: the violation of 'public contracts, which can be assumed to affect the interests of all nations. For they are a threat to their freedom and a challenge to them to unite against such misconduct and to deprive the culprit of the power to act in a similar way again'.[9]

The mere fact that this passage came in for stern criticism from Carl Schmitt speaks reams about it. Schmitt saw in it the premises of developments that in the twentieth century were to put an end to the ancient 'Nomos of the Earth' – the foundation for Schmitt of a sort of golden age of international law and 'circumscribed' war, at least in relations among European states – and plunge it into the disorder and confusion of the contemporary world, manifested by the establishment of the League of Nations.[10]

Closer to us, Jürgen Habermas responds, as is known, to Schmitt's radical criticism – the famous 'whoever invokes humanity wants to cheat'[11] – and attempts to re-found the Kantian position by replacing transcendental Reason with the practice of communication. At the heart of the polemic is the question of what Schmitt calls 'discriminatory war' waged in the name of Humanity, that denies all legal status to the enemy and leads necessarily to a war of extermination.[12] In this debate, it appears that cosmopolitanism necessarily defends the idea of humanitarian intervention as a manifestation of the establishment of the legal character of international relations and a gradual transition of international society from the state of nature to the 'civil state'.[13] In 1999 Habermas spoke out openly for NATO intervention in

[8] I Kant, 'The Metaphysics of Morals' [1797], *The Theory of Right*, pt II, § 60, in *Kant. Political Writings*, ed HS Reiss, tr HB Nisbet, 2nd edn (Cambridge, Cambridge University Press, 1970) 131–75, 170.

[9] ibid.

[10] C Schmitt, *The* Nomos *of the Earth in the International Law of the* Jus Publicum Europaeum [1950], tr GL Ulmen (New York, Telos Press Publishing, 2006), 168 for the critique of Kant and ibid Part IV for the description of dissolution of *jus publicum europaeum* and the emergence of the concept of discriminatory war.

[11] See C Schmitt, *The Concept of the Political [1932]*, tr G Schwab (Chicago, IL, University of Chicago Press, 1996, 2007) esp at 54–55.

[12] J Habermas, 'Kant's Idea of Perpetual Peace with the Benefit of Two Hundred Years' Hindsight' in J Bohman and M Lutz-Bachmann (eds), *Perpetual Peace. Essays on Kant's Cosmopolitan Ideal* (Cambridge, MA, MIT Press, 1997).

[13] ibid 140: '[T]the police actions of a democratically legitimate world organization capable of taking action would better earn the title of the means for "civilizing" international conflicts than would limited war. Establishing a cosmopolitan order means that violations of human rights are no longer condemned and fought from the moral point of view in an unmediated way, but are rather prosecuted as criminal actions with the framework of a state-organised legal order according to institutionalised legal procedures. Precisely such a juridification of the state of nature among states would protect us from a moral de-differentiation of law and would guarantee to the accused full legal protection, even in cases of war crimes and crimes of humanity. Even such cases are protected from unmediated moral discrimination.'

Kosovo.[14] Conversely, he condemned US intervention in Iraq in 2003 on the strength of the same arguments.[15]

Beyond these direct sources, it can be asserted that the question of armed international intervention is central or should be central to any cosmopolitan theory in that it speaks to what is often identified as the quintessence of the notion of the modern state: the fact that it is an institution with the monopoly of violence in a given society.

The exercise of violence is the most extreme manifestation of constraint characterising public law. Theoretically cosmopolitan law should be reflected by a transfer of the monopoly of violence to the supranational institution tasked with exercising universal constraint. Such a transfer can only be gradual and partial but it marks the transition from international governance to genuine international government.[16]

The question that may then be asked is 'Can it be deduced from this that R2P emanates directly from Kantian cosmopolitanism?' Nothing could be less sure. In actual fact, the pivotal concepts of R2P have little to do with cosmopolitanism and reflect rather a patchwork of doctrines that fit together poorly.

Therefore we formulate a hypothesis: R2P is heading along the wrong conceptual track; and setting the theory of humanitarian intervention back on another track, in the case in point the track of cosmopolitanism, would not only facilitate understanding of the recent practice of interventions, but would also make it possible to adopt a less risky conception of intervention, in both practical and moral terms, than the conception that currently prevails with R2P.

We must therefore proceed in two stages. First we shall examine the pivotal concepts of R2P to show that not only are they not tied to cosmopolitan theory but that, above all, they are open to criticism. Secondly, we shall have to outline a reconstruction of the theory of humanitarian intervention in the context of cosmopolitan theory, which we hope will enable us to better

[14] J Habermas, 'From Power Politics to Cosmopolitan Society' in *Time of Transitions*, tr and ed C Cronin and M Pensky (Cambridge, Polity, 2006): 'Within the framework of classical international law, this would have counted as an interference in the internal affairs of a sovereign state, that is, as a violation of the principle of non-intervention. Premised on human rights, this intervention is now supposed to be regarded as an armed peace mission tacitly authorised by the international community – though without a UN mandate. According to this Western interpretation, the war in Kosovo could mark a significant advance on the road from classical international law between states to the cosmopolitan law of a society of world citizens.'

[15] J Habermas, 'Interpreting the Fall of a Monument' in *The Divided West*, tr and ed C Cronin (Cambridge, Polity Press, 2006).

[16] See Habermas, 'Kant's Idea of Perpetual Peace' (n 12) 146: '[T]he idea of a constitutional state demands that the coercive violence of the state be channelled both externally and internally through legitimate law; and the democratic legitimation of law is supposed to guarantee that law remain in harmony with recognized moral principles. Cosmopolitan law is thus a consequence of the idea of the constitutional state. In it, symmetry is finally established between the juridification of social and political relations both inside and outside the state' boundaries.'

understand recent practice and to contemplate it on a sounder theoretical footing.

I. Analysis of the Pivotal Concepts of R2P

R2P rests on two pivotal concepts: protection and functional sovereignty. As shall be seen, the two are totally unrelated. They might even be considered antinomical. Whereas protection relates clearly to a Hobbesian conception of authority, the idea of functional sovereignty belongs typically to the register of liberal philosophy derived from Locke. This attests to the 'rough and ready' character of R2P doctrine. In any event, both concepts must be set aside if we are to construct a cosmopolitan theory of humanitarian intervention.

A. Protection

(1) The notion of 'protection' imposed itself in the construction of R2P for two reasons:

- Political and ideological reasons related to the language of Canadian foreign policy of the time. Canada had made the idea of 'human security' its standard bearer, and at its core the idea that the state's primary duty is to 'protect its population' against all possible risks.[17] The International Commission on Intervention and State

[17] The idea of 'human security' first appears in the UNDP *Human Development Report 1994* (New York, Oxford University Press, 1994), ch 2, 23: 'Human security can be said to have two main aspects. It means, first, safety from such chronic threats as hunger, disease and repression. And second, it means protection from sudden and hurtful disruptions in the patterns of daily life – whether in homes, in jobs or in communities. Such threats can exist at all levels of national income and development.'. A little further on (ibid 24) the UNDP adds 'There have always been two major components of human security: freedom from fear and freedom from want. This was recognized right from the beginning of the United Nations. But later the concept was tilted in favour of the first component rather than the second.' Canadian diplomacy took hold of the concept in 1996 when Lloyd Axworthy became minister for foreign affairs in the government of Jean Chrétien. See especially L Axworthy, 'Canada and human security: the need for leadership' (1997) 52 *International Journal* 183–96. In 1999, Axworthy supported intervention in Kosovo on the basis of his conception of 'human security'. The notion of human security was raised, but without being defined, alongside that of 'responsibility to protect', in the Outcome Document adopted at the end of the 2005 Summit (§ 143): '[A]ll individuals, in particular vulnerable people, are entitled to freedom from fear and freedom from want, with an equal opportunity to enjoy all their rights and fully develop their human potential. To this end, we commit ourselves to discussing and defining the notion of human security in the General Assembly.' On the use of human security in Canadian and Japanese diplomacy, see E Remacle, 'Approaches to Human Security: Japan, Canada and Europe in Comparative Perspective' (2008) 66 *Journal of Social Science* 5–34. The question is followed up in the General Assembly. See most recently Resolution 66/290, 'Follow-up to paragraph 143 on human security of the 2005 World Summit Outcome'. The Resolution outlines a 'common understanding on the notion of human security', which is not very enlightening, but reflects the intention of the resolution's drafters to neutralise

Sovereignty (ICISS) that 'invented' R2P plainly wanted to head in the direction indicated by its sponsor.

– Reasons of expediency: as Gareth Evans (former Australian foreign affairs minister who co-chaired the commission) explained very clearly, they had to find a concept that would not be dismissed immediately by the 'global South' who were extremely hostile to the concept of the '*droit d'ingérence*' previously defended by France. The idea of 'protection' appeared to be neutral enough for a consensus to be created around it.[18]

Beyond these circumstantial explanations, it may be asked what the conceptual bases are for the 'protection' of populations. Certainly not cosmopolitan theory. This might possibly speak of 'guaranteeing' rights but not of 'protection'. Kantian cosmopolitanism is founded on the recognition of freedom (or autonomy) of the person as a mark of their dignity. In the Kantian paradigm, the individual does not seek 'protection' of his/her person in the civil state. What they are looking for is a legal guarantee for their liberty and the ensuing rights, rights and freedoms that are constantly under threat in the state of nature.[19] So intervention in cosmopolitan theory can be aimed only at upholding citizens' constitutional rights, not at their *survival* as such.

(2) If we wish to establish the genealogy of this concept of protection, it seems we must turn not to cosmopolitan philosophy but rather, as Anne Orford showed, to the Hobbesian model of sovereignty.[20] For Hobbes, 'Desire of Ease, and sensuall Delight, disposeth men to obey a common Power: Because by such Desires, a man doth abandon the protection might be hoped for from his own Industry, and labour. Fear of Death, and Wounds, disposeth to the same; and for the same reason'.[21] But this state of peace cannot be achieved without the introduction of a power capable of *protecting* them. On the contrary, passions can lead only to a state of war of all against all. Peace can only be the outcome of *terror* inspired by the *mortal god* that is the Sovereign Leviathan, 'able to defend them from the invasion of Foreigners, and the injuries of one another,

the interventionist potential of the concept and especially by distinguishing it clearly from the concept of responsibility to protect. See para 3 of the operative part: '(*d*) The notion of human security is distinct from the responsibility to protect and its implementation; (*e*) Human security does not entail the threat or the use of force or coercive measures …'.

[18] See especially G Evans, 'The Responsibility to Protect: An Idea Whose Time Has Come … and Gone?' (2008) 22 *International Relations* 283–98.

[19] See O de Frouville, 'Une conception démocratique du droit international' (2001) XXXIX *Revue européenne des Sciences sociales (Cahiers Vilfredo Pareto)* 101–44; and O de Frouville, *L'intangibilité des droits de l'Homme en droit international. Régime conventionnel des droits de l'homme et droit des traités* (Paris, Pedone, 2004) 13–20.

[20] A Orford, *International Authority and the Responsibility to Protect* (Cambridge, Cambridge University Press, 2011).

[21] T Hobbes, *Leviathan* (Everyman's Library, Dent & Sons, London) ch 11, 50.

> and thereby to secure them in such sort, as that by their own industrie, and by the fruites of the Earth, they may nourish themselves and live contentedly'.[22] The Sovereign's authority is based on this power of protection, which is the result of pure fact and not of any *right*: for the Sovereign is not party to the compact instituting it. Similarly, the Sovereign is not removed from office because it has lost legitimacy based on a compact that is not binding on it. It only loses its power by losing its *capacity to protect* its subjects: 'The Obligation of Subjects to the Sovereign, is understood to last as long, and no longer, than the power lasteth, by which he is able to protect them.'[23]

R2P refers back to this figure of the Sovereign protector. The Sovereign is not instituted with a view to guaranteeing freedoms. In the terms of a line of reasoning the tactical mainspring of which can be clearly seen in the polemical context of the time,[24] Hobbes claims that the exercise of the power of protection, including by terror, is not incompatible with freedom, but it is protection that is sought in creating the Sovereign and not freedom as it is in Locke, Kant or even Rousseau.

Anne Orford shows clearly in this regard that the introduction of the R2P concept was an important philosophical turning point in contemporary international law.[25] The adoption of the United Nations Charter had introduced an element of legality in the appreciation of the legitimacy of power, whereas before that legitimacy had rested primarily upon effectiveness; effectiveness of a government over a territory and a population. In attacking the legitimacy of the power of colonial states over certain territories, the Charter placed new emphasis on the right to self-determination. It might be added that the promotion of the concept of human rights, the representation of such rights as constitutional rights on an international scale gives rise, universally, to the figure of the rule of law, in other words, the ring-fencing of power by rights. With the Charter, power is in the service of rights and Sovereignty becomes, as in Kant, the medium for achieving liberty.

R2P wrong-foots this cosmopolitan approach and brings effectiveness back to the forefront. Except that it is no longer effective *control* (exercised over a territory and a population), as in classical international law, but effective *protection*, within the meaning Hobbes gave to it. The state and

[22] ibid 17, 89.

[23] ibid 21, 116.

[24] Q Skinner, *Hobbes and Republican Liberty* (Cambridge, Cambridge University Press, 2008).

[25] See Orford, *International Authority* (n 20) esp 16: 'The responsibility to protect … is premised on the notion that authority, to be legitimate, must be effective at guaranteeing protection, and that the failure to protect a population is a factual matter that can be determined by the international community. The responsibility to protect concept thus grounds authority – both of states and of the international community – on the capacity to provide effective protection to populations at risk. This de facto grounding of authority marginalises the more familiar claims to authority grounded on right, whether that right be understood in historical, universal, or democratic terms.'

the international community have the *responsibility to protect* its population against genocide, crimes against humanity, war crimes and ethnic cleansing. It is not a question here of defending *human rights*, nor even of the self-determination of peoples, but of saving populations from massacre.

This change of tack is open to post-modern criticism combining Carl Schmitt and Michel Foucault in particular.

Anne Orford thus denounces the authoritarian potential of R2P doctrine, consolidating as it does dictatorial United Nations practice in areas hit by instability. Insistence on protecting life arguably enables the international community to place itself outside of the law, in a state of exception: it supposedly immunises international action against any criticism based on human rights. Anne Orford cites in this respect the decision of the European Court of Human Rights in the case of *Berhami and Saramati*, which seems to her to issue immunity of jurisdiction for any act that might be justified by a Security Council mandate in the name of the 'essential' character of the mission conferred on the Council by the international community.[26]

Hence 'losses' and blunders, violations of human rights are invariably understood as the price to pay to achieve the end of protecting the population. Law no longer applies to such operations because their biopolitical claim sets them outside of any legal appraisal. More specifically, 'War or police action may be necessary – and thus individual lives may have to be sacrificed – in order to protect a population at risk. The population here functions as a "transcendental form of life" in the name of which mere "biological life" can reasonably be sacrificed.'[27]

These conclusions fall in broadly with the arguments of Giorgio Agamben.[28] Let us recall briefly that Agamben begins with the classical distinction in philosophy between *zoē* and *bios*. He refers to *zoē* by the term 'bare life'. *Homo sacer*, sacred man, is the legal prototype of this bare life: the man who cannot be sacrificed and yet may be killed. Relying on a conception of biopolitical drawn from Foucault, Agamben defends the idea that the inclusion of bare life in the domain of the political is the hidden essence of sovereign power.[29] Thus he dissociates himself from Schmitt's theory of

[26] ECHR, Grand Chamber, Decision as to the admissibility of application 71412/01, esp para 149: '[T]he Convention cannot be interpreted in a manner which would subject the acts and omissions of Contracting Parties which are covered by UNSC Resolutions and occur prior to or in the course of such missions, to the scrutiny of the Court. To do so would be to interfere with the fulfilment of the UN's key mission in this field including, as argued by certain parties, with the effective conduct of its operations.'

[27] A Orford, 'The Passions of Protection: Sovereign Authority and Humanitarian War' in D Fassin and M Pandolfi (eds), *Contemporary States of Emergency: The Politics of Military and Humanitarian Interventions* (New York, Zone Books, 2010) 344.

[28] It is rather difficult to address the work of Giorgio Agamben in just a few lines, because it is a refined and complex work and because it has given rise to prolific debate and commentary for which there is no room here. I shall try to cut to the quick, without oversimplifying matters, but I apologise in advance for what will seem a hasty summary.

[29] G Agamben, *Homo sacer. Sovereign Power and Bare Life*, tr D Heller-Roazen (Redwood City, CA, Stanford University Press, 1998): '[T]he inclusion of bare life in the political realm

the political: the definition of the political does not stem from the distinction between friend and enemy but between *zoē* and *bios*. The very project of liberal democracy stems from this conception, particularly through the recognition of 'human rights' which are intended to take 'sacred man' from 'bare life' to the status of citizen.[30] But taking up Hannah Arendt and her celebrated critique of human rights, Agamben shows the ambivalence of such a policy: human rights being recognised and protected on national scale, inclusion produces exclusion at one and the same time. On the grounds of extending the personal scope of rights of citizenship, certain individuals see their enjoyment of such rights excluded. To what is, after all, this well-known paradox, Agamben adds an extra feature relying on the eighth thesis of Walter Benjamin's concept of history: the state of exception has become the rule.[31] Since the state of exception is permanent, the distinction between *zoē* and *bios* becomes clouded, insofar as the *decision* to include or exclude that constitutes the political is arbitrary and not subject to law.

And it is at this point that criticism touches on the question of armed intervention – beyond R2P itself: it is always part of the state of exception, it fits inevitably into the context of an exceptional situation which in its essence leaves room for the sovereign's arbitrariness. Humanitarian intervention is the violent manifestation of the liberal project. It is always a question of including bare life in the political. But such inclusion in a state of emergency actually produces just as much exclusion: on the grounds of extending the reign of democracy and the political, civilian populations are subjected to bombing, causing streams of refugees who are put into camps – in other words, 'bare life' is produced on the pretext of including it.

Although Agamben's critique clearly goes much too far in certain respects,[32] it is difficult to set it aside completely when considering not just

constitutes the original – if concealed – nucleus of sovereign power. *It can even be said that the production of a biopolitical body is the original activity of sovereign power.*'

[30] ibid 17: 'If anything characterizes modern democracy as opposed to classical democracy, then, it is that modern democracy presents itself from the beginning as a vindication and liberation of *zoē* and that it is constantly trying to transform its own bare life into a way of life and to find, so to speak, the *bios* of the *zoē*.'

[31] W Benjamin, *Œuvres* vol. III (Paris, Gallimard, Folio Essais) 433. W Benjamin, *Illuminations*, tr H Zohn) (New York, Harcourt, Brace & World, 1968): 'The tradition of the oppressed teaches us that the "state of emergency" in which we live is not the exception but the rule. We must attain to a conception of history that is in keeping with this insight. Then we shall clearly realize that it is our task to bring about a real state of emergency, and this will improve our position in the struggle against Fascism.'

[32] In particular the comparison Agamben makes between Nazi death camps and refugee camps, which to my mind is both morally and scientifically unacceptable. The idea of hidden solidarity between liberalism and totalitarianism also seems to me to be sophistry and manipulation. Yet it is one of the most cited propositions in Agamben's philosophy. While he himself is rather cautious in his formulations, some of his supporters are less wary (see esp D Bigo and A Tsoukala, *Terror, Insecurity and Liberty: Illiberal Practices of Liberal Regimes after 9/11* (London, Routledge, 2008)). It is typical to find in this kind of reasoning Schmitt's art of the reversal that makes the executioner the victim and vice versa. But as in Schmitt, in Agamben too we find true ideas that with a dash of political agenda and emotional subjectivity finish up becoming false.

the practice of contemporary democracies since 11 September 2001 but also the emergence of concepts such as 'human security' and R2P. Beyond the fact that the 'war on terror' has provided without doubt a perfect illustration of Agamben's theories about 'bare life' and the state of exception, the highlighting of concepts based on the primary requirement of fighting suffering and saving life and limb seems to confirm the emergence of bio-politics on a global scale. This is all the more so because R2P is placed in the hands of an institution – the Security Council – which, through its capacity to decide totally at will, cannot fail to be reminiscent of Schmitt's sovereign. Ultimately, we come back to what Habermas had spied as the 'core' of truth in Schmitt's discourse on war conducted in the name of Humanity, namely that 'the unmediated moralization of law and politics' can only lead to lawless wars, because the moral condemnation of the unjust enemy places him outside of humanity.[33] Likewise, a war conducted in the name of the physical protection of victims would be 'absolutely moral' and so would justify the suspension of law, including the legal status of persons. Once again, the 'war against terror' and the arguments made by the Bush Jr administration to justify both the invasion of Iraq (security of the United States) and torture of persons subjected to forced disappearance – the negation of their personhood *par excellence* – are a striking demonstration of this. But it should also be emphasised that Habermas replied to this argument by recalling that the project of contemporary international law since the League of Nations was aimed indeed at reducing the scope of moral arguments in international relations, especially by lending a legal character to human rights but also by instituting *individual* criminal responsibility for state crimes (rather than having a whole people bear moral responsibility for those crimes): 'Fundamentalism about human rights is to be avoided not by giving up on the politics of human rights, but rather only through the cosmopolitan transformation of the state of nature among states into a legal order.'[34] And it implies that one must conduct action based on the defence of rights and not on the defence of *security* as R2P proposes.

The concept of protection that is at the centre of R2P doctrine is therefore alien to cosmopolitan theory and vulnerable to the post-modern critique of power that denounces the expression of 'liberal imperialism' in any armed intervention. It is understandable that the idea of protection was introduced into discussions for reasons of expediency, but it is unacceptable in a cosmopolitan theory of intervention. The same goes for the theory of functional sovereignty.

[33] Habermas, 'Kant's Idea of Perpetual Peace' (n 12) 146.
[34] ibid 149.

B. *Functional Sovereignty*

The functional sovereignty concept is described perfectly in the context of intervention theory by Antoine Rougier in his 1910 article.[35] Functional sovereignty for him means sovereignty being subjugated to certain essential functions and the obligation for the sovereign only to use public force to ensure these essential functions. Rougier identifies two such functions: maintaining the existence of a duly appointed government and the protection of inhabitants' human rights.[36]

The consequence of this conception could not be clearer: when a government uses public force other than for the assigned functions, it commits what Rougier calls a *misappropriation of sovereignty* (*détournement de souveraineté*). And this misappropriation in turn vindicates the exercise of 'international control', that is, the substitution of the guilty government's sovereignty by foreign sovereignty.[37] Rougier specifies that such control cannot go so far as the substitution of sovereignty among civilised states. However, it may be longer lasting for 'semi-civilised' or 'barbarian' states: 'Plain intervention is then replaced by a standing law of intervention or right of tutelage. This is the right European powers have taken upon themselves with respect to the Porte. Tutelage may be replaced by an even narrower form of control, consecrating the political dependence of the state under control, such as the protectorate. Lastly, with respect to the most backward tribes of Africa, some jurisconsults seek to recognise the states of Europe have a special right, the right to civilise, and those states implement it through pseudo-protectorates that serve merely to disguise their territorial annexations.'[38]

The idea of 'sovereignty as responsibility' that is the crux of R2P follows from the same reasoning. Sovereignty is subjugated to a function of 'protection' of its population. Should the Sovereign fail in its protective function then it falls to the members of the international community to stand in for it and exercise the function of protection that is otherwise no longer provided. When the Sovereign does not consent thereto, such substitution is effected by means of provisional or permanent *intervention* allowing the 'control' necessary for the exercise of sovereign functions.

Plainly such ideas owe nothing to Hobbes but are in the line of liberal philosophy inherited notably from Locke and reinterpreted in light of the

[35] See n 6.

[36] ibid 495: 'The Sovereign appears to be invested with certain functions for accomplishing which it disposes of the forces of law and order, and for accomplishing which the use of those forces is alone legitimate. … Every state sees two categories of functions fall to it. The ones are the functions necessary to the existence of any organized society; they are resumed in the two grand ideas of order and justice and presuppose essentially the existence of a regular government and the protection of the inhabitants' human rights.'

[37] ibid 495–96.

[38] ibid 496–97.

colonialist ambitions of Western powers in the nineteenth century. In the idea of functional sovereignty, we can make out the idea of Lockean *trust* or, in other words, fiduciary power: the government is formed to act to promote the interests of its trustees. As Locke emphasises in his *Second Treaty of Government*, the Legislator acting against such interest would be guilty of malfeasance, which causes power to return to the hands of the People, who may use it to appoint a new Government.[39]

But intervention theory is already, before R2P, a patchwork of doctrines. It admixes to this liberal conception of Sovereignty a throw-back to the theory of just war developed by sixteenth-century theologians.[40] When Rougier queries the 'criteria' vindicating intervention, he is led almost naturally to take up the criteria characteristic of just war theory: just cause, legitimate authority, upright intention. Tying back with the universalist ideal of the Second Scholasticism, he describes a theory of just war put in the service no longer of the community of Christian states but the community of 'civilised European states' impelled by their imperial project. Thus Rougier theorises beyond any doubt about what one might consider to be the bases of 'liberal imperialism'.[41] Besides, Rougier was no dupe and concluded his presentation with what could hardly be a more realistic observation stating simply what Schmitt was to try to show much later in a round-about way and by dint of ambiguous sophisms.[42]

It may be queried, however, whether this expression 'liberal imperialism' is not an oxymoron. By 'adding' the theory of just war in an imperialist

[39] J Locke, 'The Second Treatise of Government', para 222 in P Laslett (ed), *Two Treatises of Government* (Cambridge, Cambridge University Press, 1960) 267–428, 412–13: 'Whensoever therefore the legislative shall transgress this fundamental rule of society; and either by ambition, fear, folly or corruption, endeavour to grasp themselves, or put into the hands of any other an absolute power over the lives liberties, and estates of the people; by this breach of trust they forfeit the power, the people had put into their hands, for quite contrary ends, and it devolves to the people, who have a right to resume their original liberty, and, by the establishment of a new legislative (such as they shall think fit) provide for their own safety and security, which is the end for which they are in society.'

[40] To which certain technical features of public law must be added – the ideas of 'control' and 'substitution' – and it is probably this aspect that is the most interesting as shall be seen below.

[41] See B Delcourt, 'La séduction du concept d'impérialisme libéral auprès des élites européennes: vers une redéfinition de la politique étrangère de l'Union européenne ?' in E Jouannet and H Ruiz-Fabri (eds), *Impérialisme et droit international en Europe et aux Etats-Unis* (Paris, Société de Législation Comparée, 2007) 73–114, commenting especially on 'new liberal imperialism' described by British diplomat Robert Cooper.

[42] Rougier, 'La théorie de l'intervention d'humanité (n 6) 526: '[I]t is practically impossible to separate humanitarian motives for intervention from political motives and to ensure the intervening states are entirely disinterested. … Whenever one power intervenes within another power's sphere in the name of humanity, it will only ever oppose its conception of the just and the social good to the latter's conception thereof, sanctioning it where need be by force. Its action will tend ultimately to encompass a state within its sphere of moral and social influence until such time as it can encompass it within its sphere of political influence. It will *control* it so as to make ready to dominate it. In this way, humanitarian intervention appears to be an ingenious legal way to chip away progressively at a state's independence to make it lean gradually towards semi-sovereignty'.

perspective to the liberal theory of functional sovereignty, Rougier fundamentally alters the consequences of the latter. In Locke, the government's malfeasance leads to the devolution of power to the people, without the people returning to the state of nature. In the theory of humanitarian intervention, as in R2P, the 'misappropriation of sovereignty' or 'failure in the responsibility to protect' does not a priori engender any new process of self-determination, but outside 'intervention' or 'control', either by 'civilised states' in Rougier or by the international community upon a Security Council decision.

What is at issue here is the possible acclimatisation of the liberal theory of functional sovereignty in the conceptual environment of international law. As is known, the classical theory of international law (that is, 'Vatellian' theory if you like) duplicates the concept of Sovereignty, correlative to the assertion of autonomous power of states over their territory and their population. *Internal sovereignty* as power of command exercised with regard to subjects is distinguished from *external sovereignty* as equal liberty of state-persons in the state of nature, in other words as the equal non-subordination to any power of command. While the idea of functional sovereignty is meaningful when applied to internal sovereignty, it is an aporia when applied to external sovereignty. Internal functional sovereignty, means that, as Rougier explains, the state's power of command cannot be exercised unless exercised for the use of certain functions. But external functional sovereignty would mean that the *liberty* of the state-person is *conditional* upon the exercise of certain functions, which is conceptually impossible, because liberty in the state of nature cannot be bounded or conditional upon the terms of some *legality* which by definition cannot exist. In the state of nature, the only *boundary* on the exercise of freedom is the concurrent exercise by another person of his freedom which is imposed by force. But there cannot be any freedom that is *finalised* or subjugated to the exercise of any function: in the state of nature, *freedom* is necessarily ... *free*.

In actual fact, the concept of functional sovereignty applied to external Sovereignty amounts to denying the very concept of external Sovereignty, by making the action of the controlled state conditional upon terms defined by the controlling states, which thereby infringes the principle of equality that is consubstantial with the principle of Sovereignty. To imagine a functional sovereignty in international law, it would have to be considered that the state's external sovereignty was a liberty limited to the civil state by some power of constraint. One would have to presuppose the existence of a Sovereign on an international scale.

The upshot is that any intervention conducted on the basis of functional sovereignty theory is an intervention conducted in the name of a Sovereign able to exercise its power of constraint over the offending state. Only the presupposition of a Sovereign can explain why the *misappropriation of sovereignty* does not lead to a devolution of power to the people, but rather to substitution of the legitimate Sovereign (the 'community of civilised states' or the international community) for the ousted Sovereign.

Such a conception is not just aporetic it is also dangerous insofar as it leads to the negation of the right to self-determination of the people formed into a state. The danger is particularly great if we think of the actual conditions for implementing such an intervention, because it arises from a *decision* taken by an organ exercising its powers on a discretionary basis: the United Nations Security Council, which is the only organ in international law where inequality among states can be exerted par excellence in the form of institutionalised violence.

In other words, R2P as it is formulated, entails a major danger of making the Security Council into an authority capable of depriving a people of its right to self-determination. One must question, in this respect, the legitimacy of transitional solutions set up, of international administrations established after interventions, which may sometimes be likened to true international dictatorships. The powers conferred on these provincial 'governors' of the universal Republic that were the special representatives of the Secretary General in Bosnia, Kosovo or Timor suggest that there is a very real danger of sinking into the arbitrary exercise of international supervision, whose action, in addition, escapes any control as to its legality or compliance with human rights.[43] This is a genuine subject of concern that invites us to think again about the foundations of humanitarian intervention and consequently to abandon R2P as it is presently conceptualised.

The two pivotal components of R2P are not just totally alien to cosmopolitan theory but also open to entirely convincing criticism necessitating their exclusion from the construction. Besides, they stem from different, even opposing, philosophical inspirations that make R2P an unsatisfactory patchwork conceptually.

Our job now is to try to outline a reconstruction of a cosmopolitan theory of humanitarian intervention.

II. Outline Reconstruction of a Cosmopolitan Theory of Humanitarian Intervention

The starting point for the reconstruction is to understand the international legal order on the basis of an appropriate theory of the Federation, grounded on Kant's antinomy of a Federation of Free States (section A).

[43] M Forteau, 'Le droit applicable en matière de droits de l'homme aux administrations territoriales gérées par des organisations internationales' in SFDI, *Journées d'études de Strasbourg: La soumission des organisations internationales aux normes internationales relatives aux droits de l'homme* (Paris, Pedone 2009) 7–34. C Stahn, *The Law and Practice of International Territorial Administration. Versailles to Iraq and Beyond* (Cambridge, Cambridge University Press, 2008) esp 479ff.

In the context of that theory, it becomes possible to understand humanitarian intervention as a federal form of execution, which is of a nature to guard it against the criticisms that could be levelled at the responsibility to protect (section B).

A. The Federation of Free States: Framework for Intervention Theory

First of all, it ought to be explained what is meant by Kant's antinomy of the *Federation of Free States*.[44] It is often construed as a sort of realistic position of retreat for Kant. After contemplating the hypothesis of a World State and observing that it would not only be unachievable but also dangerous because potentially despotic, Kant fell back on a sort of compromise solution, a halfway house in the form of a 'Federation of Free States', which would be neither a Federation nor an international organisation.

And yet the concept contains far more than the expression of a straightforward compromise. It takes the form of an antinomy, in that it brings together two opposing and contradictory concepts: anarchical society on one side (the juxtaposition of free states) and the world federal state on the other (the Federation). Upon closer scrutiny, the reality of world institutions, at least since the establishment of the League of Nations, has always lain between these two concepts and is constantly being defined and redefined through reference to them.

Perpetual peace (peace *and* security, that is positive peace and not merely the absence of war) has been the regulating Idea of world organisation ever since the League of Nations. And the rules on the prohibition of the use of force and the protection of human rights are the direct consequences of this inclusion of the Idea of perpetual peace in positive law. At the same time,

[44] This is the title of the second definitive article on perpetual peace: 'The law of nations shall be founded on a federation of free states' ['Das Völkerrecht soll auf einen Föderalism freier Staaten gegründet sein' in the original]. From the outset Kant replaces the expression in a historical perspective, which is also the perspective of his philosophy of history in which the *original contract* like the Idea of Reason is far more a goal to be reached (the goal towards which we move without ever knowing if it is attainable) than a starting point. For the 'they ought to advance out of' the state of nature which holds for individuals cannot hold for states, which wish to maintain their freedom and independence. But 'Meanwhile, however, reason, from her throne of the supreme law-giving moral power, absolutely condemns war as a morally lawful proceeding, and makes a state of peace, on the other hand, an immediate duty. Without a compact between the nations, however, this state of peace cannot be established or assured. Hence there must be an alliance of a particular kind which we may call a covenant of peace (*foedus pacificum*), which would differ from a treaty of peace (*pactum pacis*) in this respect, that the latter merely puts an end to one war, while the former would seek to put an end to war for ever'. I Kant, *Perpetual Peace. A Philosophical Essay* [1795], tr M Campbell Smith (London, George Allen & Unwin, 1917) 133–34. In other words, for Kant, the solution does not lie as is so often claimed in a mere confederation of states or league of peoples, but in an evolving institution designed to establish cosmopolitan law.

allowance for this regulating Idea is made in the fundamentally centrifugal, heterogeneous and conflict-ridden environment of the society of 'free' states.[45]

Kant's antinomy of the Federation of Free States therefore provides a prism through which it is possible to understand the entire evolution of contemporary international law.

It is therefore in the context of an appropriate theory of the Federation that we must try to understand contemporary international law and, as concerns us here, the theory of humanitarian intervention. What do we call an 'appropriate theory' of the Federation? It is a theory that accounts for Kant's antinomy of a 'Federation of Free States'. In other words, a theory that conceives of the 'federation' not as a particular type of organisation of the state, with universally valid characteristics – the federal state – but rather as a *process* governed by the antinomy between the particular type that the federal state represents and the anarchical society of 'free' states.

So we must from the outset set aside the classical dualist theories that rest on the distinction between 'federal state' and 'confederation of states'. As Elisabeth Zoller showed, such theories were born at the same time as dualism in system relations with a view to establishing the Reich's authority after the unification of Germany. They subsequently fulfilled an identical role in Italy.[46]

One must look rather on the side of alternative theories to dualist voluntarism, that take as their starting point the refuting of a strictly dualist approach to the problem and consider the Federation as a particular type in itself, that cannot be assimilated either to the federal state or to the international organisation or to the Confederation. Two major theoretical currents can be identified.

First, the objectivist theories of the first half of the twentieth century. Based on what are partly similar presuppositions (objectivism, dismissal of Sovereignty), and partly radically opposed presuppositions, Kelsen on the one hand and Duguit and Scelle on the other developed autonomous theories of the Federation relying on the rejection of the dichotomy between the federal state and the Confederation of states and asserting the continuity of the federative phenomenon from the most decentralised structure to the most centralised federal state. In this respect the League of Nations itself appears to be part of the federative phenomenon.[47] Closer to us, Elisabeth

[45] See de Frouville, 'Une conception démocratique du droit international' (n 19).

[46] E Zoller, 'Aspects internationaux du droit constitutionnel. Contribution à la théorie de la fédération d'Etats' (2002) 294 *Collected Courses of the Academy of International Law* 39–166, 51.

[47] H Kelsen, *General Theory of Law and State*, tr A Wedberg (Cambridge, MA, Harvard University Press, 1945) 316: 'Only the degree of decentralization distinguishes a unitary State divided into autonomous provinces from a federal State. And as the federal State is distinguished from a unitary State, so is an international confederacy of States distinguished from a federal State by a higher degree of decentralization only. On the scale of decentralization, the federal

Zoller joins with this strand when examining the 'international aspects of constitutional law', in other words when she declines to draw any sharp methodological boundary between what pertains to the state and what to international law. Elisabeth Zoller infers from the American example that 'a federation of states is less of a structure than a process. Being a form of government that is constantly reconstructed and redefined, it is a ship seeking a channel between two reefs, consolidation and dismemberment'.[48] These theories share a central point, namely that the Federation must be analysed as a concept in itself, independently of the concept of federal state. The Federation is a type that includes all sorts of practical experiences historically, ranging from the most decentralised Confederations to the most centralised federal states. Based on such a definition of the federative phenomenon, the UN may therefore be understood as a super-federation on the world scale and the Security Council as a federal organ endowed with particular executive powers.

Another theoretical current is represented by Carl Schmitt, with the developments devoted to the theory of the Federation in his *Constitutional Theory*.[49] Exploiting this very rich seam, Olivier Beaud follows up Schmitt's thinking to develop a *Théorie de la Fédération*, the challenge of which is to explicitly 'remove the Federation from the orbit of the State' and envisage it as an autonomous political-legal entity.[50] And yet Carl Schmitt like Olivier Beaud refuses to include the League of Nations (and so the UN) in the federative phenomenon.[51]

For the purposes of the present demonstration, it is therefore a priori the first strand of thought that we need to draw upon. If our aim is to apply the tools and techniques of Federation theory to found humanitarian intervention as practised in the 'society of the law of nations' and more specifically in the context of the United Nations, it must necessarily be observed that *only* objectivist theories authorise us to do so. Both Kelsen and Scelle contemplate possible armed action as exercise of executive power by the Federation's organs. However, they do not dwell on the conditions for implementing this

State stands between the unitary State and an international union of States.' G Scelle, *Précis de droit des gens. Principes et systématique*, Première Partie (Paris, Sirey, 1932) ch III, 'Le phénomène fédératif', esp at 200: 'There are not one but several forms of federal state: none can be considered the exclusive type form. The federal state itself is but the most thorough-going integration of federalism, but in studying positive law, it can be noticed that it is not always in the federal state that the genius of federalism is best observed, nor the independence of federalized groups best ensured.' See also Section IV of the chapter on 'La Société des Nations comme organisation fédérale'.

[48] Zoller (n 46) 71.

[49] C Schmitt, *Constitutional Theory [1928]*, tr J Seitzer (Durham, NC and London, Duke University Press, 2008).

[50] O Beaud, *Théorie de la Fédération* (Paris, PUF, 2007).

[51] See Schmitt, *Constitutional Theory* (n 49) 400; Beaud, *Théorie de la Fédération* (n 50) 272.

form of action in the event of violation of the fundamental principles of the constitutional pact. They focus on the prevention of disorder (administrative police) or the enforcement of arbitral awards or decisions of the international court (enforcement procedure, sanctions).

But what interests us here is something else, for humanitarian intervention is not executive technique in the general sense. It relates more specifically to the question of the guarantee of fundamental rights on the federal scale and beyond that on the form of governments that, by Kant's precept, must be 'republics'. In other words, what is at stake behind the issue of humanitarian intervention is the typically Kantian problem of the homogeneity of political regimes, the first definitive article in view of perpetual peace. Now, both Schmitt and Beaud tackle this question head on. The point is that Schmitt is eager for tactical reasons to exclude international organisations – and especially the League of Nations – from the federative phenomenon.[52] He is therefore led to problematise the question of regime homogeneity as a *solution* to what he himself calls 'antinomies of federation' and which attach – Schmitt does not say as much obviously – to the Kantian antinomy of the *Federation of Free States* we described above. The question Schmitt seeks to answer is 'How can a free state be made to bend to federal requirements? How can a state that holds to its autonomy be made to accept federal intervention in its internal affairs?' The problem of the Federation is therefore that the global existence of the Federation cannot result in the suppression of the existence of the member states *and* that the particular existence of the member states cannot suppress the existence of the Federation (third antinomy). The solution to this question and these antinomies lies in '*the homogeneity of all federation members*, in particular on a substantial similarity that justifies a concrete, existential agreement of member states and ensures that the extreme case of conflict does not emerge within the federation'.[53] It is only on this condition of homogeneity that intervention can be considered not to be outside interference.[54] Schmitt's tactical goal is to prove that because the League of Nations is not of a homogeneous character, its interventions cannot be perceived as legitimate. But he is thus led to look more closely at the technique of federal enforcement as *guaranteeing the homogeneity* of regimes within the Federation.

The proposal I make here is that, in this context, humanitarian intervention must be understood as a particular type of federal enforcement.

[52] See Beaud, introduction to Carl Schmitt, *Théorie de la Constitution* (Paris, PUF, 2013) 110–11; and Beaud, *Théorie de la Fédération* (n 50) 267–68, fn 5: 'It was crucial for Germany, as it pondered the necessity of joining [the League of Nations], to know whether or not it was a Federation because if it was so characterized then extensive rights of intervention in its member states' internal affairs could be conferred on it'.

[53] Schmitt, *Constitutional Theory* (n 49) 392.

[54] ibid 394.

B. Federal Enforcement and Substitution Theory

The notion of federal enforcement is inherent in the theory and practice of the federal institution. It is an instrument guaranteeing the obligations in the basic federal compact, an instrument available to the Federation's authorities against a federated group.[55]

Contrary to *federal intervention*, which is an intervention that is consented to, made at the request of the federated group, *federal enforcement* is interference that is not consented to, that is forced in reaction to a breach of a constitutional undertaking by the governors of the federated group.[56]

In 'federal republics', federal enforcement is designed essentially for defending the republican form of regime of the federated group.[57] In other words, it is a question no more and no less of guaranteeing what is one of the conditions of cosmopolitanism in the Kantian project for perpetual peace: that all member governments of the Federation have a republican regime.

Historically the institution has played an essentially dissuasive role in already homogenous Federations. This is true of the United States where the threat of federal enforcement was brandished against attempts to change the regime by force (as in the rebellion by Thomas Wilson Dorr in 1841–1842, described by Olivier Beaud).[58]

But what is even more interesting for our discussion is that federal enforcement has also been used when governments have been heterogeneous. This was particularly the case in Switzerland between 1815 and 1848, culminating in the *Sonderbund* war of 1847, opposing troops of the Federation to armies of the seven Catholic and conservative cantons. In this instance federal enforcement was openly conflict-ridden as it sought to impose on the federated authorities a form of republican government they rejected.[59]

In this form (enforcement in the context of a federation with heterogeneous governments), the institution of federal enforcement is a rather accurate description of the interventions in Libya and Ivory Coast. That is, fundamentally reactions by the federal organ to grave violations of the Federal Compact – or to use Kant's formula, reactions against those whose maxim would have made the state of nature an everlasting one.

The case of Ivory Coast is particularly interesting because the international community reacted not only to crimes against the civilian populations but also an attempt to subvert the republican form of regime by refusing to accept the results of an electoral process that was conducted under United Nations authority.

[55] ibid 397.
[56] Beaud, *Théorie de la Fédération* (n 50) 368.
[57] ibid 368ff.
[58] ibid 370.
[59] ibid 373ff.

Federation theory helps us therefore to better understand the nature of interventions conducted today in the name of R2P. But it allows us above all to avoid the major pitfall identified in R2P doctrine; namely, the use of the functional sovereignty concept which, it should be recalled, threatened to lead us directly to the negation of the principle of peoples' right to self-determination.

This may seem paradoxical but it is nonetheless true that a model based on Sovereignty is less protective of the independence of states than a model based on the antinomy of the Federation of Free States. Because in line with the democratic principle underlying Federation theory, the theory radically limits the powers of federal authorities in the context of federal enforcement. Such limitation can be very well explained in the light of substitution theory.

Kant once again shows us the way philosophically when he deals with the forms of intervention and its limits as follows: all nations, he says, must take from the enemy the power to act in similar way again, '[b]ut this does *not* entitle them *to divide up the offending state among themselves* and to make it disappear, as it were, from the face of the earth. For this would be an injustice against the people, who cannot lose their original right to unite into a commonwealth'.[60]

That is it. It remains to translate this philosophical directive into legal theory. For this, we shall return to classical French public law theory of control (often abusively called 'tutelage') exercised by centralised or federal authorities over decentralised or federated authorities. It is this same theory of substitution that is found in the *patchwork* of humanitarian intervention theory developed by Rougier. And in truth it is the most useful part of this theory, provided that we detach from it the concepts of functional sovereignty and the remnants of the theory of just war which are the other two components of this motley construction.

Substitution theory is classically and very clearly expounded by Léon Duguit in the second part of his major work on the theory of state concerning governors and agents.[61] Duguit identifies two characters which, he says, 'are common to decentralized and federalized agents and distinguish them from centralized agents'. First, 'they are instituted by an act in which governors are neither directly nor indirectly involved', that is generally a local election which confers autonomy on them with regard to centralised governors. Secondly, 'they are subject to control and not to some hierarchical power. This control authorizes the superior agent to not approve, to suspend, to cancel, but never to reform'.[62]

[60] Kant, 'The Metaphysics of Morals' [1797], *The Theory of Right*, pt II (n 8) § 60, 170.
[61] L Duguit, *L'Etat, les gouvernants et les agents* (Paris, Albert Fontemoing, 1903; new edn Paris, Dalloz, 2005).
[62] ibid 733.

This is Kant's idea of the limitation of the powers of the federal authorities referred to above applied to legal acts. If this substitution theory is transposed to federal enforcement, it must be inferred that federal authority can admittedly stand in for the federated authority that is wanting or fails in the exercise of its powers; but under no circumstances can it, as Kant said, go so far as to take from this federated group 'their original right to unite into a commonwealth'.

In other words, autonomy and the right to self-determination of the federated entity are preserved because the authority of this entity derives from an act in which, as Duguit says, centralised governors are not involved either directly or indirectly.

I have endeavoured here to explicate the complex ties between R2P and cosmopolitan theory. Yes, cosmopolitan theory can justify humanitarian intervention. However, it cannot do so starting from the conceptual components that make up R2P, like a patchwork. There cannot be any cosmopolitan theory of humanitarian intervention other than under the banner of the antinomy of the Federation of Free States, and in the context of an appropriate theory of the Federation. Such a theory includes contemporary international society as a Federation of Free States, whose Constitution is composed in part of customary norms, general principles of law, the United Nations Charter and charters of other international organisations which lay down both substantive norms and institutional arrangements of a nature that contributes to the exercise of basic social functions. In this context, the Security Council exercises an executive function when it decides that constraint, including armed constraint, must be used against a member of the Federation. That may legally occur when the Security Council, by virtue of article 39 of the Charter observes the existence of 'any threat to the peace, breach of the peace, or act of aggression'. On this basis, the Security Council may decide on measures of constraint in reaction to any manifest breach or threat of manifest breach of federal public order – meaning all fundamental norms of the Constitution that reflect the common values of international society. This reaction is the reaction of a guarantor of the human rights of 'citizens' of the Federation. The action decided on is designed to end the disorder and restore the primacy of the constitutional order. What the Security Council decides on, consequently, as the federal organ with executive power, is to substitute the international community for the government that is failing in the implementation of its federal obligations.

The role of the international community must end when the crimes themselves have ended. That may involve a removal of the government in power, when the government leaders themselves are the criminals. However, such dismissal from office does not infringe the right to self-determination of the people of that state. On the contrary, any dismissal must necessarily be followed by a process of self-determination, allowing the people of the state to establish democratic institutions in agreement with the fundamental rules of the federal constitution. This may take some time and it is then that, beyond the intervention, there arises the problem of the international administration of the territory, which means nothing other than a more lasting substitution of the local government. During this substitution phase, the international administration delegated by the federal order is duty bound to ensure and enforce the federal constitutional rights of the citizens of the state. Any international administration must also be accountable for its failing with regard to federal constitutional law.

Obviously, these few lines of enquiry are far from settling everything. In particular, they do not deal with the question of the legitimacy of the federal enforcement decision in an institutional environment that is that of the United Nations and in a context where the state of exception has become the rule, in the absence of any control over the Security Council's discretionary power.

This question is part of the theoretical tools of cosmopolitan theory that deals with the question of democracy. As said, this is not the subject matter of this chapter.

The aim of this chapter has been more modestly to put reflection on the practice of interventions in the current context back on the right theoretical track. R2P lays down a mistaken conceptual context, which does not help us to think out this practice correctly and to reflect on the reforms required to make it credible and escape the criticisms of its detractors.

In moving away from R2P talk and in understanding humanitarian interventions as measures of federal enforcement it becomes possible to thwart postmodern critiques based on the notion of bio-power and the creation of 'bare life'.

Humanitarian intervention is aimed at compliance with the federal compact and human rights conceived of as constitutional norms of the Federation. What is sanctioned by federal enforcement is the massive violation of these rights, through characterisations that relate as much to public order norms as they do to criminal law.

In other words, what is presupposed behind such action is the recognition of the rights of the populations attacked and it is to restore those rights that the action is conducted. The collateral victims of the attack do not expose the ambivalence of the plan, but only the difficulties inherent in implementing it: all wars are dirty, no violent action can promise there will be no victims.

At least such a theory provides an outline of an answer – although only an outline – so that Truth might not be a subject only bombs discuss.

4

Justifying International Law, Defending Cosmopolitanism

'But if you believe you're a citizen of the world, you're a citizen of nowhere.'
Theresa May

'From this day forward, a new vision will govern … it's going to be only America first, America first.'
Donald Trump

At the time I first met Emmanuel Decaux at the University of Nanterre, we were living in a very different world. It was the early 1990s and the pictures that best conveyed the spirit of the time were those of Berliners sitting astride the Wall or tearing it down block by block. Some believed they could feel the wind of a future change for the better. This was plainly not the case of Emmanuel Decaux, too imbued with the 'tragic sense of History'[1] to believe that it could end in any universal reconciliation. The stage play was obviously not over, because it was forever beginning anew. But things had shifted, the data were fresh, History had opened up the field of possibilities. At the very least, we could observe that these possibilities were reflected by the unprecedented expansion of international law in its cosmopolitan dimension. The oldest of cosmopolitan ideas, the European idea, was going through new and decisive stages and the fall of the Berlin Wall meant it was possible to imagine a Europe unified around a federal type of common project. And the United Nations and the collective security system were experiencing previously unknown activity, which although disorderly and full of pitfalls was promising, even so. Even the crises that shook Europe and the world in the course of the 1990s – the break-up of former Yugoslavia with the crimes that attended it, the genocide in Rwanda, etc – all of this could still be viewed as the monstrous manifestation of the 'work of the negative': the world could still learn from its failures and improve.

More than 20 years later, this confidence in the future is behind us and it is uncertainty that prevails instead. The only certainty that remains may be

[1] Emmanuel Decaux recalled this expression of Raymond Aron's in his address when Sir Nigel Rodley was made a doctor *honoris causa* at Panthéon-Assas University. See www.youtube.com/watch?v=l0VJBt3H9o0&t=3s.

that what 20 years ago we thought was the legal and moral underpinning of a world order under construction is no longer self-evident. On the contrary, it seems that we have moved into a new era – an era that confusingly some already name after the President of the United States of America the 'Trump era'. An era in which we are supposedly no longer called on to *explain* international law but summoned to *justify* it. An era in which we again need to *defend* cosmopolitanism as the future of international law; and to reaffirm aloud our determination 'to save succeeding generations from the scourge of war, which twice in our lifetime has brought untold sorrow to mankind'.[2]

In writing a new conclusion to the 10th edition of his textbook *Droit international public*, Emmanuel Decaux makes an incontestable observation:

> So, on the threshold of the twenty-first century, international law is to be reinvented over and again. From the terrorist attacks of 11 September 2001 that marked the birth of the new century through to the chain effects of the 2008 financial crisis, it is the certainties of the Western world – based on the illusion of the 'end of history' with the triumph of the market and 'felicitous globalization' – that have been shaken.[3]

Emmanuel has a way of capturing in a few lines 20 years of History and the spirit of the age at a time *t*. In one way, we can rejoice over the end of a certain teleology of History that was overly systematic and ultimately left little scope for human freedom. Gradually the economic face of globalisation has come to colonise its political and cultural dimension. It is self-evident that such a process of creative destruction should be curbed or ended. Yet, the difficulty is that the sometimes violent challenge to the expansionary process of capitalism does not seem to open up the way to any politicisation of the world. Oddly enough, the condemnation of market globalisation has not sparked any resolute action to bring about legal and political globalisation, that is, to draw up norms and institutions capable of governing globalised economic activity. The term 'globalisation' itself no longer seems to designate one of the lofty aspirations of the human mind but, on the contrary, to be reduced to a plot hatched by a few oligarchs. Few people nowadays still evoke the idea of globalisation as federalisation, in accordance with Kant's cosmopolitan model of the 'federation of free states'; and those who do so are usually looked upon at best with the sympathy afforded to the weak-minded or to daydreamers.

From now on, the response from populists of all stripes is for communities and nations to turn inwards and to shelter behind borders and walls. Could it be that 'felicitous globalisation' is to give way to 'felicitous re-nationalisation'? Yet the experience of history tends to show that nationalism

[2] Preamble to the United Nations Charter, first paragraph.

[3] E Decaux and O de Frouville, *Droit international public*, 10th edn (Paris, Dalloz/Hypercours, 2016) 589.

and protectionism have never been factors for peace. The only certainty is that, on the contrary, they have twice plunged the world into total war.

Scholars of international law cannot fail to be intrigued by such a development. Even those of us who are keenest to maintain state sovereignty and the will of the state as a principle of international law do not go so far as to challenge the developments of contemporary international law head on. And yet these developments are directly inspired by the cosmopolitan project. The League of Nations and thereafter the UN are a direct response to the Kantian aspiration to go beyond the provisional and precarious peace of treaties and to achieve a state of perpetual peace;[4] disarmament law is an attempt to be rid of the risk of a war of extermination 'which would bring about perpetual peace only in the great graveyard of the human race';[5] and the international proclamation of human rights confers the value of positive law on the idea of cosmopolitan citizenship, or citizenship of the world.[6] David Held, starting from the perspective of international relations, is right to remind us that '[c]osmopolitanism is not made up of political ideals for another age, but is embedded in rule systems and institutions that have already altered state sovereignty in distinct ways, and in societies of diverse faiths'.[7]

Populists are not thinkers but they use – or even instrumentalise – a number of strands of thought and of ideas developed by intellectuals, who either choose to impoverish and popularise their thinking or are in turn echoed by certain media or certain media figures, who often command a large audience.[8] The fact of the matter is that contemporary thought is incontrovertibly witnessing a resurgence of movements which, if some common ground were to be found for them despite their wide diversity, might be said to be characterised by a more or less far-reaching critique of modernity: an 'external'

[4] I Kant, *Perpetual Peace. A Philosophical Essay* [1795], tr M Campbell Smith (London, George Allen & Unwin, 1917), Second definitive article: 'A treaty of peace makes, it may be, an end to the war of the moment … but not to the conditions of war which may at any time afford a new pretext for opening hostilities …'.

[5] ibid First section, 6.

[6] ibid Second section, introduction, note no 1: 'A legal constitution is, according to the nature of the individuals who compose the state: (1) A constitution formed in accordance with the right of citizenship of the individuals who constitute a nation (*jus civitatis*). (2) A constitution whose principle is international law which determines the relations of states (*jus gentium*). (3) A constitution formed in accordance with cosmopolitan law which determines the relations of states (*jus cosmopoliticum*).'

[7] D Held, 'Le cosmopolitisme dans un monde multipolaire et saturé' in O de Frouville (ed), *Le cosmopolitisme juridique* (Paris, Pedone, 2015) 189–205, 190–91. English version in D Held, 'Cosmopolitanism in the Face of Gridlock in Global Governance' in R Bearsworth, GW Brown, and R Shapcott (eds), *The State and Cosmopolitan* Responsibilities (Oxford, Oxford University Press, 2019) 243–58, 246.

[8] Like the journalist Natacha Polony, surrounded by the 'comité Orwell', which claims to be a 'sovereignist think-tank promoting the pluralism of ideas'. See N Polony and the Comité Orwell, *Bienvenue dans le pire des mondes. Le triomphe du* soft *totalitarisme* (Paris, Plon, 2016). Not to mention a media polemicist like Eric Zemmour or an *éminence grise* like Patrick Buisson who has emerged from the shadows into the limelight.

critique that rejects the gains of modernity wholesale and recommends either a return to pre-modernity or a move beyond modernity through a form of post-modernity to be defined; and an 'internal' critique, in that it is indignant that the promises of modernity have been betrayed and in particular that its promises of emancipation have been hijacked by what is in actual fact a bourgeois and conservative discourse.[9] More specifically, all of these movements set themselves up as critics of the cosmopolitan dimensions of contemporary international law. What are particularly targeted are the universal and therefore 'non-national' proclamation of human rights and the institutionalisation of power beyond the sway of states.

One may be disgusted by the use made of these critical ideas in the mouths of new populists and of extremist political movements. Even so, they deserve as such to be discussed in terms of the thinking behind them. Within the confines of this contribution, I would like to try to pinpoint a few features common to all these philosophical and political discourses which find considerable resonance in the domain of law. To do this, I might well begin with a populist speech, given by former British Prime Minister Theresa May at the Conservative Party Congress of 2 October 2016, which was a concentrate of many of the critical themes I shall be examining:

> But if you believe you're a citizen of the world, you're a citizen of nowhere. You don't understand what the very word 'citizenship' means.
>
> So if you're a boss who earns a fortune but doesn't look after your staff …
>
> An international company that treats tax laws as an optional extra …
>
> A household name that refuses to work with the authorities even to fight terrorism …
>
> A director who takes out massive dividends while knowing that the company pension is about to go bust …
>
> I'm putting you on warning. This can't go on anymore. A change has got to come. And this party – the Conservative Party – is going to make that change.[10]

May's speech prompted many reactions and some did not fail to detect in it echoes of other speeches of the twentieth century, with openly anti-Semitic undertones, ranging from the 'Protocols of the Elders of Zion' to the Stalinist anathema cast on the 'rootless cosmopolitans'.[11] Philosopher Kwame Anthony Appiah reminded us there was no reason to posit that there was any incompatibility in a double allegiance to the nation and to humankind.[12]

[9] For an inventory of these critiques from the standpoint of human rights, see especially the outstanding book by J Lacroix and J-Y Pranchère, *Le procès des droits de l'homme. Généalogie du scepticisme démocratique* (Paris, Seuil, 2016).

[10] The conference speech was published on the Internet by several British media outlets, e.g. *The Independent*: www.independent.co.uk/news/uk/politics/theresa-may-speech-tory-conference-2016-in-full-transcript-a7346171.html. The excerpts cited are from this source.

[11] See the reactions in *The Guardian* of 9 October from Jeremy Adler and Rob Sykes.

[12] BBC, 29 October 2016, '"Mrs May, we are all citizens of the world", says philosopher'.

At least three erroneous ideas – one might almost say three prejudices – about cosmopolitanism can be identified in these words and should be examined and subjected to criticism themselves: (I) cosmopolitanism is allegedly nothing but the other face of neoliberalism; (II) cosmopolitanism supposedly contributes to the formation of rootless individuals driven by personal interests alone; and lastly (III) any world politics is supposedly impossible in both theory and practice. I shall end this review with a few seemingly inconsequential thoughts by way of an inconclusive conclusion (IV) ….

I. Cosmopolitanism as the Flip Side of Neoliberalism

The first feature common to these critical discourses lies in the systematic connection they make between cosmopolitanism and economic liberalism. The cosmopolitan dimensions of international law supposedly have as their essential function to act as an additive to the neoliberal project, whether through the exercise of disciplinary action (especially by way of the UN Security Council) or through the implementation of programmes and norms leading to the individualisation of societies, the reduction of intervention by states and the dissolution of national identities ('globalism'). More specifically, human rights, which are the legal and ideological heart of cosmopolitanism, supposedly work to expand capitalism by generalising the demand for individual rights. This critical theme recurs in numerous discourses, which are in appearance somewhat remote from each other, even if they are all aimed at globalisation as an economic process conducted for the benefit of the United States of America or for a 'world hyper-class'. There is a convergence beyond political identities, since such denunciation of liberalism in its twin economic and political components can claim to hail as much from Marx as from Schmitt or Heidegger.

We find this argument of 'the unity of liberalism' in particular underpinning the critical work of a philosopher whose ideas have growing resonance, Jean-Claude Michéa. His thinking is derived from Marxism but he is nowadays cited more often than not in 'conservative' intellectual circles.[13] Michéa argues there is a consubstantial link between the 'liberalism of the market' and the 'liberalism of law' or political liberalism. In this respect, human rights are said to be ultimately nothing more than the legal reverse side of economic liberalism, and this connection supposedly extends to a process that goes beyond state sovereignties and makes states no more than 'points of passage', a sort of functional unit of the world capitalist system.[14]

[13] See the article by Ariane Chemin published in *Le Monde* (11 January 2017), 'A la rencontre des jeunes conservateurs sans complexe'. See also the responses from the interested parties challenging this characterisation and especially 'Le Comptoir: socialistes et décroissants mais pas conservateurs', published in the online journal *Le Comptoir*.

[14] See especially J-C Michéa, *L'Empire du moindre mal. Essai sur la civilisation libérale* (Paris, Flammarion, 2010) 109–10: 'What does it take, *from a liberal standpoint*, to build a modern

But among recent contributions, I would like to dwell a little longer on that of Marcel Gauchet. The critique of the 'individualism' of human rights runs right through this philosopher's work.[15] However, in the fourth volume of *L'avènement de la démocratie*, published in 2017, he makes a connection between the juridicisation of human rights in contemporary societies and the unprecedented expansion of 'neoliberal globalisation'. First, Gauchet argues, democracy has changed under the effect of the juridicisation of human rights into a 'democracy of human rights' the purpose of which is 'to protect private individuals against the collective rules that fail to recognize their own prerogative, their particular interests or their specific identities'.[16] Thus 'the problem is no longer' as in 1789, one of 're-thinking the body politic based on individual rights, it is to ensure individuals a right of appeal against the authority of the community of citizens'.[17] Now, this renewal of the democratic idea, in that it generalises 'the repulsion towards the constraining verticality of an overhang guidance system, becomes conflated with the idea of a market-based political society'.[18] In other words, there is a consonance between the juridicisation of human rights and the objectives of neoliberalism. Now such consonance 'opens up, with globalization helping, to the prospect of a reign of the universality of rights and interests that challenges head on the bounds set to it by the particularities of political communities'.[19] For henceforth the universality of human rights, once devised 'to apply within the framework of and from within predefined political spaces' tends to become exteriorised and so becomes the 'source of a thoroughgoing destabilization of identity'.[20] Even if this 'cosmopolitan escape', this 'passion for dis-belonging' apparently has consequences in everyday life, if only that it lends itself to a pleasant enough 'tourist view of the world', its true effects are in fact felt, Gauchet maintains, in economics: '[the] opening here has what could not be a more concrete and pressing aspect of the organizing principle of neoliberal globalization in the form of free-trade and of the constraint placed on national economies to turn outward'.[21] With as the corollary the unlimited freedom of movement

community? … It takes, on the one hand, *a common market*, that is, a space in which human monads can freely exchange their goods and services by the rules of free and fair competition. And, on the other hand, *a set of legal rules and regulations* (or space of Law) that can both protect this competition and ensure each monad (or each free association of monads) the right to live by their *private* definition of the good life. … As, besides, these very minimal conditions of belonging are now becoming globalized … an advanced liberal society must therefore logically end up seeing itself as a simple *point of passage* implying no particular moral allegiance from those who have provisionally opted to live there and that each should be free to leave for some other point whenever some or other calculation shows it is to their advantage.'

[15] See in this respect the developments on his work and his dialogue with Claude Lefort in the book by Lacroix and Pranchère, *Le procès des droits de l'homme* (n 9) 65ff.

[16] M Gauchet, *L'avènement de la démocratie IV. Le nouveau monde* (Paris, Gallimard, 2017) 571.

[17] ibid.

[18] ibid 667.

[19] ibid 670.

[20] ibid 671.

[21] ibid 673.

and settlement of individuals worldwide and the emergence of a 'democracy without *demos*'. Hence Gauchet's argument that '[t]he question raised by migratory movements reveals itself here to be, then, the fulcrum around which the deconstitution of politics by law acquires its systematic scope'.[22]

Finally, we come back more or less to Michéa's conclusions: political liberalism cannot be dissociated from economic liberalism; human rights promote both individualism and competition among economic agents and denationalisation, that is, the formation of 'citizens of the world', detached from any national allegiance and reduced to the condition of pure economic agents. What of the role of international law in this context? In point of fact neither Michéa nor Gauchet seem very well informed or even very interested in the developments of contemporary international law. This can probably be explained by a degree of 'methodological nationalism' that still prevails in the social sciences, at any rate in France, and that certainly contributes to problems of understanding and apprehending the phenomenon of globalisation.[23] Even so Marcel Gauchet draws a clear distinction between what he calls the 'law of nations', which refers by and large to 'classical' international law based on sovereignty – which he seems to think is still fully current[24] – and the phenomenon of international organisations, both governmental and non-governmental. These organisations, he claims, have as their purpose to organise cooperation among nations aimed at 'facilitating exchanges and communications of all kinds by codifying them'.[25] The exponential development of NGOs as from the 1970s is supposedly concomitant with the surge in the neoliberal project.[26]

So it is as if everything were interconnected. Human rights and institutions of world governance and NGOs all contribute to the accomplishment of globalised capitalism – according to a description that is somewhat reminiscent of Heidegger's criticism of the 'world of technology'.[27]

Let us ignore for the time being the mistaken view of human rights as the legal component of liberal individualism – we shall return to it in section II.

[22] ibid 675.

[23] See the journal *Raisons politiques* (2014) 2(54), special issue 'Les sciences sociales sont-elles nationalistes?'; and esp Speranta Dumitru, 'Qu'est-ce que le nationalisme méthodologique? Essai de typologie' ibid 9–22. The author defines methodological nationalism as 'a cognitive bias' which 'consists in understanding the social world by taking the nation state as the unit of analysis'. See also the contribution by Isabelle Delpla, 'Cosmopolitisme ou internationalisme méthodologique' ibid 87–102, who defines *a contrario* a 'methodological cosmopolitanism'.

[24] Gauchet, *L'avènement de la démocratie IV* (n 16) 287–91.

[25] ibid 256.

[26] ibid 258.

[27] See especially M Heidegger, 'What is Metaphysics' and 'The Question Concerning Technology' in DF Krell, *Martin Heidegger: Basic Writings* (London, Routledge, 1993) 89–110 and 307–341 respectively.

What must be specifically challenged here is the fuzzy idea that the internationalisation of human rights and the development of international organisations for cooperation are supposedly in the service of neoliberal globalisation. As concerns international organisations, this clearly ignores their diversity and the variety of their specialisations and even the historical conditions in which they developed. First, international organisations do not comply with some blueprint and any single will, but are created as and when initiatives arise from states in different contexts and on different levels. Since the end of the Cold War, it is incontrovertible that the institutions created at Bretton Woods and the GATT, succeeded by the World Trade Organization, have had as their purpose and goal the promotion of an economic world order obeying the precepts of economic liberalism. But such an outlook is far less clear for the organisations of the galaxy of the United Nations and the International Labour Organization, which have their own dynamics that mean they are very often opposed to the directions taken by the international economic organisations. The argument about convergence is even further from the truth when it comes to international human rights law. Here again, it amounts to a misunderstanding of the conditions in which this legal corpus was created and has developed, especially since the early 1990s, making possible the surge in power of the category of economic, social and cultural rights and the emergence of a critical discourse about economic globalisation *in the name of* human rights.[28] If our critical authors had taken the trouble to look at the works of the Committee of Economic, Social and Cultural Rights,[29] or those of the various special rapporteurs to the UN Human Rights Council,[30]

[28] Which explains the 'turn' taken by most major organisations for the defence of human rights like Amnesty International or the FIDH, which began in the early 1990s to address the violations of economic and social rights engendered by economic globalisation and the responsibility of multinational firms. On this approach to globalisation by human rights, see D Kinley, *Civilising Globalisation. Human Rights and the Global Economy* (Cambridge, Cambridge University Press, 2009). For a legal approach to the confrontation between international trade law in services and the right to education, see S Grosbon, *Le droit à l'enseignement supérieur et la libéralisation internationale du commerce des services* (Brussels, Bruylant, 2010).

[29] M Odello and F Seatzu, *The UN Committee on Economic, Social and Cultural Rights: The Law, Process and Practice* (Abingdon, Routledge, 2014); B Saul, D Kinley and J Mowbray (eds), *The International Covenant on Economic, Social and Cultural Rights: Commentary, Cases and Materials* (Oxford, Oxford University Press, 2004). And see the declaration from the Committee: 'Public debt, austerity measures and the International Covenant on Economic, Social and Cultural Rights', UN doc E/C.12/2016/1, 22 July 2016, esp para 8: 'The Committee is fully aware that, in the case of the IMF or the IBRD, the relevant Articles of Agreement establishing these organisations have sometimes been interpreted by these organisations as excluding human rights considerations in making their decisions. The Committee does not agree with such an interpretation.'

[30] See eg the work of the Special Rapporteur on the right to food, Olivier de Schutter and esp Mission to the World Trade Organization (25 June 2008), doc A/HRC/10/5/Add. 2; 'Guiding principles on human rights impact assessments of trade and investment agreements', Report of the Special Rapporteur, doc A/HRC/19/59/Add.5, 19 December 2011.

they could easily have observed that, far from supporting the movement for out-and-out liberalisation, human rights provide suitable legal tools not just for limiting its effects but for challenging its very basis. From that point on, it is easy to observe that the conception of world citizenship, that implicitly arises from the discourse and programmes of international organisations, is not one that advocates the unlimited freedom of movement of all actors worldwide. In truth, far from representing the apex of the 'deconstitution of politics', the issue of migration reveals above all the incapacity of governments, but also of many of the intellectual elite, to shake off their nationalist tensions in order to think through this question calmly as a global problem. And if there is a solution to this question, it does indeed involve systematising consideration within a globalised and decompartmentalised framework, that is open to all actors and no longer just to states alone.[31]

Equally absurd is the accusation levelled at NGOs *in general* of being both the product of economic liberalisation and the henchmen of its worldwide expansion. This is to overlook and to despise the wide diversity of civil society and the capacity for self-organisation of social movements, many of which pursue a cosmopolitan agenda that has as its purpose to counter the effects of liberal globalisation or to promote alternative models.[32]

Ultimately, the criticism of 'complicity' between cosmopolitanism and neoliberalism arises from a misunderstanding of the intentions and goals of cosmopolitanism, at any rate such as it is expressed in the works of most authors who adhere to it, but also in contemporary international law and the programmes and ideas defended by international organisations. In particular it is on the basis of the observation that states are powerless to govern a globalised economy, including by the traditional means of international cooperation, that the proponents of cosmopolitanism advocate developing new forms of global governance.[33] But it is as though the proponents of the 'complicity' argument were unable to conceive a domestication of the world market by a policy that would be itself globalised. There are two essential reasons for this. First because, for most of them, the individual cannot be conceived of as a 'monad' torn from their community (usually

[31] See C Wihtol de Wenden, *La question migratoire au XXIè siècle. Migrants, réfugiés et relations internationales* (Paris, Les Presses de Sciences Po, 2010); and O de Frouville, 'Les instruments universels de protection: quelle effectivité ?' in H Gherari and R Mehdi, *La société internationale face aux défis migratoires* (Paris, Pedone, 2012) 94–115.

[32] See O de Frouville, 'La place de la société civile dans les organisations internationales: quelle stratégie pour la France au XXIè siècle?' in G Cahin, F Poirat and S Szurek, *La France et les organisations internationales* (Paris, Pedone, 2014) 295–325.

[33] See especially J Habermas, 'The Postnational Constellation and the Future of Democracy' in J Habermas, *The Postnational Constellation. Political Essays*, tr M Pensky (Cambridge, Polity Press, 2001) 58–112; D Held, *Cosmopolitanism. Ideals and Realities* (Cambridge, Polity Press, 2010); and D Held, *Global Covenant. The Social Democratic Alternative to the Washington Consensus* (Cambridge, Polity Press, 2004).

national community) of origin. Secondly because it would be theoretically and practically impossible to conceive forms of devolution of the exercise of power in a 'supranational' framework – the expression 'supranational' itself revealing that it is impossible to think of politics outside of the state-based framework. These two objections form the other two common features of anti-cosmopolitan discourse that shall now be contemplated.

II. Cosmopolitanism as the Construction of a Rootless Individualist

The second feature common to the critical discourses of interest to us lies in the denunciation of the 'abstract', 'rootless' and 'unsettled' character of the norms arising from cosmopolitanism. The critique of human rights in particular argues that the sense of belonging or national identity is a condition for true freedom to flourish as opposed to universal and therefore abstract rights. Here again there are many variants. In support of the critique of universal human rights, Joseph de Maistre is readily cited and the irony-ridden passage of his *Considerations on France*:

> I have seen Frenchmen, Italians, Russians [...]; I know, too, thanks to Montesquieu, that one can be a Persian. But as for man, I declare that I have never met him in my life; if he exists, he is unknown to me.

A first variation on this theme puts on the garb of twentieth-century nationalism. It is more the stuff of extremist or populist politicians and actually finds little support, at least explicit support, among academics. Conversely, a number of intellectuals who are media figures to some degree readily take up the nostalgia for the 'Nation' as the only cradle capable of procuring security and well-being for the citizens of the state. For these 'new' nationalists, the Nation forms the ultimate or even the exclusive community to which individuals can belong and should impose its primacy in terms of norms over other forms of belonging or allegiance. Nationalism purports to oppose cosmopolitanism almost term for term, the latter being considered as the ideology of 'rootlessness' *par excellence*.[34] But nationalism also opposes other forms of communitarianism that claim infra-national or transnational membership and tend to dissolve or break up the 'basic (national) community'. Now, cosmopolitan human rights are designated in this respect as being guilty, too, of defending or being 'instrumentalised' so as to defend

[34] Among the literature produced by the think tanks of extreme-right movement, see eg the contributions published online in the journal of the 'Club de l'Horloge', *Polemia*, for the XXIXè Université annuelle du Club de l'horloge on 'Cosmopolitisme, idéologie dominante mondiale', and in particular Pierre Milloz, 'Le cosmopolitisme, voilà l'ennemi' and H. de Lesquen, 'Les douze champs de bataille de la guerre contre le cosmopolitisme'.

individual rights claimed by these infra-national or transnational communities against the national community. Universal human rights seemingly thus become the instrument of an active 'minoritarianism', a false universality as it were, undermining the foundations of the only true universality, that of the Nation.[35] Accordingly cosmopolitanism is guilty of both uprooting and of rooting too deeply.

But the theme of rootlessness has a more widespread variation in philosophical and political discourses that seeks to avoid the accusation of a return to the demons of the past. By virtue of this criticism, cosmopolitanism, through fully subjectivised 'law' – transformed by human rights – supposedly atomises individuals and separates them artificially from their community affiliations, and in particular but not exclusively from their national affiliation. In doing so it allegedly intensifies society's tendencies towards fragmentation that have already been induced by the colonisation of the world as experienced by economics. These critical themes are found again, from what are often different perspectives, not just among French political philosophers like Jean-Claude Michéa[36] and Marcel Gauchet,[37] who have already been cited, but also Pierre Manent.[38] They can be found more recently in Axel Honneth, in the search for a 'democratic ethicity', which it seems must involve an inch-by-inch criticism of legal 'subjective rights' in society.[39] They are also

[35] See, eg, Polony and Comité Orwell, *Bienvenue dans le pire des mondes* (n 8) at, eg, 186–87, which contains all the commonplaces – and untruths or *Alt-Facts* – of the far right on the subject, including the hatred of Islam: 'The multicultural revolution has gone hand in hand with the advent of the religion of human rights. In Western societies, the rights of man and the citizen have thus changed into the rights of individuals and minorities in defiance of national interests and the common good. The courts, and especially the supranational courts of Brussels, have sped this change. Through their case law, they have created ever more new fundamental rights, hunting down discrimination on the way to the point of obsession. Political Islam has rushed into this breach and gradually imposed its norm.' See also N Polony, *Nous sommes la France* (Paris, Plon, 2015) 143, which very clearly makes nationalism an antidote to neoliberalism, with which cosmopolitanism is supposedly complicit.

[36] See Michéa, *L'Empire du moindre mal* (n 14) esp at 99–100: 'The programme of liberal cleansing of Law (or as left-wing and far left liberals prefer to say, the "fight against *all* forms of discrimination and *all* forms of exclusion" therefore discovers that it too is bound by nature to endless movement'. See also J-C Michéa, 'Droit, libéralisme et vie commune' *Journal du Mauss* (November 2015) at www.journaldumauss.net/?Droit-liberalisme-et-vie-commune.

[37] See especially the passages cited in section I above.

[38] See P Manent, *La raison des nations. Réflexions sur la démocratie en Europe* (Paris, Gallimard, 2006) esp at 55–66 and, eg, 58: 'Governed by these instruments of governance and not of government, the peoples of Europe are becoming the instruments of their instruments, the disgruntled but docile stuff of a stack of tiers of governance which, from the local council to the United Nations, have the sole purpose of heading off any individual or collective action that is not the mere application of a legal rule. … The time of enlightened despotism has returned, this being the right term for the sum total of agencies, administrations, courts of justice and commission that, randomly but unanimously ever more meticulously lay the rule on us.' And more recently, in a more openly polemical tone, P Manent, *Situation de la France* (Paris, Desclée de Brouwer, 2015).

[39] A Honneth, *Freedom's Right. The Social Foundations of Democratic Life* tr J Ganahl (New York, Columbia University Press, 2014) esp at 81ff on the developments on the 'The limitations of legal freedom'.

found in the writings of international law scholars who claim to make a (left wing) 'critical' reading of international law.[40] None of these authors proposes directly to re-found society by freeing themselves from human rights but all of them question the cosmopolitan component of contemporary international law in that it is supposedly the accomplice of a liberal rationale leading ultimately to the dissolution of the 'political', that is, ultimately, as these authors see it, the accomplice of the precedence of the community over the individual. We come back in this way to the previous criticism, about conflating cosmopolitanism and neoliberalism, since the argument is ultimately that the atomisation of society supposedly forms part of the neoliberal 'scheme' to achieve its ends, that of a world without borders and without nations and focused entirely on trade.

Such criticisms can only puzzle if not the citizen at least the jurist who can claim a good working knowledge of international human rights law and of the case law of the organs for the protection of human rights.[41] Anything more than a cursory study of that case law should suffice to show that concerns about a potential breakdown of society boosted by human rights are if not totally unwarranted at least largely to be nuanced. In particular, reducing human rights to the liberal individual rights of 1789 and considering their uses only in a war of rights among individuals seems quite anachronistic to say the least and seems to overlook two important developments. First, the question of balancing rights against the general interest and therefore the social dimension of individual rights was developed throughout the twentieth century in the case law of national courts and included from the outset in the language of the founding international texts.[42] Secondly, the dynamic of equality – inherent for that matter in the development of democratic societies as Tocqueville had observed[43] – far from being intensified by human rights and the principle of non-discrimination has been curbed under the influence of the universalist principle inherent in the very concept of human rights. Thus, it was reaffirmed in Vienna in 1993 that women's rights were part of 'universal human rights'.[44] The question of minorities, which, after

[40] See, eg, M Koskenniemi, 'The effect of rights on political culture' and 'Human rights, politics and love' in M Koskenniemi, *The Politics of International Law* (Oxford, Hart Publishing, 2011); D Kennedy, *The Dark Sides of Virtue. Reassessing international humanitarianism* (Princeton, NJ, Princeton University Press, 2004).

[41] For a more political critique of these discourses, see Lacroix and Pranchère, *Le procès des droits de l'homme* (n 9).

[42] See the developments on the 'human rights regime' in my book, O de Frouville, *L'intangibilité des droits de l'homme en droit international. Régime conventionnel des droits de l'homme et droit des traités* (Paris, Pedone, 2004).

[43] A de Tocqueville, *Democracy in America*, tr JT Schleifer ed E Nolla (Indianapolis, Liberty Fund, 2010), vol II, pt two, ch XIII: 'When inequality is the common law of a society, the greatest inequalities do not strike the eye. When all is nearly level, the least inequalities offend. This is why the desire for equality always becomes more insatiable as equality is greater.'

[44] See the Vienna Declaration and Programme of Action, pt I, para 18: 'The human rights of women and of the girl-child are an inalienable, integral and indivisible part of universal human

the League of Nations, was the subject of a specific legal regime, was taken up after World War II in the context of universal human rights.[45] And more recently it is the same universalist approach that has prevailed, not without tension, with respect to the rights of indigenous populations and their members.[46] Likewise, the principle of respect for cultural diversity, rather than serving as a guarantee for cultural relativism, has been constructed in international law as a tool designed to 'better understand' and apply the principle of the universality of human rights.[47] In other words, the critics of human rights and of cosmopolitanism have got the wrong target. They wrongly liken human rights to the Tocquevillian dynamic of equality inherent in the democratic process. They fail to see that in some sense human rights are, in this context, and provided they are properly interpreted – that is, that they are not themselves submerged by the dynamic of equality – the eminent legal instrument for limiting the excesses of the frenzied individualism that has taken hold of some of our contemporaries.

III. The Theoretical and Practical Impossibility of World Politics

A third feature common to the critiques of international law in its cosmopolitan dimension lies in the certainty that it is both theoretically and practically impossible for there to be any devolution and any exercise of power on an international scale. By the precepts of Thomas Hobbes, international society remains in a state of nature and there is no going beyond that state. In this respect there is a radical opposition between Hobbes' argument and that made by Kant which rests on the hypothesis of states going beyond the state of nature. Again it is Carl Schmitt, himself a reader of Hobbes, who is the most common reference for anti-cosmopolitan critical discourse.

rights.' On the approach to women's rights as human rights, see the works of the Committee on the Elimination of Discrimination against Women: Diane Roman (ed), *La Convention pour l'élimination des discriminations à l'égard des femmes* (Paris, Pedone, 2014).

[45] See especially the 'Commentary of the working group on minorities to the United Nations Declaration on the rights of persons belonging to national or ethnic, religious and linguistic minorities', UN doc E/CN.4/Sub.2/AC.5/2005/2, and in particular para 4: 'The Declaration builds on and adds to the rights contained in the International Bill of Human Rights and other human rights instruments by strengthening and clarifying those rights which make it possible for persons belonging to minorities to preserve and develop their group identity. The human rights set out in the Universal Declaration of Human Rights must at all times be respected in the process, including the principle of non-discrimination between individuals.'

[46] See especially M Weller and J Hohmann (eds), *The UN Declaration on the Rights of Indigenous Peoples: A Commentary* (Oxford, Oxford University Press, 2017).

[47] See especially the 'conceptual and legal framework' of the independent expert on cultural rights, Mrs Farida Shaheed, UN doc A/HRC/14/36, para 3. And more generally on cultural rights as human rights, see M Bidault, *La protection internationale des droits culturels* (Brussels, Bruylant, 2009) esp at 53 and 76.

First for his axiom that situates the criterion of the political in the friend-foe relationship from which it ensues that 'the world is no political unit but a political universum'. This supposedly confirms the impossibility in theory and in practice for there to be a 'universal state' or even any possibility of a world political form that would not come down to the coexistence of political units.[48] What is most troublesome in this theory is precisely its axiomatic character, namely that it begins with a premise that is accepted as right and draws consequences from it that would therefore necessarily be right. Now, the idea that the political is consubstantial with the friend-enemy relationship surely cannot be validated without discussion. At any rate, one might prefer to it the idea of politics defined as an art of living together in the *polis* accepting and respecting the plural character of humankind. If we follow this definition, there is nothing to oppose the idea of a *political universum*, provided that the idea of universality is not caricatured, as in Schmitt or again, in his footsteps, Alain de Benoist,[49] by deliberately conflating universality and unity, cosmopolitanism and a dream of merging humanity. Cosmopolitanism has never claimed to build the 'universal state'. Quite the contrary. It has always fitted in with plurality and in its legal and political form with the federalist idea. Immanuel Kant explicitly dismissed the hypothesis of a universal state in his *Doctrine of Right*[50] and in *Perpetual Peace*[51] preferring instead the antinomy of the *Federation of Free States* (second definitive article for perpetual peace). While in contemporary times, Jürgen Habermas conceives of his cosmopolitanism outside of any project for a world government, preferring the idea of a 'world domestic policy'.[52]

[48] C Schmitt, *The Concept of the Political* (Chicago, IL, University of Chicago Press, 1996).

[49] A de Benoist, 'Le cosmopolitisme bute sur une aporie', *Philitt* (15 June 2016); and V Fontan-Moret, 'L'Etat universel en échec', ibid, which mistakenly likens cosmopolitanism to the plan to construct a world state.

[50] I Kant, *Metaphysics of Morals II. Doctrine of Right*, tr Mary Gregor (Cambridge, Cambridge University Press, 1996).

[51] Kant, *Perpetual Peace* (n 4) 156: 'The idea of international law presupposes the separate existence of neighbouring and independent states; and, although such a condition of things is in itself already a state of war, (if a federative union of these nations does not prevent the outbreak of hostilities) yet, according to the Idea of reason, this is better than that all the states should be merged into one under a power which has gained the ascendency over its neighbours and gradually become a universal monarchy. For the wider the sphere of their jurisdiction, the more laws lose in force; and soulless despotism, when it has choked the seeds of good, at last sinks into anarchy.'

[52] Habermas, 'The Postnational Constellation' (n 33) 109–10: 'A politics that can catch up with global markets, one that will be able to change the mode of locational competition, cannot simply be introduced at the top level of a multilevel politics organized into a "world state". Rather than a state, it has to find a less demanding basis of legitimacy in the organizational forms of an international negotiation system, which already exist today in other political arenas. … The international negotiating systems that make agreements between state actors possible communicate on the one side with internal state processes that respective governments depend on; on the other side they also connect up with the contexts and policies of the world organization. The result is at least a prospect for a world domestic policy without a world government.'

From its beginnings, cosmopolitanism has seen in the plurality of humans the very essence of universality. '[M]y city and country, so far as I am Antoninus, is Rome, but so far as I am a man, it is the world. The things then which are useful to these cities are alone useful to me', wrote Marcus Aurelius.[53] In other words, there is no access to the universal in itself outside of the experience of the individual; and there is no cosmopolitanism that is not in fact rooted.[54] The attainment of cosmopolitanism does not therefore in any way imply the merging of humankind and the indifferentiation of peoples, quite the opposite. Kant refuted this hypothesis from the outset. There cannot be any federation of peoples, he wrote, in the form of a federative state since a state implies a relationship between a government and a people, yet *peoples* cannot be reduced to a single people.[55] Yet later, Emmanuel Levinas took this dialectic further, or brought it closer, as you wish, on the level of a phenomenology of the relationship with others which shows no longer that the universal is indissociable from the singular but that sameness and otherness are consubstantial:

> Otherness of the unique and the incomparable, because everyone belongs to the human race, which, ipso facto and paradoxically, supposedly cancels itself out, precisely to leave everyone unique of their kind.[56]

It is the same thread, it seems to me, that runs from Marcus Aurelius to Lévinas, from the pre-political relation between the I and the Thou to the plan for a Federation of Free States. The conception of politics as a friend-foe relationship is ultimately an obsession: an obsession about homogeneity not to say purity. It stems from the idea that there is no political relation outside of a process of inclusion–exclusion which itself engenders a propensity for conflict that is inherent in the human species. It is about choosing your own anthropology: that of Marcus Aurelius, like those of Kant or Lévinas, emphasise the unsocial sociability,[57] the repulsion the other feels with respect to

[53] Marcus Aurelius, *Meditations*, bk VI, XLIV, tr George Long (White Plains, NY, Peter Pauper Press, 1957).

[54] See KA Appiah, *Cosmopolitanism. Ethics in a World of Strangers* (London, Penguin Books, 2006). See also U Beck, *Cosmopolitan Vision* (Cambridge, Polity Press, 2006); and U Beck, ' Nationalisme méthodologique – cosmopolitisme méthodologique: un changement de paradigme dans les sciences sociales' (2014) 2(54) *Raisons politiques* 103–20, esp at 107: 'Cosmopolitanism seeks neither to rank differences nor dissolve them. On the contrary, it accepts them as such, and even assigns a positive value to them. … It makes room for what is excluded by hierarchical difference and universal equality by presenting the Others as both different *and* equal'.

[55] Kant, *Perpetual Peace* (n 4).

[56] E Levinas, 'Les droits de l'homme et les droits d'autrui' in *Hors sujet* (Paris, Fata Morgana, 1987) 157–70, 160.

[57] Kant's fourth proposition in 'Idea of a Universal History from a Cosmopolitical Point of View' in *Kant's Principles of Politics*, tr W Hastie (Edinburgh, Clark, 1891): 'Man has an inclination to *socialise* himself by associating with others, because in such a state he feels himself more than a natural man, in the development of his natural capacities. He has, moreover, a great tendency to *individualise* himself by isolation from others, because he likewise finds in himself the unsocial disposition of wishing to direct everything merely according to his own mind; and

the same and at the same time the attraction the same has for the other …. Politics is the endless beginning again that consists in striking a precarious and always fleeting balance in this dialectic applied to all areas of human activity. Seen in this way, the political problem, which itself leads to the problem of law, is the same whatever the society. Wherever and at whatever level this unsociable sociability manifests itself, it is reflected by political and legal institutions that form a synthesis of the universal and the particular and, ultimately, recognise the otherness of the like. It is obviously no matter of chance that Carl Schmitt should construct a theory of the federation that refuses this name to the League of Nations, to reserve it for 'homogenous' units.[58] And indeed, from a purely static perspective, the effort of the plural world, of a world of sovereign states to put an end to wars, cannot be reflected other than by a 'negative equivalent' to the idea of a world state, namely an 'alliance against war'. And yet, at the same time as it comes into being, this alliance is already one step further on. It extends 'ever further' because it aspires to its transformation into a true positive alliance. It is worked on by the antinomy of the Federation of Free States, which postulates both the freedom of the components and the federative character of the institutions it brings together, and therefore the coexistence of two irreconcilable sovereignties.[59]

This antinomic political form, that is embodied today in the European Union, is the proof that it is possible for there to be political construction within a *pluriversum*.

IV. A Few Seemingly Inconsequential Thoughts by Way of an Inconclusive Conclusion …

A. A New 'Betrayal of the Intellectuals'?

Hannah Arendt in *The Origins of Totalitarianism* recalls the bitterness of humanists of the years between the wars when confronted with the complicity of intellectual elites with totalitarian ideologies:

> What the spokesmen of humanism and liberalism usually overlook, in their bitter disappointment and their unfamiliarity with the more general experiences of the time, is that an atmosphere in which all traditional values and propositions had evaporated … in a sense made it easier to accept patently absurd propositions than the old truths which had become pious banalities, precisely because nobody could be expected to take the absurdities seriously. Vulgarity with its cynical dismissal of respected standards and accepted theories carried with it a frank admission of

hence he expects resistance everywhere just as he knows with regard to himself that he is inclined on his part to resist others.'

[58] See in this volume ch 3, 'A Cosmopolitan Perspective on the Responsibility to Protect'.

[59] See Kant, *Perpetual Peace* (n 4).

> the worst and a disregard for all pretenses which were easily mistaken for courage and a new style of life.[60]

Might we now be seeing a resurgence of what Julien Benda called in 1927, the 'betrayal of the intellectuals' that he perceived in the unbridled adhesion of some 'intellectuals' of his time to nationalism?[61]

We might obviously multiply the comparisons between the times we are living in and the inter-war period and there are many such comparisons in recent works in the social sciences.[62] In any event, the intellectuals who delight in denouncing 'human-rightism' and NGOs and who continue to accord an irrefutable presumption of innocence to the state and sovereignty might want to ponder these parallels.[63]

In an article published in 1935, Paul Morand, a 'cosmopolitan' writer if ever there was one, began the shift that was to lead to his collaboration with the Vichy regime. He was coming to realise that the aristocratic cosmopolitanism[64] that he was fond of and engaged in personally was nearing extinction, caught between the rise of nationalism and an 'internationalism' (that of the League of Nations) that he reviled:

> The birth of internationalism dates from the decline of cosmopolitan culture. By a strange paradox, internationalism began to grow at the same time as did nationalities, from which it borrowed their mysticism. The religion of nationalism required the sacrificing of the individual to the state; internationalist faith requires nations to sacrifice themselves to a super-nation. Thus that faith is increasingly opposed

[60] H Arendt, *The Origins of Totalitarianism* [1951], pt III 'Totalitarianism' (Cleveland and New York, The World Publishing Company, 1958) 334.

[61] J Benda, *La trahison des clercs* (Paris, Grasset, 1927) published in English as *The Treason of the Intellectuals*, tr R Aldington (London, Transaction Publishers, 2007) 99: 'The cult for the particular and the scorn for the universal is a reversal of values quite generally characteristic of the teaching of the modern "clerks"'.

[62] See the literature cited by Emmanuel Mattiato in the 'Introduction' to U Lemke, M Lucarelli and E Mattiato (eds), *Cosmopolitisme et réaction: le triangle Allemagne-France-Italie dans l'entre-deux-guerres* (Chambéry, Université Savoie Mont Blanc, 2014) 15–43.

[63] Emmanuel Decaux draws a distinction between 'primary' and 'secondary' anti-human-rightism. The latter, theorised in particular by his friend Alain Pellet, is primarily epistemological in its scope. It comes from an academic who can hardly be suspected of wanting to challenge the foundations of contemporary international law. But Emmanuel Decaux warns against the risks of instrumentalisation of one by the other: 'When Alain denounces "human rightism", he does so as a jurist, eager to defend the integrity of international law and its coherence in the face of any risk of fragmentation. But he is all too often heard in the area of international relations, where the "like-minded" denounce the influence of democracies, although they are very silent, or the action of foreign NGOs, now made to toe the line in Russia as in China.' E Decaux, 'Relations internationales: introduction au droit international' in *Dictionnaire des idées reçues* (Paris, Pedone, 2017) 484–85. Putting 'human rightism' on trial is one of the favourite themes of a number of extreme and anti-modern discourses. This is all the more worrying when the expression is used by politicians in high office, including among those who lay claim to a degree of intellectual authority or who are perceived in the medias as enjoying such authority.

[64] That is the cosmopolitanism of a small, cultivated, world elite that was French-speaking and shared a common culture.

> to cosmopolitanism, which, far from being a faith, is a form of scepticism; which, far from being a passion, is an experience; which, far from being demagogical, is peculiar to an elite; which sets out selfishly and disinterestedly only to acquire fuller knowledge of the world and a clear awareness of its values; which, far from taking fright at incoherence and disparity sees the charm in them and seeks it out. A cosmopolitan would not have invented the League of Nations; Geneva leaves him aghast just as much as does mass international stultification by the wireless, Fordism, the cinema, or war; 'war is the popularization of travel', thinks the cosmopolitan in disgust, for whom travel is the reward of enlightened minds and war, twenty million poor souls becoming acquainted in spite of themselves amid a deluge or iron and a chaos of endless talk drawn out by the crises to which wars give rise.[65]

Oddly, the idea that the internationalism of the League of Nations might serve to democratise the cosmopolitan experience reserved until then to an elite did not occur to Morand. That the international law of the League of Nations might defend diversity and be in the service of the continuing and endless expansion of the maxim of the broader Kantian thinking;[66] that the cosmopolitan spectator of the world might converge with the cosmopolitan actor in a single infinite quest for otherness;[67] that human rights should not be just machine tools of Fordism and mass culture, plainly seemed beyond his conception. His loathing of modernity, including Kant, was getting the upper hand. Perhaps because, as Emmanuel Decaux recently told me with his usual wry humour, 'Morand was a magnificent writer ... but he wasn't terribly bright!'

B. The Courage of Truth in the Post-truth Era

The Oxford English Dictionary chose 'post-truth' as its word of the year in 2016. As if the language had been marked by the double impact of Brexit and the election of Donald Trump as president of the United States. As the daily newspaper *Le Monde* explains:

[65] P Morand, 'L'enfer des cosmopolites' in *Chroniques 1931–1954* (Paris, Grasset, 1935) 526. I became aware of this article by reading the Introduction by Emmanuel Mattiato cited above (fn 62). See his analysis ibid at 34.

[66] One of the three maxims of *sensus communis* identified by Immanuel Kant, *Critique of Judgement*, tr JH Bernard (London, MacMillan and Co, Ldt, 1914) § 40: 'to put ourselves in thought in the place of everyone else'. This maxim refers to everyone's ability 'if he disregards the subjective private conditions of his own judgement, by which so many others are confined, and reflects upon it from a *universal standpoint* (which he can only determine by placing himself at the standpoint of others)'.

[67] See the very fine book by O Rémaud, *Un monde étrange. Pour une autre approche du cosmopolitisme* (Paris, PUF, 2015) and esp the magnificent passages at 189–202 on Kant's *Anthropology from a Pragmatic Point of View* and on Hannah Arendt's commentary on para 40 of the *Critique of Judgement* (H Arendt, *Juger. Sur la philosophie politique de Kant* (Paris, Seuil, 1991) 116).

> In the age of post-truth news, … facts are no longer fundamental. Public figures may now announce fake news knowingly, without any care for the truth – and may benefit therefrom.[68]

This form of politics that cares not a whit for the truth is perhaps not as new as it seems. Dialectics and sometimes the opposition between what is true and what is politic is as old as Socrates.[69] If there is anything new, it may lie more in the paradox that, in the act of communication unleashed by new information technologies, lies can continue to spread and whole sections of the population remain impervious to the simple exposition of the facts. The explanation for this paradox may be sought in the fact that, while contributing to create an entirely decompartmentalised public space on a world scale, the Internet seems to have reproduced and more seriously fragmented epistemic communities, with each now being able to filter the type and nature of information that is likely to come to its attention.

In some countries, this fragmentation compounds the totalitarian control of information through the surveillance and censorship of news broadcast over the network. Thus, the totalitarianism of information manipulated by a single censor is compounded or, as the case may be, replaced by an atomism that seems equally harmful to the truth in the fight against lies in politics and consequently in the establishment of communication that is capable of engendering individual decisions and rational collective agreements.

Does the 'post-truth' era close the period of expansion of the cosmopolitan dimension of international law? Does it not rather open up a period of resistance to the dismantling of international law, understood not just as the law of co-existence but as the legal order of a world common to all nations and all individuals? But what resistance can an intellectual or an academic put up in a world in which truth is no longer important?

The pre-eminent act of resistance lies precisely in attempting to display that 'courage of truth' that Michel Foucault studied[70] and not giving in to the

[68] 'Les risques de la société "post-vérité"', editorial, *Le Monde* (2 January 2017). See also *The Economist* (10 September 2016), issue entitled 'Art of the Lie. Post-Truth Politics in the Age of Social Media'.

[69] See the study by Hannah Arendt written further to the polemic and campaign of defamation following the publication of *Eichmann in Jerusalem*, 'Truth and politics', originally published in *The New Yorker* (25 February 1967). Arendt reminds us from the outset that 'The subject of these reflections is a commonplace. No one has ever doubted that truth and politics are on rather bad terms with each other, and no one, as far as I know, has ever counted truthfulness among political virtues. Lies have always been regarded as necessary and justifiable tools not only of the politician's or the demagogue's but also of the statesman's trade.'

[70] See the study of *parrhesia* by Michel Foucault in his courses at the Collège de France 1982–83, *Le gouvernement de soi et des autres* (Paris, Seuil/Gallimard, 2008) and 1984, *Le courage de la vérité. Le gouvernement de soi et des autres II* (Paris, Seuil/Gallimard, 2009). In particular, in the last volume, ibid at 14 (our translation): '*Parrhesia* is therefore, in a word, the courage to speak the truth for he who speaks and takes the risk, despite everything, of telling the whole truth as he sees it, but it is also the courage of the person he is speaking to to accept as true the hurtful truth he hears.' One might think, too, of Denis de Rougemont, *Lettres sur la bombe atomique* (Paris,

reign of post-truth, to the primacy of emotions and to the powerlessness of rationality. It is essential therefore to reiterate facts, to tirelessly recall principles, to decipher the twisting of arguments, to expose the manipulation of words, not to yield on any point. For the jurist, it means not confining oneself to law as a 'game for the mind'; not hesitating to intervene in the field of law, that is, understanding law as a social practice. Emmanuel Decaux likes to quote Bergson: 'act like a man of thought and think like a man of action'.[71] This is a way of saying that his 'practice' as a UN expert is not an answer to any aspiration for a change of scenery or, worse still, to turn an academic from his calling. There is an internal consistency between thought and action, since thought guides action and action nurtures thought. 'It is easy for an intellectual to be right in his ivory tower. It is more exalting for an academic to try to implement what he knows and what he believes.'[72] A philosophy of academic life for our times.

La Différence, 1991) 72: 'What it takes to be free is, alone and quite simply, courage. … A free man is a courageous man, not a man who has received (from whom?) three or four or a thousand-and-one freedoms. We hear people says, "X is a free spirit". Who does he get his freedom from? Neither from the state, or the revolution, or the soviets, or democracy, and especially not from their experts. He gets it from his vision alone and from his courage to fight to join it. … We shall not be free in peace unless we fight on.' (our translation). It is a fearsome lesson and a difficult path that the author lays before us. Our freedom is not given to us, we do not receive it; nothing is for granted. We must fight endlessly. 'Will we have courage enough?' then becomes the true question. A question that those who live under the yoke of dictatorship keep on asking. A question that in our democracies we all too often forget to ask ourselves.

[71] Conclusion to the Grenoble colloquium organised by Mihaela Anca Ailincai on *Soft law et droits fondamentaux*, 5 February 2016.

[72] E Decaux, 'La Sous-Commission des droits de l'homme des Nations Unies, de 1947 à nos jours' (2007) 4(32) *Relations internationales* 59–77, 62.

5

A Critical Defence of Human Rights

Ever since human rights were first recognised and set out, philosophical strands have formed to criticise both their underpinnings and their scope.[1] Are there equivalent strands in the legal domain? And more specifically, because they now have the status of positive legal norms, are human rights immune from any form of criticism?

Any attempt to answer this question must begin by observing that the 'legal field' is not unequivocal and that it is characterised even by a wide diversity of approaches.

For the purposes of this communication, I feel it is helpful to distinguish between two main critical approaches:

- an 'internal' critical approach, purporting to pertain to legal positivism. The objections it raises are part of *the framework of positive law* and supposedly refrain from any judgement based on criteria derived from other disciplinary fields or non-legal normative orders; and
- an 'external' critical approach which, conversely, seeks input from judgment criteria from outside positive law. This notably involves 'judging' law in the light of its social, political and economic effects or its 'morality'.

It can be considered that this second approach is itself divided into two sub-schools. One exhibits more or less explicitly and more or less overtly *an intention to contest and call into question human rights discourse* and another – which is no less critical – sets itself the objective of *defending* human rights and more broadly the discourse of modernity that underlies them both in philosophy and as legal norms. It will be understood that in the limited context of this presentation, I shall confine myself to the discourses produced by *scholars trained in law*, leaving aside authors versed in other sciences even if these 'external' critical discourses often come from specialists of other disciplines such as philosophy.[2]

[1] For an excellent analysis and criticism of critiques, see J Lacroix and J-Y Pranchère, *Le procès des droits de l'Homme. Généalogie du scepticisme démocratique* (Paris, Seuil, 2016).

[2] In this respect, about a rather philosophical critique of modernity and especially of human rights and the cosmopolitan side of international law, see in this volume ch 4, 'Justifying International Law, Defending Cosmopolitanism'.

I. The Critical 'Positivist' Approach

I use the term 'positivist' in inverted commas because there is obviously no question here of speaking of positivist authors in general – of which I am one – but instead of a situated scholarly discourse that developed in the course of the 1990s and produced a critical discourse of international human rights law (IHRL) inasmuch as its interpretation is supposedly characterised by 'autonomist' or even 'separatist' tendencies and allegedly creates inconsistencies with other norms of international law or internal law.

This approach is based on a presupposition, namely that the positivist method should refrain from 'judging' law by the standards of anything other than strictly legal considerations. From this perspective, criticism of law is not non-existent but should be made in light of law itself and so should be expressed through the categories of evaluation drawn essentially from *logic* aimed at evaluating the *coherence* of legal discourse. Consequently, what this 'positivism' looks to determine is the validity of an interpretation of law and therefore its *rationally ordered* character, in particular with the *legal syllogism* as a landmark.

It is therefore an 'internal' critique, a criticism within the framework of the 'rules of the game', that refrains from criticising those rules or from challenging them on the basis of factors from outside the system. What is criticised is any failing by the players to abide by the rule laid down beforehand, including when the rule is produced by the players who, in doing so, impose additional future constraints on themselves.

This approach is complicated in the domain of human rights because the statements that purport to be human rights (or the general obligation of the state with respect to a right) are always at a high level of abstraction, that is, at the level of abstraction of a principle. Think for example of the wording of the right to life in article 6(1) of the International Covenant on Civil and Political Rights: 'Every human being has the inherent right to life. This right shall be protected by law. No one shall be arbitrarily deprived of his life.' Obviously many other examples may be given to show that these statements are characteristic of the 'open texture' of the law HLA Hart spoke of. The outcome is that IHRL is primarily judge-made-law: it is even the prototype of such law and the development of independent bodies, of 'third parties' whether judicial or expert bodies (like committees), has enabled the court-driven expansion of IHRL for more than 50 years both regionally and universally.

The method claiming to derive from 'positivism' therefore essentially sets about criticising judge-made interpretations of IHRL in the name of interpretations that purport to have a degree of 'scientificness' about them, being based on a degree of logical formalism. What is criticised is just as much the normative work of the judge or the expert (the development of IHRL on the basis of texts and then of the existing interpretations) as their work of application of judge-made rules to specific instances (and in particular through the technique of weighing up interests).

'Criticism' defined in this way is not absent from legal discourse. It is even, in a first variant, a commonplace. It is the criticism all 'commentators' on legal judgments engage in, unthinkingly, especially in 'case-law reviews'. Beyond the description of case law (which includes providing perspective with relation to precedents, not only of the body that laid down the case law but sometimes also of other bodies in a comparative approach), 'criticism' of case law is a set figure in the exercise of reviewing. It may sometimes be supported in the dissenting opinions appended by judges to majority decisions. It is a matter of criticising some interpretation that supposedly gives too narrow or too broad a content to a notion, or of considering that a poor balance is struck between individual rights and public interests, often by drawing on precedents derived from similar situations. In this variant, the criticism of the interpretation of human rights is therefore set out by reference to IHRL in the name of the rights themselves, that is, an earlier case-law interpretation of the 'legislated' rights. In this context, legal discourse is often articulated around an opposition between legal 'progressivism' and 'conservatism', and therefore between the proponents of a continual evolution of interpretation and proponents of maintaining the 'classical' or initial interpretations, including by way of reference to preparatory works or to the 'will' of the parties to the treaty.

In a second variant – which is more specific and is more specifically of interest to us here – criticism purporting to be from legal positivism is still made relative to pre-established norms, but norms arising from other sets of norms than IHRL. This variant is especially pointed in the domain of human rights and takes the form of criticism of IHRL and of its interpreters in the name of 'general international law' or again of a methodological criticism of what Alain Pellet has mocked rather as 'human rightism' (*droits-de-l'hommisme*).[3] Although it seems somewhat outmoded today, the debate was at its height in the mid-1990s especially in connection with the application to human rights conventions of the 'general' regime established by the 1969 Vienna Convention on the Law of Treaties.[4] It was all the talk at the 1997 Strasbourg conference organised by the *Société Française pour le Droit International*.[5]

[3] A Pellet, '"Droits-de-l'hommisme" et droit international', *Conférence commémorative Gilberto Amado*, 18 July 2000, United Nations. And on criticism of the critique, B Simma, 'Droits-de-l'hommistes: fondamentalistes' in *Dictionnaire des idées reçues en droit international* (Paris, Pedone, 2017) 211–14.

[4] My PhD dissertation took as its starting point the debate on the 'specificity' of human rights in international law and the quarrel then raging over the treaty regime; see O de Frouville, *L'intangibilité des droits de l'Homme en droit international. Régime conventionnel des droits de l'homme et droit des traités* (Paris, Pedone, 2004).

[5] SFDI, *La protection des droits de l'homme et l'évolution du droit international. Colloque de Strasbourg* (Paris, Pedone, 1998).

The late Jean-François Flauss introduced the colloquium by recalling that 'the evolution of the international protection of human rights has crystallized a truly scholastic quarrel on the ground of the theory of international law'. He argued there were three opposing camps: the 'fundamentalist' or 'traditionalist' strand looking to 'neutralize or at least' to 'smooth over' the 'atypical rough edges of the international regimes of protection of human rights'; on the other side an 'autonomist' or 'secessionist' strand considered general international law as 'an obstacle … to the development of the international protection of human rights'; and a third camp (undoubtedly that of the author) supposedly advocated 'moderate evolutionism', preferring to 'pay tribute to empiricism rather than to dogmatism' and emphasising 'existing complementary features'.[6]

The debate crystallised in the following years around the regime of reservations to treaties, at the initiative of Alain Pellet, who was then the special rapporteur on the topic of the UN International Law Commission.[7] In a way, the exchanges and discussions that ensued – including among members of the treaty bodies such as the Human Rights Committee and the International Law Commission, between the proponents of a 'specific' approach and the 'generalists' – eased the controversy, which nowadays seems to be a thing of the past.

It is now more the question of the consistency of IHRL with national legal orders that is posed. If 'human rightism' is challenged, it is not so much because it supposedly subverts general international law but more because it allegedly interferes too deeply in internal legal orders, including in the domains that a number of states look to ring-fence through the concept of 'constitutional identity'.[8] But this new criticism, although directed specifically at human rights, is also aimed indirectly at all law 'of international origin', since it tends to call into question the primacy of international law over internal law and the principle, recalled especially by article 27 of the Vienna Convention on the Law of Treaties, that states cannot invoke domestic law in order to avoid performing their international obligations. Moreover, this new critical discourse resonates with a more political discourse reaffirming sovereignties and consequently a degree of legal nationalism.

Beyond this 'internal' critical positivist discourse and sometimes as an extension of such criticisms or in conjunction with them, are other *external*

[6] J-F Flauss, 'Introduction', ibid 13–14. See also Pellet's intervention in the concluding round table discussion, ibid 294–98 and the general conclusions of G Cohen-Jonathan, 'La protection des droits de l'homme et l'évolution du droit international', ibid 306–41.

[7] See my PhD dissertation (n 4) and, after the adoption of the *Guide de la pratique sur les réserves aux traités*, my comments in O de Frouville, 'Commentaire (I)' in SFDI, *Actualités des réserves aux traités. Journée d'études de Nanterre* (Paris, Pedone, 2014) 39–44.

[8] See especially the very complete overview by P-F Laval, 'Les limites constitutionnelles à l'exécution des arrêts de la Cour européenne des droits de l'homme à la lumière de la jurisprudence nationale comparée' (2017) 3 *RGDIP* 662–82; and the proceedings of the conference on 'L'identité constitutionnelle de la France et le droit international' (2014) 3 *RGDIP* 481–662.

perspectives. These see human rights as a legal object that can be criticised *per se* against the yardstick of factors external to law, that is, philosophical, historical, sociological or political considerations. Here the discourse of jurists concurs with or borrows the arguments from other disciplines in order to articulate a critical discourse on law and on 'rights' – since this is very often the way that 'criticism' refers to human rights.

II. The External Critical Approach Contesting 'Rights'

'Rights': probably to avoid writing 'human rights', that is, substantively so as not to be open to the criticism of the *fable* of rights inherent in human nature, of would-be natural 'subjective rights'. And to set rights against law, (bad) rights against (good) objective law.

External critical discourses about rights are largely conflated with a critical discourse of the key concepts of modernity and modernity itself as a project and an accomplishment. In point of fact, it could be said that all discourses that are critical of human rights purport to be either pre-modern or post-modern and are unanimously anti-modern. To supplement this scheme, it seems to me we can add a second right–left axis that combines with the former.

It may seem somewhat strange to use this political categorisation especially in a discourse on legal doctrine and moreover at a time when people would have us believe that the distinction between right and left is no longer meaningful (although this attempt is contested and encounters some resistance). But I have to say that I have not found anything better to date. However, the use of this distinction can be accompanied by a careful use of language to specify what I mean by it in the present context. By 'right/left', I do not necessarily mean a positioning on the political chessboard but I refer more to themes, and also to a bent, a temperament or even a style. The right: looking rather towards the past, celebrating authority (not necessarily or exclusively the authority of the state) and fearing or deploring chaos, magnifying willpower and individual autonomy, and for pessimists revelling in an aesthetic of decadence or decline. The left: rather forward looking, contesting authority and authorities (but not always and only the authority of the state) and calling for 'emancipation', sometimes celebrating disorder and chaos, magnifying social forces and devaluing the individual compared with society and, for pessimists, fascinated by an aesthetic not of decline or decadence but of catastrophe.

We thus find ourselves with a horizontal axis opposing pre-modernity and post-modernity; and a vertical axis with left and right as its poles. There are therefore four categories in a typology that is worth what any typology is worth, that is, not much: right/left-wing pre-modern; right/left-wing post-modern. In the limited context of this contribution I shall look exclusively at the 'post-modern' side of criticism, which seems to exert a genuine influence over the thinking of jurists, including internationalists. This seems to be less the case for 'pre-modern' criticism.

Unlike pre-modern criticism, post-modern criticism does not call for a *return* to something prior to modernity. One of the characteristics of post-modern thought, or one of the common points of thinkers who may claim to be part of this line, is the rejection of the great narratives, of major theories, of concepts with capital letters, be they God, Reason or History.

Post-modernity is written under the sign of complexity, of the plurality of a net-like web. By this yardstick, it does not accept Greek or Mapuche holism any more than the Reason of the Enlightenment. The modern explanation of the world like the pre-modern explanations of the world is dismissed, because it is the explanation of the world in itself that has to be dismissed. There are only *explanations* and *discourses* about the world that are tangled and usually conflicting.

Post-modernity also condemns modernity in that it has supposedly changed into a project of unbridled *modernisation*, with instrumental reasons as its prime force, blinded to questions of ethics and justice.

Lastly, post-modernity has a passion for the genealogy of concepts (within the meaning of Nietzsche) and deconstruction (with a meaning Derrida would not accept paternity for, or at least that he would wish to be carefully distinguished from *la déconstruction*[9]), namely, the exposure of hidden and underlying logics and hidden meanings in language. In this sense, it sets about a critical work on the major narratives of modernity, which are that much harder to deconstruct because they often assert themselves as deconstructive (of tradition and oppression and more generally of any form of heteronomy).

But paired with certain political obsessions, this passion for deconstruction turns into the hermeneutics of suspicion, introduced by Heidegger and Carl Schmitt, which unfortunately quite often characterises post-modern discourses in particular when it comes to IHRL or cosmopolitanism, in short, the ideals of the Enlightenment.

As with pre-modern criticism, it is possible, however, to identify a right-wing and a left-wing post-modern criticism.

A. Right-wing Post-modern Criticism

This underscores the fallacious character of the universalism of the language of human rights. That universalism relates to an anthropology that is supposedly

[9] See his conference at the Cardozo Law School attended by proponents of Critical Legal Studies in J Derrida, *Force de loi. Le 'Fondement mystique de l'autorité'* (Paris, Galilée, 1994) esp 24–25.

valid for everyone whereas human communities are not all one and the same. Universalism as an identity or as equality is a lie. It is even a totalitarian temptation for a way of thinking that emphasises the radical otherness of each being and above all of each historically and culturally grounded group and in particular for the Nation.

What right-wing post-moderns cannot accept in view of their presuppositions is the rationalist ambition of the foundation of a community and therefore the very possibility of universal communicability. The political bond in particular can only be found within communities that are situated and historically constructed or even, for Schmitt, construct themselves only in opposition to other communities. Schmitt claims that the essence of politics lies in the friend-foe relationship and therefore there can be no universal community as human rights postulate.

Human rights are therefore bound to failure as a principle of action directed at the Common Good or Justice. Conversely, they serve as a mask for hegemony (and this is where one of the favourite themes of post-modernity can be seen to re-emerge, which is also taken up by left-wing post-modernists for that matter. In this, right and left merge when it comes to denouncing 'hegemony' and in particular that of a state on the North American continent that we shall not name). Again it is Schmitt who is evoked with his supposed deformed citation from Proudhon: 'Whoever invokes humanity wants to cheat'.[10]

It seems to me that these themes are to be found notably in the writings of a US conservative jurist, Professor Eric A Posner of the University of Chicago, who published what he probably hoped would be a firebrand in 2014 and which turns out to be a rather foolish book, *The Twilight of Human Rights Law*. The book's starting point is clear and completely axiomatic, as the author explains on page 7:

> The starting point for this book is that human rights law has failed to accomplish its objectives.[11]

And the aim is to explain this presupposed failure.

> [M]y major argument is that human rights law reflects a kind of rule naiveté – the view that the good in every country can be reduced to a set of rules that can then be impartially enforced. Rule naiveté is in part responsible for the proliferation of human rights, which has made meaningful enforcement impossible.[12]

It is indeed Reason that is on trial here and with it the modern belief in change through law. What Posner calls 'rule naivety' is the idea that abstract

[10] C Schmitt, *The Concept of the Political*, tr G Schwab, exp edn (Chicago, IL, University of Chicago Press, 1996).
[11] E A Posner, *The Twilight of Human Rights Law* (Oxford, Oxford University Press, 2014) 7.
[12] ibid.

principles such as human rights might exert a hold on what is of its essence a more complex and plural reality that is actually impenetrable to reason.

Posner recommends, then, a form of pragmatism coloured by utilitarianism. He asks the question of the best means to use to achieve the maximum good in a situation in which financial resources are limited. He adds to that the belief that the development of freedom in a country is not necessarily correlative to economic development which, he argues, is the only true guarantee of the 'public good' that is sought. Accordingly, the promotion of law and of abstract principles such as human rights is costly in resources and does not necessarily lead to the public good, because all countries are different. It is a mark of 'rule naivety' to believe, for example, that combatting torture in some country will necessarily contribute to the public good. It is better to undertake concrete actions with visible effect rather than try to tackle practices such as torture, that Posner thinks might be so deeply ingrained in a country's culture and habits that it would be impossible to root them out:

> Rather than devise general rules or theoretical approaches, consider each country on its own terms. All countries are different and all countries have different needs. It might make more sense for Western donors to help a country build a reliable road system than to force it to abolish torture. It may well be easy to build the road using donors' funds and local labor. Once built, the road may spur economic development, and even lead to greater political liberty by allowing people to travel to voting booths and enabling candidates to stump about the country. Meanwhile, if torture is an entrenched practice of the police force, no amount of aid for retraining the police and improving the judicial system will make any difference. If the goal is to help people in poor countries, and limited funds are available, then those funds should be used in ways that do the most good, not to compel the country to submit to an abstract formulation of human rights that Westerners imagine are right for everyone in the world.[13]

What Posner has to say therefore combines pragmatism with cultural relativism, all through the prism of post-modern complexity. He condemns in essence Enlightenment 'systems' and 'theories' as being both ambitious and necessarily hegemonic. On this plane we find again the Schmittian criticism of hegemony under Posner's pen in conclusion to his book, when he compares, to finish off, human rights with nineteenth century missionary policy and colonisation. Again he emphasises the insurmountable character of cultural differences and that one culture is illegible for another.

This decisive judgement ends with a very post-modern appeal to modesty by contrast with the supposed *hubris* of the Enlightenment:

> With the benefit of hindsight, we can see that the human rights treaties were not so much an act of idealism as an act of hubris, with more than a passing resemblance to the civilizing efforts undertaken by governments and missionary groups

[13] ibid 145–46.

> in the nineteenth century, which did little good for native populations while entangling European powers in the affairs of countries they did no understand. A more humble approach is long overdue.

It is 70 years of human rights history that are trashed in this way. It is not insignificant that Posner uses the term 'hubris', (deliberately?) establishing a sort of complicity with pre-modern criticism. Hubris for the Ancients was an act caused by someone because they lost sight of the *proper* place of things and beings in the Universe. There follows from it the *disproportion*, literally the misjudgement of the proportions of things that entails the fall (and divine punishment, *nemesis*: Tantalus, Icarus, Prometheus, etc).

Modernity comes across necessarily as hubris precisely because it is *a sometimes peaceful and sometimes violent transgression of the established order of the world*. Modernity is as such criticism in that it unmasks the fact that what appears behind the face of Nature is actually part of Culture or History and so can be changed. Modernity is an affront to tradition, hierarchy and authority. It forces tradition to doff its threadbare finery and reduces it to what it is – a set of rules and habits inherited from History and social relations.

B. Left-wing Post-modern Criticism

This is more widespread in literature, perhaps because it is less aggressive on its face than right-wing post-modern criticism. Often left-wing post-modernists do not announce the death or at any rate the 'twilight' of human rights (as Posner may do without any misgivings), but come across rather as defenders of freedom and above all of emancipation. They denounce rather the fact that human rights 'make too many promises' and do not form a satisfactory policy of emancipation. They may even be instrumentalised by the middle class or the dominant class (world hyperclass, capitalist oligarchy) to appease demands while maintaining them within a framework that is not liable to harm the interests of the privileged few.

This left-wing post-modern criticism can be read essentially among authors from the *Critical Legal Studies* movement such as Duncan Kennedy and, more specifically for international law, David Kennedy, Martti Koskenniemi, Anthony Anghie or Anne Orford.

Obviously there are points in common among all these authors but also nuances. I shall rely within the bounds of this discussion on the most important contributions from David Kennedy and Martti Koskenniemi on the subject.[14]

[14] D Kennedy, *The Dark Sides of Virtue. Reassessing International Humanitarianism* (Princeton, NJ, Princeton University Press, 2004); M Koskenniemi, 'The Effects of Rights on Political Culture' and 'Human Rights, Politics and Love' in M Koskenniemi, *The Politics of International Law* (Oxford, Hart Publishing, 2011) 133–52 and 153–68, respectively.

The hermeneutics of suspicion is often taken further still among left-wing post-modernists than their right-wing counterparts when it comes to human rights. Perhaps because the deconstructive (again, not within the meaning of Derrida) passion among them is mixed with Marxist criticism of human rights but also with a particularly virulent allergy to Empire, neo-colonialism and hegemony in general. There is also a *smack* of paradox in the aesthetic sense: these authors clearly delight in flushing out potential for alienation in any discourse with emancipatory aims. One gets the impression that even if there were no such potential, they would invent it for the sake of unmasking it. The point is primarily to unmask the domination behind the apolitical discourse and to find again the politics behind the law.

In *The Dark Sides of Virtue*, David Kennedy leads a headlong charge against human rights. He draws up a list of 10 'pragmatic worries'. And while denying any wish to challenge the principle of human rights, that is exactly what he does on several subsequent occasions. The main complaints summarised are that:

- human rights occupy the field of discourse on emancipation and de-legitimate alternative discourses; they are hegemonic in their essence;
- they oversimplify social life by designating Good and Evil, Victims and Torturers;
- they are inexpressibly attached to the West and its categories of thought and not necessarily exportable;
- they make promises they cannot keep;
- they come across as objective knowledge about Justice, Good, and Universality, whereas they are actually vague, indeterminate and conflict-ridden; this ultimately amounts to giving excessive power to ('fetishised') judges and more generally to experts; in short to an elite that decides for others;
- finally the legal regime of human rights, taken as a whole, does more to produce and excuse violations than to prevent and remedy them (an affirmation I still do not really understand the justification for).

Martti Koskenniemi takes what I feel is a more coherent stance. Ultimately his arguments come down to a fundamental point derived from an observation already made by Jürgen Habermas (but obviously not for the same purpose) and that Koskenniemi puts as follows:

> [R]ights 'straddle' between legal positivity and naturalism. To demonstrate their independence from the political passions of the day, rights appear as ahistorical and universal. Yet, to disclose their concrete (and democratic) content, they are translated into positive constitutions (fundamental rights) and other legal enactments. Hence, the extraordinary rhetorical power of rights: on the one hand, they are 'outside' the political community in the sense that the legislators's task is merely to declare their presence in positive law, not to create them. On the other

> hand, they are also 'inside' the community by being fixed in constitutions and other positive legal enactments and thus amenable to objective confirmation.[15]

But instead of seeing a force for democracy, society, social progress and emancipation in this 'rhetorical power', Koskenniemi sees above all[16] a ground for suspicion and consequently an object to set his critical mind to work on.

Basically Koskenniemi criticises human rights discourse for engaging in politics under the appearance of neutrality: the formation of the 'field' of human rights is the subject of political decisions; decisions about the limitations of human rights and about conciliation among rights and so on are political decisions. And people are given to believe that these are objective natural rights that prevail as such, that are apolitical and universal and consequently escape any critical appraisal.

Koskenniemi sees this as a tremendous vehicle of domination and power, a vehicle for the elimination of politics which – of course – promotes the interests of globalised capitalism that seeks to transform all political citizens into disciplined consumers (one also detects fragments of Foucault's critique of power).[17]

Lastly, Koskenniemi also takes up the cultural argument found in Kennedy and, on the right, in Posner too: 'rights' do not do justice to the diversity of cultures, but also to that which in public life cannot be transposed into subjective law, such as civil passions like nationalism. Above all universality is ontologically unthinkable. There is no centre, no unity. Just subjectivities and points of view. And any claim to universality is bound to fail. It is always the particular (the West) that advances under the mask of the universal and generally with unpraiseworthy intentions (domination, hegemony, imperialism, etc).

[15] Koskenniemi, 'The Effects of Rights on Political Culture' (n 14) 136. This passage is a reworking (consciously or not) of an argument previously supported by Habermas and that was one of the starting points for my analysis of human rights treaty law in my PhD dissertation: 'As human rights can only be "claimed" as civil rights within a state order, they are dependent on the will of a political lawgiver; but to the extent that they are at the same time the basis of any democratic community, the sovereign lawgiver itself cannot make free use of these fundamental norms.' J Habermas, 'Le débat interculturel sur les droits de l'homme' in J Habermas, *L'intégration républicaine. Essais de théorie politique* (Paris, Fayard, 1998) 245 (our translation). Further to this affirmation and as part of the debate between universalism and relativism in the West, Habermas deconstructs the 'two variants' of the hermeneutics of suspicion initially introduced by Heidegger and Carl Schmitt – and to which 'post-modernists' of both right and left lay claim.

[16] This is clearly the conclusion of the first article. But in the second article ('Human Rights, Politics and Love' (n 14)) Koskenniemi is less radical in his criticism, see below.

[17] A reference noted by Pranchère and Lacroix in *Le procès des droits de l'homme* (n 1) 75. Even if it should be observed that Foucault's position on human rights – and more generally liberalism – was far from so directly critical. See especially his admirable M Foucault, 'Face aux gouvernements, les droits de l'homme' in *Dits et écrits* (Paris, Gallimard, 1994) vol IV, text no 355. A refoundation of human rights from the very Foucaldian: 'After all, we are all "the governed" and as such we stand united.' (our translation).

At the end of his book, after excoriating human rights by 10 abstract proposals followed by a few amusing accounts of his own experiences, David Kennedy makes 10 suggestions in all modesty to 'help international humanitarians who wish to work to develop such a posture informed by the vertiginous experience of disenchantment, of seeing that one is responsible and yet does not already know. That we must act on faith and hope for grace.'[18]

Is it to capture a larger audience in militant spheres that he declares his own wish to work for a fairer world and, with visible rhetorical pleasure, he uses several times over the wording 'Imagine a humanitarianism …', giving a utopian tone to what he has to say and a little of a mix of Martin Luther King and John Lennon. What is his message?

'International humanitarianism rules' and 'is powerful' (so human rights are political), 'weigh outcomes, not structures', 'tools are tools' (pragmatic and consequentialist moral), 'progress is not program' (reject Enlightenment illusions and rhetoric, the narrative of Progress is against liberty).[19]

The only conclusion on which we shall agree in part – not entirely because Kennedy pushes it too far with his aesthetic taste for the paradox – can be captured in the idea of 'humanitarianism as critique':

> Imagine instead a humanitarianism whose end was criticism, whose knowledge was critique. Imagine a human rights movement which was not the vehicle for what we know justice to be, but a network for criticizing the pretense of justice as it is. Imagine human rights training in the technologies of critical reasoning, treaty instruments reminding us to ask again what justice requires. (…) With criticism as our objective rather than our tool, we might imagine international humanitarianism – or a human rights movement – as an antiestablishment establishment, invigorating our political life for heterodoxy.[20]

Something of the same turn of the tables can be found in Koskenniemi – as if these left-wing post-moderns were unable to find it in themselves to declare human rights dead or in their twilight. In the presentation of the French version of 'Human Rights, Politics and Love', he specifies that he gave this conference in Oslo 'on the eve of the attack on the World Trade Center in New York in September 2001' and that since then 'this message has become increasingly important: human rights are both impossible and necessary'.[21] And he concludes his paper in an almost Habermassian way:

> Rights may not always bring emancipation. But often they can because they are split against themselves: particular and universal at the same time, strong in waging hegemonic struggles, weak in maintaining hegemonic positions.[22]

[18] Kennedy, *The Dark Sides of Virtue* (n 14) 347.
[19] ibid 348–57.
[20] ibid 353–54.
[21] M Koskenniemi, 'Les droits de l'homme, la politique et l'amour' in M Koskenniemi, *La politique du droit international* (Pedone, coll. Doctrine(s), Paris, 2007) 203. Our translation from the French text.
[22] Koskenniemi, 'Human Rights, Politics and Love' (n 14) 166.

III. The External Critical Approach Defending Human Rights

As can be seen, human rights are far from being immune to critical legal discourse. What I would now like to broach is another form of external legal discourse. It too rests on concepts and reasoning from other disciplines but it is a discourse of defence of human rights and more specifically of *critical defence of human rights*. In other words, it is not an *apologetic* discourse and even less a discourse of *propaganda* in favour of one legal form rather than another, a 'legal ideology' as critics sometimes like to say. It is rather a discourse that turns to account the self-critical potential of human rights; or more profoundly, that sees in this potential for self-criticism the trump card of human rights compared with any other legal form.

Put otherwise, there is not any denial of criticism. Instead the criticism is incorporated by legal human rights that are continually called upon to be reinterpreted to achieve their emancipatory potential in an era that is marked by the 'disenchantment of the world', pluralism and globalisation. In a way, this approach responds (without having heard it or waited for it) to the call from David Kennedy for a conception of human rights that would make criticism the purpose of human rights. In point of fact, this critical potential is *contained* in human rights, as also is their hegemonic potential by universalising the particular.

The error of the authors I have ranked here in the category of post-moderns, which was well seen by Habermas, is the *reduction* of human rights discourse to hegemony, that is, the attempted expansion of the particular under the mask of the universal. This is what obsesses the post-moderns. Universality is necessarily a lure, because the forms of life specific to each culture, to each people, cannot be reduced to the same thing in all their aspects.

Habermas opposes to this something that 'eludes' these 'reason-levelling' criticisms, namely 'the particular self-referentiality that characterises Enlightenment discourse. The debate on human rights, too, is supposed to give everyone their say. That is why it itself puts forward the criteria in light of which infringements, even latent ones, of its own requirements may be spotted and corrected'.[23] And he cites another authority which speaks to the 'detective' side of human rights discourse: 'indeed, these rights, which require that the other should be included within their scope, work at the same time like sensors capable of detecting any disbarment in their name'.[24]

The characteristic of the external critical discourse defending human rights is to bring into play this 'detective' or 'sensor' effect of human rights.

[23] Habermas, 'Le débat interculturel sur les droits de l'homme' (n 15) 247–48 (our translation).
[24] ibid (our translation).

In this sense, the external critical discourse defending human rights and the left-wing post-modern external critical discourse contesting human rights share affinities.

In fact the critical defence sets about the same genealogical enquiry as critical contestation does. It too poses questions continually not just about the risks of instrumentalisation by the power(s) of human rights but also about the means for further advancing the emancipatory potential of human rights or again about how to make room within human rights or alongside human rights discourse for separate emancipatory strategies or discourses.

Moreover, the critical defence discourse acknowledges the *political* character of human rights (and even of law in general) but does not for all that draw the conclusion that human rights are doomed to lie or mislead. It considers human rights as just one among other forms of political activity and debate within democratic institutions.

Ultimately, those who denounce the 'political' character of human rights are positivist critics who, to pick up on one of Duncan Kennedy's themes,[25] have 'lost faith'. They realised at one point that law was not a mere language game, an arrangement of norms related by logical connectors, but a social practice.

By contrast, the defence critique has not lost faith because it never had any. Or if it has lost faith, it has not been embittered by it. It has drawn conclusions from the fact that law is primarily a social practice and that legal norms are primarily perceived by social actors as instruments for defending interests and resolving conflicts.

Thus a critical defence discourse considers:

- that cultures (of what groups, at what levels, homogeneous in what way?) are not incommensurable and that consequently a principle that is formulated abstractly but implemented in some context is not destined to be of no practical consequence;
- that on this basis there is a possibility of universal communicability and that universality may have concrete and real content and is not necessarily the way in which one particular experience seeks to prevail over others;[26]
- that the virtue of human rights is precisely that they create the conditions for possible discussion which is liable to give rise to universal conceptions and understanding, because human rights require everyone to shake

[25] D Kennedy, 'The Critique of Rights in Critical Legal Studies' in W Brown and J Halley (eds), *Left Legalism/Left Critique* (Durham, NC, Duke University Press, 2002) 178–227, esp 191ff on 'Loss of Faith in Legal Reasoning': 'To lose your faith in judicial reason means to experience legal argument as "mere rhetoric".'

[26] On universality and the particular see D Lochak, *Le droit et les paradoxes de l'universalité* (Paris, PUF, 2010) esp 184–85.

off their natural solipsist attitude and to engage in a dialogical type of relationship with others;[27]

- that human rights, far from promoting individualism, may through their complex mechanism for balancing different competing interests, reinforce individual inclusion in social interplay;
- that, if human beings are to escape their state of tutelage,[28] there is no alternative to acknowledging that everyone is autonomous, which can only be reflected in legal terms by subjective rights that can be upheld by the courts;
- that criticism can only be fuelled by thorough knowledge of the *terrain*, that is, of the actual implementation of human rights in different contexts each time; in this respect, an approach of this kind acknowledges post-modern complexity and the inanity of grand narratives, albeit without dismissing the relevance of a governing ideal.

Ultimately, the fundamental difference between the two approaches, is that the critical defence discourse does not give way to the dual temptation of a hermeneutics of suspicion and an aesthetics of despair. In this sense it remains true to the spirit of the Enlightenment and continues to trust in the liberating potential of the discourse of modernity in general.

[27] See also in this volume ch 1, 'What is Legal Cosmopolitanism?'.

[28] According to Kant's celebrated description of the Enlightenment project, 'Enlightenment is man's release from his self-incurred tutelage'.

6

Natural Law, Human Rights, the Law of Nature: Towards a Revived Modernity

After having heard a presentation on positive law,[1] the law in force here and now, you are probably expecting some sort of history lesson on legal doctrines: natural law, well, it smells a little musty, like some old material from a trunk that has not been opened for years ….

Well, this might come as a surprise to you, but I am going to show you quite the opposite applies: natural law remains very topical. It has not become topical 'again'; it *remains* topical. That is, international law today is still thought about and talked about in the terms of natural law.

Practitioners of international law – diplomats, experts, officials in international organisations and so on – all use natural law terminology all the time. Natural law remains today the common vernacular of international law.

But we still have to agree on what we mean by natural law. Not, for sure, the natural law of the Ancients, which does indeed seem far behind us or, as we shall see later, perhaps just up ahead of us. But natural law of the modern period, which Michel Villey rightly saw as a betrayal of the natural law of the Ancients, as a dangerous vector of excess that might lead to social break-up;[2] that natural law of the eighteenth century Enlightenment, focused entirely on the subject, the individual, the Cartesian *cogito*;[3] the natural law which, from

[1] This article is based on a conference given during a workshop that took place in Aix-en-Provence in September 2014. I was given the floor after a brilliant paper by Olivier Corten on 'Legal positivism today: science or science-fiction?'. Thus the initial reference to a 'presentation on positive law'. I thought I should keep the almost oral style of my presentation, which was also a response to Olivier Corten. All the papers given during the workshop were published in J Ferrero and T Démaria (eds), 'Théorie et réalités du droit international public au XXIè siècle', Hors-série (March 2016) *Revue Québécoise de droit international.*

[2] M Villey, *Le droit et les droits de l'homme* (Paris, Presses universitaires de France, 1983).

[3] On the difference between 'classical' natural law of the Ancients and natural law of the modern period, see especially L Strauss, *Droit naturel et histoire* (Paris, Flammarion, 1953). On natural law of the modern era and social contract theories, see J Terrel, *Les théories du pacte social. Droit naturel, souveraineté et contrat de Bodin à Rousseau* (Paris, Seuil, 2001).

Grotius to Vattel, served as a guideline for the School of the Law of Nature and of Nations, to finally give rise to the conceptual framework of modern international law.[4] It is this discourse on modern natural law that remains ubiquitous today and essentially in two forms: on the one side is the discourse of sovereignty and voluntarism and on the other side the discourse of human rights.

I shall begin by attempting to shed some light on the connection between voluntarism and jusnaturalism, because it is not necessarily self-evident for everyone. Then I shall attempt to show in what way the other discourse of natural law – human rights – deconstructs the discourse of voluntarism in international law. And lastly I shall show how human rights in turn are called into question, again in the name of natural law, or more exactly in the name of nature, but this time by a discourse at the point where the natural law of the Ancients meets with postmodern law.

I. The Discourse of Sovereignty and Voluntarism

What voluntarism tells us is a fable. It is a well known fable for that matter, since it is drawn from social contract theories and the infinite variations thereon from Hobbes down to Kant. It is the fable of the state of nature.[5]

Underpinning the legal and political order, voluntarism imagines a person in a pre-political state, the state of nature. In the state of nature, it is said, individuals are born free – that is, they have at least this fundamental quality specific to subjectivity: they are autonomous, they are capable of laying down norms for themselves. They have freedom to act according to their own will and therefore freedom of contract.

[4] See E Jouannet, *Emer de Vattel et l'émergence doctrinale du droit international classique* (Paris, Pedone, 1998).

[5] For Terrel, *Les théories du pacte social* (n 3) 135, the invention of the state of pure nature as opposed to a civil state, actually goes back to Hobbes. The state of *pure nature* cannot be likened to any actual historical situation. Jean-Jacques Rousseau took up the image, but with a caveat from the outset. J-J Rousseau, 'The Second Discourse: Discourse on the Origin and Foundations of Inequality Among Mankind' in J-J Rousseau, *The Social Contract and The First and Second Discourses (Rethinking the Western Tradition)*, ed and with an Introduction by S Dunn (New Haven, CT, Yale University Press, 2002) 88: 'Let us begin then by laying facts aside, for they do not affect the question. The researches, in which we may engage on this occasion, are not to be taken for historical truths, but merely as hypothetical and conditional reasonings, fitter to illustrate the nature of things, than to show their true origin, like those systems, which our naturalists daily make of the formation of the world. Religion commands us to believe that men, having been drawn by God himself out of a state of nature, are unequal, because it is His pleasure they should be so; but religion does not forbid us to draw conjectures solely from the nature of man, considered in itself, and from that of the beings which surround him, concerning the fate of mankind, had they been left to themselves. This is then the question I am to answer, the question I propose to examine in the present discourse.'

In the classical doctrine of international law, this model is transposed imperfectly, but the fable is the same to begin with. States are born free and equal in law in the state of nature; they are said to be equally sovereign. Sovereignty is the freedom of the state personified. The only difference is that the transition to the civil state is either impossible as in Hobbes,[6] or problematic and problematised as in Kant.[7]

Therefore this state-person is free in the state of nature and, as an individual, it is a reasonable being. In the language of philosophers of modern natural law, this means that it has freedom to act according to its own will; it can lay down its own norms for itself, it has the capacity to will, to consent, in other words to set itself norms of conduct.

The state of nature is an a-political state, that is, power is not organised, but it is not an a-legal state; in other words, in the state of nature, no public law is to be found (which is specific to the political state) but there is on the other hand private law to be found, that is, contracts.[8] Since individuals or states have the freedom to act according to their own will, they can mutually recognise rights and duties on a horizontal basis; they constrain each other. They bind themselves by their consent and by their consent alone: this is voluntarism.

The problem obviously – and Kant recognises it just as Hobbes did – is that such contracts are but scraps of paper, because ultimately there is no public guarantee that they will be performed, no power of constraint. The only way to ensure their performance, in the absence of any organised power and any public constraint, is the private justice exercised between states in the form of war and reprisals.[9] This is the supposedly 'primitive' character of international law as Kelsen said of it.[10] Scelle also emphasised the inorganic

[6] T Hobbes, *Leviathan*, 1651, ed with an introduction by JCA Gaskin, Oxford World's Classics (New York, Oxford University Press, 1996) pt II, ch XXI, 'Of the Liberty of Subjects', 8, 142–43.

[7] See O de Frouville, 'Une conception démocratique du droit international' (2001) 29 *Revue européenne des sciences sociales* 101, 101–04.

[8] I Kant, *The Philosophy of Law. An exposition of the fundamental principles of jurisprudence as the science of right* [1797], tr W Hastie (Edinburgh, T&T Clark, 1887), 58: 'The highest Division of the System of Natural Right should not be – as it is frequently put – into "Natural Right" and "Social Right" but into NATURAL RIGHT and CIVIL RIGHT. The first constitutes PRIVATE RIGHT; the second PUBLIC RIGHT. For it is not the "Social state" but the "Civil state" that is opposed to the "State of Nature;" for in the "State of Nature" there may well be Society of some kind, but there is no "civil" Society, as an Institution securing the Mine and Thine by public laws.'

[9] Kant, *The Philosophy of Law* (n 8) 218: 'Viewed as in the state of Nature, the Right of Nations *to go to War* and to carry on hostilities is the legitimate way by which they prosecute their Rights by their own power when they regard themselves as injured; and this is done because in that state the method of a juridical *Process*, although the only one proper to settle such disputes, cannot be adopted.'

[10] H Kelsen, *General Theory of Law and State*, tr A Wedberg (Cambridge MA, Harvard University Press, 1945) 338–39.

character of international society, its 'institutional shortfall' (*carence institutionnelle*) that the law of role splitting (*dédoublement fonctionnel*) was designed to palliate.[11] As has often been said, Vattel was probably the one who presented this jusnaturalist theory of international law in its fullest form.[12] He clearly makes the cross-over of the jusnaturalist model in the following very clear passage, echoes of which can still be heard in the UN Charter:

> Since men are naturally equal, and a perfect equality prevails in their rights and obligations, as equally proceeding from nature, – nations composed of men, and considered as so many free persons living together in the state of nature, are naturally equal, and inherit from nature the same obligations and rights. Power or weakness does not in this respect produce any difference. A dwarf is as much a man as a giant; a small republic is no less a sovereign state than the most powerful kingdom.[13]

This is a fine definition of the principle of equal sovereignty that underlies and continues to underlie all of current discourse, that is taught in law schools and that is used daily by the actors of international law, beginning with diplomats. For this discourse incontrovertibly holds numerous advantages for states. If a slightly more strategic point of view of law is taken, it is easy to see that it is discourse that handles states' interests with care, however powerful they may be. Understandably then, they revel in this. It is less understandable, though, that legal scholarship should share in this revelry.

Kelsen and Scelle, each separately, had called for the removal of these hangovers from natural law, of that doctrine of subjectivity which, besides, it seemed should be swept away by the advent of the social sciences. Scelle, in particular, acknowledges there is no free individual in the state of nature, there are only individuals already there, who are born, live and die in society, and society is immediately a political society, and every political society produces its law.[14] Oddly enough, though, it is not these positivist interpretations that got the upper hand. Paradoxically, if voluntarism has been weakened, it is not through positivist scruples but under the impact of another product of modern natural law: human rights.

[11] G Scelle, *Manuel de droit international public* (Paris, Domat-Montchrestien, 1948) 21.

[12] See Jouannet, *Emer de Vattel* (n 4).

[13] E de Vattel, *The Law of Nations, Or, Principles of the Law of Nature, Applied to the Conduct and Affairs of Nations and Sovereigns*, ed and with an Introduction by B Kapossy and R Whatmore, tr T Nugent (Indianapolis, IN, Liberty Fund, 2008) §18, 75.

[14] G Scelle, *Précis de droit des gens. Principes et systématique. Deuxième partie. Droit constitutionnel international* (Paris, Recueil Sirey, 1934) 16: 'Individuals cannot possess fundamental subjective rights, nor can collectivities have fundamental rights, if by fundamental rights one means legal conditions ("*situations juridiques*") which precede any society, which are superior to any social rule, and in respect of which the legislator would be legally powerless. For the rule of law and for legislation to exist, there must first be society; this social reality is anterior and superior to any legal right.' tr from H Thierry, 'The Thought of Georges Scelle' (1990) 1 *EJIL* 193, 204.

II. The Discourse of Human Rights

The birth of human rights was concomitant with that of 'Vatellian' modern international law. They shared the same roots, the same fount: modern natural law, the idea of autonomy.[15] It was a clean break with natural law; law was no longer heteronomous, no longer divine law or the law of nature that was imposed on humans. People become capable of laying down their own law for themselves. Internally, this idea gave rise to the theory of human rights and democracy; internationally it gave rise to modern international law. But why this separation between internal and international? Because the problem of sovereignty internally was different from the problem of sovereignty internationally. Internally the aim was to legitimise the state's power of constraint over its subjects. Internationally the aim was to bring about the peaceful coexistence of states within the Holy Roman Empire in a period of wars of religion. How was this to be set about? By imposing a principle of indifference.

The idea was that each ruler should choose the religion of his subjects: *cujus regio, ejus religio*, whose realm, their religion – a principle enshrined in the constitution of the Holy Roman Empire from the time of the Peace of Augsburg in 1555 and that was to become one of the central clauses of the Peace of Westphalia in 1648.[16] And it is not for nothing that the Peace of Westphalia is often considered, in historiography, as the starting point of modern international law.[17]

Upholding peace means imposing mutual toleration, coexistence among beliefs that hold themselves to be absolute. The way to do this is to impose a water-tight separation between the internal and international spheres. It is the division between the polity and the home that is replicated, which highlights in passing the deeply gendered dimension of international law.[18] Each state is the master in its own household, like the *pater familias*. In addition to the sovereign's freedom to choose his subjects' religion, each state is acknowledged by extension to have the right to choose its own political regime, its economic, social and cultural model.

[15] See S Rials, 'Ouverture : généalogie des droits de l'homme' (1985) 2 *Droits* 3, 3–12; L Ferry and A Renaut, *Des droits de l'homme à l'idée républicaine* (Paris, Presses universitaires de France, 2007) 489ff.

[16] See B Nicollier, *Le Saint Empire romain germanique (1495–1648)* (Paris, Ellipses, 2012) 83 and 169.

[17] For a critical perspective see esp D Gaurier, *Histoire du droit international. Auteurs, doctrines et développement de l'Antiquité à l'aube de la période contemporaine* (Rennes, Presses universitaires de Rennes, 2005) 382.

[18] H Charlesworth, 'Le sexe de l'État en droit international' in H Charlesworth, *Sexe, genre et droit international* (Paris, Pedone, 2013) 159; E Tourme-Jouannet, *What is a Fair International Society? International Law Between Development and Recognition* (Oxford, Hart Publishing, 2013) 175ff.

In 1986, in the *Case concerning Military and Paramilitary Activities in Nicaragua* (merits), the International Court of Justice forcefully asserted this principle of internal autonomy by highlighting the intrinsic tie binding it to the principle of sovereignty:

> [A]dherence by a State to any particular doctrine does not constitute a violation of customary international law; to hold otherwise would make nonsense of the fundamental principle of State sovereignty, on which the whole of international law rests, and the freedom of choice of the political, social, economic and cultural system of a State.[19]

And here we see emerging one of the fundamental corollaries of the principle of sovereignty: the principle of non-interference prohibiting any intervention by one state in the 'internal affairs' of another, which is to be understood as in the processes of devolution and exercise of power in the internal order.

In the same spirit, classical international law does not accept that individuals can be the subjects of international law. They may only be 'mediate' subjects – that is by way of the state's mediation – but never immediate. In this respect let us re-read a major voluntarist author of the early twentieth century, Hans Triepel, who is most eloquent on this:

> The private individual, from the point of view of a legalistic community binding States as such, cannot be invested with his own rights and duties emanating from a legal system of that community. In the context of international law proper, the individual can only be conceived of as an object of international rights and duties.[20]

That is as clear a statement as can be and replies fully to states' main needs from the seventeenth to nineteenth centuries: the need of coexistence, the necessary mutual tolerance, to each his own. That is all well and good. Or is it? The ambivalence of sovereignty was not long in emerging and then breaking out in its full horror. The very same conditions that make it possible under international law to make the state an autonomous subject turn against the individual, who becomes the victim of the indifference of international law with regard to the form of political, economic and cultural regimes. The consequence of all that is the negation of the individual purely and simply, their reduction to the state of an object in the view of international law.[21]

[19] *Military and Paramilitary Activities in and against Nicaragua (Nicaragua v United States of America)*, Merits, Judgement, [1986] ICJ Rep 133, para 263.

[20] H Triepel, *Droit international et droit interne*, tr René Brunet, with a Foreword by Olivier Beaud, (Paris, Panthéon-Assas, 2010) 20.

[21] ibid. Triepel also writes, following on from the passage cited above, 'The agreements between States in favour of African negroes do not raise blacks, whose well-being they must protect, to the rank of persons of the legal community, the institutions of which take care of them [*sic*]. The individual can then only be conceived of, in the framework of international law that is assumed possible for us, as an *object* of international rights and duties'.

The individual is at the sovereign's mercy; and the sovereign may turn into a criminal and even a mass murderer. As Mario Bettati put it: 'sovereignty is the mutual guarantee of torturers'.[22]

It is this point of awareness that was reached after World War II. The state had lost its presumption of innocence for good, wrote Habermas – namely the presumption of innocence that sovereignty granted it.[23] The sovereign state had been understood as a protector of freedom; it now became the executioner.

The reaction to this abuse of sovereignty was the proclamation of human rights internationally. In 1945, in a burst of moral indignation, states proclaimed universal human rights. In doing so they were sawing off the branch they were sitting on; they torpedoed the conceptual foundations that gave them existence as states in international law, as defined in classical international law.

The declaration of human rights meant the end of the very principle of a water-tight separation between the internal and international spheres. Not only did the individual become a subject of international law but it was the whole constitutional substance of internal law that came within the compass of international law and its guarantee mechanisms.

What is interesting here is to see how one discourse of modern natural law came to be opposed head-on with another discourse of modern international law and in the end to undermine its foundations.

With human rights, states no longer relinquish just their religious autonomy but also more widely their autonomy in terms of freedom of thought or belief, free speech, in terms of judicial and prison administration, in social and economic matters, and so on. States failed to see that with human rights they were engaging in a process of federalisation. With human rights reputedly a part of natural law, states saw their own natural rights gradually stripped to their bare bones. They held tight to the voluntarism of treaties but it was a hopeless struggle and one that was already largely over.[24]

The first discourse of natural law – that of voluntarism – was therefore strongly destabilised by the second offspring of modern natural law, human rights. Will human rights have the last word? Are they the basis on which international law should henceforth be constructed? I do not wish to answer this question here, but what interests me more is the criticism human rights have come in for in their turn in the name of nature.

[22] M Bettati, *Le droit d'ingérence : Mutation de l'ordre international* (Paris, Odile Jacob, 1996) 17.

[23] J Habermas, 'Kant's Idea of Perpetual Peace with the Benefit of 200 Years' Hindsight' in J Bohman and M Lutz-Bachmann (eds), *Perpetual Peace: Essays on Kant's Cosmopolitan Ideal* (Cambridge, MA, MIT Press, 1997) 178.

[24] O de Frouville, *L'intangibilité des droits de l'homme en droit international. Régime conventionnel des droits de l'homme et droit des traités* (Paris, Pedone, 2004).

III. The Discourse of Nature

Much criticism has been levelled at human rights but none as powerful and convincing as this: the criticism that denounces the anthropocentrism of human rights and the fact that they are part of a line of modern thought that leads straight to contempt for and destruction of everything that is not human. With natural law, we are in a Cartesian scheme of things. Everything begins with the *cogito*, with individual consciousness, with the subject. Modern natural law, and all of modernity with it, is a 'metaphysics of subjectivity' to use the expression of Martin Heidegger, one of its greatest detractors.[25]

The result of this is that the relationship with nature is always thought of as a relationship of subject and object. I am and nature is merely the object of my consciousness. It follows from this, again for Descartes, that Man makes himself '*as* masters and owners of nature'.[26]

And so nature is merely our 'environment'. It is not nature in itself. It is nature only with respect to the subject of knowledge, who knows nature as that which literally 'environs' the subject.[27] Consequently, the 'right to a healthy environment' for example, if ever it is actually fully recognised and put into application as a human right, will never make it possible to accede to a proper concept of a legal code of nature. Ultimately such a right will simply slow the destruction of nature without preventing it. In this respect, human rights are inadequate.[28]

What is interesting is to see that this criticism comes from two fronts that might seem wholly opposed but that actually have many points in common: pre-modernity and post-modernity.

There is a pre-modern critique, a critique in the name of the natural law of the Ancients: we must go back to natural law as the law ruling the cosmos, the whole, take the point of view of the whole, have a holistic rather than a subjective view of things. And then there is on the other side a critique of modernity by strands of thought that seek to challenge subjectivism, the centrality of the *cogito*, for the benefit of a return to the world or even of an ontology of 'being there' (*dasein*) that escapes from the metaphysics of subjectivity … a conception, in other words, that denounces in human rights

[25] Notably in his letter on humanism. See M Heidegger 'Letter on Humanism', trs AFA Capuzzi and J Glenn Gray, in DF Krell (ed), *Martin Heidegger: Basic Writings*, rev and exp edn (London, Routledge, 1993) 217–65. See the critical commentary in defence of legal humanism by L Ferry, *Philosophie politique*, I: *Le droit: la nouvelle querelle des anciens et des modernes* (Paris, Presses universitaires de France, 1996) 273–90.

[26] R Descartes, 'Discours de la méthode' in *Œuvres philosophiques*, I: *1618–1637* (Paris, Classiques Garnier, 2010) 634.

[27] G Mairet, *Nature et souveraineté* (Paris, Presses de Sciences Po, 2012) 18.

[28] In truth, to be fair, we should also develop the criticism that the discourse on the law of nature addresses to sovereignty and therefore the voluntarist/jusnaturalist conception of international law; that criticism is developed by Gérard Mairet in his book.

the continual assertion of the 'I' of subjectivity, whether that *I* is the selfish bourgeois individual or the dominating and imperialistic Westerner.

With an author like Judge Antonio Cançado Trindade, as I had the opportunity to show in another conference,[29] these two trends cleverly combine. Judge Cançado draws his sources from the second scholastic of Saint Thomas Aquinas, but he also borrows from post-modernity his enthusiasm for native cultures, for a necessary respect for cultures and conceptions that are not modern, precisely because they are part of a vision of the cosmos, of the whole, of nature, that goes beyond and encompasses human beings. As Judge Cançado summarised it so well at that conference: 'I hate modernity!'

The principle of autonomy of human beings – and the idea that the dignity of human beings lies in their autonomy – seems to me a valuable inheritance from modern natural law that we should preserve for reasons of all kinds. But how can we preserve this heritage of autonomy without reifying nature, without reducing it to the condition of an object and therefore of a thing that is not worth respecting and can consequently be exploited without limitations?

In his book *Nature et souveraineté*, Gérard Mairet highlights two fundamental orientations of philosophical discourse on nature, to finally propose a 'cosmopolitics of Nature'. Here I will reword these two orientations as I understand them in light of a number of other readings.[30]

The first orientation does not extend beyond the schema of modernity. It consists in considering that we have a duty of respect that extends beyond humankind for everything that is part of nature. One does not escape the subject/object relationship, one just widens the circle of holders of this right to respect. The philosophical question is, however, to determine on what basis such a right is recognised? The practical question is how far to widen the circle. This approach is criticised and I think rightly so by Gérard Mairet because it tends to ignore 'the unity of the biota' and in particular the fact that human beings are part of nature just as much as other living beings are.

The second approach is to abandon the subject/object relationship and replace natural law with a biotic law that 'expresses the bond natural living things maintain among themselves within the ecosystems of which they are the inhabitants; such that it is an obligation for humans to enforce, maintain and protect that right'.[31] This is ultimately the approach explored in the

[29] O de Frouville, 'Libres propos autour du livre d'Antonio Cançado Trindade: Le droit international pour la personne humaine' (October 2012), online at www.frouville.org.

[30] See esp C Larrère and R Larrère, *Du bon usage de la nature. Pour une philosophie de l'environnement* (Paris, Flammarion, 2009); M Serres, *Le contrat naturel* (Paris, Flammarion, 2009); F Flipo, 'Pour les droits de la nature' (2012) 2(70) *Mouvements* 122. Gérard Mairet's book alone would be worth an entire contribution for a detailed critical commentary.

[31] Mairet, *Nature et souveraineté* (n 27) 58. See also ibid 61: 'If human societies are not outside of nature and if thereby they are unable to draw up norms, having lost their overarching and exterior posture, then recognition of a *biotic law* is made necessary. There is no longer any subject or object. There is an infinity of processes at work tying and untying the universality of beings,

line of the *World Charter for Nature*,[32] the ideas of which were taken up and promoted in the form of declarations proposed by Bolivia and Ecuador at the Rio+20 Conference.[33]

But the problem posed by a solution of this kind is whether it does not finally bring us back to a form of holism? Are we not sacrificing all the gains of modernity? If humans are a part of the whole, are they not in some sense subject to nature, whose law applies to them whether it be called natural law or biotic law?

We come back to the crucial question: how can nature be acknowledged as having a status that frees it from anthropocentrism without destroying human rights by the same stroke? For Gérard Mairet,

> [i]t is worth noting here that a declaration of biotic right would not come into conflict with the principle of 'human rights' in general, provided that this principle were understood in a biotic sense, that is, pursuant to the conception of the human/nature relationship that biotic law calls for.[34]

What does this mean? How might human rights, which are anthropocentric by definition, be understood in a 'biotic sense'? For Fabrice Flipo, there are in fact two understandings of modern humanism: the first 'is conflated with man's absolute right over this biotic community' whereas the 'practical humanism of the proponents of the "rights of nature" is that the world is not human if it confers no dignity on the beings of nature. Humanists are those who seek to defend a human relationship with the world and not a barbarous or exploitative relationship.'[35] He adds that the defendants of the 'rights of nature' have never claimed 'that these rights should be strictly identical to human rights'.[36]

human and non-human, the ultimate effect of which, still largely unknown to humankind today, is the production of nature itself.'

[32] *World Charter for Nature*, UN General Assembly, 28 October 1982, A/RES/37/7, 37th session. The Charter opens with the following principles: 'The General Assembly: … *[a]ware* that: (a) Mankind is a part of nature and life depends on the uninterrupted functioning of natural systems which ensure the supply of energy and nutrients, (b) Civilization is rooted in nature, which has shaped human culture and influenced all artistic and scientific achievement, and living in harmony with nature gives man the best opportunities for the development of his creativity, and for rest and recreation, *Convinced* that (a) Every form of life is unique, warranting respect regardless of its worth to man, and, to accord other organisms such recognition, man must be guided by a moral code of action, (b) Man can alter nature and exhaust natural resources by his action or its consequences and, therefore, must fully recognize the urgency of maintaining the stability and quality of nature and of conserving natural resources'.

[33] On the *Charter* and the proposals from Bolivia and Ecuador, see Flipo, 'Pour les droits de la nature' (n 30). On the implications of this particular (and limited) orientation of international environment law, see S Emmenegger and A Tschentscher, 'Taking Nature's Rights Seriously: The Long Way to Biocentrism in Environmental Law' (1994) 4(3) *Georgetown International Environmental Law Review* 545–742.

[34] Mairet, *Nature et souveraineté* (n 27) 87.

[35] Flipo, 'Pour les droits de la nature' (n 30) 131.

[36] ibid 130.

These remarks suggest a solution that I shall simply outline here but that should certainly be explored further. There is one thing we seemingly fail to understand despite the earthquakes, hurricanes or more mundanely the vegetation that little by little covers over gardens when we are not attentive – we say that 'nature reclaims its rights'; we fail to understand that nature can get along very well without us! One might say that nature is 'autonomous' with respect to us. Not in the sense that nature lays down its own laws for itself at the end of some deliberation, that is, in the sense of human autonomy, of self-legislation; but in the sense that nature has its own laws of evolution, its own agenda. Ultimately we come back to the dualism that leads to a line being drawn between the natural and normative sciences. As Kelsen explained, the former obey a causal principle while the latter resort to the principle of imputation.[37] Each in their own order. Does not the Cartesian problem arise simply from the belief whereby everything could be known and explained using the principle of causality? If humanism is ailing, is it not from this belief in absolute knowledge? In other words from the belief that humanity could actually *be* 'master and owner of nature'? We now know that the complexity of nature prohibits this; it is in this that lies, as it were, the principle of its autonomy with respect to humanity. Humanity will never be able to fully make nature its own; nature will always elude us in part, or alternatively the consequences of human acts on nature will always be partly unpredictable. Now, here too Kelsen teaches us, relinquishing this mirage of absolute knowledge is the beginning of positivist thinking.[38]

This autonomy of nature compels us, it constrains us both physically and morally. We shall never fully control nature and in particular predict catastrophes or entirely counter their effects. Moreover, this puzzle of the world forces a degree of humanity on us: there is in this a reign of ends that eludes us. In saying that, we are not making things sacrosanct, we are merely acknowledging the bounds of our positive knowledge so as to shore up its foundations. Thus the 'autonomy' of nature is for us not a norm but a fact.

Nothing in all of that encroaches upon our own human autonomy, on what for Kant gives us our dignity: namely our capacity for self-legislating,

[37] See esp H Kelsen, *Pure Theory of Law*, tr from the 2nd (rev and enlarged) German edn by M Knight (Berkeley, CA, University of California Press, 1967) III.18, 'Causality and Imputation: Law of Nature and Legal Law'.

[38] H Kelsen, 'Natural Law Doctrine and Legal Positivism', Appendix to Kelsen, *General Theory of Law and State* (n 10) 433–34: 'Even a philosophy which is free of metaphysics and based only on scientific experience must remain conscious of the eternal secret which surrounds the world of experience on all sides. Only blindness or delusion could presume to deny the riddle of the universe, or declare it scientifically soluble. It is the attitude of the philosophical ideal type under discussion, which alone deserves to be called "scientific", that it stops before the ultimate enigma which it freely recognize, because it is conscious of the limitations of human knowledge. It is a self-discipline of the human mind which is as conscious of its vigor as of its unsurpassable limitations.'

our capacity for collectively deliberating and for deciding, against the causal laws of nature. It needs to be reasserted: going against nature, going against what might seem to be 'the order of things' is what constitutes our dignity. This does not mean that we should disregard the de facto constraint that these causal laws lay upon us; that we can believe ourselves to be all powerful over nature reduced to the status of an object. There is no longer any object and subject but a whole of which we are a part; nature is 'autonomous' without for all that being a person. As such, there is indeed a 'biotic law', which is not a natural law that forces on us a heteronomy that is incompatible with our autonomy, but rather a set of rules, defined by humans and founded on what in nature is both known to us and remains unknown to us.

How else might I conclude this contribution other than by taking leave of natural law, whether ancient or modern? Heteronomy on one side, incompatible with the democratic ideal and the rights of individuals; exclusive subjectivisation of humankind, on the other side, to the detriment of other living beings and of nature in general. On both sides, natural law leads to a dead end. Does that mean we must also say goodbye to modernity and to human rights? I do not believe so. The project of modernity is not conflated with natural law, which serves as an explanatory fable; it pertains instead to the constitution of power according to the principle of autonomy. A project so well described by Kant in his *What is Enlightenment?*[39] Likewise, although human rights use the language of natural law (rights 'inherent' in 'human nature', etc), it is to represent the point that, although part of positive law, they are not at the lawmaker's disposal, because they are, as legal norms, the condition rendering the democratic exercise of power possible.[40]

To conclude: long live human rights and the rights of nature! Down with sovereignty!

[39] I Kant, 'An Answer to the Question: "What is Enlightenment?"' in *Kant. Political Writings*, ed HS Reiss, tr HB Nisbet, Cambridge Texts in History of Political Thought (Cambridge, Cambridge University Press, 1970) 54–60. Let us just recall the first sentence: 'Enlightenment is man's emergence from his self-incurred immaturity.'

[40] J Habermas, 'Le débat interculturel sur les droits de l'homme' in J Habermas, *L'intégration républicaine. Essais de théorie politique*, tr R Rochlitz (Paris, Fayard, 1998) 245.

7

Towards a Democratic Theory of International Law

What is a democratic theory of international law?

For the purposes of this exposition, a theory can be defined as a set of ideas and concepts forming a system and intended to explain reality – phenomena, in the sense of that which is apparent. A theory provides an interpretive framework, a frame of reference for understanding the real. A theory also has a retroactive effect on the real: dominating theories tend to frame the real because social actors are consciously or unconsciously influenced by them.

A *democratic theory of law* can be defined as a system of concepts explaining the phenomenon of law based on the principle of autonomy of the human person. Law is defined essentially as a technique aiming at the reconciliation between the freedoms of each and every persons. In this, a democratic theory of law can be opposed to theological theories of law or theories of law based on natural law.

A *democratic theory of international law* is a theory that understands the phenomenon of international law through the prism of the principle of autonomy of the human person.

The first argument I shall defend runs like this. The *classical* theory of international law, which I shall refer to also as 'Vatellian' theory, based on the concept of external state sovereignty was adapted to describe the phenomenon of international law as it developed in Europe from the seventeenth century to the early twentieth century. This is what professors at the time referred to as 'European public law', which was the law of a society of sovereign states that was secularised by *exclusion of values* (I shall explain what I mean by that later; but one might also say a society based on indifference to values or even based on 'tolerance', that is, the refusal to address the question of values in the public arena).

This theory lost all its explanatory force as from the second half of the twentieth century and especially from the early 1990s under the impetus of three major historical transformations: (1) the efforts made since the late nineteenth century to *create* a peaceful international order based on law, at first European, and then global; (2) the process of decolonisation that led to the *universalisation of the nation state* as a political form of organisation and consequently to the universalisation of public international law; (3) the process of economic globalisation, begun as far back as the eighteenth century but which brought about the worldwide extension of the capitalist model in the period following the end of the opposition between the eastern and western blocs.

The second argument is that, under the impetus of these major transformations, there began a process of formation of a world-society secularised *by adhesion to* (and no longer by exclusion of) *the values of modernity* and in particular the principle of autonomy. One might call this society in the process of formation *cosmopolitan society* (that is, a political society on the scale of the cosmos, the world). Like any society, this cosmopolitan society engenders law, which might be termed *cosmopolitan law*. Lastly, this process of formation of a cosmopolitan society might be called a *cosmopolitan process* or process of the federation of free states.

The *democratic theory of international law* is thus the theory that takes note of these transformations, that is, it takes note of the fact that international law, which has become law of the cosmopolitan transition, can no longer be thought of in terms of the concept of state sovereignty (the founding principle of European public law) but must now be thought of in terms of the *principle of autonomy* of the human person as the founding principle of modernity.

Finally, then, the democratic theory of international law might be defined as *the theory that seeks to describe the phenomenon of law in a world-society having engaged in a process of cosmopolitan transition.*

This definition should now be explained in three stages. First we must look into the theoretical structure of 'classical' or Vatellian international law by explaining what might be called the paradox of modernity, a paradox which leads to the search for a new basis for international law.

Secondly we shall set out the main lines of the democratic conception of international law which has progressively penetrated public international law, concomitantly with the development of international society itself.

And thirdly, we shall provide a glimpse of the theoretical underpinnings of the democratic theory of international law proposed.

I. The Theoretical Structure of Classical International Law

Classical international law is law of the modern era. What does that mean? It means that the classical theory of international law was constructed at the same time as political theories of the modern period and therefore at the same time as the theory of the state and the theory of human rights and of the social contract.

I shall begin by explaining this principle of autonomy that lies at the heart of the revolution of the modern era. Then I shall go on to explain the consequences of this principle of autonomy for the classical theory of international law, then for political theory in democratic states of modern times. That will enable me to formulate the paradox of modernity.

A. The Principle of Autonomy

What was the fundamental feature of the modern age? The principle of autonomy. Autonomy contrasts with heteronomy. The thinking of the Ancients was dominated by the principle of heteronomy, meaning that social or legal norms were dictated *from outside* and imposed on human beings. The order of the world arose out of either *Nature* or *God.* Consequently, law was either divine law or natural law (in the sense of law dictated by the order of the Cosmos, the law of nature, that imposed itself on Man as both a natural and a cultural being).

The modern era broke with this representation of the world. Grotius (1583–1645), in particular, laid down the bases of modern natural law through two conceptual revolutions that were clearly set out in his book *De Jure Pacis et Belli*:

- The first conceptual revolution was that of the autonomy of 'volitional' human law as against volitional divine law and natural law. Grotius made these three branches of law separate and autonomous. He said especially that volitional divine law could do nothing to change natural law. God could not bring it to be that 2 and 2 should not make 4.[1] God created nature, but, once created, nature obeyed its own laws. Likewise, human law was the outcome of conventions among men and not necessarily consistent with natural law or divine law.
- The second revolution was that natural law was no longer an 'objective' law. It was expressed essentially by subjective law, that is, the right of each individual to consent to the norm. This was the principle of autonomy: I lay down my own norm for myself. One could not therefore ascertain the rules of natural law either by reading the word of God or by observing the Cosmos; instead it involved delving within ourselves through resort to Reason, to the faculty we possess for formulating universalisable norms. Reason worked by questioning oneself and others, too: What is the rule that applies to everyone? A natural law rule could be established 'when we cannot with absolute certainty, yet with very great probability, conclude that to be by the Law of Nature, which is generally believed to be so by all, or at least, the most civilised, nations'.[2]

[1] H Grotius, *The Rights of War and Peace* [1625], ed and with introduction by R Tuck, from the edition by J Barbeyrac (Indianapolis, IN, Liberty Fund, 2005) bk I, ch I, X, 5, 155.

[2] ibid bk I, ch I, XII, 155.

The principle of autonomy gave birth on the one side to the modern-era theory of the state and on the other to the theory of international law. And it is important to understand that the two were intrinsically linked and gave rise to the two sides of the concept of sovereignty: internal and external sovereignty.

To grasp this, it must be remembered where the theory of modernity came from in Grotius, Hobbes and the others. It was grounded in an historical event: the Reformation and the wars of religion in Europe. It was fundamentally a quarrel over the question of truth.

Each side thought it held the truth and that the other side was in error, that they were heretics. Modernity was the attempt made in that context to peacefully reconcile irreconcilable views, to entertain two mutually exclusive conceptions of truth.

A first form of peaceful reconciliation was *tolerance*. This means that I think you are wrong because you think that the norm is such, whereas I think that the truth (the one truth) is that the norm is otherwise; but it is prohibited by law to try to impose what I think is truth on others, in the name of the peaceful coexistence of a divided society.[3] Society founded on tolerance was already a post-metaphysical society *by exclusion of values*. The question of values was excluded from public debate and tended to be confined to the private sphere.

A second stage that was progressively to be adopted in European states in the modern period in various forms was the autonomisation of law with respect to religious and moral laws. Law became the pre-eminent point of application of the principle of autonomy that involved a relativisation of truth in the sphere of law and politics (whereas the absolute character of truth could be preserved in the sphere of morality and in the private sphere). This was what might be called a post-metaphysical society *by adhesion to the values* of the modern era, or to the principle of autonomy that implied the legal protection of differences (without necessarily any moral acceptance of those differences).

B. Classical International Law

Historically, this recognition of autonomy *first* involved the affirmation of early modern states. It took the form of the principle *cujus regio, ejus religio* (whose realm, their religion) enshrined by the Peace of Augsburg of 1555 and reaffirmed in the Peace of Westphalia of 1648, which is often perceived in historiography as the birth certificate of international law in the

[3] See in particular Yves Charles Zarka, commenting on Pierre Bayle, in YC Zarka, F Lessay and J Rogers, *Les fondements philosophiques de la tolérance*, vol 1 (Paris, PUF) xii. See also J Habermas, 'Religious Tolerance – The Pacemaker for Cultural Rights', Royal Institute of Philosophy Annual Lecture 2003, *The Royal Institute of Philosophy*, 79, 2004.

modern era – when speaking of classical international law, we often say 'Westphalian international law'.[4]

This principle meant that religious peace was restored to Europe by the recognition that each ruler enjoyed autonomy in the domain of religion: each sovereign had the right to choose the religion of their subjects. Domestically, therefore, it was the confirmation of internal sovereignty as the sovereign's power of command over their subjects, as the subjection of domestic subjects to the command of the ruler.

Internationally, it meant something else; namely, the sovereign's right and freedom to choose for themselves the religion of their subjects, with no interference from other sovereigns. Autonomy here was freedom of choice and it is what is called the *external or international sovereignty of the state*, which was the foundation of classical international law.

At its high point, classical theory was to formalise this conception of international sovereignty by analogy with individual freedom in social contract theories. It was therefore to proceed by *incorporation of the state*. The state became a person – a legal entity but the analogy was often taken further with the legal entity being viewed as an actual individual – Hobbes' Leviathan – with its own will and with rights of its own.

It was Emer de Vattel who best formalised this analogy between sovereignty and freedom in the state of nature – which is why when I speak of classical international law I also speak of 'Vatellian' international law:

> Nations being composed of men naturally free and independent, and who, before the establishment of civil societies, lived together in the state of nature, – nations or sovereign states are to be considered as so many free persons living together in the state of nature.[5]

Vattel compounded this affirmation of sovereignty as freedom with the principle of legal equality – since the recognition of autonomy was the recognition of equal autonomy, which alone justified mutual respect among subjects (the fact that I can no more impose my own conception of truth on you than you can impose yours on me, because neither one of us can lay claim, in law, to absolute truth):

> Since men are naturally equal, and a perfect equality prevails in their rights and obligations, as equally proceeding from nature, – nations composed of men, and considered as so many free persons living together in the state of nature, are

[4] For a critical perspective see esp D Gaurier, *Histoire du droit international. Auteurs, doctrines et développement de l'Antiquité à l'aube de la période contemporaine* (Rennes, Presses universitaires de Rennes, 2005) 382.

[5] E de Vattel, *The Law of Nations Or, Principles of the Law of Nature, Applied to the Conduct and Affairs of Nations and Sovereigns, with Three Early Essays on the Origin and Nature of Natural Law and on Luxury*, ed with an introduction by B Kapossy and R Whatmore, tr T Nugent [1797] (Indianapolis, IN, Liberty Fund, 2008) Preliminaries, §4.

> naturally equal, and inherit from nature the same obligations and rights. Power or weakness does not in this respect produce any difference. A dwarf is as much a man as a giant; a small republic is no less a sovereign state than the most powerful kingdom.[6]

Freedom plus equality – you recognise in that the principle of equal sovereignty of states and it can be said that all of classical public international law is contained in these two assertions.

It is important to fully understand the implications of this classical theory of international law:

- International law is *a law of indifference or tolerance*: it therefore forms an international society of sovereign states that is *post-metaphysical by exclusion* of all discussion about values. And the subjects of discussion excluded were obviously to extend beyond religion. The state's freedom of choice covered not just the religion of its subjects but subsequently the political and economic regime, and so on. The traditional formulation of the *principle of non-intervention* is re-stated for example in the UN Charter and developed in UN General Assembly resolution 2625 (XXV).[7]
- This results in *dualism*: the dissociation between internal and external sovereignty and the indifference of international law to the forms of political and social organisation within states implies dualism. This means there are two clearly separated international and domestic legal orders, 'two circles touching each other but never overlapping' to cite Heinrich Triepel.[8] Moreover, the validity of one legal order with respect to the other is always relative, as it is necessarily founded on the provisions of the domestic legal order. This dualism means that solipsism is the natural attitude of the sovereign state: the world/other legal order is formed in and from the state's legal order. As a consequence, there are potentially as many international legal orders as there are states. This is generalised relativism.
- There results from this too the *negation of the individual as a subject of international law*. International law is a fiction of two separate world-societies: internal society made up of individuals governed by the domestic legal order and international society made up of states governed by the international legal order whose subjects are states. Consequently, the individual has no rights in classical international law but only with respect to the domestic order or by way of international law: individuals are

[6] ibid Preliminaries, § 18.

[7] Resolution no 2625(XXV), Declaration on Principles of International Law concerning Friendly Relations and Co-operation among States in accordance with the Charter on the United Nations, 24 October 1970.

[8] One of the most eminent theoreticians of dualism as applied to the relation between international law and domestic law, author of *Völkerrecht und Landesrecht* (Leipzig, Hirchfeld, 1899).

therefore 'mediate' subjects of international law through the intermediary of the will of the state.

C. The Theory of the Democratic State

Alongside the birth of international law, the principle of autonomy also renewed the question of the exercising of internal sovereignty, that is, of the vertical relationship between the modern state and its subjects.

The affirmation of man's natural freedom led on the one side to the affirmation of the principle of equality among citizens of the state and on the other side to the principle of self-legislation, that is, to the democratic principle.

i. Principle of Equality

If everyone is autonomous, then each individual can lay down their own norm for themselves and consequently no one can impose their truth on anyone else or, more generally, assert the primacy of their rights over those of others. This was obviously the end of the aristocratic era and the onset of the democratic era, which Tocqueville described so well as the growing and endless expansion of the principle of equality. With several major consequences that Tocqueville plainly saw:

> In democratic centuries, men rarely sacrifice themselves for each other; but they show a general compassion for all the members of the human species. You do not see them inflict useless evils, and when, without hurting themselves very much, they can relieve the sufferings of others, they take pleasure in doing so; they are not disinterested, but they are mild.[9]

Therefore:

- the impossibility of heteronomy (since each subject was worthy of equal respect);
- the universalisation of compassion towards those like oneself (but still 'other') and therefore the emergence of the possibility of a cosmopolitan feeling;
- the loss of intensity of compassion for those like oneself and the surge in interest, in other words the transition from community to society.

[9] A de Tocqueville, *Democracy in America*, historical-critical edn of *De la Démocratie en Amérique*, ed E Nolla, tr JT Schleifer (Indianapolis, Liberty Fund, 2010) vol IV, pt III, ch I, 'How Mores Become Milder as Conditions Become Equal'.

ii. Principle of Self-legislation

The relationship with authority also changed. The affirmation of personal autonomy dismissed the principle of heteronomy, including on the part of the sovereign. The question of sovereignty was posed anew. It raised the question of the legitimacy of legal constraint in a society made up of individuals who, by nature, were also free. This problem of democracy was that of all who wrote on the social contract, from Hobbes to Kant, and none raised it better than Rousseau:

> 'To find a form of association that may defend and protect with the whole force of the community the person and the property of every associate, and by means of which each, joining together with all, may nevertheless obey only himself, and remain as free as before.' Such is the fundamental problem of which the social contract provides the solution.[10]

Social contract theories, of course, answered this question in different ways.

Empirically and historically, solutions were provided in the context of the nation state by:

- on the one hand, democratic political institutions with the ambition to implement the principle of autonomy more or less comprehensively;
- on the other hand, human rights as rights protecting citizens against interference from the state.

Progressively, human rights came to underpin all democratic institutions by setting out all guarantees of the principle of autonomy in the form of subjective rights.

Not only did human rights require the citizen to recognise others as being like them (by virtue of the principle of equal rights) but they conferred on others a *right* to be different and to lay claim to their difference (for example, through the freedom of religious belief or freedom of speech but also through cultural rights). In this way, law in the modern era compelled citizens at least not only to tolerate but to fully accept the difference of others in the public sphere, even if, deep down, their conviction was no more than mere tolerance of others and of their difference.

Although these rights were developed nationally, they were always thought through in the universalist language of social contract theorists – a *necessarily universalist* language, because the question of co-existence – and especially religious co-existence – could not be confined to the recognition of equality among citizens of the same nation. The combination of this universalist language of human rights as developed domestically with the concept of sovereignty conceived as the foundation of international law

[10] J-J Rousseau, 'The Social Contract' in *The Social Contract and The First and Second Discourses (Rethinking the Western Tradition)*, ed and with an introduction by S Dunn (New Haven, CT, Yale University Press, 2002) bk I, ch VI, 149–254, 108.

explains how at some point we come to a paradox that might be termed the paradox of modernity.

D. The Paradox of Modernity

The paradox of modernity lies in the fact that the recognition of state sovereignty, which underlies classical international law, both *brings about* and *eliminates* autonomy in the same movement.

First, the emancipatory promise of modernity – in other words, the promise of autonomy for all – is achieved in the modern era by peoples acceding to the status of sovereign state and therefore via *the medium of sovereignty*. This can readily be seen in the process of decolonisation. Decolonised peoples did not look to found an alternative model of political organisation to the modern state and the sovereign state of international law. On the contrary, they all made this form their own. For peoples subject to colonial domination, the call for a right to self-determination corresponded to the deep-seated conviction that a people could only achieve freedom through the medium of the sovereign state. Since, with the recognition as a state, these peoples or rather their governments, acquired a legal status conferring on them the same rights and obligations as other states and a protective status of their self-determination in all areas: economic, political, religious and cultural.

Secondly, at the same time as sovereignty brought about this autonomy – the self-determination of peoples – it eliminated it. This ensued from the character of international law: sovereignty in international law bestowed self-determination on a people, but at the very moment that people came to form a state, it ceased to be a subject of international law, just as the individuals who made it up ceased being recognised as having any autonomy in the eyes of international law. The 'cut-off' was made between international and internal sovereignty, leaving the individual subject to the power of the government, which was the 'organ' of the state in international law.

The formation of the state in international law turned the individual into an 'object' of international law. Moreover, it strengthened the tie between individual and state. In a period of rising nationalism in Europe, this effective bond between the state and the individual under its jurisdiction by virtue of nationality was reflected by a principle of belonging, which was very clearly expressed by the PCIJ in the case of *Mavrommatis*:

> By taking up the case of one of its subjects and by resorting to diplomatic action or international judicial proceedings on his behalf, a State is in reality asserting its own rights – its right to ensure, in the person of its subjects, respect for the rules of international law.[11]

[11] *The Mavrommatis Palestine Concessions*, 30 August 1924, PCIJ Series A, no 2, 12.

The wording had *paternalist and patriarchal overtones*: it evoked the position of those struck by 'legal incapacity' – women and children – who were dependent on and under the 'protection' of the father of the household. And this is exactly what individuals were in international law: in a state of incapacity and unable to defend their rights in the 'international sphere' and who, to do so, had to seek *their* state's 'protection'.

Their right was not their right, it was 'in reality', the right of the state that they were asserting. For any infringement of the right of 'one of its subjects' was an infringement of the rights of the state itself.

The wording was also *politically highly significant* because it meant individuals were assigned to a 'nation', which was itself associated with the intrinsic identity of the state. To be a 'national' of the state was to be part of the nation. Such an assignment to a group was naturally based on a principle of inclusion/exclusion meaning that 'foreigners' were those who were not nationals.

And this foreshadowed the mode of conflict of the modern era, international warfare, no longer wars of religion or wars between sovereigns, but mass war opposing entire peoples. Jean-Jacques Rousseau had seen this development coming:

> Political bodies, thus remaining in a state of nature among themselves, soon experienced the inconveniencies that had obliged individuals to quit it; and this state became much more fatal to these great bodies, than it had been before to the individuals who now composed them. Hence those national wars, those battles, those murders, those reprisals, which make nature shudder and shock reason; hence all those horrible prejudices, which make it a virtue and an honor to shed human blood. The worthiest men learned to consider cutting the throats of their fellows as a duty; at length men began to butcher each other by thousands without knowing for what; and more murders were committed in a single action, and more horrible disorders at the taking of a single town, than had been committed in the state of nature during ages together upon the whole face of the earth. Such are the first effects we may conceive to have arisen from the division of mankind into different societies.[12]

Modern international law failed, then, just at the point it became successful: at the very time individuals achieved a form of recognition by acquiring the status of a sovereign state in international law, they became reified by the same international law.

War, as Rousseau had clearly seen, was no longer a relationship of man to man but of state to state. Individuals tore each other apart and killed each other as 'nationals' and *because they were nationals* (and not out of any

[12] J-J Rousseau, 'The Second Discourse: Discourse on the Origin and Foundations of Inequality Among Mankind' English translation from: in Rousseau, *The Social Contract* (n 10) 69–148, 126.

personal hatred). Moreover, individuals became mere *objects of law* and so potentially could be destroyed by the sovereign state holding sway over them. They did not have, they could not have any rights under international law. They were the things of the state and the state could do whatever it wanted with its 'things'.

Beyond the chronicle of wars between states and of crimes perpetrated by states against their own 'nationals', two problems highlighted this flaw in international law of the modern period. First the problem of *national minorities*, which was the cause of the Great War in a context of growing nationalism. Then the problem of *stateless peoples* – that is, peoples that were left literally unrecognised by the formation of sovereign states as they were not in the majority in any state or at least were not officially assimilated under any particular nation-state.

At the heart of this paradox, modernity came under strain. The classical theory of international law aimed at ending wars of religion but proved equally lethal to the freedom of individuals and potentially a cause of war, with the help of nationalism. It was this observation that led a number of thinkers to develop a cosmopolitan project that stood apart from the project of classical international law.

II. Cosmopolitan Projects: A Democratic Conception of International Law

A. The Two Theoretical Traditions of International Law

There were two separate theoretical traditions in the history of thought: that of the 'law of nations', which was to lead to the theory of international law formalised by Vattel and that of the projects of perpetual peace, from Henri IV's Grand Design to Kant's project for perpetual peace.[13]

The 'law of nations' tradition was not aimed at prohibiting war, which was considered rather as a normal means of enforcement or a form of sanction that the state might use when its rights were infringed. In their way, the 'law of nations' theorists pursued a form of utopia in the idea of domesticating power through law, within a system based solely on the (good) will of states themselves, which implied making sovereignty a legal and not a political concept. Sovereignty was the capacity to consent to be bound (the autonomy of will).[14]

[13] See D Archibugi, M Croce and A Salvatore, 'Droit des gens ou paix perpétuelle? Deux théories internationales fondatrices sur l'usage de la force', tr Louis Lourme, in O de Frouville (ed), *Le cosmopolitisme juridique* (Paris, Pedone, 2013) 71–97.

[14] 'The Court declines to see in the conclusion of any Treaty by which a State undertakes to perform or refrain from performing a particular act of abandonment of its sovereignty. No doubt

The theorists of plans for perpetual peace had a more radical objective. They wanted to put an end to all wars and therefore to establish a general state of peace, which implied eliminating the causes of war and introducing a public body of law (and not just a *consensus-based private* body of law) that was valid and applicable in relations among states, called cosmopolitan law.

Whereas the law of nations doctrine made its object autonomous through the separation between the internal and international orders, the theorists of perpetual peace refused such an artificial separation by marking the continuum that meant that injustices within the state led to war between states and, vice-versa, the establishment of the conditions for a pacified society within the state was the precondition for peace among states.

We shall look more specifically here at Kant's cosmopolitan project.

B. *Kant's Plan for Perpetual Peace*

Kant began by observing that international law of the modern period was a failure: the constitution of sovereign states enabled on the one hand the introduction of a degree of order in relations among sovereigns but on the other hand it multiplied the impact of conflicts by setting Nations against other Nations. Consequently the only peace that could be contemplated under that system was 'in the vast graveyard of the human race'.[15] Kant besides did not think at all highly of the theorists of the law of nations he cited – Hugo Grotius, Pufendorf and Vattel – and whom he dismissed as 'sorry comforters as they are'.[16] Ultimately it could be said that Kant criticised the theorists of the law of nations for having misconstrued the principle of self-legislation applied to relations between states.

The whole construction of international law was based on an analogy which was itself a mind-boggling fiction. The state was thought of as a person, a sort of superman. Consequently the society of states was thought of as a society in the state of nature: all states were individuals with their own autonomous will. The problem of autonomy was therefore duplicated: the question of autonomy *in the internal order* differed from the question of autonomy *in the international order*.

any convention creating an obligation of this kind places a restriction upon the exercise of the sovereign rights of the State, in the sense that it requires them to be exercised in a certain way. But the right of entering into international engagements is an attribute of State sovereignty.' *Case of the SS 'Wimbledon'*, 17 August 1923, PCIJ Series A no 1, 25.

[15] I Kant, 'Perpetual Peace. A Philosophical Sketch' in *Kant. Political Writings*, ed HS Reiss, tr HB Nisbet, Cambridge Texts in History of Political Thought (Cambridge, Cambridge University Press, 1970) Ak 8:347, 96.

[16] ibid Ak 8:355, 103.

Kant proposed to overhaul this logic. Against the original dualism of international law, he set up a form of legal monism. In point of fact, the problem of law in the modern period, that is with autonomy as its principle, was the same in both internal and international law. It was a problem of human freedom and not of the freedom of an imaginary state-person. The question of law was both one of reconciling everyone's liberties in accordance with a universal rule and of reconciling everyone's liberties and a public constraint exercised on them.

Kant believed this double reconciliation could easily be achieved in a democratic state. It was just that this would only be a half-way point because the peace thus implemented internally would still be threatened by the persistence of war among states. Likewise, in legal terms, the perfecting of a body of public law respecting the liberties of each and everyone at the state's level would always be *provisional*, until such time as a body of public law could impose peace among states.

> What is the use of working for a law-governed civil constitution among individual men, i.e. of planning a commonwealth? The same unsociability which forced men to do so gives rise in turn to a situation whereby each commonwealth, in its external relations (i.e. as a state in relation to other states), is in a position of unrestricted freedom. Each must accordingly expect from any other precisely the same evils which formerly oppressed individual men and forced them into a law-governed civil state.[17]

In other words again, if autonomy was the principle behind the modern period, that autonomy could only be fully achieved through the medium of an international law that was itself based on and aimed at the autonomy of individuals – and not of states.

It can readily be seen that on the contrary an international law with the autonomy of states as the principle behind it would negate the autonomy of individuals and, moreover, perpetuate the state of war of all against all. Kant therefore proposed two things:

- The first of these was to expand the democratic regime within states. All states would need to become progressively democratic because in that way they would become just and peaceful.
- The second was to go beyond classical international law by means of a cosmopolitan law in the context of a 'Federation of Free States'.[18] Let us dwell on this second proposal, which is the harder to understand of the two but the more fundamental.

[17] I Kant, 'Idea for a Universal History with a Cosmopolitan Purpose' in *Kant. PoliticalWritings*, ed HS Reiss, tr HB Nisbet, Cambridge Texts in History of Political Thought (Cambridge, Cambridge University Press, 1970) Seventh Proposition, 41–53, 47.

[18] See the Second Definitive Article of a Perpetual Peace, 'The Rights of Nations shall be based on a Federation of Free States': Kant, 'Perpetual Peace. A Philosophical Sketch' (n 15) 102–05.

The Federation of Free States is an antinomical concept. This can easily be seen with a moment's thought. Federation is traditionally opposed to confederation. In a confederation, the component parts maintain their sovereignty. It is actually an advanced form of integration and distribution of competences. Conversely, the federation refers to a form of state in which the components (the federated states) lose their sovereignty to the profit of the federal state exclusively. Kant spoke of a 'Federation of Free States'. In other words, he contemplated the hypothesis of a federation in which the federated states would not lose their freedom, which seems to be a contradiction in terms.

Why this antinomy? Because Kant was aware that cosmopolitanism could only operate in the plural. Cosmopolitanism was not the equivalent of a merger of humankind, much less was it the universal state, which Kant said would be both despotic and ineffective.[19]

So what did this antinomy mean? It meant that the Federation of Free States was a *process* and not a particular form of state that could be set up. It was a goal towards which one should work, an Idea of Reason, which one should strive tirelessly to bring about.

C. Positive International Law and the Democratic Conception of International Law

Is this conception, this cosmopolitan project, encompassed by international law today? Of course it is! Contemporary international law is a mixture of conceptions of classical international law (Vattel's law of nations) and of cosmopolitan theories.

At the great peace conferences at The Hague in 1899 and 1907, the principles of a cosmopolitan outlook were integrated into international law. The League of Nations founded by the Treaty of Versailles in 1919 was symbolically, if not materially, the accomplishment of Kant's alliance against war. The International Labour Organisation (ILO), also created by the Treaty of Versailles is explicit in its Kantian philosophy:

> Whereas the League of Nations has for its object the establishment of universal peace, and such a peace can be established only if it based upon social justice;
>
> And whereas conditions of labour exist involving such injustice, hardship and privation to large numbers of people as to produce unrest so great that the peace and harmony of the world are imperilled;

[19] See Kant, 'On the Common Saying: "This May be True in Theory, but it does not Apply in Practice"' in *Kant. Political Writings*, ed HS Reiss, tr HB Nisbet, Cambridge Texts in History of Political Thought (Cambridge, Cambridge University Press, 1970) 61–92, 90; Kant, 'Perpetual Peace' (n 15), First supplement, Ak 8:367, 113.

The entire part of international law aimed at preventing and prohibiting war between states and at disarmament comes under cosmopolitan law. Similarly, all of the international organisations whose purposes extend beyond purely instrumental cooperation among states and pursue ends on the scale of humankind or on a transnational dimension belong to cosmopolitan law. In truth, that covers virtually all the organisations of the United Nations family. Lastly, more than any other corpus of contemporary international law, the proclamation of human rights embodies the ideal of the Federation of Free States because it enshrines recognition of the individual in international law and the idea of constitutional protection of the individual's rights as a citizen of the world (without distinction as to nationality).

International law has indeed therefore embarked upon a cosmopolitan process.

With two visible consequences which are incomprehensible when measured against the yardstick of a classical theory of international law:

- first the objectivisation of international law – meaning that international law is elaborated and imposed on subjects without requiring the consent of states;
- second the hierarchisation of international law, with the continuing enhancement of the contents of an international constitution the norms of which frame the process of elaboration of other (legislative) norms but also the emergence of an idea of public policy, with norms defended by a common public interest – because they convey common values of society.

An axiological content can therefore be seen to arise in the heart of international law, which was excluded by principle from the realm of classical international law.

This cosmopolitan process is not only deliberate, it is carried along by the development of events, and especially the growth in the world's population and issues involving common goods such as climate change and pandemics; but also by the globalisation of the economy, which has outpaced political globalisation.

The result is a growing interdependency which, in a way, no longer leaves states with any real choice, as Habermas explains in *The Postnational Constellation* and for whom globalisation processes

> [...] introduce us to *another* perspective, from which we see the growing interdependence of social arenas, communities of risks, and the networks of shared fate ever more clearly. The acceleration and the intensification of communication and commerce sharing spatial and temporal distances; expanding markets run up against the limits of the planet; the exploitation of resources meets the limits of nature. These narrowed horizons rule out the option of externalizing the consequences of many of our actions: it is increasingly rare that costs and risks can be

> shifted onto others – whether other sectors of society, other geographical regions, other cultures, or future generations – without sanctions of one kind or another.[20]

Another consequence of globalisation is the growing powerlessness of states which follows from their ever narrower margin for manoeuvre in the context of an economy directed essentially by transnational actors:

> The broad renunciation of the power of politics to shape social relations, and the readiness to abandon normative points of view in favor of adaptations to supposedly unavoidable systemic imperatives, now dominate the political arenas of the Western world. Clinton or Blair, relying on empty formulas such as 'It's time for a change,' pitch themselves as efficient managers for the reorganization of failing business ventures. The truly programmatic vacuity of a political platform that has been whittled down to 'political change' corresponds, on the side of voters, either to informed abstinence or to the thirst for 'political charisma' …[21]

These two factors prompt Habermas to say that '[w]e will only be able to meet the challenges of globalisation in a reasonable manner if the postnational constellation can successfully develop new forms for the democratic self-steering of society'.[22]

No more than Kant does Habermas contemplate the creation of a world state, but instead what he terms 'a world domestic policy possible without a world government'.[23]

So where are we in his view?

> Global powers no longer operate in the state of nature envisioned by classical international law, but on the middle level of an emerging world politics.[24]

This observation of fact leads to the final point, which is meant to outline what a democratic theory of international law involves.

III. The Bases for a Democratic Theory of International Law

This observation as to the state of society and international law illuminates the proposed definition of a democratic theory of international law as *a theory that seeks to describe the phenomenon of law in a world society that has engaged in a process of cosmopolitan transition*.

It is also probably easier to understand why it was asserted from the outset that a classical theory of international law, founded on the principle

[20] J Habermas, 'Learning from Catastrophe? A Look Back at the Short Twentieth Century' in J Habermas, *The Postnational Constellation. Political Essays*, tr, ed and with an introduction by M Pensky (Cambridge, MA, MIT Press, 2001) 38–57, 55.

[21] J Habermas, 'The Postnational Constellation and the Future of Democracy' in Habermas, *The Postnational Constellation* (n 20) 58–112, 79–80.

[22] ibid 88.

[23] ibid 104.

[24] ibid 109–10.

of sovereignty, had *nothing more to say* about contemporary international law, that is, international law caught up in a cosmopolitan process. Such a theory no longer has anything to say because it is confined to founding and explaining a society aimed at co-existence among sovereign states. Therefore it cannot explain or describe an international law incorporating common values as norms of public policy and recognising individuals as subjects alongside states.

It is necessary therefore to forge a new theory of international law. Not a democratic *conception* of international law but a democratic *theory* of international law. By conception we understand a normative representation *prescribing* a transformation of existing law. By theory, however, we designate a set of concepts whose purpose is the *descriptive* presentation of existing law in its shifting and dynamic aspects.

As a cosmopolitan theory, a democratic theory of international law necessarily takes on the form of a *theory of the process of Federation of Free States.* The two poles of the antinomy, it will be noticed, articulate the principle of autonomy differently.

The *Federation*, because it is the political form that enables reconciliation between unity and diversity. More exactly, it is the political form of unity *for* diversity, the object of which is to unify so as to maintain the diversity – and therefore the autonomy – of each of the component parts. It is the political form of a pluralism (cultural, political) that refuses to merge while seeking unity of action.

Democracy because it is the political regime that brings about autonomy through the implementation of the principle of self-legislation, which Habermas, further to Rousseau, formulates in this way: *each addressee of the norm should be able to think of themselves at the same time as its author.*

Let us take up these two categories again to make them more explicit.

A. The Concepts Related to the Theory of the Federation

There are two major understandings of the federative phenomenon.

The first contemplates the federation only in relation to the political form of the state. Hence the opposition between confederation and federation, which designates two poles of the federative phenomenon, thought of in terms of sovereignty and therefore of the theory of the state. The confederation is the form that lets the sovereignty of the component parts remain but to which specific competences are deferred. The federation is the form that is sovereign – therefore a federal *state* – and that abolishes the sovereignty of its component parts.

We must therefore turn rather towards theories that do not assimilate the federation to a federal state but that see in the federation a non-state, de-statified and de-nationalised phenomenon, defined by its techniques far more than by its institutions. This second series of theories does not therefore force us to choose between the loss of sovereignty of the component parts to the federal state and the maintaining of the sovereignty of the component parts and the consequent comparative powerlessness of the confederation.

In interpreting international law through a democratic theory of international law, then, we shall use the key concepts of federalism:

1. the principle of autonomy of the component parts, which is the precondition for maintaining diversity in unity;
2. the principle of participation of the component parts, which ensures the principle of self-legislation;
3. the principle of the immediate effect of federal law and therefore the fact that the individual is the subject of several legal orders and at any rate of both the federal order and the order of the component entity;
4. the principle of subsidiarity and/or complementarity making it possible to distribute and/or share competences by virtue of the principle that each competence is attributed to the level(s) best able to exercise it, which ties back in with the concept of 'multi-level governance';
5. the principle of substitution, which enables the federal level to stand in for the federated level should the latter fail to implement the competences attributed to it.

It is with these concepts, it seems to me, that it is now possible to understand the nesting of competences at several levels among states and the various international organisations and to potentially put the different competences of these different levels in order. For example, we can reinterpret the entire institution of the International Criminal Court in the light of these different principles and thereby reach a far better understanding of the working of international criminal justice than could be done by using classical international law as our yardstick[25] (the only thing that classical international law could say on this subject is that the obligations under the Rome Statute, which is a treaty, are binding only on the states that have ratified the treaty).

B. The Concepts Related to the Theory of Democracy

In the same way as we use a de-statified theory of federation, not related to the form of the federal state, we need to resort to a theory of democracy that is also de-statified and de-nationalised. Furthermore, we should draw

[25] For a cosmopolitan understanding of the ICC and the process that led to the adoption of the Rome statute, see O de Frouville, 'La Cour pénale internationale: une humanité souveraine', *Les Temps modernes*, no 610, *La Souveraineté*, Fall 2000, 257–88.

on a theory of *democracy without demos*, to take up the expression coined by Catherine Colliot-Thélène.[26]

This expression may look like an oxymoron. Democracy, etymologically, is indeed power conferred on the *demos*, the people. How then could there be a democracy without a people?

This is possible provided we view democracy not as a constitutional form (in the classification of regimes alongside aristocracy, oligarchy, and so on) but as a set of techniques and concepts designed to reflect the principle of self-legislation in terms of law and institutions. Democracy is fundamentally the techniques and concepts that make it so that in practice anyone who is the addressee of a norm can at the same time think of themselves as its author. And there is no reason why such techniques and concepts cannot be implemented not just in the context of a state but also in other social frameworks; not only in a social unity – a nation-state – but also in a multiplicity of societies in their interrelations.

Besides, if you sit and think about it, this is what happens including in states with very classical regimes of representation, in which democracy comes into play on several levels of government (local, regional, central) corresponding to different societies that cannot be summarised as part of a great whole.

In truth, only the *national* election of representatives (president, parliament) or national referendum can reflect the literal idea of a democracy as a practice of self-legislation of the *demos* constituted as such. For the rest, it has been well understood since Tocqueville that democratic life and democratic practice relate to multiple instances whose capacity for action is itself guaranteed by subjective rights often exercised collectively and including freedom of expression, freedom of association and freedom of assembly. All of these are rights that the European Court of Human Rights for example designates as being intrinsically related to the concept of 'democratic society'.

We need, therefore, to make this transposition of democracy in the cosmopolitan process, and rid ourselves of an overly subjective vision of democracy as residing, on the one side, in the individual with their autonomy of will and, on the other side, in a Leviathan type of macro-subject capable of expressing the *general will*. Hence the importance of de-subjectivising the conception we have of law and its foundations.

In this respect, the path long pointed out and followed is that first trodden by Jürgen Habermas, who replaces the reason of the transcendental subject as the foundation of law by a rational agreement based on *the social practice of communication*.

[26] C Colliot-Thélène, *La démocratie sans 'demos'* (Paris, PUF, 2011).

> Communicative reason differs from practical reason first and foremost in that it is no longer ascribed to the individual actor or to a macrosubject at the level of the state or the whole of society. Rather, what makes communicative reason possible is the linguistic medium through which interactions are woven together and forms of life are structured.[27]

Such substitution makes it possible to rid oneself again of all too excessive state-morphism that leads some proponents of cosmopolitanism to propose, for instance, the establishment of a second representative chamber of peoples alongside the General Assembly of states.

Obviously it is not a question of that: there is no longer any need to locate the general 'will' in a macro-subject. It is a question rather of looking to benefit from and channel the strength of legitimation of interactions among different organs and actors on different levels. Where necessary, a formal validation of the norm may ultimately be effected through the intermediary of a specific organ, as a formal condition for labelling a rule as 'law' thereby bestowing on it a formal mark of validity which will enshrine its legitimacy and without which it might not actually exist (the fact that its implementation may be backed by a form of public constraint).

It seems to me that this model can explain the way international organisations actually operate in this day and age and in particular that it can provide an explanatory framework for the involvement of private actors and organisations of civil society, whether or not their involvement is formalised as such.[28]

When all is said and done, a democratic theory of international law provides a better understanding of contemporary international law. It also provides a useful interpretive framework from a reformist perspective for speeding up the cosmopolitan process and making up ground as everyone would like so that we can take our destiny back in hand by bringing the globalised economy back under control through the globalisation of politics.

[27] J Habermas, *Between Facts and Norms*, tr W Rehg (Cambridge, Polity Press, 1996) 3–4.
[28] See ch 8 of this volume.

Part II

Towards World Citizenship: ‘Cosmopolitan Building Sites’

8

Civil Society's Role in International Organisations. Theory(ies) and Practice(s)

I first took an interest in the role of civil society in international organisations when representing a non-governmental organisation (NGO) – the International Federation for Human Rights (FIDH) – as part of the ECOSOC working group tasked with negotiating in New York the reform of the consultative status of NGOs. Those negotiations were to lead to the adoption of resolution 1996/31 superseding resolution 1296 (XLIV) of 23 May 1968.[1]

The negotiations had got underway after what Antoine Bernard, then FIDH Executive Director, called the 'Big Bang' of NGOs in the early 1990s, especially at the 1993 Vienna World Conference on Human Rights.[2]

The 'Big Bang' was so called because an unprecedented number of *national* NGOs for the defence of human rights made their way to Vienna. This upwelling of national NGOs was something new. It fell in line with the processes of democratic transition in Eastern Europe and the Global South, and with the concomitant development of civil societies. They disrupted the routine of the major international NGOs which had until then been the only ones or almost the only ones entitled to take the floor and intervene in international organisations in Geneva or New York. There was an atmosphere like there must have been when the French Revolutionaries abolished feudalism on the night of 4 August 1789, with all these national NGOs challenging in a sense the international NGOs *privilege* of representation – an undue privilege in their view. Beginning in the early 1990s, national NGOs wanted to attend the UN themselves to conduct their own advocacy, to put their messages across in person and to use its mechanisms. Their demands were encouraged and furthered by certain international NGOs which, by their nature or their calling, thought those demands were both a right and a necessity. Among them were the FIDH, as a federative international organisation, and so an emanation of its members, but also the International Service for Human

[1] cf the report on this mission, O de Frouville, 'La réforme des relations avec les ONG: entre conservatismes et démagogies', *La Lettre de la FIDH*, nos 595–596, 1320 July 1995, 8.

[2] See A Bernard, 'Le big bang des ONG', *Autrement vivre*, ENDA, Vienne 93, 5.

Rights (ISHR), whose task was to 'service' national NGOs and human rights defenders coming to Geneva and to guide them in the United Nations corridors and institutions.

Now the younger members of the audience, sitting here listening to these old timer's recollections, are entitled to ask whether what I refer to as 'international civil society' does not correspond to a very precise 'moment' in the history of international law, a small historical window, somewhere between 1990 and 1995? They might ask whether the topic is still relevant. Is 'civil society' not a concept attached to those heady days in the early 1990s when we might well have been tempted to entertain the illusion of an 'end of History' based on human rights, the rule of law and the market economy? 'Civil society, so 90s ?' to take up the ironic title of a conference by Marti Koskenniemi on human rights.[3]

The (barely veiled) criticisms like the comparison are not without their relevance. There is both a historical and a conceptual connection between the upsurge of human rights and the upsurge of civil society – because at the same time as the waves of democratisation were liberalising political regimes in the East and South they were opening up a public space for citizens' participation and for demands for human rights without discrimination.

Similarly it is probably fair to say that what we now blushingly call the 'shrinking' of the space of civil society in many countries[4] goes along with backtracking on human rights and even in some instances challenges to the relevance of human rights norms.

And yet in both instances – call me an incorrigible optimist if you like – it seems that recent backtracking is part of a continuum characterised by the expansion of national civil societies and democratic space as much as by the discourse of appropriation surrounding universal human rights.

Let us take just one example, at the crossroads of these two movements of civil society and human rights: the idea of 'human rights defenders'. Negotiation of what is often called, in short, the *Declaration on Human Rights Defenders* took 13 years.[5] I was personally involved in the last four years of

[3] Conference given at the University of Oxford in 2014, available in full at www.youtube.com/watch?v=9hFdZRYZhkg.

[4] The expression is used in many recent reports reflecting a shared observation among government, non-government and inter-government observers. See eg United Nations, Report of the United Nations High Commissioner for Human Rights, *Practical Recommendations for the Creation and Maintenance of a Safe and Enabling Environment for Civil Society, Based on Good Practices and Lessons Learned*, A/HRC/32/20; European Union/Directorate-General for External Policies, *Shrinking Space for Civil Society: The EU Response*, 2017; European Union/EU Agency for Fundamental Rights (FRA), *Challenges Facing Civil Society Organisations Working on Human Rights in the EU*, 2017; Council of Europe: Report of the Consultative meeting. *Shrinking Space for Civil Society: The Impact on Young People and their Organisations*, Strasbourg, 7–8 November 2018, CMJ(2019)7, 11 February 2019.

[5] Declaration on the Right and Responsibility of Individuals, Groups and Organs of Society to Promote and Protect Universally Recognized Human Rights and Fundamental Freedoms, adopted by the General Assembly in Resolution 53/144, 9 December 1998.

the talks from 1995 to 1998 as a representative of FIDH. On completion of the negotiations in 1998, it should be recalled that the idea of human rights defenders barely existed; it was forged during the talks with NGOs themselves and become more substantial when they began to build protection and action programmes around the Declaration, especially the Observatory for the Protection of Human Rights Defenders and then the appointment of the United Nations Representative of the Secretary General on the situation of human rights defenders.[6] Nowadays there is no escaping the concept of 'human rights defender' in word and deed both internationally and nationally.[7] Alongside the identification of 'whistle-blowers', the characterisation of 'human rights defenders' shows that it has now become very complicated for authoritarian governments to close down public space completely: the genie got out of the lamp 20 years ago; it will be difficult if not impossible to bottle it up again.

More generally it is becoming difficult now to deny the role of civil society organisations (CSOs) within international organisations (IOs). This is plain to see for anyone who takes part in IO negotiations or actions, be they diplomats, experts or members of the secretary's office.

Conversely, it is interesting to see that the scope of such participation by CSOs in the work of IOs is still talked down. The gist of the argument is that IOs remain primarily intergovernmental mechanisms and that CSOs have at best a decorative role or provide a ready guarantee for decisions that are actually negotiated and made by states alone.

In actual fact, the role of CSOs in IOs is an obvious point, but it remains largely an unthought-of point of international law.

I would like to ponder this paradox. I shall first go back over a few examples of this obvious point of the role played by CSOs in IOs before returning to the unthought-of point and uncovering the theoretical reasons for it.

I. The Obvious Point

The role played by CSOs in IOs is as plain as day and one need only read the discourse of the IOs themselves on the issue to realise this. I shall therefore look at a few examples of IOs to see what they have to say about CSO participation in their work – first I want to see how IOs identify CSOs, particularly

[6] Subsequently the Special Rapporteur. Successive office holders have been Ms Hina Jilani (Pakistan), 2000–08; Ms Margaret Sekaggya (Uganda), 2008–14; Mr Michel Forst (France), 2014–19.

[7] See recently, eg, the adoption by consensus of UN Human Rights Council Resolution 40/11, 21 March 2019, recognising the contribution of environmental human rights defenders to the enjoyment of human rights, environmental protection and sustainable development.

as opposed to other types of actors. We shall then see how IOs define the role of these CSOs with respect to them.

First, though, a word of caution that is not unimportant: here as elsewhere, discourse alone does not create its object. It is not IOs that have created CSOs, it is CSOs that have come to IOs. They are a sociological reality that pre-exist their recognition by IOs. What we are going to examine here, then, is but a part of reality; it is CSOs viewed very narrowly through the eyes of IOs, if I might put it that way. But I believe that this view of things, however narrow, is revealing. It shows how IOs have been led to react when confronted with this reality.

A. Identification of CSOs

Let us look first how CSOs are identified or defined by IOs. And first off, it is interesting to observe that there have been two recent changes in this respect.

i. From NGOs to CSOs

Until the mid or even late 2000s, we spoke rarely of CSOs but rather of NGOs. At present the term CSO has become widespread and NGO is used by a few organisations in reference to a status adopted prior to this development.

The development itself can probably be explained by the fact that most IOs realised that NGOs were a category that failed to cover all of the organisations with which they were led to work, because the term 'NGO' often refers to a legal status at national level whereas many organisations are not necessarily recognised by the authorities or are not constituted in any clearly defined legal form.

ii. Widening of the Range of 'Partners'

The second notable development is that CSOs are perceived as *just another category* of private actors with which IOs maintain ties. This development is most striking. It follows on from the gradual generalisation of relations forged between IOs and the private sector, the business world, notably further to the UN's introduction of the *Global Compact*,[8] but also thinking begun at the turn of the century at the instigation of Secretary-General Kofi Annan,[9] on the

[8] See esp L Boisson de Chazournes and E Mazzuier (eds), *Le Pacte mondial des Nations Unies 10 ans après* (Brussels, Bruylant, 2011).

[9] See the report *We the peoples: the role of the United Nations in the twenty-first century*, A/54/2000, 27 March 2000 and General Assembly Resolution 55/215 of 21 December 2000, 'Towards global partnerships'. The UN General Assembly Resolution 68/234, 'Towards global partnerships: a principle-based approach to enhanced cooperation between the United Nations and all relevant partners' provides the following definition: 'partnerships are voluntary and collaborative relationships between various parties, both public and non-public, in which all

formation of 'global partnerships'. From that point on, many organisations set about distinguishing various categories of actors which they sometimes recognised as having different statuses and different rights.

The development is visible, for example, with UNESCO. The cultural organisation had long had a consultative status for NGOs, which was completely overhauled in the course of the 1990s, as it was for virtually all IOs, and led in 1995 to the adoption by the 28th General Conference of updated guidelines on UNESCO's relations with NGOs. But in 2013 UNESCO adopted a 'comprehensive strategy'[10] centred on the notion of 'partnerships'[11] with both an *umbrella statement* applicable to all actors and 'separate strategies for engagement with individual categories of partner', namely the private sector, bilateral funding partners, media, NGOs, parliamentarians, associations, centres and clubs for UNESCO, universities and other higher education institutions and a few other more specific actors.

The same development occurred in other organisations which now carefully distinguish between CSOs and other actors and especially states or other public institutions and the private sector. UNICEF, for instance, distinguishes between the public sector, business partnerships and relations with CSOs. Similarly the United Nations Population Fund recognises various strategic partnerships with the business sector, philanthropic foundations, parliamentarians, CSOs, academia, high net worth individuals, individuals, etc.[12] According to a 2019 working paper written for the Development Co-ordination Directorate of the OECD, this distinction has become a common feature of the policies of most if not all member states, and in the OECD itself.[13]

This is an interesting development because it shows that CSOs are not understood as just any private group; notably they stand clearly apart from the private or commercial sector.

participants agree to work together to achieve a common purpose or undertake a specific task and, as mutually agreed, to share risks and responsibilities, resources and benefits'. The idea of partnership was taken up again in the Millennium Development Goals (goal 8: 'global partnership for development') and then in the Sustainable Development Goals (goal 17: strengthen the means of implementation and revitalize the global partnerships for sustainable development) and more specifically goals 17.16 and 17.17 concerning 'multi-stakeholder partnerships'.

[10] Comprehensive partnership strategy, updated in 2019, see doc 207 EX/11, adopted by the Executive Board at its 207th session, 207 EX/Decisions, 23 November 2019.

[11] The updated document on the comprehensive partnership strategy (para 5) states that 'The definition of partnership to which UNESCO adheres is that set out by the United Nations, as defined in United Nations General Assembly (FA) Resolution 68/234 …'.

[12] See www.unfpa.org/strategic-partnerships, consulted in July 2020.

[13] J Wood and K Fällman, *Enabling Civil Society for Sustainable Development: Select Survey Findings*, OECD Development Cooperation Working Paper 57, May 2019, 16, 'Member definitions of CSOs are quite similar. Recurring themes in members' CSO definitions include that they are distinct from state and private sector, and non-profit.'

But what is it that makes them distinctive? Few organisations venture onto this ground. UNICEF has a stab at a definition that is rather successful and worth setting out in full:

> What is 'civil society'? The civil society net is broad. For the purposes of partnering with UNICEF, CSOs are defined as associations independent of the public and for-profit sectors and designed to advance collective interests. Some of the civil society partners with which UNICEF has worked include: International and national non-governmental organization; Community-based organizations; Social movements; Faith-based organizations; Advocacy groups; Trade unions; Women's groups; Professional voluntary associations; Foundations; Independent media; Social networks; Think-tanks and research institutes.[14]

It is worth noting in particular the idea of a dual independence with respect to the public sector (the state, the administration) and the private sector (for-profit businesses) and this functional conception: the purpose of CSOs is to promote collective interests and ideas as opposed to private interests. The distinction was not self-evident initially. For several years, the opening of IOs to private businesses left room for ambiguity by encompassing under the term 'civil society' both NGOs (humanitarian, environmental, for the defence of human rights, etc) and commercial undertakings.[15]

Now this distinction fits in well with the development of civil society in ordinary language and in the conception we now intuitively have of the concept.

Formerly, in line with Hegelian philosophy, civil society related to everything that was not the state, not just private economic actors but also citizens. Today this definition seems to be beside the point because it is obvious that NGOs like Amnesty International or Greenpeace cannot be likened in their vocation, their purposes or their forms of action to private enterprise. The most common meaning given to civil society today sees it foremost as a 'third sector' separate from both the state and the private sector. But this position as a third sector alone is not enough to characterise it. Civil society is also defined by the quality or nature of its interventions, in other words it is defined on a more functional basis: it promotes and defends 'public' interests, that is, its interventions are intended to defend a certain conception of the general interest – the general interest in national terms or even, when it comes to participating in the world of IOs in the context of a global-scale public policy, a worldwide general interest.

[14] See www.unicef.org/about/partnerships, consulted in July 2020.

[15] See the concerns voiced in 2003 by Antoine Bernard, FIDH Executive Director, in his contribution to the CEDIN conference in Nanterre, in H Gherari and S Szurek (eds), *L'émergence de la société civile internationale. Vers la privatisation du droit international?* (Paris, Pedone, 2003) 34.

It can be asserted therefore that the discourse of IOs is consistent with that of philosopher Jürgen Habermas when he looked to define the notion of civil society in his book *Between Facts and Norms*:

> What is meant by 'civil society' today, in contrast to its usage in the Marxist tradition, no longer includes the economy as constituted by private law and steered through markets in labor, capital, and commodities. Rather, its institutional core comprises those nongovernemental and non-economic connections and voluntary associations that anchor the communication structures of the public sphere in the society component of the lifeworld. Civil society is composed of those more or less spontaneously emergent associations, organizations and movements that, attuned to how societal problems resonate in the private life spheres, distill and transmit such reactions in amplified form to the public sphere. The core of civil society comprises a network of associations that institutionalizes problem-solving discourses on questions of general interest inside the framework of organized public spheres. [...] Such associations [...] do form the organizational substratum of the general public of citizens. More or less emerging from the private sphere, this public is made of citizens who seek acceptable interpretations for their social interests and experiences and who want to have an influence on institutionalized opinion-and-will-formation.[16]

Now that we have a clearer idea of just how IOs think of civil society, let us turn to the role that CSOs are liable to play according to IOs.

B. The Role of CSOs

In an effort to understand the role of CSOs in IOs, the forms of intervention must be distinguished from the nature of interventions.

i. Forms of Intervention

When it comes to the type of interventions by CSOs, again the discourse of IOs is quite enlightening. The striking feature at first glance is the diversity of roles contemplated. CSOs are seen as intervening from an instrumental perspective at almost all levels of action. UNESCO, for example, explains that:

> Combining expertise and resources with NGOs allows the Organization to: create strategic alliance; enhance efficiency and effectiveness of programme/activity implementation; strengthen visibility and impact of its action and presence, globally, regionally and at country level; reinforce the implementation and

[16] J Habermas, *Between Facts and Norms*, tr William Rehg (Cambridge, Polity Press, 1996) 366–67. See also B Frydman, 'Habermas et la société civile contemporaine' in B Frydman (ed), *La société civile et ses droits* (Brussels, Bruylant, 2004) 123–44.

monitoring of its normative frameworks; enhance its capacity to reach all segments of societies which should be beneficiaries of its action; multiply the effects of UNESCO's actions.[17]

If all of this is brought back to the theory of social function, it can be seen that while IOs fulfil *normative*, *jurisdictional* and *executive* functions, CSOs contribute actively to all three functions:

- *Participation in the normative function*: this may be the most familiar aspect because it is the best studied of the actions of CSOs within IOs, since it is also the most accessible.[18] One need merely to sit in on discussions or negotiations to see that: (1) very often it is CSOs that instigate new norms; (2) the actual drafts are often written or inspired by CSOs; (3) CSOs participate in negotiations, with or without standing.
- *Participation in the jurisdictional function*, which is fairly familiar too,[19] including the strategic litigation activity that leads CSOs to bring cases before national or international courts or tribunals[20] so as to highlight an issue – for example some form of discrimination – and if possible to further the judiciary's interpretation of norms.
- *Participation in the executive function*, whether the supervisory function essentially powered by the documentation provided by CSOs both in their fact-finding and advocacy role,[21] or the implementation of programmes 'on the ground'.[22]

[17] See http://en.unesco.org/partnerships/non-governmental-organizations, consulted in July 2020.

[18] See esp O de Frouville, 'La Cour pénale internationale: une humanité souveraine ?', *Les Temps Modernes*, n° 610 La souveraineté, automne 2000, 257–88, 260, fn 11; S Szurek, 'La société civile internationale et l'élaboration du droit' in Gherari and Szurek (eds), *L'émergence de la société civile internationale* (n 15) 49–75; H M'rad, 'La participation des acteurs non étatiques aux conférences internationales' in R Ben Achour and S Laghmani, *Acteurs non étatiques et droit international* (Paris, Pedone, 2007) 79–99.

[19] See esp L Vierucci, 'NGOs before international courts and tribunals' in P-M Dupuy and L Vierucci, *NGOs in International Law. Efficiency in Flexibility?* (Cheltenham, Edward Elgar, 2008) 155–80.

[20] See H Duffy, *Strategic Human Rights Litigation: Understanding and Maximising Impact* (Oxford, Hart Publishing, 2018); and the report of the Open Society Justice Initiative, *Strategic Litigation Impacts. Insights from Global Experience* (2018).

[21] See in particular M Keck and K Sikkink, *Activists Beyond Borders* (New York, Cornell University Press, 1998).

[22] CSOs are now generally viewed by international organisations and countries providing development public aid as 'implementers', meaning both practical implementation of programmes, but also promotion and implementation of international standards. At the level of the European Union, see the Council conclusions on the roots of democracy and sustainable development: Europe's engagement with Civil Society in external relations, 3191st Foreign Affairs development Council meeting, Luxembourg, 15 October 2012, which recognises CSOs 'as autonomous development actors in their own rights' (point 3), and acknowledges 'the key role of CSOs in promoting human rights' (point 7). For a study on how the EU works practically on the field in partnership with CSOs, see CONCORD (European NGO confederation for relief and development), *EU Delegations Unwrapped. A Practical Guide for CSO Engagement with EUDs* (2019). See also the OECD Working Paper on policies of member states and the

The role of CSOs is therefore extremely diverse and is not confined to a contribution to the normative function as is often read. CSOs like other actors are acknowledged to have specific *competences* that are attributed to them by IOs or that are rather the legalisation by IOs of action by CSOs.

Beyond the diversity of the forms of intervention of CSOs, the nature of those interventions must be investigated.

ii. The Nature of Interventions

The discourse of IOs brings out two models corresponding to two very different ways of conceptualising CSOs' contributions to IOs' work: a consultative model and a participatory model.

The *consultative model* corresponds to an *instrumental* conception of the role of NGOs: NGOs are allowed physical access and a right to speak with respect to the United Nations to *serve* the purposes of IOs. In other words, they are there because they can make a contribution that can be drawn on by states and by IOs to achieve their own purposes.

On a deeper level, such a conception of the role of NGOs sees them as non-autonomous entities that do not have the capacity of rational agents able to participate in decision making or to be attributed their own operational competences.

This is the 'classical' model to be found, for example, in ECOSOC resolution 1996/31 on the consultative relationship between the UN and NGOs. The institutional practice of the United Nations shows how far this instrumental perspective is completely outdated. In most areas of competence of the UN and of IOs, NGOs and CSOs more broadly play a major role at all stages of the decision-making and implementation processes.

As opposed to this consultative model, another model has been emerging for some years now that may be termed the *participatory model.* In a number of instances, the term 'participation' is replacing the term 'consultation', with 'consultative' status becoming 'participatory' status. This is the case, for example, of the status of NGOs in the Council of Europe as a result of resolution (2003)8 of the Committee of Ministers.

The relationship between CSOs and states is no longer seen in instrumental terms but as a 'partnership' – and it has been seen that this is the term that is becoming more widespread to designate all of the interactions of IOs with multiple actors in line with Kofi Annan's proposals on the Global Compact and Millennium Development Goals.

In terms of the actual modes of participation, the characteristic of the participatory model is to recommend the introduction of decompartmentalised or inclusive instances for deliberation and/or discussion. CSOs and other stakeholders are no longer there just as observers but as participants.

organisation itself towards CSOs in development co-operation: Wood and Fällman, *Enabling Civil Society for Sustainable Development* (n 13).

CSOs may be integrated into a deliberative organ of the organisation. There are long-standing examples of this as with UNAIDS, which was considered a pioneering structure when first set up in 1996 because it included five NGO representatives, one per region (Asia/Pacific, Africa, Europe, Latin America/Caribbean, North America).[23]

A more recent example is the *Global Fund to Fight AIDS, Tuberculosis and Malaria*, which presents itself as a global public/private partnership for collecting and then allocating additional resources to prevent and treat HIV/AIDS, tuberculosis and malaria. The Fund is directed by a Board with representation by 'implementers and donors. Non-governmental organisations; communities affected by HIV, TB and malaria; the private sector; and private foundations'.[24] More specifically of the 20 voting seats on the Board (eight others are attributed to non-voting 'partners') 10 are allocated to implementer constituencies (as opposed to 'donors'), three of which are held by 'community' and 'civil society' representatives: one seat is attributed to nongovernmental organisations from 'the developed world' and one to NGOs 'from the developing world' and a third for 'communities living with or affected by the three diseases'.[25]

A variant on the participatory model is that in which CSOs are not integrated in the governance but are acknowledged to have a central role in the working of the regime or institution. A familiar example is the Ottawa Convention on the banning of anti-personnel landmines and the International Campaign to Ban Landmines, especially through the annual report of the Landmine Monitor, which plays a fundamental part in supervising application of the Mine Ban Treaty and more recently of the Convention on Cluster Munitions.[26]

[23] See www.unaids.org/en/aboutunaids/unaidsprogrammecoordinatingboard/ngocivilsociety participationinpcb.

[24] See www.theglobalfund.org/en/board/.

[25] The website presentation clarifies the distinction drawn between 'civil society' and 'communities', with the latter category referring to members of civil society who are 'particularly affected': '"Civil society" is the term the Global Fund uses to designate all those stakeholders who are neither government bodies nor private sector enterprises – groups such as international and national nongovernmental organizations, advocacy groups, faith-based organizations, networks of people living with the disease and so on.'; '"Communities" is used to refer to people who are connected to each other in varied and distinct ways, such as people who are particularly affected by a given health problem or people who share particular characteristics or vulnerabilities due to gender, identity, geography, behavior, ethnicity, religion, culture or age. Community groups are also part of broader civil society.'

[26] B Stern, 'La société civile internationale et la mise en œuvre du droit international: l'exemple de la Convention d'Ottawa sur l'élimination des mines antipersonnel' in H Gherari and S Szurek (eds), *L'émergence de la société civile internationale. Vers la privatisation du droit international?* (Paris, Pedone, 2003) 103–123, 117. See also *Disarmament Forum*, 1999, no 4, 'Framework for a Mine-free World', with contributions from D Atwood, 'Implementing Ottawa: Continuity and Change in the Role of NGOs' and S Goose and M Wareham, 'Landmine Monitor: Citizens' Verification in Action'. See also the International Campaign to Ban Landmines – Cluster Munition Coalition.

The difficulty with this 'new' participatory model is that it is not conceptually articulated. There is a development in practice but not in the conceptual framework, with the risks which that may entail of poorly controlling the development of such participation and ending up with unwanted results.[27] The very idea of 'partnerships', which is very often used to refer to those new forms of interaction between CSOs and IOs, is seldom warranted as such or, if it is, we very often come back to the same arguments that justify a consultative model, namely the idea that by having NGOs participate, IOs seek merely to further their own purposes.

But it can be felt that this search for a more efficient or more effective instrumentalisation of CSOs by IOs cannot be the only justification for the transition from a consultative to a participatory model. There is an unthought-of point that needs to be brought to light in order to set about looking for a more appropriate theoretical model to account for these practices.

II. An Unthought-of Point

When I speak of an unthought-of point, I am obviously not saying that today there are no scholarly works attempting to conceptualise the role of civil society in IOs. There are such works and they are even tending to multiply. But their multiplication does not really seem to affect the way states or IOs conceptualise the role of CSOs and other actors in the context of global public space.

This is because all too often states and IOs remain prisoners of a classical theory of international law that is no longer suitable for describing the phenomenon that is generally called the globalisation process and which I choose to call the process of cosmopolitan transition.[28]

I would like to return quickly to a specific aspect of this process, which I feel accounts for the phenomenon of CSO participation in IOs while explaining why the classical theory is unsuitable and prompts the search for one or more alternative theories.

Strategy 2017–2021: 'The Monitor has become the de facto monitoring regime of the Mine Ban Treaty and Convention on Cluster Munitions' (available at www.stopclustermunitions.org/media/2397469/Strategy-2017-2021-English-Final.pdf).

[27] See, eg, the nuanced record of CSO participation in works on amending the appendices to the Convention on the International Trade of Endangered Species (CITES): DWS Challender and DC MacMillan, 'Investigating the influence of non-State actors on amendments to the CITES Appendices' (2019) 22(2) *Journal of International Wildlife and Policy* 90–114.

[28] See in this volume ch 7, 'Towards a Democratic Theory of International Law'.

A. The Realities of Globalisation

The new role of CSOs cannot be taken into consideration without an understanding of the unprecedented development of IOs' activities.

This development results in explicit or implicit transfers of competence in an ever growing number of areas of social life that were previously the preserve of states. There is therefore a gradual loss of control by states over the development of norms and also over their implementation.

The problem of such transfers is that they raise the question of *participation* in the sense of the guarantee of the right to self-determination and, ultimately, of democracy – an argument that is very often bandied about nowadays including in populist discourse to *contest* the legitimacy of IOs.[29]

From the standpoint of CSOs themselves, the demand for access and participation in IOs' activities begins with the observation that IOs may have a very concrete impact and in three different ways: in the sense that they represent an alternative *public authority* to an often failing state, or sometimes even a *possible resort* against a persecuting state; in the sense that the norms they adopt and the programmes they implement have a growing impact on the day-to-day lives of populations; to the extent that some *global* issues demand intervention beyond the national framework and on a global level.

In other words, the movement for participation arises from a genuinely democratic concern: the challenge is for people who are affected by norms and programmes to be able to *contribute* to their design and implementation in order to satisfy what is the core of the democratic principle, namely the principle of self-legislation: each addressee of the norm must be able to see themselves at the same time as its author.[30]

B. The Difficulties of Classical Theory

The difficulty is that the classical theory of international law prohibits thinking about the institutional and legal developments that have arisen from this democratic concern.

[29] On the democratic deficits in international law and its challenges, see S Wheatley, *The Democratic Legitimacy of International Law* (Oxford, Hart Publishing, 2010).

[30] On the centrality of the principle of self-legislation in the modern conception of democracy, see Habermas, *Between Facts and Norms* (n 16) 33: 'For without religious or metaphysical support, the coercive law tailored for the self-interested use of individual rights can preserve its socially integrating force only insofar as the addressees of legal norms may at the same time understand themselves, taken as a whole, as the rational *authors* of those norms.' On the principle of autonomy in a theory of deliberative democracy, see also D Held, *Models of Democracy*, 3rd edn (Stanford, CA, Stanford University Press, 2006) esp ch 10.

First, classical theory of international law includes insuperable limits as to its theory of subjectivity: states alone are the original subjects of international law, and therefore other 'actors' can only be secondary subjects and not autonomous subjects – IOs themselves are not thought of as institutions of global governance but as organisations in the service of common purposes of the inter-state community. As for private persons, they are 'granted' rights and obligations solely from a functional and utilitarian perspective, with a view to serving these common purposes as defined by states – which explains why their utility and their status cannot be contemplated beyond a mere consultative function.

Secondly, classical theory also presents insuperable limits in terms of the classical constitutional theory which promotes the idea of a process of formation of norms that takes place within the framework of institutions whose legitimacy is based on their being representative. This argument is widely challenged in modern democracies: few people still assert that democracy lies essentially in the power of citizens to designate their representatives.

Transposed to the international level, this argument consists in viewing inter-state organs as the only possible forum for the formation of norms and in considering states or IOs as the agents of the implementation of international law, to the exclusion of other actors including civil society.

In the light of this argument it is easier to understand the reproach regularly levelled at CSOs that they cannot claim to accede to IOs for want of 'representativeness'. Their participation is seen only from the standpoint of this criterion of 'representativeness' which seems to be the only criterion of legitimacy for participating in IOs' activities. As states alone are considered 'representative', they alone can legitimately participate unless they themselves decide to provide access to individuals, but obviously in this case, the input from such actors will be secondary.

C. Another Approach Based on a Democratic Theory of International Law

The outcome is that we cannot go any further within the framework of a classical theory based on sovereignty. This theory has not much to tell us about the development of IOs in the context of the globalisation process or the cosmopolitan transition process.

In order to understand and conceptualise the intervention of CSOs in IOs, we need to resort to a different theoretical model that is able to take on board the reality of the development of the activity of IOs and the transnationalisation of democratic issues, that is, the search for the principle of self-legislation beyond borders.

Today article 25 of the International Covenant on Civil and Political Rights recognising the right to participate in public affairs cannot be limited to national borders.[31] 'Public affairs' are also decided and implemented by 'international'/non-national/supranational organs, which call for recognition of a right to participation in these mechanisms. The participation of CSOs and more widely the logic of opening up or of partnerships of IOs to other actors meets this requirement.

Understanding and conceptualising the intervention of CSOs therefore requires having a theory that makes it possible to understand the working of what is called a 'multi-level' system in which different actors at different levels are assigned different competences for the purpose of achieving common goals. To my mind such theoretical tools can be found in the theories of Federation.[32]

Understanding and conceptualising the intervention of CSOs also means having an alternative theory to the representative model that situates the place where the general will is formed in a clearly determined institution made up of 'representatives' of the community under consideration. Such tools are to be found in the theory of deliberative democracy as conceptualised notably by Jürgen Habermas.[33]

It should be recalled that from the perspective of deliberative theory, the development and implementation of a *global* law does not require the setting up of a new *Sovereign* on an international scale: global law is developed within a public discussion space on a global scale, organised around a number of institutions that allow ideas and contributions of various kinds to circulate and be freely discussed.

If we place ourselves in the context of deliberative theory, the old questions of 'legitimacy' of CSOs take on a new meaning. In a model based on Sovereignty, things were deadlocked, because it was plainly impossible

[31] cf General Comment no 25 of the Human Rights Committee on article 25 of the International Covenant on Civil and Political Rights (Participation in public affairs and right to vote), 56th session (1996), para 5 (emphasis added): 'The conduct of public affairs, referred to in paragraph (a), is a broad concept which relates to the exercise of political power, in particular the exercise of legislative, executive and administrative powers. It covers all aspects of public administration, and the formulation and implementation of policy at *international*, national, regional and local levels.' See also the Draft guidelines for States on the effective implementation of the right to participate in public affairs drawn up by the Office of the High Commissioner for Human Rights, A/HRC/39/28, 20 July 2018. And my comments on the process and the text in O de Frouville, 'Vers une démocratie continue à l'échelle globale? Nouvelles perspectives sur le droit de participer aux affaires publiques' in *Mélanges en l'honneur du professeur Dominique Rousseau. Constitution, justice, démocratie* (Paris, LGDJ, 2020) 395–407.

[32] I use the term 'Federation' here to refer to an autonomous political form as developed in a number of theories. On this genealogy and the issues surrounding it, see in this volume ch 3, 'A Cosmopolitan Perspective on the Responsibility to Protect'. More generally, on the idea of a federal multilevel system of governance at the global level, J Habermas, 'Does the constitutionalization of international law still have a chance?' in *The Divided West*, ed and tr C Cronon (Cambridge, Polity Press, 2006) 115–93.

[33] There is plentiful literature on deliberative democracy based on Habermas' ideas. See especially the collection of writings compiled by C Girard and A Le Goff, *La démocratie délibérative* (Paris, Hermann éditeurs, 2010).

to establish the legitimacy of actors other than the state, with the state alone being deemed both intrinsically legitimate (because sovereign) and potentially representative. In the context of the discussion model, legitimacy to participate in political processes is no longer based on political autonomy, nor necessarily on representativeness, or else on other forms of representativeness than those of the state.

The question is therefore no longer whether such groups should or should not participate in talks at international level alongside states. The question is instead *which actors* can legitimately claim to participate in *what types of activity* and in each instance *under what arrangements*.

It is important to answer this question precisely not just for theoretical reasons or in terms of abstract knowledge. It is of practical importance too. Without proper conceptualisation there shall be no proper regulation, no good practice and there may well even be poor practice that will be grist to the mill of those who continue to restrict public space to state representatives alone. We shall not manage to establish the institutions of effective global governance without an effective status for civil society.

At the present time, states are essentially reactive, with a reflex to defend their own patch based on an outdated theory of representativeness. This has the double consequences of deterioration of the status of civil society and of the quality of international institutions themselves.

The example of the consultative status with ECOSOC is instructive in this respect: this system is in its death throes today, the victim of the double strategy of entrism of GONGOs (*Governmental NGOs*) and of repression of NGOs making use of freedom of expression, which I described in a paper some years ago,[34] and that is now the subject of more sustained attention.[35]

The question of the status of civil society is therefore one of those cosmopolitan building sites we should set about as a matter of urgency!

[34] O de Frouville, 'Une société servile à l'ONU ?' (2006) 2 *Revue Générale de Droit International Public* 391–434; and in a revised English version O de Frouville, 'Domesticating Civil Society at the United Nations' in Dupuy and Vierucci (eds), *NGOs in International Law* (n 19) 71–115.

[35] See esp the report of the High Commissioner for Human Rights, *Procedures and practices in respect of civil society engagement with international and regional organizations*, A/HRC/38/18, 18 April 2018. See in particular the developments and recommendations on the works of the NGO Committee of the Economic and Social Committee. See also the Draft guidelines for States on the effective implementation of the right to participate in public affairs, cited above. See also the report by the Special Rapporteur on Rights to freedom of peaceful assembly and of association, Mr Maina Kiai, on the exercise of such freedoms in the context of multilateral organizations, A/69/365, 1 September 2014. The Special Rapporteur acknowledges (at para 86) that 'In today's globalized world, the meaning and practice of democracy stretches beyond national boundaries.' He recommends (at para 88) 'Reform[ing] the Committee on Non-Governmental Organizations to prevent Member States from blocking accreditation applications with perpetual questioning and to unilaterally vetoing applications'. See also the supervision by the International Service for Human Rights at www.ishr.ch/news/ecosoc-and-ngo-committee and the round-up in the report *The Backlash against Civil Society Access and Participation at the UN. Intimidation, Restrictions and Reprisals: 10 Case Studies* (Geneva, 2018).

9

Building a Universal System for the Protection of Human Rights: The Way Forward

'States have sought membership of the Commission not to strengthen human rights but to protect themselves against criticism or to criticize others.' Those words from Kofi Annan, then Secretary General of the United Nations spelled the end of the Commission on Human Rights.[1]

In his 2005 report 'In Larger Freedom: Development, Security and Respect for Human Rights', the Secretary General, while recognising that the Commission on Human Rights was a unique global forum for the discussion of human rights issues, expressed strong criticisms. Kofi Annan stressed that the Commission '[had] been increasingly undermined by its declining credibility and professionalism'. He then proposed the replacement of the Commission by a 'Human Rights Council' that would be 'a principal organ of the United Nations or a subsidiary body of the General Assembly' and whose members 'would be elected directly by the General Assembly by a two-thirds majority of members present and voting'. Annan moreover suggested that '[t]hose elected to the Council should undertake to abide by the highest human rights standards'.[2] This idea was taken up by some states and promoted by the then High Commissioner for Human Rights, Louise Arbour. The United Nations General Assembly, on the occasion of its September 2005 High-Level Plenary Meeting, proposed the creation of a new Human Rights Council. One vague and general section of the Outcome Document, which did not reflect the Secretary General's proposals stated:

> 157. Pursuant to our commitment to further strengthen the United Nations human rights machinery, we resolve to create a Human Rights Council.

[1] This chapter was originally published in 2011 and thus covers the first years of the functioning of the Council (2006–11). I have chosen not to try to update it in light of the subsequent practice of the Council – which would have meant writing a new article. Many developments have occurred and my evaluation of the institution has changed on some points – although the main thread and conclusions in the chapter remain valid.

[2] Doc A/59/2005, paras 182–183.

158. The Council will be responsible for promoting universal respect for the protection of all human rights and fundamental freedoms for all, without distinction of any kind and in a fair and equal manner.

159. The Council should address situations of violations of human rights, including gross and systematic violations, and make recommendations thereon. It should also promote effective coordination and the mainstreaming of human rights within the United Nations system.

160. We request the President of the General Assembly to conduct open, transparent and inclusive negotiations, to be completed as soon as possible during the sixtieth session, with the aim of establishing the mandate, modalities, functions, size, composition, membership, working methods and procedures of the Council.[3]

One must remember the prevailing atmosphere at that time. A conflictual consensus had emerged. For different reasons, sometimes for totally opposing reasons, nearly all states demanded the end of the Human Rights Commission (Commission). At the eve of the twenty-first century, there was a frenzy for reform. Unfortunately, there was no consensus on the kind of reform to be adopted: reforming the Security Council is still in debate today; and bringing other than strictly technical adjustments to the General Assembly or the Economic and Social Council seemed hopeless. The only body about which a consensus seemed possible was the Commission, because everyone agreed that it should disappear! The Commission was not *credible anymore*. It was wholly 'discredited'.

Once the deed was done, it was time to think about what should happen next. The expectations were clearly stated: the Commission had been too politicised, so the Human Rights Council (Council) would have to be non-politicised; the Commission had been an arena for political confrontation among states, so the Council would have to be an effective tool for human rights protection, responding to serious human rights violations in a spirit of impartiality and non-selectivity. The diplomats in New York and Geneva[4] would invent the new structure and somehow make it workable. Tribute should be paid to the diplomats, because they succeeded, in a short time and on a somewhat thin foundation, to build an institution that is indeed workable.

Five years after its creation, this chapter reviews the initial promises to see whether the expectations have been fulfilled. In this chapter, I explain why the creation of the Council did not bring a qualitative change to what existed

[3] Resolution 60/1, 16 September 2005, paras 157–160. Compare with the draft outcome document, dated 22 July, prepared by the Secretariat, paras 130–132.

[4] In New York, General Assembly Resolution 60/251 of 15 March 2006 established the Human Rights Council; while in Geneva, the Council itself, after difficult negotiations, adopted Resolution 5/1 of 18 June 2007 containing the 'Institution Building Package' – better known as the *IB Package* or *IBP* – which sets more precise rules on a certain number of topics.

before. While recognising that some improvements have been achieved, including those acknowledged in the recent reviews,[5] the major modifications sought by the Secretary General were not forthcoming (section I). This chapter explores the case of the emblematic innovation brought by the establishment of the Council, the *Universal Periodic Review* (UPR). This chapter argues that, in its present form, the UPR does not constitute a major innovation in the human rights system (section II); and then reflecting on the notion of 'progress' of the system, identifies the deficiencies of the Council that prevent it from achieving real progress (section III). Defending the idea that any reform should be based on sound theoretical basis, I will conclude by trying to make some constructive proposals on how the system should evolve in the future.

I. Change or Continuity: Has the Establishment of the Council Really Changed Anything in the Universal System of Human Rights Protection?

It was hoped that the Council would help to resolve the main problem that hampered the Commission's ability to effectively protect human rights: its politicisation. I will argue in this section that one characteristic of the recent evolution of this system is that there is generally no vision for its future (although this probably began to change with the review processes). One needs to say that actually the Commission has been in a constant process of reform since the late 1990s. The most important of these reforms – the so-called 'Selebi reform' (named after the South African ambassador of that time who chaired the Commission), had also been prompted by criticisms of the Commission's politicisation and selectivity.[6] At that time there was a broad division between those who wanted to limit the number and powers of special procedures, and those who, on the contrary, promoted the development of those procedures for the protection of human rights. A balance was reached at the end of the process. Some argued that 'les meubles ont été sauvés', but the 'reform' was not based on any specific concept of how to improve the organisation of the system or how to enable it to protect human rights more efficiently.

[5] There have been two reviews of the HRC, one in Geneva and the other in New York. The outcome of the 'Geneva Review' is included in the resolution of the Council 16/21 of 25 March 2011, adopted without a vote; the outcome of the 'New York Review' is found in General Assembly Resolution 65/281 of 17 June 2011, adopted with 154 votes in favour and 4 against (Canada, Israel, Palau, United States of America).

[6] See O de Frouville, 'Les organes subsidiaires de la Commission des droits de l'homme des Nations Unies. Rapport general' in E Decaux (ed), *Les Nations Unies et les droits de l'Homme: enjeux et défis d'une réforme* (Paris, Pedone, 2006) 171–99.

In 2005, the Secretary General submitted a concrete – although brief – proposal in order to reach that goal: the creation of a smaller body, composed of states whose human rights records would be undisputable.[7] Although supported by the US and some other states, the proposal was both unrealistic and unconvincing. Unrealistic because it was unbelievable to think that the great majority of the 193 member states of the UN would accept to see their cases considered by a small number of their peers, no matter how virtuous they could be. Unconvincing because the proposed solution did not attack the main cause of the identified problem as being the previous 'politicisation' of the system. In its essence, the proposal consisted in changing the size of the body, but not its nature: the new Human Rights Council would still be an intergovernmental body, just as the Commission. Since states are, in essence, politicised institutions, in the sense that their acts are mainly driven by their national interest, the truth is that, in a body composed of states, the public discussion on any topic, but strictly technical, can only be politicised. Even though human rights as such are part of the legal discipline, this topic is of course particularly sensitive to politicisation.

Nevertheless, this very thin proposal was sent as a working basis to diplomats in New York and Geneva, who did their best to make something out of it. The result is certainly totally different from what was initially expected, as confirmed by the practice of the Council in the first years of activity. The Council appeared to be a highly politicised and polarised body, focussing on certain country situations while ignoring others, failing to react to certain crisis, while over-reacting to others .... At the same time, the General Assembly Resolution 60/251[8] and the Council's Resolution 5/1[9] brought a certain number of novelties, some of which can be considered as improvements, others as drawbacks, and most of them having both positive and negative aspects.

This chapter does not discuss the details of this assessment[10] but selects a few striking examples for discussion (the UPR will be specifically discussed in the next section).

First, on the negative side, the creation of the Council meant the end of the *Sub Commission for the Promotion and Protection of Human Rights* and its replacement by the 'Advisory Committee'. The Sub Commission had virtually no one to defend it. Some states found that it was too pro-active and took too many (disturbing) initiatives; some others felt, on the contrary, that its

[7] See the Introduction above.

[8] 'Human Rights Council', 15 March 2006 (n 4).

[9] *IB Package* (n 4).

[10] For a detailed assessment with regards both to the 'acquis' of the Commission and to the innovations introduced through the Council, see the Opinion of the French National Commission for Human Rights (CNCDH), September 2010, on the Commission's website at www.cncdh.fr/.

members were not independent and that it was also too 'politicised', particularly when it insisted on the importance of economic, social and cultural rights, the rights of minorities or the protection of Indigenous Peoples.

Despite its shortcomings – which were real – the Sub Commission had also been a very creative think-tank, which not only initiated most of the standard-setting procedures that took place within the Commission, but also gave the impulse for the creation of a great number of special procedures, such as the Working Group on arbitrary detention, the Special Rapporteur on freedom of expression or the Special Rapporteur on adequate housing. Not to mention the work done by the Sub Commission on countries which, far from duplicating the work done by the Commission, complemented it in dealing with countries that, in a political body, were totally immune to criticisms or supervision.[11]

The Advisory Committee is deprived of what made the Sub Commission such a creative body: its unique one-month session in August, its capacity to initiate studies and appoint special rapporteurs or working groups, its power to vote resolutions on themes or countries .... No need to say more: for those who knew the days of the Sub Commission, it's enough to have a walk in Room XX of the Palais des Nations. The room is almost empty, states have almost deserted the place and, what is even more striking, very few NGOs are attending those meetings. The members of the Advisory Committee have, since the beginning, done their utmost to make their institution meaningful again, but the situation remains challenging. It is to be hoped that the Advisory Committee will, in the future, be able to gain more autonomy vis-à-vis its parent body – the Human Rights Council.

Secondly, other measures taken by creating the Council can be considered as improvements, at least if properly implemented. In this regard, the review processes conducted at the end of the first five years of activity of the Council helped to set the potential for this mechanism in motion. Among other positive elements, one can note:

(i) **The upgrading of the status of the Council**, which is now a subsidiary body of the UN General Assembly, as compared to the Commission which was a subsidiary organ of the Economic and Social Council, is on its face an improvement, as it places an institutional foundation below the concept put forward by the UN Secretary General of the indivisibility between Security, Development and Human Rights. However, even if we put aside the controversial fact that the closing down of the Commission without amending the UN Charter and its article 68 could be considered unconstitutional, still other problems resurfaced.

[11] See de Frouville, 'Les organes subsidiaires de la Commission des droits de l'homme des Nations Unies. Rapport general' (n 6).

Some of the problems were solved from the very beginning – such as the issue of participation of NGOs in the session of the Council[12] – whereas others are still pending, such as the mode of interaction between the Council, the UN General Assembly, and its third Committee. On this issue, the General Assembly Review process failed to reach a consensus and the present status quo was more or less preserved with some slight modifications, which bring little to the main issue: the dispute about whether the Council should report to the 3rd Committee or directly to the plenary will probably go on in the near future.[13] The funding problem is also still pending, essentially because some decisions of the Council having financial implications can only be approved once in the year by the UN General Assembly, following deliberations by the 5th Committee. However, as many decisions requiring funding are taken as the events unfold throughout the year, this creates insurmountable problems for the budget of the Office of the High Commissioner.[14]

(ii) **The principle of election of the members of the Council by a majority of the General Assembly's members and the practice of 'pledges' by states**[15] can also be considered as improvements. This raised great enthusiasm in the beginning among observers. However, it soon appeared to be quite ineffective, mainly for two reasons: first, the regional groups would in general present 'single already agreed candidates' to the elections (so-called 'clean slates'), thus leaving no space for competition between states on the basis of their pledges; secondly, the UN General Assembly or the Council did not set any mechanism to assess the effective implementation of the pledges. These two shortcomings were much discussed during the New York Review Process, although eventually no consensus could be reached on a way to enhance the election procedure. Despite the fact that we are very far from the initial idea of a Council made up of virtuous states, the practice in the General Assembly, under the influence of some states, has discouraged the candidacy of a number of states whose human rights records were particularly poor. But while this could be considered 'progress' for someone who knows the system well, the same view would certainly not be shared by an outside observer ('the general public'), who would still

[12] In Resolution 60/251, the General Assembly decided that 'the participation of and consultation with … non-governmental organizations, shall be based on arrangements, including Economic and Social Council resolution 1996/31 of 25 July 1996 and practices observed by the Commission on Human Rights, while ensuring the most effective contribution of these entities'.

[13] See operative para 6 of Resolution 65/281 (New York Review).

[14] See operative paras 8 and 9 of Resolution 65/281.

[15] That is the States' commitments to undertake certain reforms or to take certain measures to promote and to protect human rights during their term, if elected to the Council.

ask why other states whose records are not particularly brilliant, but who are more influential in world's politics, continue to have a seat on the Council.

(iii) **The initiation of special sessions has been facilitated.** Whereas special sessions of the Commission could only be initiated by a majority of states,[16] now only one third of the Council member states (at least 16) can agree to convene a special session ... with the result that, since 2006, 17 special sessions have been held, mostly on country situations (compared with the five special sessions held by the Commission during its entirety). This is certainly a major improvement, although the 11th special session on Sri Lanka in May 2009 has showed that the most difficult issue remains to find a consensus on an appropriate reaction to a situation of violations of human rights. Faced with the recent political unrest in certain countries, the Council took effective action on Ivory Coast, Libya and Syria. But it remained silent on Tunisia, Egypt and Bahrain (and is less proactive in the case of Yemen, not to speak about China) .... It is a fact that special sessions did not totally cure the 'selectivity syndrome'.[17]

(iv) **The selection process of Special procedures mandate holders has been totally reviewed, in order to make it more formal and transparent.** This is clearly an improvement if compared to the opaque procedure that prevailed under the Commission. The early practice, however, created quite a lot of discontent, with what seemed often to be arbitrary selections either by the 'Consultative Group' of ambassadors, or by the Chair, who would sometimes choose another candidate rather than the one recommended by the Group, without any apparent or rational justification. This is one of the issues streamlined by the Geneva Review process.[18] The last appointment report of the Consultative Group is a clear evidence of this qualitative step.[19]

(v) **The consolidation of the practice set by the Commission to hold 'interactive dialogues' with the Special procedures** is also a positive contribution of the reform process. Still the practice of

[16] See the ECOSOC Resolution 1990/48 of 25 May 1990, authorising the Commission to hold special sessions.

[17] See Human Rights Watch, *Curing the Selectivity Syndrome: the 2011 Review of the Human Rights Council* (24 June 2010).

[18] See the outcome of the review contained in Resolution 16/21 of the Council, para 22: from now on, each candidate shall submit an application for each specific mandate and is to be interviewed by the Consultative Group. The Group, on its side, shall 'consider, in a transparent manner, candidates having applied' whereas the President 'shall justify his/her decision if he/she decides not to follow the order of priority proposed by the Consultative group'.

[19] See the Letter of the Chair of the Human Rights Council transmitting the report of the Consultative Group relating to the Special Procedures mandate holders to be appointed at the 18th session of the Human Rights Council.

interactive dialogue by the Council has been so far disappointing, with the 'clustering' of several Special procedures which makes the debate very confusing and difficult to follow. Besides, time constraints result in the 'interactive dialogue' not being a real 'dialogue' and even less an 'interactive' dialogue: each mandate holder has only 10 minutes to present its report (plus two minutes for each addendum). Thereafter the states take the floor for hours, and then the 'other stakeholders' (NGOs and NHRIs). The process leaves only five minutes for each mandate holder to respond at the end of the statements!

Finally, one can identify some 'trends' that appeared in the last years of the Commission and which were strengthened in the first years of the Council.

A first trend is the challenge to the Special procedures' independence and impartiality. Statements by states against Special procedures mandate holders were already frequent in the late years of the Commission, but became almost general practice in the Council. This trend materialised in the adoption of the *Code of Conduct for Special Procedures Mandate Holders of the Human Rights Council*[20] and in the more recent proposal to set up a 'supervisory body' that would deal with state complaints of violations of the *Code* by special procedures mandate holders. This issue was seriously discussed during the Geneva Review process. The need for mandate holders to scrupulously respect the *Code of Conduct* was counterbalanced with the obligation of states to fully cooperate with the special procedures. This obligation – which, by the way, can be inferred from articles 55 and 56 of the UN Charter – was recalled in the *outcome document*,[21] a wording which appears to be one of the most important achievements of the Geneva Review process.

A second more worrying trend takes the form of progressive restrictions imposed on the NGOs' contributions to the Council. NGOs have always been the object of attacks during the Commission period, when they criticised the human rights situations prevailing in some countries. Furthermore, the phenomenon of 'GONGOs' (ie, 'Government Operated NGOs', NGOs aligning their positions with that of their national governments) has always been of some concern, as it contributed to discredit the whole NGOs community which the result that their speaking time is being reduced now.[22] The overall situation for NGOs in the Council instead of improving became even worse in certain aspects, so much that nowadays NGOs at times are simply

[20] Resolution 5/2 of the Human Rights Council, 18 June 2007.

[21] See Resolution 16/21, para 26: 'States are urged to cooperate with and assist special procedures by responding in a timely manner to requests for information and visits, and to study carefully the conclusions and recommendations addressed to them by the special procedures.'

[22] See O de Frouville 'Domesticating Civil Society in the United Nations' in P-M Dupuy and L Vierucci (eds), *NGOs in International Law. Efficiency in Flexibility?* (Cheltenham, Edward Elgar, 2008) 71–115.

left out of the negotiations, to what attests the last Geneva Review process.[23] The fact that the Council is now holding three sessions, in addition to the UPR working groups, and the special sessions, has been straining NGOs resources. At a time when even Geneva-based NGOs experience difficulties following the work of the Council, it is not difficult to presuppose that the situation has become much worse for national or small international NGOs. NGOs, which used to attend systematically the sessions of the Commission on human rights, have to use alternative means to monitor the activities of the Council. The Webcast has certainly been playing a significant role in this respect. So did those NGOs which specialised in informing about the activities of the UN in the field of Human rights, notably the already veteran *International Service*, but also some others, whose creation was prompted by the setting up of the Council. Nonetheless, the modalities of participation of NGOs remain unsatisfactory, compared to the recent practice of other institutions. Resolution 96/31 of the ECOSOC (which serves as a basis for NGOs participation in the work of the Council) seemed very advanced for its time,[24] but is now mostly outdated and needs reviewing.[25]

II. Is the UPR a Real Added Value to the System?

The UPR needs special attention, as it appears to be the 'flagship' of the Council, its most visible innovation. The 'Human Right Council' concept was initially quite empty as we have seen (except the Secretary General proposal described above related to the composition of the Council), but the idea of setting up a 'peer review' helped to give it more substance. It was also, apparently, a correct answer to the critics of 'politicisation', as the UPR would impose some kind of supervision of human rights situation in all states of the United Nations, on an equal footing. It's a fact that the UPR formally gives no room for selectivity, as the review program is systematic and does not reflect the concerns of particular states or groups of states at a certain moment. This systematic character can also create discontent or difficulties: what would happen, for instance, if a state goes through a serious crisis, with

[23] See the account by the International Service for Human Rights, (2011) 2 *Human Rights Monitor Quarterly* 8.

[24] See S Guillet, 'Les relations entre les ONG et l'ONU dans le domaine des droits de l'Homme: un partenariat en mutation', *L'Observateur des Nations Unies* (Winter 1999) no 7.

[25] In fact such a process was started in 2004 when the Secretary General decided to 'assemble a group of eminent persons representing a variety of perspectives and experiences to review past and current practices and recommend improvements for the future in order to make the interaction between civil society and the United Nations more meaningful'. (A/57/387, § 141.) The report was handed down to the Secretary General in June 2004 (A/58/817). The Secretary General responded to it in a report published in September 2004 (A/59/354). The reports were transmitted to the General Assembly for consideration. But no action was ever taken.

numerous human rights violations that prompt, for instance, the holding of a special session and the appointment of a special country mechanism? A recent example is Syria (the human rights situation in that country was reviewed at the 12th session, in October 2011, following two special sessions on Syria that had previously taken place).

The UPR was supposed to give an overview of the human rights situation in the world. It was also supposed to be a tool to trigger work towards the 'improvement of the human rights situation on the ground'[26] by subjecting all states to a continuing oversight of the measures taken. As fears were expressed that the UPR may somewhat duplicate existing mechanisms (in particular the treaty bodies and the special procedures), language was included in resolution 5/1 to ensure that the future procedure would 'complement rather than duplicate' other human rights mechanisms, thus offering an 'added value'.[27]

In fact, the UPR has failed to live up to expectations. Certainly, some may argue that a real assessment will only be possible at the end of the second cycle. That is partially true, since the Council will be following up on the recommendations made during the first cycle. However, it is possible at this stage to draw three preliminary conclusions.

(a) *The 'complementarity' and the 'added value' of the UPR is far from being proved.* There is no real complementarity because there is no real interaction between the UPR and the other mechanisms for the protection of human rights. For sure, one of the three reports used as a basis for the review is a 'compilation prepared by the Office of the High Commissioner for Human Rights of the information contained in the reports of treaty bodies, special procedures, including observations and comments by the state concerned'.[28] But this ten page document is not a real 'compilation' but a brief and sometimes selective summary of some observations and comments made by the independent experts' bodies. Additionally it is only one of the three reports used as a basis. Two others are the state's report, and the report compiling the documents submitted by 'other stakeholders', ie mainly NGOs and NHRIs. Furthermore, the reviewing states would only pick up, among those recommendations, a few that they consider to be consistent with their own purpose. Ultimately, the hard work of the treaty bodies and the special procedures is totally simplified, summarised, diluted.

But this is certainly not yet the worst that could have happened. The worst is that far from being complementary, the UPR is overshadowing the work of the treaty bodies and of the special procedures. It is

[26] See Resolution 5/1, Annex, para 4-a.
[27] See Resolution 5/1, Annex, para 3-f.
[28] See Resolution 5/1, Annex, para 15-b.

overshadowing it in the most immediate sense, through the media and the general public, who now tend to identify the UN human rights system with the UPR. As a result the UPR session of one country usually attracts much more media and general public attention than the review of the periodic report of that same country before a treaty body, for example the Human Rights Committee. This means that, for a given country, the UPR outcome documents adopted by the Council's 47 member states are more visible than the 'concluding observations' of a committee of independent experts. This is all the more unfortunate since, when one compares the two documents (ie, the UPR outcome document and Treaty Body Concluding observations), one is left at times with the impression that they do not address the same country situation. Pre-revolutionary Tunisia was a striking example, when the representatives of Mr Ben Ali's regime presented almost simultaneously their UPR report to the Human Rights Council and their periodic report before the Human Rights Committee. The comparison between the two documents coming out from those procedures speaks for itself, and it is shameful for the UPR ….[29] Whereas the Committee pointed out areas of concern and made recommendations in the most accurate manner, the immense majority of the states taking the floor during the UPR focused on praising this country for its great achievements in the field of human rights, including its 'pluralist' democracy, the freedom of the media and the interaction with civil society ….

This situation is all the more worrying since the working group's meetings have in some cases been below the required level because of the complacency of the statements made by some states. The procedure originally set to establish the list of speakers aggravated this phenomenon: the principle 'first come, first served' allowed the most 'friendly' states to register before the others, in an attempt to monopolise the speaking time.[30] Fortunately, this is one of those 'technical' issues that the Geneva review has fixed by imposing the passage of speakers in alphabetical order.[31] Retrospectively, watching the UPR of Libya is surrealistic (as well as reading the outcome document), with a series of statements congratulating the Jamahiriya for its progress in the field of human rights! Is it really the image that the United Nations wants to give of itself? Wouldn't it be better to webcast the meetings of the Human Rights Committee or of other committees, during which good questions

[29] Report of the UPR Working Group: A/HRC/8/21 and Corr 1 (2008) and Concluding observation of the Human Rights Committee on Tunisia, CCPR/C/TUN/CO/5.

[30] It must also be said that, on the contrary, it happened sometimes that the most 'unfriendly' would do their best to register first. See for instance the UPR of the US where Cuba took the floor as the first speaker during the working group and the plenary meetings.

[31] See the Appendix of the Outcome and Decision 17/119 of 17 June 2011, para 8.

are put to the government in relation to the real state of human rights in the country? To this regard, how can it be explained that all the Council's sessions and all the UPR working groups' session are 'webcasted', and not the sessions of the treaty bodies?

It is somehow ironic that, today, the treaty bodies and some special procedures are quoting 'accepted' recommendations by states during their UPR, in what seems to be an attempt to give some legitimacy to their own identical recommendations, which had been previously released, sometimes years before. Can someone call this circular type of cross-references, when different organs cite each other's recommendations 'complementarity'?

The UPR is also materially overshadowing the other mechanisms and I can testify, as a member of the Working Group on Enforced or Involuntary Disappearances, one of the Council's special procedures, that we have often waited for translations of important documents for months, because the translators were all busy translating the hundreds of documents needed for the UPR process.[32] It is not only the victims of human rights violation that are prejudiced by these delays, but also the states, whose answers to our questions and requests are not translated in time to be taken into account by us, and thus are sometimes not even included in our annual report. By the way, how can someone explain that mission reports by special procedures are not translated in all official languages of the UN? That follow-up reports and communications reports are not translated either? If the means put in the UPR process would have been applied to the special procedures (including staff members which are always scarce), this would have certainly given much more strength to those procedures. There is, here, a cost/benefit test to implement, to see whether the funds used for the UPR would not be used with more benefit to human rights if diverted to other activities.

(b) *The global efficiency of the mechanism is wholly dependent upon the good will of the state under review.* In that sense the UPR is not as equalitarian as it pretends to be. States who want to take it seriously will be very much involved in the process and will certainly profit from it. That is certainly the case for those who held prior consultations with civil society in preparation of the report at the domestic level, and who would

[32] In 1947, the Commission of Human Rights decided not to respond to human rights complaints that were addressed to it. The Secretary General of the UN was only tasked to transmit those complaints to the members of the Commission once in a year, but no action would ever be taken. John Humphrey, who happened to be the first 'Director of Human Rights' in the UN and one of the inspirers of the UDHR 'characterized the restrictive procedure as "probably the most elaborate wastepaper basket ever invented"', quoted in H Tolley Jr, *The UN Commission on Human Rights*, Westview Special Studies in International Relations (Boulder, CO, Westview Press, 1987) 18. One can wonder whether the UPR has not broken the record set by this previous procedure.

thereafter set up a domestic inclusive process oriented to the implementation of the recommendations. This is also true of those who would present a mid-term assessment on the implementation to the General Assembly, and, hopefully, take some positive steps in conformity with the recommendations. But on the contrary, it is very doubtful that the UPR can be of any use in the case of those who are not really willing to participate and who only will be striving to escape criticism as much as they can. One aspect that seems crucial, in particular, is how the state will interact with its domestic civil society during the process. The participation of national civil society is key to getting positive results. But this will never happen in states where the only kind of relationship existing between the government and the civil society is that of repression or denial.

In the state's point of view, it may seem a bit paradoxical that the states who take it the most seriously and who are the most honest are also those who may carry the heaviest burden in terms of obligations and who may get the most criticism in the end. Debating with civil society, committing itself to implement recommendations at the national level, setting up some specific mechanisms to this regard is costly. On the other hand the dishonest state whose firm intention from the very beginning is only to 'look as if' might get a bit stressed before the working group's debate, but will shortly be reassured when all its 'friends' take the floor to congratulate it on its achievements (expecting they will get the same treatment in return). Those states are fundamentally unequal: the honest state is punished while the dishonest state is rewarded. This cannot happen before the treaty bodies or the special procedure. On the contrary, the non-cooperative state will be clearly singled out and 'punished', for instance by having its periodic report reviewed in its absence. It is the same price for all. Thus, whereas the UPR is formally 'non selective' and equalitarian in nature, it in fact treats some states 'more equally than others'.

(c) *The third remark concerns the nature of the process.* It is a 'political' process, in the sense that, as the *Institution Building Package* (resolution 5/1 of the Council) puts it, it is 'an intergovernmental process, United Nations Member-driven' (para 3-d). There is nothing bad in this: again, the UN is an intergovernmental organisation and, as such, aside from the Secretariat, is composed of political organs, and it is quite logical that political debates are held in those political organs. However, human rights are legal norms and the UPR, according to the IBP, also aims at '[t]he fulfilment of the State's human rights obligations and commitments' (para 4-b). Furthermore the 'basis' of the review are:

(a) The Charter of the United Nations;
(b) The Universal Declaration of Human Rights;

(c) Human rights instruments to which a State is party;
(d) Voluntary pledges and commitments made by States, including those undertaken when presenting their candidatures for election to the Human Rights Council (hereinafter 'the Council').

It is obviously very difficult for a political entity to address legal norms, as the interpretation it will give of those norms will always be oriented by extra-legal considerations and in particular, as far as states are concerned, by their national interest. This can be seen clearly in the practice of the UPR. One concern which has been often raised, even by some states, is that the 'recommendations' made by individual states may be infra standard, ie it would impose a lesser degree of duty than what the legal obligation requires. This is all the more worrying since states, according to the UPR rules, can either 'accept' or 'reject' recommendations, with the risk that some recommendations, in fact corresponding to a legal obligation of the state, would be rejected. It is not only here that the UPR would not be 'complementary' to the treaty bodies of the special procedure: in these cases, the UPR would really undermine the work of these mechanisms in allowing the state to reject obligations which are binding on it.

It is all the same clear that it is almost impossible for an intergovernmental body to formulate a genuine legal assessment of a situation, devoid of any political resonance. Besides, in general, those types of bodies would be reluctant to express such an assessment. The IBP provides that the outcome document of the review must contain '[a]n assessment undertaken in an objective and transparent manner of the human rights situation in the country under review, including positive developments and the challenges faced by the country'. But this has never happened. The result of this is that the legal dimension of the process gets totally lost in the middle, with the effect that state's obligations are in fact diluted and weakened by the UPR process. States can now play the UPR against the treaty bodies and the special procedure. And they can do that all the more now that, as we have said above, the public's attention is focussed on the UPR and not on the work of the independent experts.

After this short review, it appears clear that the Council has not lived up to its promises. The Council is a politicised body, just as the Commission was. A certain number of improvements have been achieved, but the creation of the Council has not really changed the human rights protection system. The nature of the system is still fundamentally the same.

This chapter will now identify the reasons why there has been no real progress in creating the Council. The final section will give some insights on how the system for the protection of human rights could evolve in the future.

III. Why the Council does not Represent a Real Progress for the Universal Human Rights Protection System

The notion of 'progress' might seem to be mostly subjective. It is difficult to speak of progress when applied to certain matters, like art, for instance. But when applied to other objects, like tools or technologies, progress has a clearer meaning. Of course, one may say that each 'progress' has its positive and its negative sides. For instance, the discovery of nuclear fission certainly represented progress for science, but among other applications, some of them 'positive', it also led to the invention of the nuclear bomb.

But still progress is something objective (apart from any value judgement) when, in relation to a certain univocal purpose, the method used to reach this purpose has improved in terms of efficiency.[33] For instance, if the purpose is to travel as fast as possible from point A to point B, high speed trains are clearly a 'progress' in comparison to steam trains. This kind of notion of 'progress' can be applied to procedures: as procedures are a set of rules oriented towards the realisation of certain purposes, a procedure can be said to have made progress when it is more efficient in realising its own purpose, at least when this purpose is clearly identified and univocal.[34] Progress is of course a function of certain external parameters (like the political situation prevailing at a certain time that favours the realisation of the said goal), but it is also a function of internal parameters, like the composition of the organs of the procedure and how the relationship between those organs is organised. Since Montesquieu, we know for instance that the balance of powers between the different organs of the state is a key element in constitutional engineering. The same kind of principles holds true for other types of institutions and procedures.

The purposes of the Human Rights Council are stated in General Assembly resolution 60/251, paragraph 5:

(a) Promote human rights education and learning as well as advisory services, technical assistance and capacity-building, to be provided in consultation with and with the consent of Member States concerned;
(b) Serve as a forum for dialogue on thematic issues on all human rights;

[33] See the discussion of notion of progress by R Aron, *Dix-huit leçons sur la société industrielle* (Paris, Idées Nrf-Gallimard, 1962) 82.

[34] The notion cannot be applied in relation to procedures that would have a plurality of purposes, some of them conflicting with the others. For instance, one can speak of 'progress' in relation to a procedure whose relation is the 'settlement of dispute' or the 'protection of the physical integrity of persons who are threatened in their lives and limbs'. But one would find it hard to speak of 'progress' for a procedure which purpose would be both to 'make justice' and to bring peace, two purposes which are often found to be conflicting, even though they might coincide in some cases. Measuring 'progress' would then need to address both purposes separately. See Aron, *Dix-huit leçons* (n 33) about the plurality of purposes of the economic activity and thus, the difficulty of applying the concept of 'progress' to it.

(c) Make recommendations to the General Assembly for the further development of international law in the field of human rights;
(d) Promote the full implementation of human rights obligations undertaken by States and follow-up to the goals and commitments related to the promotion and protection of human rights emanating from United Nations conferences and summits;
(e) Undertake a universal periodic review, based on objective and reliable information, of the fulfilment by each State of its human rights obligations and commitments in a manner which ensures universality of coverage and equal treatment with respect to all States; the review shall be a cooperative mechanism, based on an interactive dialogue, with the full involvement of the country concerned and with consideration given to its capacity-building needs; such a mechanism shall complement and not duplicate the work of treaty bodies; the Council shall develop the modalities and necessary time allocation for the universal periodic review mechanism within one year after the holding of its first session;
(f) Contribute, through dialogue and cooperation, towards the prevention of human rights violations and respond promptly to human rights emergencies;
(g) Assume the role and responsibilities of the Commission on Human Rights relating to the work of the Office of the United Nations High Commissioner for Human Rights, as decided by the General Assembly in its resolution 48/141 of 20 December 1993;
(h) Work in close cooperation in the field of human rights with Governments, regional organisations, national human rights institutions and civil society;
(i) Make recommendations with regard to the promotion and protection of human rights;
(j) Submit an annual report to the General Assembly;'

I don't think that any of these multiple purposes are in conflict with each other. They all have the same global goal which might be summed up as the 'universal respect for, and observance of, human rights and fundamental freedoms for all without distinction as to race, sex, language, or religion', to take up the language of article 55-c of the UN Charter.

The main argument here is that the Council has not achieved real progress in comparison with the Commission, because its efficiency in reaching that purpose has not fundamentally improved. This is so because the system's structure remains essentially the same.

Schematically the system has four components: the 'states' component, the 'independent experts' component, the 'institutional' components (that is to say the UN as an 'integrated' organisation, represented by its Secretariat) and the 'civil society' component. The 'states' component is composed of individual states and of intergovernmental bodies: as we have seen above, states are mainly driven by their national interests and see human rights as vectors to defend their own interests (including when their own interest is closely linked to the defence of human rights, where then a situation of 'dédoublement fonctionnel' occurs[35]); their approach of human rights is thus mainly politicised – and not legal – and the debate they have on human rights has a political character and finds its conclusion in political compromises. The 'independent experts' component is composed of individuals and collective independent bodies, whose mandate is to give a legal interpretation of legal norms and to apply those norms to particular cases in a systematic and non-selective manner. In certain cases, those experts can also have a broader mandate of proposing new standards for states to approve. They can also have a more 'mediator'-like mandate in certain country situations, however always within the framework of the international legal order. Independent experts, as long as they are truly independent, do not serve any state's interest or even institutional interest (for instance the UN's interest as an integrated organisation). Of course that doesn't mean that the experts are not part of the political debate, this term being understood in a broad sense – discussions on public affairs, ie on how should people live together in a society. But their intervention in the political debate is normally restricted to the reassertion and implementation of the general constraints (among others, legal) within which political decisions can be taken.

The 'institutional' component is formed by the members of the Secretariat of the United Nations, who will always tend to represent the Organisation as a person, with its own interests and purposes. The Secretariat also has an obligation of 'neutrality' towards states that makes its work particularly difficult and sensitive. That is what fundamentally differentiates the work of the 'independent experts' from the work of the international bureaucracy: if both serve 'international' interests as displayed in international legal norms, the international bureaucracy cannot take sides without being suspected of failing to live up to its mandate. Whereas the independent experts are expected to take sides, as their role is precisely to remind states of their obligations and to denounce the violations.

Finally, the 'civil society component' is composed of individuals and organisations representing the diversity of the international society and of the domestic societies. Civil society organisations may represent a great range of interests, sometimes purely private but in some other cases of a

[35] 'Dédoublement fonctionnel' refers to the French publicist Georges Scelle's doctrine which showed that the 'inorganic' nature of the international legal order was compensated by states who would, in certain matters and circumstances, act as 'organs of the international society'. Of course, for that to happen, the national interest of the state and the 'international interest' of the international society have to coincide at a certain point. See also O de Frouville, 'La Cour pénale internationale: une humanité souveraine?', *Les Temps Modernes*, n° 610 La souveraineté, automne 2000, 257–88; O de Frouville, 'Le paradigme de la constitutionnalisation vu du droit international' in S Hennette-Vauchez (ed), *Les droits de l'Homme ont-ils 'constitutionnalisé le monde'? Retour sur la construction savante du droit européen des droits de l'homme, à l'occasion du 60ème anniversaire de la Convention européenne des droits de l'homme*, 5–6 mars 2010, Maison de l'Europe (Brussels, Bruylant, 2011), 193–216.

public nature.[36] More importantly, they produce a great diversity of point of views, interpretations and factual information on a number of subjects of public interests. Faced with the univocal discourse of the state, civil society discourse clearly represents a precious alternative, which is necessary to reach a reasoned assessment of a situation and thus, rational decisions.

Based on the foregoing, it is possible to identify two main deficiencies in the present system.

(a) **The first aspect concerns the status and participation of civil society**. As we have said above, the universal system for the protection of human rights has given some space to civil society to express itself and participate. Successively, resolution 1296 (XLIV) and resolution 96/31 of the ECOSOC on the 'consultative status' of NGOs have set up the legal framework under which accredited organisations of the civil society could come and actively participate the intergovernmental meetings held in Geneva. The relative 'liberal' atmosphere prevailing in Geneva as far as NGOs participation is concerned (if compared to the more restrictive attitude of states in New York) was a major factor of development for the human rights regime, both normative and institutional. NGOs participation gave the impulse for a number of new treaties and instruments, as well as most of the new protection mechanisms, from the Convention (and the Committee) against torture to the Convention (and the Committee) against enforced disappearances, from the 'Joinet' Principles on impunity to the Declaration (and the Special Rapporteur) for the protection of human rights defenders, among many other examples. In the middle of the 1990s, the ECOSOC-NGO consultation scheme was still one of the most evolved in all international organisations. However, this came to evolve very fast: as new and more 'participatory' models were developed in different regimes and organisations,[37] the participation of NGOs to the Council became more difficult. It sounds like an extraordinary paradox and at the same time is quite revealing that NGO participation was easier in the 'New-York Review Process' than in the Geneva Review Process, although the General Assembly has no special arrangements for the participation of NGOs.[38] This of course

[36] Here we understand 'civil society' as including both business organisations and non-profit organisations. For a more thorough study of the notion of 'civil society', see O de Frouville, 'La place de la société civile dans les organisations internationales: quelle stratégie pour la France au XXIème siècle?' in G Cahin, S Szurek and F Poirat (eds), *La France et les organisations internationales au XXIème siècle* (Paris, Pedone, 2012).

[37] See N Angelet et al, *Société civile et démocratisation des organisations* internationales (Ghent, Academia Press, 2005); L Boisson de Chazournes and R Mehdi (eds), *Une société internationale en mutation: quels acteurs pour une nouvelle gouvernance?* (Brussels, Bruylant, 2005).

[38] See the account by the International Service for Human Rights on this point in the *Human Rights Monitor Quarterly* (July 2011) 7.

does not affect the special arrangements made with expert bodies, which in general have evolved in a satisfactory way, even if this evolution is far from being homogenous, taking into account that each body sets its own rules on the matter.

If the purpose of NGO participation is also to enhance the efficiency of the UN machinery for the protection of human rights, progress would imply that the rules for NGOs participation in the Council should be drastically improved. This would mean at least suppressing the UN intergovernmental body deciding upon the NGOs' applications for consultative status to the UN – the 'NGO Committee' and replacing it with a more appropriate body of supervision. It would also imply the definition of new arrangements, promoting the participation of NGOs, rather than their 'consultation', and whereby NGOs could be considered not only as 'stakeholders' but as both counter powers and partners. *Counter powers* because NGOs bring the contradiction in the public debate of human rights and provide alternative views and information to those delivered by the states and the UN system; *partners* in the sense that the civil society is a key factor in the process of implementation of human rights and in the supervision of this implementation by international bodies.

(b) **The second aspect concerns the relationship between the 'states' component and the 'independent experts' component**. During the history of the UN human rights system, states have progressively set up – very often under the pressure of NGOs – a range of procedures and bodies composed of so-called 'independent experts'. Why have they done so? Why haven't they given those competences to interstate bodies? Because they thought that it was appropriate to trust independent experts and not states to fulfil such mandates: they decided themselves to 'de-politicise' part of the activity of the human rights system, with the clear understanding that this would produce more efficiency in terms of protection of human rights. At the same time, in this process of continuous creation, the issue of the relationship between those independent bodies and the intergovernmental organs was never reflected upon. This was probably caused partly by the empirical character of the process, and also partly by a wilful omission on the part of the states, who were not very keen to bind themselves to the decisions of experts. The result was the creation of what can be depicted as almost two separate and isolated systems: a 'states system' and an 'independent system'. The truth is that today the two components coexist side by side, but do not interact effectively, because the states component is not clearly coordinated with the independent component. The instances where this absence of coordination and interaction are the more obvious are the situations in which urgent action would be needed, because serious violations are either on the verge of occurring, or are already taking place. In these situations, the independent experts would 'ring the alert bell' in order to trigger preventive measures, or call to the political component to take measures of sanctions and intimidation against the faulting state. But in the present state of things, no specific mechanism is set for these signals to be taken into account and to trigger action on the part of the political body. There is no clear articulation between the two, no systematic inter-relation. Thus the two components, in a way, live a life on their own, independent from each other: the political component might or might not use the information and the signals brought to it by the independent component; conversely, the independent component is only erratically relayed by the state component in its recommendations and its pressures towards member states.

If a real change is to take place, it should tackle this specific problem by establishing systematic links between the two components, at all levels. For instance, the UPR, as we have seen, should not be seen as a quasi-autonomous process, almost totally disconnected from the conclusions and recommendations of the independent experts bodies. The UPR should be mainly conceived as an intergovernmental process aimed at supervising the implementation of recommendations and decisions made by those independent expert bodies. It is only by conceiving the peer review in close link with the independent component that it would be able to give some 'added value' to the system.

Similarly, the syndrome of selectivity can only be cured by setting automatic triggering mechanisms under which, for instance, the special procedures or the treaty bodies would be in a position to put on the agenda some situations according to specific criteria.[39] And this would be just the beginning of a necessary evolution ....

[39] See the specific proposal made by the French National Consultative Commission in its opinion:

> 'R35. Allow a set number of Special Procedures or the Coordination Committee called upon for this purpose by one or more members, or even a treaty body with majority rule, to put an issue or situation on the Council's agenda or, in emergency cases, to summon an extraordinary Council session.
> R36. On this basis, authorise the Council to hold a debate, either in an ordinary session or an extraordinary session summoned for this purpose. Following the debate, the Council would determine a procedural resolution that contains modalities of monitoring the situation based on the proposal issued by the mandate holders that initiated the referral or by the coordination committee or the members of the committee who issue the referral. The monitoring methods could in particular take the form of creating a special geographic mechanism, including regionally (special rapporteurs, special investigation commission, etc.) or a joint visit based on several thematic mandates.
> R37. Allow a set number of Special procedures or the Coordination Committee called upon for this purpose by one or more members, or even a treaty body with majority rule to make an emergency referral to the Council President so he may take appropriate measures and, in particular, take action against the State in question. More specifically, this procedure could be implemented when individuals cooperating with members are the victims of threats or reprisals.

IV. Towards Progress: How Could the System for the Protection of Human Rights Evolve in the Future?

It is a well-known fact to any international lawyer that states do not like to be bound by the decisions of 'independent' personalities. States want to preserve their 'sovereignty'. That is why they would like to keep the privilege of the interpretation of law. At the same time, law only comes to life in society, among a plurality of persons with diverging interests. The function of law is precisely to conciliate those diverging interests and to allow the subjects to exercise their freedom while respecting the freedom of others, whatever their strength and their general ability to impose their will. So even the 'sovereign' state knows that, in certain instances, where there is a conflict of interpretation, the best solution is to entrust a third party with the authority to give an interpretation of law that might have the chance to be accepted by all. Still, in the interstate relations, the state will remain cautious and would generally prefer to use its power or influence to impose its point of view, if it may, and, if it may not, use other sorts of 'non judicial' and non-binding procedures for the settlement of disputes, like mediation or conciliation. The case of the international law of human rights is, however, specific in many ways. Some specificities are shared with other fields of international law, like its transnational character. Like matters relating to the environment, issues of human rights often have consequences outside the borders of a state, when, for instance, it provokes a flow of refugees. Serious human rights violations generally affect the global peace and security and governments who persecute their own population are a threat to humanity as a whole. Another specificity of human rights is the triangular character of the relationship it establishes between subjects of law: turning human rights into an obligation of international law first creates an interstate obligation. Each state bound by the obligation has an obligation towards the other states bound by the same obligation to respect human rights. And conversely, each other state has a right to demand respect for those rights (this is generally what is known as the *erga omnes* character of the norm, either *erga omnes omnium* if the norm pertains to international customary law, or *erga omnes partes* if the norm is contained in an international treaty). Furthermore, the international law of human rights also creates an obligation of the state towards the persons who are under its jurisdiction. Correlatively, each individual depending on the

See also, in the context of the Review, the proposals made by Human Rights Watch in *Curing the Selectivity Syndrome* (n 17) and by Amnesty International in *Making it Work: the Reviews of the UN Human Rights Council* (2011). See also de Frouville, 'Les organes subsidiaires de la Commission des droits de l'homme des Nations Unies. Rapport général' (n 6); and the 1998 report of FIDH., co-authored with Sara Guillet in the context of the 'Selebi' reform process: *Strengthening the Mechanisms of the Commission on Human Rights: Towards a More Effective Protection of the Victims. A contribution to the Review of the Mechanisms of the Commission on Human Rights* (July 1998).

jurisdiction of the state has a right towards that state to see his/her rights respected, protected and fulfilled.

This specificity of the structure of human rights makes it practically more difficult to avoid third party settlements of disputes in case of a violation of human rights. Indeed, in both cases, it is very difficult to imagine how such a dispute could be settled efficiently by an interstate mechanism. There are schematically two possibilities: (a) the other state(s) have an interest in the case – because, for instance, the victim is one of their nationals, or because the orientation of their foreign policy makes it interesting for them to criticise the violating state, or even, more genuinely, to 'act in favour of human rights': in any case, the intervening state will be exploiting the case – or at least be perceived as exploiting the case for its own interests; or (b) the other state(s) have no interest in the case, and will not intervene at all, leaving the victim to face his/her persecutor alone. This specificity probably explains why the development of independent-third parties mechanisms went faster in this field of international law than in others. In fact, if we take some time to look backward into the history of human rights in the international sphere, what do we see? First, the development of a normative *corpus* of norms, that allowed the passage of human rights from the status of moral norms to the status of legal norms – thus being subject to 'objective' determination.[40] Secondly, the creation of a number of independent bodies, ranging from 'special rapporteurs' to international tribunals, at the regional or universal level, to assess, monitor and decide upon, in an 'objective' manner, whether states have implemented their obligations in the field of human rights.

One aspect of the progress of the international human rights regime can thus be clearly identified: it is realised when individuals and groups gain the capacity to refer their case to a body which has no state-like interest and which can make an objective determination of whether a legal right has been violated or not.

The way the regional systems for the protection of human rights evolved are, to this regard, significant. The three existing systems – European, American, African – progressively saw their centre of gravity displaced from the political bodies of the organisation, to the independent bodies that were progressively set up, and which competences were slowly diversified.

My argument is that the same should happen at the universal level. Not because there is some kind of predestination. But because it corresponds to the internal logic of such kinds of institutional regimes, taking into account

[40] This was a key to the development of a truly international order: as long as human rights were not part of positive international law, it could be easily used to serve the national interests of those states who would invoke it against other states. 'Humanity' appeared to be the pretext of intervention and imperialism. As Habermas has rightly shown, the fact that human rights have become legal norms is a first step against that trend, although it needs to be completed by effective procedures: see J Habermas, 'La paix perpétuelle. Le bicentenaire d'une idée kantienne' in J Habermas, *L'intégration républicaine* (Paris, Fayard, 1998) 161–204, 199.

its specific purpose and constraints. Of course, there are external factors that may affect this evolution, the more obvious being the state of international relations. September 11th took us ten years backward. It seems today (although one should remain *very cautious* when talking about the future, see below) that the 'Arab Spring' might impulse a leap forward ….

It is then probably high time to do again, as Jean Rivero proposed in 1950, 'l'apologie des faiseurs de systèmes'.[41]

The main sin of the 2006 reform is that it was led without any clear vision or plans. There was no concept and no sense of progress behind those words 'human rights council': only a slogan that was used to satisfy an urgent political need for reform at the eve of the 60th anniversary of the World Organization.

What should then the universal system of protection of tomorrow look like?

First, the empirical development of the treaty bodies has reached its limit. Furthermore, most of the 'core conventions' are now widely ratified and should be universally ratified in the coming decades. It is thus high time to think about and to work on how to give this coherent body of law a stronger institutional basis.

Secondly, the reform must preserve the various functions presently undertaken by the existing bodies, that is to say, among others: the review of periodic reports, in order to follow up on progress made and put a constant pressure on implementation; the review of individual complaints, in order to settle particular disputes; the provisory measures in the form of urgent actions, so as to preserve the life, physical or mental integrity of those who are threatened; the onsite visits for different purposes (global evaluation of the situation; monitoring of trials; visits of prisons); the follow-up on individual cases and general situations; the reviewing of specific issues, in particular 'new' or unexplored topics with a view to develop and codify international law.

Thirdly, it is necessary to find a new balance between the states component and the independent experts component, so that the states component can be used as means to implement the recommendations or decisions made by the independent experts.

Under those principles, there is no single scheme, and one scheme, however sophisticated, may not exactly become reality. Building a house can always cause some surprises and need some adjustments. This said, I would make an attempt, although it is not possible, given the limits assigned to this contribution, to get into many details at this stage. This might be the subject of another contribution.

The idea of *creating a World Court of Human Rights* immediately comes to mind. To this regard, the works of Manfred Nowak and Martin Scheinin

[41] J Rivero, 'Apologie pour les faiseurs de systèmes', *Dalloz*, 1951, Chronique, 99.

should be commended.[42] The Court would be based on an autonomous treaty, negotiated within the UN. It would be composed of permanent judges and would undertake the 'individual complaint' function presently devoted to some committees. States would have the choice to recognise its competence to do so and would in consequence withdraw the acceptation of the competence of the corresponding committee. It would of course be attributed the competence to issue provisional measures in relation to the cases which are transmitted to it. It would have its own secretariat (a Registry).

But, as a judicial body, the World Court would not be the appropriate organ to undertake monitoring functions, such as the review of periodic reports, the onsite visits (except if needed for the establishment of facts in a particular case, of course) and continuous dialogue, follow-up of general issues, or development of international law. To undertake such functions, a *World Commission of Human Rights* should be created as a subsidiary body of the General Assembly. It should be composed of a certain number of independent experts. This Commission would act as a collective body, with its own opinions and decision, but the commissioners may also be appointed for special mandates, as appropriate, country or thematic oriented, to fulfil the role which is generally attributed to special procedures.

In front of these two independent bodies, the Council would keep its general competences and attributions, but generally reoriented towards the implementation of the recommendations and decisions taken by the Court and the Commission. The UPR would thus become a peer review mechanism that would greatly enhance the effectivity of those recommendations and decisions. Similarly, in case of urgent matters, the Council would be called to use its political influence either to ensure the security of a threatened individual, or to try to stop a government perpetrating serious human rights violations against its own people. The Council would also be at the interface between the independent bodies and the other political bodies of the UN. But again, triggering mechanisms based on specific criteria should be set up, so as to ensure that the Council would not be in a position to withhold information. On the contrary, the Human Rights Council should be expressly tasked with the mission to implement mainstreaming within the organisation, which means, for instance, more regular contacts and exchanges with the Security Council and the General Assembly.

This chapter concludes with responses to two possible objections that will certainly immediately come to the mind of the reader. The first one would be that this framework is deeply marked with the illusion that the work of the 'experts', that is to say of rational agents, can replace politics and political decisions in solving the problems of society. Of course, experts are no better

[42] See J Kozma, M Nowak and M Scheinin, *A World Court of Human Rights – Consolidated Statute and Commentary* (Vienna, Neuer Wissenschaftlicher Verlag, 2010).

human beings than statesmen and the proposal is certainly not that philosophers become kings, to take up Plato's utopia. Politics is the art of making humans live together in the same society. The temptation to replace politics by pure rationality is of course not only a utopia but also a dangerous idea, leading us straight to the 'brave new world'. This is not what it is about. In the field of human rights, the political discussion has been ongoing for almost 70 years and it led up to the adoption, by political actors, of a certain number of rules: the UDHR and all the human rights conventions are among those, as well as the UN Charter and its principles. Legal rules are made in order to keep the political activity within a certain framework. Doing politics can never be understood as an activity that would allow the rules to be violated. Rules can be changed, but once they are settled, they must be respected, taking into account the instances where those rules provide for their derogation. To this regard, it is not the role of experts to do politics in the place of the political players, but to remind those of the rules they have given themselves, and which are meant to serve as a framework for their political debates and decisions.

A second objection would be to say that this framework is 'utopian', ie that in a 'realistic' perspective it has no chance to be ever implemented. However, it is not realistic to pretend that one can predict the future. Many said during the Cold War that the Berlin Wall would never fall, and it fell. Some realists predicted that there would never be such thing as a 'permanent criminal court', and the International Criminal Court was created .... A 'utopia' is, at first, a model on the basis of which the existing institutions can be criticised; it is also a model to be followed when one tries to bring reforms, something that was cruelly missing in 2006. It can also mean an ideal which might be out of reach, but which should nevertheless be kept in mind when taking decisions. Caution is required before launching the 'realist' anathema, for the utopians of today might well become the realists of tomorrow.

10

Why Do We Need a United Nations Court of Human Rights?

Tribute must be paid to the organisers of this conference for their initiative in gathering so many eminent human rights specialists to discuss a few fundamental questions for the future. The first part of the colloquium focused on the central question of universality and on whether human rights are 'a regional concept'. It seems to me there are two possible answers to this question.

The first answer is a theoretical one; human rights *cannot* be a 'regional' concept because it there be a contradiction in terms. Human rights are the rights of all of the Earth's human inhabitants and not only the rights of some inhabitants of a particular region. Universality is therefore a postulate of their very concept.

The second answer is both *institutional* and *descriptive*. It begins with the observation of the *relative primacy* of regional systems over the universal system. *Primacy* not in the sense of any hierarchy of norms or systems as there are none in this domain; but primacy in terms of visibility and authority of institutions and in terms of influence over their case law. This is true above all of the European system. Its primacy is particularly clear, both quantitatively – with respect to the number of judgments entered annually – and qualitatively because the case law of the European Court of Human Rights – to speak of it alone among all the mechanisms of the Council of Europe and the EU – influences the interpretation of international (or European) human rights law, including beyond the borders of the Council of Europe's member countries. But without even stopping at the ECtHR, one fact should be observed, which is that the other two regional systems both have judicial organs too: the Inter-American Court of Human Rights for the Organization of American States and the African Court on Human and Peoples' Rights for the African Union.

By this measure it can legitimately be wondered whether the concept of human rights impresses itself on minds and national legal systems not just being a concept from some regional rather than universal source? And ultimately, almost counter-intuitively, do we not progressively come to a situation in which there is *more than one concept* of human rights, with each region producing its own, with potential normative divergences?

I believe it would be rushing into things to slide from this observation of fact to that speculative conclusion ....

The factual primacy spoken of is actually all relative as things stand. It is false to bluntly assert that regional systems are 'stronger' than the universal system; if only because the regional systems are disparate. It is true that the ECtHR has entered and continues to enter a large number of judgments and it registers more applications every year. But the other two regional systems fall short of that level of activity and experience. And with close to 3,000 cases registered and more than a thousand 'views' to its name since 1976,[1] the UN Human Rights Committee needs, in no way, to envy the African Court (some 50 finalised cases) or even the Inter-American Court (about 350 cases). One point that should, however, be observed in future is the development of the African Court's case law especially since it has recognised its jurisdiction, under article 7 of the Ouagadougou Protocol, to interpret 'any other relevant human rights instruments' ratified by the states that recognise its jurisdiction, including treaties concluded within the United Nations framework such as the two Covenants.[2] This extended jurisdiction is rather welcome provided that the Court remains mindful of the interpretations of the UN committees and that a two-way dialogue is engaged between the Court and the committees.[3]

When all is said and done, great caution must be shown before asserting the factual primacy of the regional system over the universal system, at the risk of lapsing into a sort of European-centred self-satisfaction. Even the argument that rests this primacy on the judiciarisation of regional systems is hardly convincing in itself: in no way can some form of equation be established between effectiveness, efficiency, the dynamic development of a system of protection of human rights, and the fact that a court figures among its mechanisms. First, it is not because a judgment is binding that the judgment is invariably complied with – which is increasingly being experienced even within the Council of Europe;[4] next, the *judicial function* may well be perfectly

[1] Figures based on a statistical survey available on the Human Rights Committee's website. In addition to these cases brought before the Committee, a further 1,000 cases are registered with the other committees with an active complaints procedure (CAT, CEDAW, CERD, CESCR, CPRD, CED, CRC).

[2] See L Burgorgue-Larsen and F-F Ntwari, 'Chronique de jurisprudence de la Cour africaine des droits de l'homme et des peuples (2015–2016)' (2018) 113 *RTDH* 140; F Ouguergouz, 'La jurisprudence de la Cour africaines des droits de l'homme et des peuples – un juste hommage à l'action normative de l'Organisation des Nations Unies' in *Réciprocité et universalité. Sources et régimes du droit international des droits de l'homme. Mélanges en l'honneur du Professeur Emmanuel Decaux* (Paris, Pedone, 2017) 859–72.

[3] cf below on the question of how regional courts and a universal court would hinge together.

[4] cf esp the 11th Annual Report of the Committee of Ministers, *Supervision of the executions of judgments and decisions of the European Court of Human Rights* (2017), particularly App 2 on 'pending cases'. And in academic works, see esp P-F Laval, 'Les limites constitutionnelles à l'exécution des arrêts de la Cour européenne des droits de l'homme à la lumière de la jurisprudence nationale comparée' (2017) 3 *RGDIP* 661–82; P Pinto de Alburquerque,

fulfilled by non-judicial organs – such as treaty committees;[5] and finally, this same judicial function, which consists in settling a legal dispute in an individual instance, is just one function among others in a process of application of the law. Here too the ECtHR has become aware of this by multiplying attempts to extend the reach of its judgments to reduce mass actions, due to more structural than strictly individual causes. It can be observed that some of these cases of non-execution of the ECtHR's judgments relate to these structural causes of violations which it is far more complex to remedy than a strictly personal prejudice.[6]

Readers therefore should be given a caveat before proceeding: the idea of a United Nations Court of Human Rights does not stem, for my own part, from what I consider a false idea, if it is reduced to itself, namely that the *judiciarisation* of a system of protection of rights would necessarily and almost mathematically improve its effectiveness. In other words, the proposal does not manifest adhesion to what I would readily characterise as the 'myth of judiciarisation'.

Likewise – and I shall have the opportunity to come back to this – it is not a matter of bringing about an institutional or legal revolution or even sweeping away what is in place to replace it by something 'new'. In this respect, the plan may be distinguished from that of an International Constitutional Court, once promoted by Tunisia and supported by a group of experts including my dear colleague and friend Professor Ben Achour.[7] It cannot be ruled out, though, that the two ideas ultimately work together.[8]

Quite the contrary. The proposal is part of an already old-established line of thought on the United Nations system of protection of human rights; besides, it fits fully into the existing institutional construction and does not claim to re-found it, or even to correct its shortcomings, but to perfect it.

I shall therefore recall the origins of the idea of a universal jurisdiction of human rights (section I) and the context in which the idea has been given

'Réflexions sur le renforcement de l'obligation d'exécution des arrêts de la Cour européenne des droits de l'homme' in S Touzé (ed), *La Cour européenne des droits de l'homme. Une confiance nécessaire pour une autorité renforcée* (Paris, Pedone, 2016) 217–26. Compare with the question of the enforcement of views of treaty committees: see S Touzé, 'L'exécution des constations des comités conventionnels des Nations Unies' (2017) 3 *RGDIP* 646–59.

[5] cf below section III(E) on the question of the comparative authority of judgments of judicial bodies and 'views' of treaty bodies.

[6] See the Report of the Committee of Ministers for 2017 (n 4) App 1B, Pending Cases, 62: 'In the overwhelming majority of these cases, individual redress has been provided, and cases remain pending mainly awaiting implementation of general measures, some of which are very complex, requiring considerable time.'

[7] cf L Callejon, 'Cour mondiale des droits de l'homme, cour constitutionnelle internationale. Analyse comparée de deux projets d'inspiration cosmopolitique' in O de Frouville (ed), *Le cosmopolitisme juridique* (Paris, Pedone, 2015) 329–51.

[8] See Y Ben Achour, 'Cour constitutionnelle international, droits de l'Homme et constitutionnalité internationale' in O de Frouville (ed), *Le système de protection des droits de l'homme des Nations Unies. Présent et avenir* (Paris, Pedone, 2018) 175–86.

fresh impetus with a view to 'reforming' the system (section II). Then I shall answer a few objections to the idea (section III) and finally offer some concrete suggestions as to how it might be realised (section IV).

I. The Origins of the Idea of a Universal Court of Human Rights

First, it should be recalled that the idea of a court or tribunal for human rights within the framework of the UN is not entirely new. It was part of the initial vision imagined by a few of the individuals and a few of the states that contributed to drafting the Universal Declaration of Human Rights.

Three major ideas were introduced during that period:

- The Convention on Genocide adopted the day before the UDHR, on 9 December 1948, provides for trying persons accused of genocide by an 'international criminal court'.[9] It is common knowledge that after many postponements, the initiative took off after the end of the East-West conflict, with the International Law Commission's project followed by Trinidad-and-Tobago's initiative that led to the 1998 Rome Conference.
- Uruguay proposed the creation in 1950–51 of a High Commissioner for Human Rights[10] in an initiative that largely concurred with Cassin's initial idea for a Human Rights Prosecutor. The idea was brought up again in 1967 and remained on the table almost without interruption.[11] Once again, it was not until the end of the East-West opposition that it came about after the 1993 Vienna Conference.
- Australia's draft resolution to the UN Human Rights Commission in February 1947 'for an international court of human rights' with jurisdiction 'to hear and determine all disputes concerning the rights of citizenship and enjoyment of human rights and fundamental freedoms provided for in the Declaration of Human Rights'.[12]

A somewhat simple (even simplistic) argument in support of the creation of a UN Court of Human Rights is to claim that the Court would be the missing part of the structure as initially envisioned.

[9] See S Rosenne, 'Antecedents of the Rome Statute of the International Criminal Court revisited' in S Rosenne, *Essays on International Law and Practices* (Leiden, Nijhoff, 2007) 391–422.

[10] See especially A Clapham, 'Creating the High Commissioner for Human Rights: The outside story' (1994) 5 *EJIL* 556–68; and A Clapham, 'The Office of the High Commissioner for Human Rights' in P Alston and F Mégret (eds), *The UN and Human Rights. A Critical Appraisal*, 2nd edn (Oxford, Oxford University Press, 2020) 667–707.

[11] See Doc E/CN.4/Sub.2/1982/26, 30 July 1982, *Summary of information regarding consideration by United Nations bodies of the question of the establishment of a post of United Nations High Commissioner for Human Rights. Note by the Secretary-General* (mentioned by Clapham in 'Creating the High Commissioner' (n 10)).

[12] Doc E/CN.4/15, 5 February 1947.

But a 'systemic' vision of the sort cannot alone be convincing. Besides, it is not the primary argument made by those who have given fresh impetus to the idea of a UN court or tribunal in recent times.

In point of fact, this new impetus is part of a highly specific context of the oft observed but invariably postponed necessity to reform the UN system of human rights protection and in particular of the treaty organs.

II. The Present Context Justifying the New Impetus Behind the Idea: The Necessary Reform of the Universal System of Protection of Human Rights

The new impetus behind the idea of a universal Court has arisen primarily from an institutional concern. So for Manfred Nowak, one of the authors of the 'World Court of Human Rights' draft statute (to which I shall return), it is time to go beyond the system of 'committees' as quasi-judicial organs and to create an organ with 'the power to decide in a final and binding manner'.[13] Nowak is not wrong in characterising the UN treaty bodies as a Cold War inheritance. It is because states were unable to agree on the Australian proposal for a judicial system that what might be called 'the committee concept'[14] was created – namely supervisory bodies exercising supervision by way of reports but also a judicial function.

It is from this original 'concept' that a highly original 'treaty system'[15] developed, the merits of which no longer need to be proved.[16] The 'committees' have played a fundamental part over these past 40 years not just in terms of the progressive development of universal human rights law but also in terms of promotion and protection. Yet it must also be recollected that the system of treaty organs is diagnosed as having been 'in crisis' for at least 30 years and the theme of its reform is equally as old.

[13] cf the Preface to the book containing the Statute of the Court, J Kozma, M Nowak and M Scheinin, *A World Court of Human Rights – Consolidated Statute and Commentary* (Vienna, Neuer Wissenschaftlicher Verlag, 2010) 4: 'It is not only feasible, but it would be extremely useful and high time for States to seriously discuss the question of establishing a World Court of Human Rights instead of further pursuing the endless discussion on treaty body reform.' For a presentation of the draft, see esp M Mubiala, 'Vers la création d'une Cour mondiale des droits de l'Homme ?' (2013) 96 *RTDH* 797–810.

[14] cf O de Frouville, 'Introduction de la quatrième partie' in E Decaux (ed), *Le Pacte international sur les droits civils et politiques. Commentaire article par article* (Paris, Economica, 2011) 627–30.

[15] cf esp, E Decaux and O de Frouville (eds), *La dynamique du système des traités de l'ONU en matière de droits de l'homme* (Paris, Pedone, 2015); de Frouville (ed), *Le système de protection des droit de l'homme des Nations Unies* (n 8).

[16] See, eg, Sir Nigel Rodley, 'Reflections on the Human Rights Committee at 40' in *Mélanges en l'honneur du Professeur Emmanuel Decaux* (n 2) 1039–52; P Mutzenberg, *Agir pour la mise en œuvre des droits civils et politiques. L'apport du Comité des droits de l'homme* (Paris, L'Harmattan, 2014); B Delzangle and M Möschel, 'Le Comité pour l'élimination des discriminations à l'égard

A first cycle of reflection occurred as part of the General Assembly mandate conferred on Philip Alston between 1988 and 1996 and under which the independent expert filed three reports, the last of which set out a number of avenues for enquiry. Back in his final report in 1997, Philip Alston thought that the system as it then stood was not viable.[17] Ever since, that observation has been recalled incessantly in the various processes initiated with the objective of 'strengthening' the system precisely so as to make it viable. Further to reflections conducted by Kofi Annan following the Millennium Declaration, the Secretary General proposed a 'single report' without securing the approval of either states or the treaty bodies themselves.[18] In 2006 Louise Arbour acknowledged that despite its accomplishments, the system was experiencing 'serious challenges' and notably that states very often failed to submit the required reports, the disparities between procedures were detrimental to the system's coherence and resulted in a lack of clarity for the state parties and other actors. She recommended a number of measures including the progressive harmonisation of working methods while observing that such measures 'would not, however, address the underlying challenges to the system. Despite its achievements, the system is little known outside academic circles, Government departments and officials directly interacting with the system, and specialised lawyers and NGOs. … The number of complaints filed with the Secretariat is low in comparison to the number of individuals living under the jurisdiction of states that have accepted individual complaints procedures, and most complaints are directed toward a minority of states parties.'[19] Consequently, Louise Arbour proposed a unified standing treaty body.[20]

Lastly, Navi Pillay wrote in 2012 in her report published at the end of the 'Dublin process':

> The treaty body system is surviving because of the dedication of the experts, who are unpaid volunteers, the support of staff in OHCHR and States' non-compliance

des femmes: tente ans d'activités en faveur des femmes' in D Roman, *La Convention pour l'élimination de la discrimination à l'égard des femmes* (Paris, Pedone, 2014) 49–80; Ph Texier, 'Le Comité des droits économiques sociaux et culturels: vers une véritable indivisibilité des droits de l'homme' in D Roman (ed), *La justiciabilité des droits sociaux: vecteurs et résistance* (Paris, Pedone, 2012) 179–85; R Sodini, *Le Comité des droits économiques, sociaux et culturels* (Paris, Montchrestien, 2000); M Bidault, *Le Comité pour l'élimination de la discrimination raciale. Analyse d'une dynamique institutionnelle* (Paris, Montchrestien, 1997).

[17] *Final report on enhancing the long-term effectiveness of the United Nations human rights treaty system, by the independent expert, Mr. Philip Alston*, E/CN.4/1997/74, para 10.

[18] cf *Strengthening of the United Nations: an agenda for further change. Report of the Secretary General*, A/57/387, 9 September 2002, para 54. MF Ize-Charrin, 'L'avenir du système de surveillance des traités: comment faire pour que le travail des organes de traités soit significatif au niveau national ?' in E Decaux (ed), *Les Nations Unies et les droits de l'homme. Enjeux et défis d'une réforme* (Paris, Pedone, 2006) 297–303.

[19] *Concept paper on the High Commissioner's proposal for a unified standing treaty body. Report by the Secretariat*, HRI/MC/2006/2, para 21.

[20] ibid.

> with reporting obligations. However, at a time when human rights claims are increasing in all parts of the world, it is unacceptable that the system can only function because of non-compliance.[21]

Among other measures, the report recommended creating a single calendar for submitting reports and a common working group for treaty bodies for examining communications.

Ultimately, it is always the same challenges that have been raised for 30 years, and the situation only grows worse.[22] In particular, constant emphasis is placed on the challenges in terms of the system's *visibility* and *legibility* and so of its *accessibility* to the individuals concerned.

The *efficiency* of the mechanisms is also called into question, that is, the cost/benefit ratio of a system that involves no fewer than 172 independent experts, with substantial costs for their travel and accommodation in Geneva during ever longer sessions because of the constant increase in their workload.

Questions are also raised about *effectiveness* because of the supposedly low rate of enforcement of observations adopted under the individual communications procedure,[23] but also because of the insufficiency of monitoring mechanisms implemented by committees that are not, for some commentators, stringent enough to get states to bring their legislation and practices into line.[24] In short, the question is raised of the capacity of the treaty bodies to 'change things' on the ground.

Lastly, the debate often relates to the legal *authority* of the treaty bodies' decisions. After examination of an 'individual communication', the committees release their 'views' and not 'judgments' with binding force. This is probably the least convincing argument on the merits, as the distinction to be drawn between the end-product of a 'court' and of a 'committee', in terms of their judicial function, is more subtle than it might seem at first sight.[25]

In fact, the system is experiencing a growth paradox. It has developed on an empirical basis, by the small steps method, so as to thwart opposition from states and make the most of the 'windows of opportunity' that opened up on such and such a subject. But this approach has produced a stratification and accumulation of mechanisms that are now detrimental to the system as a whole.

[21] *United Nations reform: measures and proposals*, A/66/860, 9.

[22] See, eg, G Ulfstein, 'Do We Need a World Court of Human Rights?' in O Engdahl and P Wrange (eds), *Law at War. The Law as it Was and the Law as it Should Be. Liber Amicorum Ove Bring* (Leiden, Martinus Nijhoff Publishers, 2008) 261–72.

[23] Supposedly because there are not actually any official statistics. This appraisal rests therefore primarily on a perception.

[24] Here again, such an appraisal should be nuanced because the low level of monitoring and implementation relates primarily to shortcomings not of the committees themselves but of the bodies that would be in a position, through their presence or their action on the ground, to promote the treaty bodies' decisions and recommendations, in particular the local presence of the UN, the resident coordinator and national or regional bureaus of the Office of the High Commissioner for Human Rights.

[25] See on this point the discussion in section III(E) below.

David Held describes the phenomenon of gridlock in international organisations. In trying to provide a solution to global problems, norms and mechanisms have been put in place which are themselves at the origin of new difficulties to be solved – difficulties that Held refers to as 'second-order problems' that are a spanner in the works of international organisation and the cosmopolitical transition process.[26]

Now, it seems difficult to solve these ensuing problems solely by a 'small steps' method – the piecemeal approach – that made it possible to *construct* the system but that seems incapable of *reforming* it – like the famous technique of the poultice on a wooden leg.

Further to the proposals of the High Commissioner Navi Pillay, the General Assembly took things in hand again, at the initiative of a few states, and adopted resolution 68/268 on 'Strengthening and enhancing the effective functioning of the human rights treaty body system'.[27] The point is to take cosmetic measures so that the treaty bodies make up some of their backlog, whether unexamined reports or communications. The approach in resolution 68/268 proves to be typically piecemeal. It is designed to provisionally keep afloat a vessel that is taking in water from all quarters. The General Assembly has made a date to review the question in 2020. States[28] and experts of the actual committees[29] or of academic institutions[30] have made multiple proposals. Some actors advocate continuing with the piecemeal approach while other support more radical measures – which some think might strengthen the system and others think might weaken it irremediably.[31]

It is in this specific context that the idea of a Court of Human Rights should be re-examined as a project that might in some respects strengthen the existing system.[32] This proposal is part of a specific institutional context from which it cannot be separated. It must also be reviewed and criticised with respect to the way it is put in place, which shall be examined later. But

[26] T Hale, D Held and K Young, *Gridlock. Why Global Cooperation is Failing When We Need it Most* (Cambridge, Polity Press, 2013).

[27] cf I Salama, 'Présentation du processus de renforcement des organes conventionnels' in Decaux and de Frouville (eds), *La dynamique du système des traités de l'ONU* (n 15) 161–64.

[28] See, eg, E Whyte Gomez, 'The UN treaty system beyond 2020' in de Frouville (ed), *Le système de protection des droits de l'Homme des Nations Unies* (n 8) 73–78.

[29] See, eg, S Cleveland, 'Human rights treaty bodies in the age of connectivity' in de Frouville (ed), *Le système de protection des droits de l'Homme des Nations Unies* (n 8) 79–94.

[30] See the report of the Geneva Academy, D Zipoli, F Kirchmeier, K Kemileva and C Callejon, *Optimizing the UN Treaty Body System. Academic Platform Report of the 2020 Review*, Geneva, May 2018.

[31] cf on the process following adoption of Resolution 68/268, I Salama, 'Strengthening the UN human rights treaty body system: Prospects of a work in progress' in de Frouville (ed), *Le système de protection des droits de l'Homme des Nations Unies* (n 8) 95–111; and E Decaux, 'Pistes de réflexion et perspectives de travail pour 2020' in de Frouville (ed), *Le système de protection des droits de l'Homme des Nations Unies* (n 8) 113–31.

[32] See Ulfstein, 'Do we need a World Court of Human Rights?' (n 22) 271: 'The establishment of a World Court would overcome several of the weaknesses of the current supervisory

before that, we have to provide answers to a few objections on principle that are often raised *in limine*, before even addressing the matter.

III. Responses to Some Objections on Principle

The idea of a Court of Human Rights raises a number of objections as a matter of principle. This is before getting round to criticism of the details of any particular proposal, and especially the proposed statute of a 'World Court of Human Rights' that shall be examined below. What are these objections? The project is supposedly utopian; it allegedly goes against a number of considerations of *Realpolitik*; the Court will not mesh properly with the regional human rights courts and tribunals; it is a megalomaniacal project that will be too expensive and attract an uncontrollable avalanche of complaints; the Court will have to solve insurmountable problems of interpretation; and lastly the Court will make promises it cannot keep.

A. The Project is Utopian

A first objection is to say that creating a Court on a universal scale would be too great a 'leap' from the position we are in today and that the project is 'utopian'. But we are well short of any utopia. The plan is only to improve a system that has been around for some 40 years already! It should be recalled that eight out of nine committees now have an active complaints procedure. The legal revolution, the utopia, the leap into the void, have already been made … 70 years ago with the adoption of the Universal Declaration of Human Rights and then again 62 years ago when the UN Covenants were adopted! The people who drafted and adopted those documents truly did revolutionary work, in the midst of an age that was not really a simpler one than ours – and that is an understatement! We are merely treading modestly in their footsteps by trying to extend their vision. Let us not try to give this project more importance than it really has in the light of the history of international human rights law.

As the sadly missed Sir Nigel Rodley said at the 2016 Paris Human Rights Centre (CRDH) colloquium:

> What we must not do is let the idea drop, it is simply unnatural that there is not such a court, and there should be such a court, whether it would have direct cases from individuals or, like the European Court of Human Rights at first, and the

mechanisms, such as the lack of visibility, professionalism and independence of its members, procedural deficiencies, and – not least – the non-binding character of its decisions. Hence the Court may be expected to extend greater availability for petitioners, enjoy higher legitimacy and exert more influence in national legal systems.'

> Inter-American Court of Human Rights still, and the African Court, on the basis of reference from treaty bodies or commissions or whatever, that's another story. But a court should be there [...].[33]

B. The Project Falls Foul of Considerations of Realpolitik

In a way, this objection comes to support the previous one. It is based on considerations related to the current state of international relations, on the balance of power, power politics, or the analysis of the interests at stake. The supposed outcome is that the project for a court would have no chance of success. Two specific objections recur often under this heading: states supposedly do not wish for a new court; such a UN court would ultimately cover only Asian countries, since all the other regions already have a regional human rights court.

i. States do not Want a New Court

This objection purports to be a 'realist' interpretation and claims to establish a firm and final truth. Incontrovertibly at the time of writing most states do not support the idea of a United Nations Court of Human Rights. Some states might have expressed a degree of sympathy for the project at the turn of the 2000s, in particular further to the Swiss initiative that led to the draft statute of a 'World Court of Human Rights' (see below). But they were too few to support it and no concrete initiative was taken to include the question on the UN's agenda. It should besides be observed that the project did not mobilise civil society organisations as was the case for the Rome Statute of the ICC or for other conventions, especially with respect to disarmament or environmental protection. Moreover, the current period is not amenable to the spread of human rights when nationalists and populists are heading the polls worldwide.

Does that mean that project will never win any support? To make any such prediction would be a bold move indeed. Besides, the idea is conceptually obvious, or 'natural' as Sir Nigel Rodley put it. It is the 'logical' extension as it were of the change that has taken place so far; it also fits in, as observed from the outset, with the initial architecture envisioned by René Cassin and others. And the regional systems have developed in a similar way with initially the principal or exclusive jurisdiction of non-judicial mechanisms. Moreover, there is nothing to say that the plan for a court that is not popular today will not become all the craze tomorrow, whether with states or with civil society.

[33] Sir Nigel Rodley, 'The Idea of the World Court on Human Rights: Some Comments' in de Frouville (ed), *Le système de protection des droits de l'Homme des Nations Unies* (n 8) 201–03, 203.

If we set aside the cycles of politics – more specifically the US political cycles – there is an obvious reason for why the project has not been on the agenda so far. It is because other reform proposals or other 'utopian' ideas were under study, beginning with another court, the International Criminal Court, that mobilised civil society and a number of states from the early 1990s until the statute came into force in 2002. The phase of regression on human rights that has followed 9/11 has also witnessed a major reform, namely the replacement of the Human Rights Commission by the Human Rights Council.[34] This complex process has mobilised the energies of government and non-governmental experts in both Geneva and New York, which explains in part the lack of enthusiasm for Louise Arbour's proposal to set up a 'unified committee' instead of the existing committees, which was already the outline of an international court. And at the time of writing, we are still in this period since the report from the former High Commissioner Navi Pillay on the 'strengthening of treaties' (see above) was followed by resolution 68/268, which was – unconclusively – reviewed by the General Assembly in 2020.[35] There is nothing to prove that a new cycle has not opened and that the court will not appear in that context as not only a logical plan but an attractive one for justice ministries who will be able to make it the new objective of their 'foreign legal policy' on human rights.

Will the political climate enable an initiative of the kind to emerge? No one can say. And I have never shared the dark and romantic pessimism of the former High Commissioner for Human Rights Zeid Ra'ad al Hussein on this point: admittedly there has been a 'push-back', but over the long term the international system for human rights protection has never been as sound, in terms both of norms and institutions. It is now firmly 'rooted' in international reality and even the battering ram of populist assemblies will find it hard to break it down entirely.[36] Moreover, the environment has also completely changed nationally. Although it is true that the space that opened up for civil society with the end of East-West opposition is now tending to close again in many countries, the opening has left many lasting marks, again both in terms of norms (with the inclusion of international human rights law in many legal orders) and institutions (with, for example, the generalisation of the 'national

[34] See C Callejon, *La réforme de la Commission des droits de l'homme des Nations Unies. De la Commission au Conseil* (Paris, Pedone, 2008).

[35] See O de Frouville, 'The United Nations Treaty Bodies in a Transition Period – Progress Review March-December 2020 Chronicle', Working Paper, Geneva Academy/Paris Human Rights Center, June 2021 at www.geneva-academy.ch/geneva-humanrights-platform/ressources.

[36] cf my piece originally published in French in the newspaper *Le Temps*, 'Zeid Ra'ad al-Hussein est-il vraiment le 'prince des droits de l'homme'?' (21 August 2018) at www.letemps.ch/opinions/zeid-raad-alhussein-estil-vraiment-prince-droits-lhomme; 'Is Zeid Ra'ad Al Hussein really the "prince of Human Rights"', Universal Rights Group, 12 September 2018 at www.universal-rights.org/blog/is-zeid-raad-al-hussein-really-the-prince-of-human-rights/.

human rights institutions' model, which are now part of the Global Alliance of National Human Rights Institutions – GANHRI network).

As shall be seen, the court may have significant advantages in terms of cost, visibility and practicability including for states. It cannot be ruled out that, within a few years, states or at least a number of states will project that they need to get out of the rut. And if the ever-present 'sovereignists' object to it head on, should it be abandoned for all that? Has any ambitious reform ever been made with the say-so of those who want none of it? We cannot move ahead with our gaze focused on what is motionless. It is better to look to the future and without imagining that the future will necessarily be worse than the present. Nor can we wait until the sky is more clement to begin making plans: Did René Cassin wait for the end of World War II to think about the world after Nazism? Let us be worthy of our forebears and the legacy they bequeathed to us.

ii. The Court will Concern Asia Only

Another 'realist' objection is to say that the project for the court will be understood as a court 'for Asia'. There would be at least two consequences to this. First, Asian states will see it as an attempt by other states (especially Western ones) to impose a system of supervision on them with respect to human rights, particularly as they have shown, especially in the context of ASEAN, that they were reluctant to go beyond a form of political supervision;[37] secondly, non-Asian states will not be interested for themselves being already subject to the supervision – or potentially so – of a regional court or tribunal.[38]

This objection would be meaningful if the court project created something fundamentally new. But it should be emphasised that the project of a court does not come within an institutional vacuum, but on the contrary in the context of a debate about the reform of the treaty bodies. It is not a question therefore of building from scratch but of perfecting an existing system to supervise the obligations that already bind states. For states, the court will only replace the committees or supplement the committees in the exercise of the judicial function to which they have already consented. In this respect it should be noted, to keep to the Covenant on Civil and Political Rights, that out of the 46 states of the Asian Group in the UN, 16 have ratified the Optional Protocol to the Covenant and therefore accepted the Committee's judicial jurisdiction. For those 16 states at least, the transition from the committee to the court will be merely a matter of complete or partial transfer of jurisdiction.

[37] cf V Muntarbhorn, 'The ASEAN human rights declaration and beyond' in *Mélanges en l'honneur du Professeur Emmanuel Decaux* (n 2) 873–82.

[38] eg, S Trechsel, 'A World Court for Human Rights?' (2004) 1 *Northwestern Journal of International Human Rights* 3–21, para 15.

C. The Court will Fail to Mesh Properly with the Regional Courts and Tribunals

This objection takes on two dimensions: one procedural and one substantive.

i. In Procedural Terms

First is a procedural question as to how jurisdictions articulate together between the world court and the regional courts. Generally this type of problem is settled by a more or less restrictive *lis alibi pendens* clause. In this way, article 5(2) of the Optional Protocol to the International Covenant on Civil and Political Rights states that:

> The Committee shall not consider any communication from an individual unless it is ascertained that: (a) The same matter is not being examined under another procedure of international investigation or settlement.

It is known that some European states parties to the European Convention have somewhat hardened the condition through a reservation by which they exclude the Committee's jurisdiction to examine matters *having already been examined* under another procedure of international investigation or settlement. Even if in the case in point the Committee has adopted a restrictive interpretation of this reservation,[39] the fact is that clauses of the sort and the reservations that may be made to them may appear as a satisfactory way of articulating jurisdictions between different universal and regional bodies in procedural terms.

What is for sure is that it is an important issue. Not only must the court not appear to be duplicating regional systems but it must appear like a system that meshes with, and supplements, the regional dynamic. Integration of that kind can only encourage states to put equivalent guarantees in place regionally – namely a judicial system for those without one and possibly an extension of substantive jurisdiction of existing systems.

ii. In Substantive Terms

The objection also has a substantive or normative dimension. What would happen in the event of a contradiction in the interpretation of rights?[40] I believe that there is no ready-made solution on this matter and in any event

[39] cf E Decaux, 'La perspective internationale au regard des organes de traités sur les droits de l'homme des Nations Unies' in J Andriantsimbazovina and L Burgorgue-Larsen (eds), *La protection des droits de l'homme par les cours supranationales* (Paris, Pedone, 2016) 215–30, 221.

[40] Decaux recalls in this respect the individual opinion of justices Zupancic and Borrego Zincic in *Folgerö v Norway* in the ECtHR: *lis alibi pendens* is not only formal but also substantive inasmuch as it is meant to prevent two separate international bodies from providing different or even contradictory interpretations of the same question (ibid 223).

no systematic solution in the form, for example, of primacy of the interpretation of one court or tribunal over the interpretation of others. The systems shall maintain a degree of autonomy and it cannot be guaranteed that interpretations shall not be free from contradiction, with 'thin end of the wedge' and opportunity effects potentially leading on some subject or other to forum shopping by the claimants. This is no bad thing because a completely hierarchised system cannot be imagined – in which the International Court of Justice would act as a sort of world supreme court.[41] Yet, it can be wagered that there will be few such conflicts. The experience of expanding judicial control of the past 30 years demonstrates this in practice.[42] Competition between courts and tribunals and the much feared 'fragmentation' has not occurred, beginning with the question of human rights. 'Judicial diplomacy' and the 'dialogue of judges' have usually made it possible to overcome tension and divergence. Admittedly there are examples of conflict but they remain scarce. Practice shows more of a growing concern on the part of the different competent bodies – courts and committees – to mutually refer matters and to set about evolving interpretations by cross-fertilisation.[43] It is for all the judges and experts tasked with interpreting an instrument to do so resolutely and in a perspective of integration and observing the requirements of consistency and legal certainty. From this point of view, it should be recalled that the International Court of Justice has shown the way in its judgment on the merits in the case concerning *Ahmadou Sadio Diallo*.[44] To these considerations must be added another requirement that ties the bodies with jurisdiction to interpret human rights: this is the requirement of universality, which prohibits the development of a 'regional' interpretation of human rights. A reminder of these principles will probably be necessary, not just for the United Nations court but also for regional courts and in particular those, similar to the African Court, that find they have jurisdiction to interpret instruments other than their regional instrument of reference including universal instruments.

[41] See M Forteau, 'La Cour internationale de Justice et les systèmes régionaux. Plaidoyer pour le pluralisme désordonné' in S Touzé and E Dubout (eds), *Les droits fondamentaux: charnières entre ordres et systèmes juridiques* (Paris, Pedone, 2010) 39–64.

[42] cf the Lille colloquium of the SFDI, *La juridictionnalisation du droit international* (Paris, Pedone, 2003) and in particular the general conclusions of M Bedjaoui, 'La multiplication des tribunaux internationaux ou la bonne fortune du droit des gens', ibid 529.

[43] See esp H Tigroudja, 'Le renvoi aux décisions des comités conventionnels des Nations Unies dans la pratique des organes régionaux de protection des droits de l'homme' in Decaux and de Frouville (eds), *La dynamique du système des traités* (n 15) 137–49; Ouguergouz, 'La jurisprudence de la Cour africaine' (n 2); L Burgorgue-Larsen, 'Les cours européenne et interaméricaine des droits de l'homme et le "système onusien"' in Touzé and Dubout (eds), *Les droits fondamentaux* (n 41) 91–115.

[44] ICJ, *Case of Ahmadou Sadio Diallo (Republic of Guinea v Democratic Republic of the Congo)* (Merits) (Judgment) [2010] ICJ Rep, 639, para 66. See in particular Sir Nigel Rodley, 'La Cour internationale de Justice et les comités conventionnels des Nations Unies' in Decaux and de Frouville (eds), *La dynamique du système des traités* (n 15) 131–36.

D. *The Project is Megalomaniac with Too Many Complaints and Too Expensive*

Another commonly recurring objection is that the project for a United Nations court is supposedly inordinate or even megalomaniac in its way. A court whose jurisdiction would potentially extend to all United Nations member states would necessarily be submerged by complaints and soon be paralysed; besides it would necessarily be excessively costly with respect to the limits states would set for themselves.

i. Too Many Complaints?

First an observation should be made about the actual reasoning that rests on a concern, not to say fear, and takes up the famous 'thin end of the wedge' argument: 'if there is an opening, then we'll be submerged …'. This could be reformulated here as 'if a court or tribunal is set up, it will necessarily be overwhelmed with claims …'. I do not believe we shall get anywhere with such reasoning when it comes to human rights. Had our predecessors thought as much, they would not have created the instances and mechanisms that exist today. For sure, if a right is created, including a right of appeal, it is to be expected that people will take advantage of it! The fundamental purpose of the international regime for the protection of human rights is precisely to broaden the possibilities of availing oneself of rights. And I fail to see therefore in what the danger of increasing the number of complaints would be a valid argument against the creation of a new court or tribunal for that purpose.

This is all the more the case because the current system does not uphold the theory of submersion by the number of complaints. There are about 600 communications per year currently recorded for the eight complaint procedures now open by the United Nations in the context of treaties. Most – some two-thirds or so – of those 600 complaints are recorded under the Optional Protocol to the Covenant on Civil and Political Rights that counts 116 states parties.[45] In 2019, since the Protocol came into force, the Human Rights Committee had registered exactly 3,624 communications concerning 93 states, of which 920 were still pending.[46] It should be recalled that the European Court of Human Rights has delivered more than 22,500 judgments since it was established and that it handed down 884 judgments in 2019, 1,014 in 2018 and 1,068 in 2017![47]

[45] Figures updated in 2020 from the Secretary General's report on the *Status of the human rights treaty body system*, the third report submitted pursuant to General Assembly 68/268, doc A/74/643, 10 January 2020. See in particular Annexes VII and VIII of the report.

[46] *Report of the Human Rights Committee*, 123rd session (2–27 July 2018), 124th session (8 October–2 November 2018), 125th session (4–29 March 2019), A/74/40, 2019, para 25.

[47] See the Court's document *Statistics Overview 1959–2019* (February 2020).

Admittedly, a court is created in particular to heighten the visibility and authority of the United Nations complaints system and it can be expected that it will mechanically lead to the system being more attractive and so to a rise in the number of complaints. However, as things stand, there is no evidence that the court would be overwhelmed.

On a deeper level, the objection raises the broader problem of how the tiers of protection hinge together. It has already been seen that a rather strict system of *lis alibi pendens* would prevent duplication with regional courts and therefore already effect a distribution of tasks between the two levels – provided that the justices maintain a dialogue in substantive terms. As for the way national and international courts and tribunals fit together, the European experience progressively extends the complementary model by securing acceptance of the idea of working international standards into domestic law including through domestic courts being called upon to serve as common judges for international conventions. It is a model that ought to be developed and the efforts of the United Nations to elicit national mechanisms for reporting and follow-up are moving in this direction.[48]

Lastly, access to the future court may be restricted by a procedural mechanism comparable to that found in other regional systems, namely filtering by one or more non-judicial bodies. In this way, at the 2016 Paris Human Rights Center conference,[49] Emmanuel Decaux suggested a way to have the committees exist alongside a court by adopting a single optional protocol by which the committees could continue to rule on most matters brought before them, in the form of 'views', while referring the most important matters to the Court, especially when questions of principle or structural issues were raised requiring either a principled judgment or a 'pilot' judgment.

ii. Too Expensive?

Another standard argument against establishing a United Nations court is the financial argument that it would cost too much.[50] In this respect, comparisons are often made with the International Criminal Court. Yet, such comparisons are meaningless: the resources required by a permanent international criminal court – with everything it implies in terms of investigations and hearings – are obviously incommensurate with the resources used by a human rights court. By way of reminder, the 2018 budget of the ICC was €147 million;[51] the budget of the ECtHR – the most 'expensive' court in the area of human rights – was around €71 million according to an official document from its

[48] cf the High Commission for Human Rights, *National Mechanisms for Reporting and Follow-Up* (United Nations, Geneva, 2016).

[49] Decaux, 'Pistes de réflexion et perspectives de travail pour 2020' (n 31) 129–30.

[50] eg Trechsel, 'A World Court for Human Rights?' (n 38) para 17.

[51] See Resolution ICC-ASP/16/Res 1, adopted 14 December 2017.

registry. Need it be recalled besides that the ECtHR handed down more than 1,000 judgments in 2017. The ICC has processed 26 cases since it was set up in 2002. Comparisons can be misleading.

In fact, the UN human rights programme is terribly underfunded under the ordinary UN budget. It should be recalled in this respect that although it is presented as one of the three pillars of the UN (alongside peace and security and development), the human rights programme receives only 3.7 per cent of the ordinary budget from the United Nations, or the equivalent of about $100 million per annum (ie, about €86 million compared with the €147 million for the ICC). It is a position that is denounced each year by the High Commissioner for Human Rights, meaning the office has to count on voluntary contributions from states, some earmarked for the purpose, others not. For some years now, the Office of the High Commissioner has received some $130 million (€111.5 million) per year in voluntary contributions (€142.8 million in 2017),[52] which is more than what is received under the ordinary budget. From this total, about $15 million (some €13 million) are assigned to the treaty organs programme, a little over one-third of which (about $6 million) goes to financing the travel and *per diem* expenses of the 172 expert members of the committees for the Geneva sessions.

This figure of $15 million must be taken as a starting point, then, observing that it only covers part of the committees' judicial functions, which is only a small proportion of their activity if we set aside the Human Rights Committee, for which it can be estimated that it devotes roughly one-third of its time (the other two-thirds being taken up by examining states' reports and various other activities including drafting general observations).

This figure should be compared with the – admittedly insufficient – budgets of the two existing regional courts, the Inter-American Court with some $11 million ($5 million of which are from the ordinary budget)[53] and the African Court with some $10 million.[54]

In other words, it cannot be claimed that we are starting from scratch and that the proposal for the UN court would be a further net expense for the existing budget attributed to the judicial function ensured by the treaty bodies. The transfers of jurisdiction from the committees to the court would release at least some of the budget required for its operation. In the longer term, it can be imagined that a reform of the committee system, with for example the creation of a unified committee – as contemplated by Louise Arbour – might free up even more resources for the court.

[52] Figures from the annual reports of the High Commissioner for Human Rights.

[53] See the Court's annual report for 2017, ch VI, 890 at www.oas.org/en/iachr/mandate/financial_resources.asp.

[54] See the Court's activity reports and especially that for 2016, doc EX.CL.999(XXX), 16 at en.african-court.org/index.php/publications/activity-reports/994-executive-council-thirtieth-ordinary-session-22-27-january-2017-addis-ababa-ethiopia-report-on-the-activities-of-the-african-court-on-human-and-peoples-rights.

E. The Court will be Confronted with Insuperable Problems of Interpretation

For the adversaries of the idea of a universal court – and in particular of the draft statute for the 'World Court of Human Rights' – such a court or tribunal would run up against the impossibility of settling on a universal interpretation of human rights. Philip Alston considers that if international crimes are excepted, 'when it comes to a great many of the rights that are recognised in the 21 treaties included within the jurisdiction of the [World Court of Human Rights], the notion that there should be a single universally valid answer to complex questions involving competing rights, and that those answers should be uniformly and strictly enforced, both by domestic law enforcement agencies and by the Security Council, goes far beyond the assumptions that have been carefully built into the existing system'.[55]

Hélène Tigroudja levels the same type of objection against the draft for a 'World Court of Human Rights' that is examined below:

> How can a consensus be reached within a court made up of twenty-one judges the statute of which says they must be representative of the 'world's main legal systems' (draft article 23(4))?
>
> On this basis, will the World Court manage to find an answer to when life begins? Or to whether there is a right to die with dignity? How will it solve the question of the treatment of an illegal immigrant with a serious disease such as AIDS? Of an individual's refusal to undergo paternity testing, of surrogate motherhood, of a teacher refusing to remove her religious veil upon arriving at university for work?[56]

I have to say that I simply fail to understand this argument. Treaty bodies – and especially the Human Rights Committee since 1976 – are confronted with exactly this type of interpretative challenge, as are regional courts for that matter and there is not necessarily any more consensus regionally over 'hard cases' than there is universally. Evidence of this are the 'societal' issues raised before the Court such as surrogate motherhood, abortion or even the question of secularism. On abortion, for example, a sensitive issue if ever there was one, there is a broader consensus universally than regionally, at least if the Court's precedents are to be believed![57] Problems of interpretation are therefore just as present for regional courts as for the committees – such is the nature of 'hard cases' that raise questions that the texts fail to answer

[55] P Alston, 'Against a World Court for Human Rights' (2004) 28(2) *Ethics and International Affairs* 197–212.

[56] H Tigroudja, 'La création d'une Cour mondiale des droits de l'Homme est-elle *contra victima*? Libres propos introductifs' in de Frouville (ed), *Le système de protection des droits de l'homme des Nations Unies* (n 8) 163–74, 170.

[57] See especially F de Londras, 'Commentary. Fatal foetal abnormality, Irish constitutional law and Mellet v Ireland' (2016) 24 *Medical Law Review* 591–607.

directly and require the court or the expert to arbitrate between conflicting interests on a case by case basis.

In any event, such issues represent only a tiny part of the litigation brought before universal bodies, which is concentrated for 99 per cent on far more 'classical' issues: conditions of detention, access to the legal system, fair trials, restriction of free speech, gender-based discrimination, and so on. Accordingly, the objection focuses artificially on 'hard cases', or exceptional cases, in order to argue that the court would simply be unable to exercise jurisdiction at all.

Can a distinction be made between the committees and a court? This is what Alston seems to argue:

> It is one thing for a treaty body, such as the Human Rights Committee, to formulate essentially nonbinding 'views' or general recommendations that take adequate account of the particularities of legal systems from Afghanistan to Zimbabwe, or Austria to Uruguay. But it is quite another for a court to hand down a binding judgment on domestically controversial and contested issues to a large group of states with hugely diverse legal systems.

This assertion presupposes that the committees' views are not binding and so their interpretation may in a sense fail to take account of the specificities of the various countries the legal systems, where a court handing down binding judgments could not do. Such reasoning is wrong on (at least) three counts. First, beyond the hypothesis of 'hard cases', Alston seems to argue that there are issues that cannot be decided because they are controversial or contested within a particular society. Now that is a very dangerous claim! So, whenever an issue is controversial or contested in any given country, the international court of human rights would be unable to make a ruling? But what exactly is a 'controversial issue'? In some sense all questions and even all individual cases raised internationally are 'controversial'. It is precisely because they are controversial or contested that they end up before a committee or a court!

Next, it is legally inaccurate to make so sharp a distinction between the non-binding 'views' of the committees and the 'binding' judgments of courts insofar as although 'views' are not formally legally binding, they do have incontrovertible legal authority based both on the binding character of the treaty and on the states' recognition of the committee's jurisdiction to rule on individual cases and to legally characterise, after adversarial debate, a breach of the said obligations.

This is not the place to take up this discussion again in detail,[58] but it should be recalled that in its General Comment No. 33, the Human Rights

[58] cf especially Decaux, 'La perspective internationale au regard des organes de traités sur les droits de l'homme des Nations Unies' (n 39); Y Kerbrat, 'La portée des obligations issues des traités universels des droits de l'homme. Introduction' in Decaux and de Frouville (eds), *La dynamique du système des traités de l'ONU* (n 15) 115–20; WA Schabas, 'On the Binding Nature

Committee,[59] while recognising that its function was not in itself that of a 'judicial body' did emphasise that its views presented 'some important characteristics of a judicial decision. They are arrived at in a judicial spirit, including the impartiality and independence of Committee members, the considered interpretation of the language of the Covenant, and the determinative character of the decisions'. Thus '[t]he views of the Committee … represent an authoritative determination by the organ established under the Covenant itself charged with the interpretation of that instrument'. Furthermore, each state undertakes under article 2 paragraph 3 of the Covenant 'to provide an effective and enforceable remedy in case a violation has been established'.

On this basis, when the Committee observes a violation of the Covenant, it uses the following wording, which highlights the mandatory character of both the characterisation and the recommended remedy: 'The Committee, acting under article 5 paragraph 4 of the Optional Protocol to the Covenant, is of the view that the facts before it disclose a violation of [the relevant provisions] of the Covenant. In accordance with article 2 paragraph 3(a) of the Covenant, the state party is under an obligation to provide the author with an effective remedy.'

The International Court of Justice besides recognised in a 2010 judgment that the Committee had:

> built up a considerable body of interpretative case law, in particular through its findings in response to the individual communications which may be submitted to it in respect of States parties to the first Optional Protocol, and in the form of its 'General Comments'.
>
> Although the Court is in no way obliged, in the exercise of its judicial functions, to model its own interpretation of the Covenant on that of the Committee, it believes that it should ascribe great weight to the interpretation adopted by this independent body that was established specifically to supervise the application of that treaty. The point here is to achieve the necessary clarity and the essential consistency of international law, as well as legal security, to which both the individuals with guaranteed rights and the States obliged to comply with treaty obligations are entitled.[60]

Lastly, Alston's distinction seems to suggest that the universal character of human rights is necessarily out of reach, at least for any 'serious' court whose decisions would be binding, because of the diversity of legal systems. But an assertion of the kind goes against the very principles on which human rights are founded, namely that despite the diversity of legal systems, there

of the Findings of the Treaty Bodies' in C Bassiouni and WA Schabas (eds), *New Challenges for the UN Human Rights Machinery. What Future for the UN Treaty Body System and the Human Rights Council Procedures* (Cambridge, Intersentia, 2011).

[59] See Human Rights Committee General Comment no 33, 25 June 2009, CCPR/GC/33, paras 11–15.

[60] *Republic of Guinea v Democratic Republic of the Congo* (n 44) para 66.

are universal rights that belong to all human beings by virtue of their being human! Whether it is a court or a committee that enforces them changes nothing! Both act like everybody is tasked with a judicial function – that is, a function consisting in applying the law in a specific instance to 'subsume' the individual instance under the general rule, as Hegel's jargon would have it: they consider the particular circumstances of the specific instance, whether circumstances specific to the complainant or 'facts' in the particular sense (alleged facts) and in the general sense (the more general context in which the facts occurred). Internationally, judges may also use techniques that tend to have a principle of subsidiarity prevail, whether it is the 'national margin of appreciation' or the principle that it is for the national court to assess the facts and evidence and that on this point the international judge should confine himself to limited supervision. It is hard to see, given these different points, in what way the transfer of the litigation from committees to a court would change anything in the enforcement of human rights.

F. The Idea Makes Promises it Cannot Keep

A final objection is that the proposal of a universal court would convey hope for victims and that those hopes would necessarily be disappointed because the future court would not live up to expectations. My colleague and friend Hélène Tigroudja takes the example of the International Criminal Court, which, she says, 'promised justice and redress for the victims of the most serious crimes' and is today unable to keep that promise.[61]

I shall not discuss what to my mind is a hasty evaluation of the impact of the ICC on impunity, or even speculations as to the psychology of victims who turn to the court. It is a point on which I have no specific data and so does not seem amenable to any considered evaluation. More fundamentally, it should be emphasised that this objection cannot readily be understood if the effort is made to see things from the rationale of human rights and even, I would say, of contemporary international law. By this standard, it is the entire system of protection of human rights that should be abandoned and beyond that the UN Charter itself that could indeed provide the – inevitably misleading – illusion that one day 'international peace and security' might be achieved. If we extend this critical view, then the creation of the United Nations, which was an idea that was 'full of fine sentiment' has presumably created more victims than it has saved, more hopes that were 'necessarily' to be dashed, and so on.

[61] Tigroudja, 'La création d'une Cour mondiale des droits de l'Homme est-elle *contra victima*?' (n 56) 173.

A view of that kind falls to my mind under passive or negative nihilism as Nietzsche understood it: it is a condemnation here below in the name of an ideal that can only be attained in the hereafter, that is, in the City of God or in Plato's other world. The project is presented as an ideal and therefore unattainable except in another world, which amounts to judging as vain (or even 'dangerous', as the road to hell is paved with good intentions …) any expending of effort in this world to achieve it.

It is in this way that I understand the analogy with the ICC and the judgment made of the institution that supposedly 'betrayed the hopes of victims'. What should be inferred from such a judgment? There would seem to be only one logical consequence: that it would have been better not to create the ICC! In other words, since the realisation of the plan (what happens in reality) fails to live up to the ideal, then it does not deserve to exist in this world.

Yet, dashed hopes and disillusionment are the daily fare of everyone who works for the United Nations or for any organisation claiming to establish peace and uphold human rights in this world. What should one say to the families of people who have disappeared who come in their hundreds to meet you, thinking that the UN will be able to defend them and force the government to hand back their friends and relatives, or even bring about a military intervention by the 'international community' (another self-deceiving concept)? What should one say to a someone sentenced to death, to torture victims or to prisoners rotting in prison for years for no reason and for whom presenting a communication to the human rights committee is the only hope left? How can one say to them that it is not because, after several years, the committee will have set out its 'views' that justice will necessarily be done?

And yet the number of communications and complaints continues to rise, ever more people appeal to the committee and to the other human rights protection mechanisms and to the ICC …. How can this be explained? Why do they fail to understand that their hopes will be disappointed? Probably because those who use these procedures do not just have 'hopes' in an ideal but see in it their own 'interest' in the context of the struggle they are engaged in, whether for their own defence or for the defence of a cause.

The idea that one should refrain from setting up a court because it might 'lack consideration for victims' might also be understood as being the reflection of a theological-political conception of power: as if the 'decision-makers' *on high* should necessarily decide for the 'victims' *below*, which would imply some form of 'responsibility' of the decision-makers who should consequently refrain (out of their great leniency) from giving victims false hope.

But the question does not arise in these terms. There are not 'victims' on the one side and 'decision-makers' on the other. There are actors with diverging interests who interact within a society and produce norms and institutions. There are power relations that are mediated to varying degrees by rules and institutions. All of these actors have differing views, interests and proposals. The question is to determine, in this game, what stance to take, how to position oneself as an individual, as a group, and which project to defend in the social game? Such positioning is necessarily taken depending on some ideal, but the condition for avoiding despair is to consider that this ideal is not ultimately 'true'. The source of negative nihilism is to *believe* in the ideal as an absolute truth with as the outcome that one is invariably disappointed.

IV. Realisation of the Idea of a United Nations Court of Human Rights

Having set aside a number of objections that hardly seem convincing, I would now like to come to the project itself. And first of all to a word of caution about the method and the practice of international negotiation. It would be materially impossible to address the idea of a universal court on the basis of a single draft. A successful negotiation takes as its starting point a certain number of practical objectives to be achieved. Only from this point on can the resources to be implemented be defined. Moreover, the range of possibilities must be left open although setting out some red lines. A red line relates to the principle of no backtracking. The first principle is to seek to improve on the current situation, not to weaken it or deconstruct it. Proposals that would ultimately weaken or downgrade things as they stand are to be ruled out.

Beginning with these principles, it is feasible to examine the draft statute for a 'World Court of Human Rights' developed by Julia Kozma, Manfred Nowak and Martin Scheinin, before defining a number of parameters that might frame negotiations around a universal court.

A. The Draft Statute for a 'World Court of Human Rights'

In 2008, under the impetus of the head of the Federal Foreign Affairs Department, Mrs Micheline Calmy-Rey, the Swiss diplomacy asked a panel of eight personalities to draft a 'human rights agenda' by identifying eight research themes, including the establishment of a World Court of Human Rights in direct line with the 1947 Australian initiative. Further to the call for contributions, three eminent specialists, Martin Scheinin on the one hand and Manfred Nowak and Julia Kozma on the other, proposed a draft statute for a World Court of Human Rights. They were then asked to come up with a single draft, which was published in 2010.[62] The draft is presented explicitly

[62] cf Kozma, Nowak and Scheinin, *A World Court of Human Rights – Consolidated Statute and Commentary* (n 13).

as a pragmatic solution to the problem of the 'reform of treaty bodies' at the same time as a 'pool of ideas' for actors who might contemplate further exploring the idea of a universal court of human rights:

> The consolidated draft Statute with a comprehensive commentary and the two original drafts as attachment is nothing but a draft for interested States and other actors to consider. At the same time, it addresses all the frequently asked questions about the purpose, usefulness and feasibility of establishing a World Court of Human Rights. The answer of the three authors to these questions is very simple: It is not only feasible, but it would be extremely useful and high time for States to seriously discuss the question of establishing a World Court of Human Rights instead of further pursuing the endless discussion of treaty body reform.[63]

'Nothing but a draft …': the statute is just another project and makes no claim to provide a 'turnkey' solution. It should come as no surprise for that matter that the draft should seem overambitious or even utopian on some points. As fine connoisseurs of the multilateral system, the authors know full well that in any negotiation one should always have a very 'high' starting point in order to reach a result that might ultimately be adopted by consensus.

The draft includes a number of what I think are very positive points that should be incorporated among the main parameters of any draft statute for a future UN court.

The main 'brainwave' of the authors of the statute was to come up with a system enabling the court to be established *without revising the existing treaties*. If there is any consensus on the reform of treaty bodies, it is that such a reform should be made without going through the extremely complex amendment procedures provided for by the treaties.[64] To make a reform conditional upon the adoption of such amendments would be virtually to condemn it to failure. The draft statute avoids this pitfall by basing the court's existence not on a revision of existing treaties but on an independent international convention constituting of the court's statute. Moreover, the articulation of jurisdiction between the court and the committees extends from an ingenious mechanism: article 7 paragraph 3 of the draft provides that the ratification of the statute by a state should be considered by the UN Secretary-General with whom it is deposited as notification of the state's suspension of its acceptance of the committees' jurisdiction to hear individual communications under the treaty in question. In this way, in the event any state withdraws from the court's

[63] ibid 4.

[64] See, eg, art 51 of the Covenant on Civil and Political Rights: after a state party files a proposal, a conference of states parties may be convened, at the request of at least one-third of states parties. The amendment is then adopted by the majority of states present and voting and passed on to the General Assembly which must in turn adopt it. However, the amendment only comes into force once accepted 'pursuant to the constitutional rules in force' by a two-thirds majority of states parties. However, the amendment is then only valid for the states that have accepted it: the other states remain bound by the provisions of the Covenant without the amendment under consideration.

statute, the committee's jurisdiction would be automatically restored.[65] One might equally contemplate, however, competing jurisdiction of the committees and the court, with a possible mechanism of referral by the committees, based on the consent of the state in question, to the court's jurisdiction and on a clause in the internal rules of the relevant committee. We shall return to this in the next section.

Another ingenious point deals with the establishment of the court's jurisdiction *ratione materiae*. Rather than 're-inventing the wheel' and trying to codify international human rights law to define the court's jurisdiction, the statute provides that its ratification by a state means that the state accepts the court's jurisdiction with respect to a very full list (I shall return to this point) of international treaties set out in article 5(1). But under article 50(1), states may, at the time of ratifying the statute, exercise an opt-out from the list. In other words, they may issue a reservation that they do not recognise the court's jurisdiction for the treaties they list. States obviously have the possibility of subsequently lifting such a reservation (article 50(2)) and may also declare at any time that they recognise the court's jurisdiction with regard to a treaty not included in the list in article 5.

Other ideas are noteworthy. This is the case of the idea of including in the statute a mechanism for supervising the enforcement of the court's judgments, which is inspired by the mechanism under the Council of Europe with the role played the Committee of Ministers. In the case in point, this role is conferred on the High Commissioner for Human Rights, with the possibility that the High Commissioner might refer the question either to the Human Rights Council or to the Security Council. In the same spirit, the statute grants practical importance to the principle of subsidiarity by providing for the establishment of a voluntary fund not just to help victims and their families but also to help states parties to improve their internal appeals (article 39). Likewise, the statute grants attention to victims – a concern that was not around when the European Convention and the Covenant were drafted. Plans are therefore in place, in addition to the fund, for the establishment of a specific unit within the registry for the protection of victims and witnesses (article 30(4)).

But alongside these points that should be noted, other aspects of the statute are more debatable. The main stumbling point that has led to most criticism is the proposal to offer both international organisations and non-state actors to accept the court's jurisdiction (articles 51 and 4(1)). The idea is revolutionary, true, but it raises both theoretical and practical problems.

[65] Art 7(3) speaks more specifically of 'suspension of the operation of complaint procedures accepted by the State in question under the human rights treaties covered by the Court's jurisdiction'. See also Kozma, Nowak and Scheinin, *A World Court of Human Rights – Consolidated Statute and Commentary* (n 13), 36–37.

Theoretical because, as things stand, international treaties are designed so as to impose obligations on states alone and not on other actors or subjects of international law. It is hard to see, then, in theory how the court might supervise the enforcement of compliance by non-state entities of obligations that are not legally binding on them. Practical problems arise also because it is very doubtful that international organisations and, for example, multinational firms should accept submitting to a court that might hold them responsible for violations of human rights with uncertain consequences both internationally and domestically, knowing that between serious violations of human rights and 'international crimes' there is only a difference in characterisation. Lastly, another difficulty relates to the list of treaties established in article 5. Always with the most ambitious aims, the authors of the statute draw up a very long list of treaties, including 'orphan' conventions – to take up Emmanuel Decaux's expression[66] – that is, conventions that do not set up supervisory bodies. It would probably be wiser, for such treaties, to provide for an opt-in rather than opt-out system, because the states did not devise or accept them as treaties that might be the subject of individual applications.

B. For a United Nations Court of Human Rights

The draft for a 'World Court of Human Rights' just presented should again be considered for what it is, namely a 'reservoir of ideas', a starting point from which to think about what a universal court of human rights might be. It is merit-worthy in that it solves what might appear to be an insuperable technical obstacle: treaty revision. With the system of 'suspension' of recognition of the jurisdiction of committees under the individual communication procedures, but also with the definition of the court's jurisdiction *ratione materiae* based on a list of treaties together with a right to opt out by stating reservations at the time of ratification, the statute provides practical solutions for a 'ready-for-use' court.

However, to my way of thinking, it is important not to remain glued to any particular statute but rather to think about the desired objectives and the corresponding parameters, which might serve as a starting point for talks about a draft statute in a multilateral framework.

As concerns the *objectives*, I can see two primarily. The first is to reinforce the visibility, accessibility and effectiveness of complaints mechanisms to UN treaty bodies by transferring the jurisdiction of committees in this area to a

[66] cf Emmanuel Decaux's report as Special Rapporteur of the Human Rights Council's Consultative Committee, *The Universal implementation of international human rights treaties. Final report prepared by the Special Rapporteur responsible for conducting a detailed study of the universal implementation of international human rights treaties*, A/HRC/Sub.1/58/5 and A/HRC/Sub.1/58/5/Add.1.

judicial body. The second is to bring about this transfer without amending the treaties, without adding substantive obligations for states and without excessive additional cost.

For the parameters that should make it possible to achieve these objectives, whatever the specific forms for establishing such a judicial body:

(1) The Court of Human Rights is not a substitute for the committees which are provided for by the treaties and which at the very least maintain their function of examining states' reports or other functions conferred by treaty (such as jurisdiction on investigations or emergency procedures). At the same time, the line of thinking begun on reforming the committee system with respect to their examination of states parties' reports should be pursued. After the stage of resolution 68/268 and its implementation, new proposals are on the table for and beyond 2020.[67]

(2) The Court of Human Rights could have alternative jurisdiction to the committees or competing jurisdiction with them. In this way, a state should be able to choose from two options. Either to confer exclusive jurisdiction on the court to hear communications presented on the basis of a treaty or to recognise only subsidiary jurisdiction to the court, which would only be able to be seized of a communication by referral from the relevant committee after having examined the matter and stated its views. Both options would seem to be possible without amending the treaties. In the first case, the jurisdiction of the relevant committee is merely suspended by acceptance of the court's jurisdiction, as in the draft statute for the World Court; in the second hypothesis, the relevant committee fulfils its function under the treaty. But on the dual basis of acceptance by the state of the court's jurisdiction and of a clause in its internal rules and regulations, the committee could refer the matter to the court to be examined anew. The former solution seems more economical insofar as all of the resources for the treaty bodies for examining complaints might be transferred to the court's budget. But the latter solution might seem more pragmatic and more progressive to states.

(3) The court's jurisdiction *ratione materiae* should encompass, by default all of the basic treaties ratified by the state in question (because it goes without saying that the court would not have jurisdiction to rule on the basis of a treaty that was not ratified by the relevant state). The state might exercise, through a reservation made at the time of ratification, an opt-out

[67] See esp the reports from the Academy of International Humanitarian and Human Rights Law: Zipoli et al, *Optimizing the UN Treaty Body System* (n 30); and C Callejon, K Kemileva and F Kirchmeier, *Treaty Bodies' Individual Communication Procedures: Providing Redress and Reparation to Victims of Human Rights Violations*, Geneva, May 2019. See also the last report of the Secretary General on the implementation of the General Assembly Resolution 68/268, *Status of the human rights treaty body system*, doc A/74/643, 10 January 2020, and its annexes.

from some of the treaties. Conversely, it should be able, at any time, to decide to submit other human rights treaties to the court's jurisdiction.

(4) The court should be made up of permanent judges, elected by the assembly of states parties. Their term of office should be comparatively long, preferably nine years, which is a guarantee of independence in itself. Their number should be determined at the time of negotiation. It is obvious, though, that there cannot be as many justices as there are states potentially parties to the statute – as in the context of the Council of Europe, with the 47 justices of the European Court – since the number could rise to the 193 members states of the United Nations. The draft for the 'World Court of Human Rights' proposes 21 judges (article 20 of the draft statute), which would make it possible to form three chambers of seven judges.

(5) The court might be financed alternatively or together in three possible ways: by the states parties to the statute; by the ordinary budget of the United Nations; or by voluntary contributions. The financing of committees is provided for by the ordinary budget of the United Nations and from voluntary contributions. The draft consolidated statute for the World Court proposed on the contrary that the court be financed by the states parties, who decide on the budget when sitting as the assembly (articles 43 and 44).

(6) To ensure the court is fully independent financially and administratively, the office of the secretary of the court should be entrusted to a registry as an administrative organisation attached directly to the court and under the responsibility of the judges and not to the Secretariat of the United Nations as is currently the case with the members of the 'petitions team', who work in the context of and under the responsibility of the High Commissioner for Human Rights.

(7) Apart from these fundamental issues, many other subjects will have to be discussed and in this respect the draft for a 'World Court' is a highly useful document. This is the case, for instance, of the court's power to order provisional measures or for its jurisdiction to give advisory opinions. Similarly, the question of the follow-up and supervision mechanism of implementation of judgments shall have to be included in the thinking together with that of subsidiarity/complementarity, by introducing support measures to help states implement the court's judgments and more generally to bring their law into line with the treaties, when the court finds there are 'structural' violations.

On the basis of these parameters, which themselves derive from the objectives stated, many possibilities are open for negotiation. It will be for the negotiators themselves to explore their pros and cons. It can only be hoped, in conclusion, that alongside ongoing reflection on the 'strengthening' of the treaty bodies, a new initiative for the creation of a United Nations Court of Human Rights will come about in order for the idea to be embodied by 2030.

Figure 10.1 below sets out the possible ways of bringing cases before a United Nations Court of Human Rights: either directly by the author of the communication or by an initial action by the relevant treaty bodies followed possibly by their referral of the matter to the court.

The committees before which a complaints procedure is active in 2018 are shown, therefore all except for the Committee on the Rights of Migrant Workers (CMW), the procedure for which has not yet come into force.

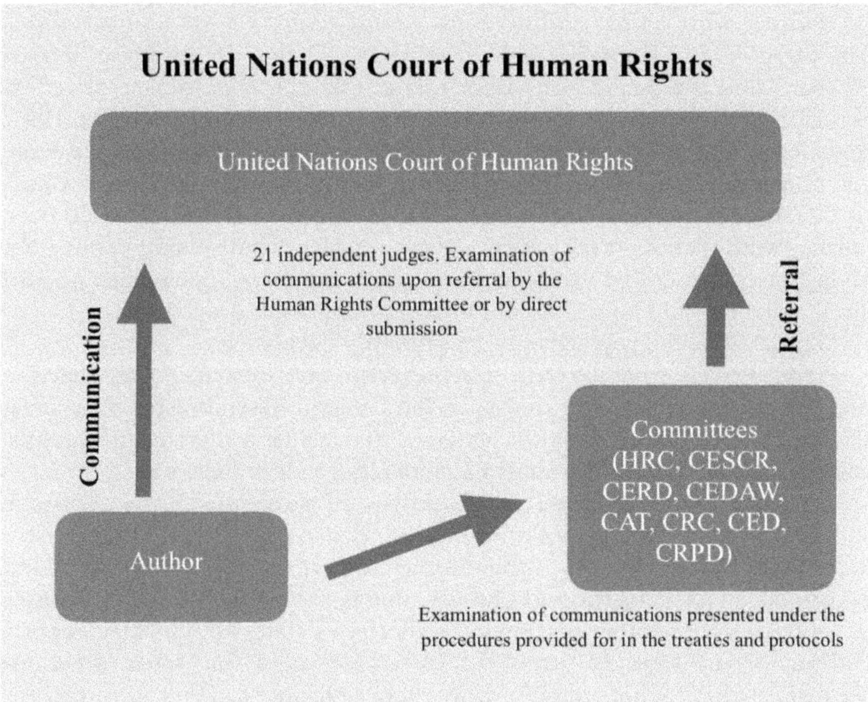

Figure 10.1 United Nations Court of Human Rights

11

The Committee System: 2020 and Beyond[1]

The treaty body system has been diagnosed as being 'in crisis' for at least 30 years, and the theme of its reform is just as old. A first cycle of reflection started with the mandate given to Philip Alston who, already in 1997, considered that the system as it existed was not sustainable.[2] Since then, this assessment has been reiterated numerous times, and ambitious proposals have followed one after another.[3] But until now stakeholders have been satisfied with makeshift repairs to prevent the ship from sinking completely. Today, being a member of a treaty body feels like being a passenger aboard the Titanic: the ship is sinking, but the orchestra continues to play!

Will 2020 be the year when we get the ship back afloat?

If this is really what we want to achieve, not only do stakeholders need to concentrate on the process started in the General Assembly, but they must also look further. In other words, we need to consider a short-term strengthening, a medium-term restructuring, and a longer-term reform.

The first cycle achieved its objectives of strengthening the system, although granted they were rather modest. For instance, treaty bodies have indeed significantly increased the number of periodic reports reviewed and have reduced their backlogs. However, this is not enough to claim victory as we have to remember that only a minority of states submit their reports on time. Navi Pillay's 2012 report thus remains valid: the system functions because states do not comply with their obligations.[4] Furthermore, the

[1] This chapter is based on a blog post originally published on 21 November 2019 on openglobalrights.org. It does not take into account subsequent developments. For an update on the '2020 process' in times of pandemia, see O de Frouville, 'The United Nations Treaty Bodies in a Transition Period – Progress Review March-December 2020 Chronicle', Working Paper, Geneva Academy/Paris Human Rights Center, June 2021 at www.geneva-academy.ch/geneva-humanrights-platform/ressources.

[2] *Final report on enhancing the long-term effectiveness of the United Nations human rights treaty system*, E/CN.4/1997/74, 27 March 1997, in particular para 10.

[3] See in particular the June 2012 report by the then High Commissioner for Human Rights Navanethem Pillay, *Strengthening the United Nations human rights treaty body system. A report by the United Nations High Commissioner for Human Rights* (United Nations, Geneva, 2012).

[4] ibid 9.

member increase within the Secretariat in charge of treaties did not happen in the proportion initially envisaged. The failure to keep these promises placed the staff of the High Commissioner (responsible for the secretariat) under considerable stress, which inevitably undermines the sustainability of the effort undertaken.

The 'strengthening' must therefore continue. First, promises to increase staff must be kept. The Secretariat is the spine of the system. Secondly, efforts relative to assisting the states need to be maintained and go even further: ensure that all the reports be submitted on time; encourage the creation of national structures in charge of preparing the reports; and more importantly, focus at least half of the next cycle's resources on the follow-up and implementation of the recommendations.

2020 must be the beginning of an extensive restructuring of the treaty system.

Indeed, the Committees each have their respective dynamics, which need to be supplemented and encouraged by the states. Last July, the treaty body Chairpersons formulated a common vision of the treaty bodies,[5] including measures to be put in place rapidly: a generalisation of the simplified procedure, the creation of a fixed and coordinated schedule for the submission of reports, new working practices to strengthen capacities such as the bodies' ability to conduct reviews in chambers .... All measures that, in the medium term, may improve the situation radically.

But the Secretariat also has to take responsibility. In accordance with all the conventions, the Secretary-General must provide the Committees with the necessary resources to implement their mandates. This involves a reflection about adapting the structures to the needs of the Committees. Therefore, we should seriously consider the proposal laid out in a report[6] from the Geneva Academy of International Humanitarian Law and Human Rights that discusses the creation of a professional structure, similar to a Registry, to effectively handle the administration of individual communications.

The salutary exercise that led the treaty body Chairpersons to formulate a 'vision' for their future was only possible as resulting from a real awareness of the existential challenge facing the system: either move forward, or perish! The proposed measures, if effectively implemented in the next five or six years, should get the ship back afloat. But we must be careful not to be lulled once again, by the regular rhythm of the engine noise! The Committees have to continue innovating. And states must assume their responsibility to

[5] See 'Position paper of the Chairs of the human rights treaty bodies on the future of the treaty body system', *Report of the Chairs of the human rights treaty bodies on their thirty-first annual meeting*, A/74/256, 30 July 2019, Annex III, 19.

[6] C Callejon, K Kemileva and F Kirchmeier, *Treaty Bodies' Individual Communication Procedures: Providing Redress and Reparation to Victims of Human Rights Violations*, Geneva, May 2019.

always improve before an international system of protection that, we must remember, was established for good reasons.

Also, we should not wait to start reflecting on what the system will be like the day after tomorrow. The periodic review must become a fully effective process for the protection and promotion of Human Rights. To that extent, two paths are possible: maintaining the plurality of the bodies, but still improving the coordination of their actions, with, for instance, 'clustered' reviews inspired by the Geneva Academy report;[7] unifying and professionalising the system, with the creation of a single Committee, as recommended by Louise Arbour in her report.[8]

As for individual communications, it is necessary to reflect rationally and without taboos about possibly transferring them, at least partially, to a judicial body – a UN Human Rights Court.[9] Matters could be referred to the Court directly or indirectly (after review by the relevant Committee, at the request of one of the parties). No need to modify the existing treaties: it would be sufficient to adopt a new convention establishing the status of the Court that states would then ratify to recognise its competence. It would constitute an improvement of the system, placing professional judges above experts, thus making decisions mandatory. Far from a 'fragmentation' of international law, such an institution would reinforce its coherence, as long as clear *lis pendens* rules be fixed with regional courts as well as an obligation to maintain a real 'dialogue of the judges.' It would also prevent any risks of case law conflicts internal to the Committee system by unifying their jurisprudence.

[7] Geneva Academy, D Zipoli, F Kirchmeier, K Kemileva and C Callejon, *Optimizing the UN Treaty Body System. Academic Platform Report of the 2020 Review*, Geneva, May 2018.

[8] *Concept paper of the High Commissioner's proposal for a unified standing treaty body*, Report by the Secretariat, HRI/MC/2006/2, 22 March 2006.

[9] See in this volume ch 10.

12

The Universal Declaration of Human Rights is 70 Years Old: What Challenges Await the United Nations?[1]

Seventy years after the adoption of the Universal Declaration of Human Rights (UDHR), we do not only have cause to complain, far from it. We must take stock of the distance we have already travelled. Before 1945 and the United Nations Charter, human rights simply did not exist in international law. An individual was only an 'object' of international law and states, except in a few specific cases, did not need to justify the way they treated their nationals: their sovereignty effectively granted them power of life or death over their citizens.

Since then, and using the Declaration as its foundation, a complete and coherent system of norms, widely accepted by states, has developed into what is often called 'international human rights law': nine fundamental UN Conventions, of which two are the covenants on civil and political rights and on economic, social and cultural rights, and seven other treaties which enumerate states' obligations regarding certain violations (torture, enforced disappearances, racial and gender-based discriminations ...) or towards certain categories of persons (children, people with disabilities, migrant workers); regional conventions such as the European Convention on Human Rights; and a multitude of other texts, treaties and other instruments.

I. A Legal Basis for Action

What is striking in this ensemble is its coherence: all these texts are grounded in the same principles, those asserted by the UDHR. To say that today human rights are not universally recognised in international law is absurd: over the

[1] This chapter was originally published online in *The Conversation* on the occasion of the 70th anniversary of the Universal Declaration for Human Rights, on 10 December 2018.

last 70 years, a process of legal universalisation has occurred, and no state seriously disputes them anymore.

Of course, these norms are not enough to end all human rights violations, but they provide everyone with a legal basis to act and oppose them. And beyond the norms, there are also implementation mechanisms. Starting in 1948, an entire apparatus has progressively been established that abounds with procedures and organs which continuously monitor human rights situations all over the world. Ten United Nations committees act as 'guardians' of the core conventions, while an ensemble of 'special procedures' – Special Rapporteurs, independent experts and working groups – work on human rights violations daily and visit countries in order to produce public reports.

Various international commissions of inquiry have also been created on a more ad hoc basis in recent years, in order to document the violations and crimes committed in Syria, Burundi, Yemen, Myanmar or the occupied Palestinian territories. Regional courts have been put in place: the European Court of Human Rights, of course, but also the Inter-American Court and the African Court of Human and Peoples' Rights. We are close to reaching what, in 1795, Kant posited as an ideal: that any violation committed in any part of the world is felt everywhere else.

Here again, this architecture is strikingly coherent: all these experts and judges apply the same standards and, if we exclude some isolated cases, have adopted the same interpretations. By patiently applying them in particular cases, in situations unique to each country, each context, they contribute to ensuring that human rights, which are universal in their principles and at the judicial level, become universal in the daily life of all citizens of the world.

However, although how far we have come in 70 years is impressive, we still face many challenges.

II. An Intellectual Challenge

The first challenge is intellectual: we are witnessing a resurgence of anti-human rights ideologies and, more generally, of what underpins human rights: principles stemming from the Enlightenment and its philosophies. Human rights have been accused by some of being complicit with economic neoliberalism, or of being a mask for certain major powers' imperialism.

For others, human rights are 'against the people' because they exclusively defend minorities against the majority or give power to 'experts' who lack democratic legitimacy. In other circles, human rights are criticised for allegedly distorting human nature by harming anthropological structures such as the family. What is often noticeable in these attacks is the ignorance or intentional distortion of what human rights as legal standards are: those who express such criticisms have rarely read a ruling by the European Court of Human Rights.

If these anti-Enlightenment schools of thought had become a minority after World War II, they are finding a new echo in today's public opinions: unscrupulous politicians do not hesitate to offer them as an answer to legitimate feelings of injustice within societies. Nowadays, defenders of democracy and human rights can no longer ignore these criticisms but must confront them and deconstruct their discourses to prove that they provide the wrong answers to what are often the right questions.

III. An Institutional Challenge

Another challenge is institutional and chiefly concerns the United Nations system: it has been said, the mechanisms which today protect human rights are numerous and play a crucial role. However, their proliferation has made the system hard to understand and complicated citizens' ability to use it, while lack of resources limits its effectiveness in practice.

Several processes are currently underway to perfect it. In 2020, the UN General Assembly is called upon to facilitate the renovation of the essential procedure by which states submit periodic reports to the UN committees, by creating a global and coordinated calendar.[2]

Beyond this, what must absolutely be improved is the procedure for reviewing individual complaints through the creation of a United Nations Human Rights Court which, standing above the relevant committees, would ensure a unified interpretation of the legal standards and strengthen their jurisprudence's authority in coordination with other regional courts and the International Court of Justice.

IV. The Normative Challenge

Finally, the last challenge is normative because, if international human rights law is particularly concrete and consistent, it must answer novel questions. New technologies in particular are challenging our relationship to freedom and dignity.

Mass surveillance, for example, has given infringements on privacy a new reach and we don't know whether our current legal standards can address it. Similarly, science's predictive capacity threatens the principle of autonomy: if science can always predict what we will be, what room do we have left to exist?

[2] For an update on the '2020 process' in times of pandemia, see O de Frouville, 'The United Nations Treaty Bodies in a Transition Period – Progress Review March–December 2020 Chronicle', Working Paper, Geneva Academy/Paris Human Rights Center, June 2021 at www.geneva-academy.ch/geneva-humanrights-platform/ressources.

Another major issue is the degradation of our environment and climate change: even as human rights are based on an anthropocentric philosophy, should we not be rethinking our relationship to Nature (and not simply to our human environment)? The challenge will be to reaffirm the principles of political modernity while also acknowledging Nature, or even recognising its own rights.

These challenges are important: we must not wait until the Declaration's 80th anniversary to rise to them!

13

Reforming the Security Council: What can be Done Without Amending the UN Charter?*

If asked 'What can be done by altering the UN Charter?' one might tend to answer 'Nothing'. But if asked 'What can be done *without altering* the UN Charter?' one might almost want to answer 'Everything' or 'Pretty much everything'. The experience already gained shows this amply. Admittedly it seems difficult for there to be an evolution that would amount to a revolution. However, reform is possible. Reform by small steps. A jurist's reform, section by section, subsection by subsection. But who is to say that such reform is not preparing the way for tomorrow's revolution? In order to see clearly in what is a somewhat complex debate for an outside observer, we need to return briefly to the concepts underlying it. Then we shall dwell a while on the reform process itself before interpreting its results in the light of the concepts extracted initially.

I. The Concepts

Most of the concepts for that matter are explicitly set out in the declarations of states and other actors as in the texts adopted by the Security Council itself. Taking a closer look, it seems as if a couple of concepts over-determine the entire question, like two guiding principles joined in a dialectical relationship. Those concepts are effectiveness and legitimacy.

On the one hand, we want a body that is able to react including in emergencies to the many challenges to the maintenance of peace and security. On the other hand, we want a body that is more legitimate. The starting point is not the same. The Security Council as it currently operates is acknowledged

* This article, even more than others, deals with a fast evolving reality. Accordingly, it has been updated to the extent possible as of June 2021. But note that I have chosen not to include specific developments related to the adaptation of the working methods of the Security Council in reaction to the COVID-19 crisis. For a full update on this issue, please see the very comprehensive reports on the website of Security Council Report at www.securitycouncilreport.org.

to have some degree of effectiveness, while it is considered that things need to go further and above all that there is a need to avoid cases of total deadlock when the Council becomes wholly inoperative. Conversely almost all the UN member states – except perhaps the Council's permanent members, and even then it is not sure – and all the other actors consider that the Council has very little legitimacy. The fear is that this deficit of legitimacy might ultimately prove detrimental to the Council's effectiveness. The dialectic between the two terms is apparent then: too much legitimacy may kill its effectiveness; but too little will kill it just as surely. Attempted reforms therefore bear essentially on efforts to lend the Council greater legitimacy. How can a balance be struck whereby the Council would gain in legitimacy without losing in effectiveness, or possibly even gain in effectiveness? There's the rub.

In the context of the debate surrounding the Security Council, the concept of 'legitimacy' relates essentially to two other concepts: 'democracy' and 'accountability', the two being interrelated in point of fact.

The concept of 'democracy' is a source of recurrent misunderstanding at the United Nations. The double meaning that prevailed during the Cold War – with popular democracies on the one side and liberal democracies on the other – left room for great conceptual confusion and sustained controversies over the meaning, the definition and the well-foundedness of this or that conception of democracy. It is understandable under the circumstances that the term is seldom encountered in what states have to say or in Security Council documents about reform. That does not mean that the concept of democracy itself or in any event the principles that derive from the concept of democracy are absent.

Alongside *accountability*, three terms recur. All three, to my mind, are closely related to the concept of democracy. They are *representativeness*, *transparency* and *participation*. The idea of *representativeness* refers to the *representative democracy* model which postulates in substance that the people (the *demos*) can only exercise power through its elected, appointed or self-proclaimed *representatives*. In the Security Council, the term representativeness covers all of the debates about the composition of the Council, namely the issue of its extension to new permanent or non-permanent members.[1] Obviously these are the debates that most mobilise not just states but public opinion too. When mention is made of 'Security Council reform', it is the question of its enlargement that generally springs to mind.

The concepts of *transparency* and *participation*, like that of *accountability*, refer more readily to the *deliberative democracy* model. While not incompatible with representative institutions, deliberative democracy considers that

[1] Although this relationship in itself can be rightly debated because states represent themselves alone. Having a permanent Latin American state or African state on the Council does not necessarily improve the 'representativeness' of Latin America or Africa. It merely strengthens the standing of one member at the expense of others.

such institutions are invariably inadequate for organising any true exercise of power by the people for the people. These institutions must be supplemented by procedures and an environment that promotes public discussion of societal issues but also constant supervision of the actions of those who govern.[2] The conditions for implementing deliberative democracy include the demands for *open and inclusive participation* and for *transparency* as the condition for any authentic and open deliberation by way of debate, discussion and exchange of ideas in a host of spheres and instances, whether state-organised or otherwise. Deliberative theory holds that such discussions are the basis for the formation of a rational agreement of citizens to legislation. It is by virtue of such agreements that everyone in a democracy can think of themselves as not just the addressees but also the authors of the rules and regulations.

Accountability covers in part this deliberative conception of democracy in its prospective aspect to the extent that it requires that the rule-making processes are both inclusive and transparent. In its retrospective aspect, *accountability* implies regular reporting obligations and means of appeal by which decisions can be challenged and those who govern possibly held liable.[3] In broader terms, accountability can be understood as relating to ways of exercising democracy. Democracy is in particular a regime in which those who hold power are held to account for their exercise of it, in a variety of ways ranging from predetermined legal procedures to free and periodic elections, by way of the work of the media who are democracy's 'guard-dogs'. The supervisory procedures – administrative or judicial – contribute to the 'answerability' of the bodies and individuals who exercise some power. In this sense, the principle of the *rule of law* – especially through the judicial guarantee of individuals' rights – is a particularly sophisticated reflection of the democratic idea of those who govern being accountable to those who are governed.

Internationally it seems the concept of representative democracy cannot readily be embodied in any effective procedures or rules.[4] Taken literally it

[2] The concept of deliberative democracy arises in large part from the works of German philosopher Jürgen Habermas. It is rooted in his *theory of communicative action* and set out especially in J Habermas, *Between Facts and Norms* (Cambridge, Polity Press,1996). See also J Chevalier, *L'Etat post-moderne* (Paris, LGDJ, 2003) 171ff; and the work of JS Dryzek, esp *Deliberative Democracy and Beyond. Liberals, Critics, Contestations* (Oxford, Oxford University Press, 2000); JS Dryzek (with Simon Niemeyer), *Foundations and Frontiers of Deliberative Governance* (Oxford, Oxford University Press, 2010).

[3] On the *retrospective accountability/prospective accountability* distinction, see S Wheatley, *The Democratic Legitimacy of International Law* (Oxford, Hart Publishing, 2010) 79. On the concept of *accountability* in international law, see the final report of the Berlin Conference of the *International Law Association* (2004) on *Accountability and International Organizations*. On the connections between *accountability* and democracy, see also RO Keohane, 'Global Governance and Democratic Accountability' in D Held and M Koenig-Archibugi (eds), *Taming Globalization. Frontiers of Governance* (Cambridge, Polity Press, 2003) 130–59.

[4] For a deconstruction of the connection between plans to enlarge the Security Council and the strengthening of its legitimacy see I Hurd, 'Myths of Membership: The Politics of Legitimation in UN Security Council Reform' (2008) 14 *Global Governance* 199–217.

would imply transposing the classic institutions of representative democracy to the international stage to form a sort of super-state, or at any rate to set up some of its bodies such as a two-tiered world parliament with a 'senate' made up of states and a 'congress' of peoples, with representatives elected by the 'world's citizens' in a universal electoral college. In my view, such a conception is not just utopian but implementing it would lead to a dead-end to the extent that the composition of such a chamber would grant excessive weight to the most populous states to the detriment of others.

Accordingly, the concept of representative democracy in the context of the United Nations refers rather to the weaker idea of 'representativeness', which is barely any easier to handle, as demonstrated by the failure of talks on the composition of the Security Council. The aim is to strike a delicate balance among the different groups of states or among the different states themselves, based on different criteria, including their 'power' in international relations. By this yardstick, a 'representative' Security Council would include states wielding a certain level of power as determined by different factors such as their geographical size, natural resources, population size, military might, cultural and linguistic influences, and so on. But it would also have to be representative of the different regional groups or of different groupings representing common interests such as the Group of 77 or the European Union, etc. In truth, striking such a balance would be tantamount to squaring the circle.

The increasingly obvious deadlock in negotiations over Security Council composition has progressively directed the debate towards the issue of deliberative democracy, with its knock-on concepts of participation, transparency and accountability. In practice, in the falsely technical language of diplomats, the UN speaks of discussions about the Council's 'working methods'.

II. The Processes

A Security Council Informal Working Group on Documentation and Other Procedural Questions had already been set up back in June 1993 to improve the workings of the Security Council as its activities exploded.[5] A number of measures were taken over the course of time and progressively consolidated in 'notes' of the Security Council's President. This process of reform by small steps was given new impetus as part of the preparations for the 2005 World Summit.

The High Level Panel on Threats, Challenges, and Change had urged the pursuit of these changes with a view to greater transparency and

[5] See www.un.org/securitycouncil/content/working-methods-handbook. On the origins and first years of the working group, see the Report of the NGO Security Council, *Security Council Working Methods: A Tale of Two Councils?* (March 2014).

accountability.[6] That recommendation was taken up by Kofi Annan in his report *In Larger Freedom*.[7] The 2005 World Summit Outcome fitted in with this dynamic:

> We support early reform of the Security Council – an essential element of our overall effort to reform the United Nations – in order to make it more broadly representative, efficient and transparent and thus to further enhance its effectiveness and the legitimacy and implementation of its decisions. We commit ourselves to continuing our efforts to achieve a decision to this end and request the General Assembly to review progress on the reform set out above by the end of 2005.
>
> We recommend that the Security Council continue to adapt its working methods so as to increase the involvement of States not members of the Council in its work, as appropriate, enhance its accountability to the membership and increase the transparency of its work.[8]

Further to the summit, the Working Group, which had been dormant for some years, was revived under the Japanese presidency. Its work led to the adoption of a note S/2006/507 recapitulating certain innovations that had emerged in practice and introducing new ones. A similar process occurred in 2010, again under the Japanese presidency, resulting in the adoption of a new recapitulative note S/2010/507, generally known as 'Note 507'. Since then updated versions of Note 507 have been adopted and debates on working methods held on a yearly basis, continuing the efforts begun by the same policy of small steps.[9]

In parallel to this, a group of 'small' states – the Small 5 (S5), headed by Switzerland, was forming in the General Assembly. Being unlikely ever to secure a permanent seat and weary of the enlargement debates, the S5 had every intention of influencing the Security Council debates on working methods in order to achieve democratisation by other means. They laid resolutions before the General Assembly on two occasions, first in 2006[10] and then in 2012,[11] which they had to withdraw largely under pressure from the permanent members. In 2013, the S5 became the Accountability, Coherence and Transparency (ACT) group of small and mid-size states that pursued the same efforts to attempt to influence Security Council debates.

[6] *A More Secure World*, A/59/565, esp para 258.

[7] Report of the Secretary-General, *In larger freedom: towards development, security and human rights for all*, A/59/2005, para 168.

[8] *2005 World Summit Outcome*, Resolution adopted by the General Assembly on 16 September 2005, A/RES/60/1, paras 153–54.

[9] At the time of revising this article, the last update was contained in doc S/2017/507, 30 August 2017. In para 100 of that Note, the Security Council 'expresses its intent to continue to hold an annual open debate on its working methods'.

[10] A/60/L.49, Documents from the Millennium Summit on improving the working methods of the Security Council, 17 March 2006.

[11] A/66/L.42/Rev.2, *Enhancing the accountability, transparency and effectiveness of the Security Council*, 3 May 2012: presented by Costa Rica, Jordan, Liechtenstein, Singapore and Switzerland.

III. The Outcomes

The outcomes of these endeavours to reform the Security Council in depth, without altering the Charter, can be arranged around the few concepts extracted above: *transparency*, *participation* and *accountability*.

A. Transparency

The first requirement is for transparency, that is, for access to information on the Security Council's activities, ongoing processes and decisions. A glance at the Security Council's website today – remembering what it was like just a few years ago – will convince anyone there has been substantial change in this respect. A large number of the innovations that can be seen on the website are the outcome of decisions taken by way of working methods and implemented, albeit somewhat erratically at times, by the successive Security Council presidencies.

Transparency involves first off the *foreseeability of the works* of the Security Council. The Security Council makes public its daily programme,[12] its provisional monthly programme,[13] and 'monthly tentative forecasts' for the following months.[14] It was decided that the questions on the agenda should be presented in the form of 'descriptive formulations', so as to avoid the cryptic wording that meant readers could not know what the Security Council was to discuss.[15] Steps were taken so that all states were advised of 'unscheduled or emergency meetings not only by e-mail but also through the Council website and by telephone if necessary'.[16] Likewise the Security Council requested the Secretariat to 'make the schedules of all meetings and provisional agenda of the subsidiary bodies of the Council available to the public, through their websites and the *Journal of the United Nations*'.[17]

Next, transparency involves *openness of the works* of the Security Council. From back in 1994, the Security Council stated it had 'heard the views of the members of the Council and many other United Nations Member states' on the need to increase the number of its public sessions so as 'to improve the flow of information and the exchange of ideas between members of the Council and other United Nations Member states'.[18] This intention led to

[12] Note S/26015, 30 June 1993: Adoption of the report of the Security Council to the General Assembly; Note S/2017/507, para 11.

[13] Note S/1998/354, 30 April 1998; Note S/2017/507, para 5.

[14] Note S/26176, 27 July 1993: Tentative forecast of the Programme of work of the Security Council; and Note S/1998/354, 30 April 1998: Reminder in the Journal re: monthly programme of work; Note S/2017/507, para 8.

[15] Note S/26812, 29 November 1993; S/2017/507, para 12.

[16] S/2017/507, para 6.

[17] ibid para 103.

[18] Statement by the President, S/PRST/1994/81, 16 December 1994.

the establishment of a typology of Security Council meetings in an attempt to extend the category of 'public meetings' and to limit 'private meetings' as far as possible.[19]

Openness also means improving the dissemination of the Security Council's works. In 1997 the Security Council revised the format and contents of its annual reports to make them more informative.[20] The President was asked to hold information meetings after plenary consultations[21] and the adoption of the work programme,[22] as well as other informal information meetings at the end of their presidency,[23] to work with the Secretariat to draw the attention of all stakeholders, including non-state actors, to the statements and decisions of the Council,[24] and to prepare a monthly assessment of their presidency in a timely manner.[25] The overhaul of the website is part of this policy to communicate regarding the Security Council's work.

Finally transparency involves *access to information and documentation* of the Security Council and its subsidiary organs. A number of measures were taken to facilitate access to all the Security Council's documentation, including for example draft resolutions or statements from the President at the stage when presented to consultations of the whole.[26] Similarly, the Security Council set out a number of measures for providing access to the works of its subsidiary bodies and especially its sanctions committees.[27]

B. Participation in Deliberations and Decision making

The second requirement for democratising the Security Council is participation. The legitimacy of decision making rests on a deliberation that is *open* to the *relevant* parties, that is, to the actors with an interest, a right or who are able to contribute their expertise. The reforms of the last 20 years have thus contributed to extending participation to a wider range of actors in *deliberation* and in *actual decision making*.

[19] Note S/1999/1291, para 5; S/2017/507, para 3 and the commitment to increase recourse to open meetings and para 21 et sq on the format of meetings.

[20] Note S/1997/451, 12 June 1997. Matters concerning the preparation of the Annual Report of the Security Council; Note S/1998/1016, 30 October 1998: Security Council working methods and procedures; Note S/2002/199, 26 February 2002, re-published on 22 May 2002, Annual report of the Security Council to the General Assembly; Note S/2012/922, para 9–12; Note S/2015/944; Note S/2017/507, para 125.

[21] S/1999/1291, para 3; S/2017/507, para 55.

[22] S/2017/507, para 4.

[23] S/2012/922, para 14; S/2017/507, § 7.

[24] S/2001/640, 29 June 2001; S/2017/507, para 87.

[25] S/2017/507, para 136.

[26] S/1994/230, 29 February 1994, § 1. S/1999/1291, 30 December 1999, para 2. S/2017/507, para 84.

[27] S/1995/234, 29 mars 1995: Procedure to improve the transparency of the Sanctions Committees; S/2017/507, paras 103 et sq.

The requirement of democratisation relates primarily on inclusive, open and transparent processes of deliberation, taking account of the points of view and interests of all stakeholders. There is no set circle for consultation but circles that vary in size with the subjects and situations. The reforms of the last 20 years have tended to open Council deliberations to states that are not Council members and to other actors too. The principle of non-member participation has been generally accepted[28] and specified in a certain number of particular instances.

First, with respect to *states*. Several measures have been recommended with a view to widening the circle and facilitating the participation of non-member states. It is planned to have newly elected states to observe all meetings of the Council for a period of three months before the beginning of their term of membership,[29] so that they can familiarise themselves with the procedure and the issues being treated.

In the periodic review of questions brought before the Security Council, the Council may decide to delete a question unless any one state, even a non-member of the Council, objects. To ensure there are no objections, the list is communicated beforehand to all UN members.[30] More specifically, the Council tends to apply the principle that any *state concerned* or affected by a question *must* be consulted: 'The members of the Security Council intend to seek the views of Member States that are parties to a conflict and/or other interested and affected parties. […] The Security Council, when it deems appropriate, may also utilise informal dialogues.'[31]

One particular question concerns the countries providing military contingents and police personnel. The Council has issued several notes on this subject, progressively organising a systematic and continual procedure of consultation of these states, with a commitment to 'ensuring the full consideration of the views and concerns of troop- and police-contributing countries'.[32] Similar recommendations are made with respect to sanctions committees, which are asked to periodically consult the states concerned or affected by sanctions.[33]

[28] S/2017/507, para 21.

[29] S/2000/155, 28 February 2000: Observance of informal consultations by newly elected members prior to starting their term; S/2002/1276: Attendance of newly elected members of the Security Council prior to the start of their term; S/2004/939: idem, supersedes the previous note. S/2017/507, paras 140–142.

[30] S/1996/603, 30 July 1996. S/1996/704, 29 August 1996; S/2017/507, §§ 15–16.

[31] S/2017/507, para 92.

[32] S/2013/630, 28 October 2013; S/PRST/1996/13, 28 March 1996, Improvement of procedures for meetings among troop-contributing countries, Council members and the Secretariat; S/1998/1016, 30 October 1998; S/PRST/2001/3; S/2002/56, 14 January 2002: Security Council Working Group on Peacekeeping Operations; Note S/2013/630, 28 October 2013; S/PRST/2015/26, 31 December 2015, on consultations between the Security Council, troop- and police-contributing countries and the Secretariat (triangular consultations); S/2017/507, pt VIII.

[33] S/1995/438, 31 May 1995: Procedures during meetings of the Sanctions Committees; S/1999/92, 29 January 1999: Proposals to improve the work of the sanctions committees, para 8; S/2017/507, para 106.

States apart, the Security Council extends the circle of deliberation to all organisations that play a functional or operational part in connection with operations decided on by the Council. This is the case in particular of regional and sub-regional organisations that the Council wishes to consult.[34]

However, the Security Council's leading interlocutor remains the UN Secretariat. Not just the Secretary-General but all the elements of the Secretariat, generally at a high level of responsibility.[35] The Secretariat is very regularly called on to give 'an ad hoc briefing … in cases in which an emergent situation which justifies a briefing arises' or 'ad hoc briefings at informal consultations on a daily basis, if necessary, when a situation justifies such briefings'.[36]

Lastly, the Security Council consults other non-governmental actors and especially independent experts – particularly Human Rights Council experts – but also actors from civil society and NGOs. To do this it uses the celebrated 'Arria-formula', named after Venezuela's former permanent representative at the UN, who sat on the Council in 1992 and 1993 and inaugurated the practice in 1992.[37] Examples of the Arria-formula are now extremely numerous.[38] The same opening with respect to non-governmental actors can be observed when the Security Council carries out missions in the field.

The question of the decision-making process is obviously more intricate and there is a die-hard tradition of secret negotiations and the primacy of the P5 in the process. The E10 (then non-permanent members) seek to ensure that all Security Council member states may have the opportunity not just to take initiatives but to participate in drafting the initiatives of others and especially P5 initiatives. This question of the *penholder* seems high on the agenda for some years and is a challenge to the P5's control over the decision-making process.[39]

In addition, the Council expresses its intention to *consult* very widely all the relevant parties in the negotiation process. It is something else to know whether these good intentions will come to be applied. A separate question – but that relates equally to a decision-making process – concerns the appointment of the presidents of the subsidiary bodies. Here too a sort of revolt against the P5's control has led to the adoption of texts calling for a more open and transparent procedure.[40]

[34] Note S/2017/507, para 96.

[35] S/1998/1016, 30 October 1998, para 1.

[36] S/2017/507, para 61.

[37] ibid para 98.

[38] See the count on the website of the NGO *Security Council Report* at www.securitycouncilreport.org/un-security-council-working-methods/arria-formula-meetings.php.

[39] S/1999/165: Participation in the preparation of the resolutions of the Council and statements by the President of the Council; S/2014/268, 14 April 2014; S/2017/507, para 78 et sq. See also the research report from Security Council Report, *The Penholder System*, 2018, no 3, 21 December 2018.

[40] S/2012/937, para 2; S/2017/507, paras 111 et sq.

C. Accountability

The question of accountability is raised as part of the reform of the Security Council's working methods so as to ensure, as far as can be done, that the decisions of the Council or its subsidiary bodies comply with international law, so that these bodies are held to due account and especially so that there are ways and means of challenging their decisions.

In truth the Council has not gone so far as to impose its own limits on its normative power much less to allow any form of appeal against its decisions. It is only insofar as greater transparency facilitates accountability that the Security Council can be said at this point in time to have taken steps in this regard. At present it is hard to see the Council accepting to submit to any judicial or even quasi-judicial review of its decisions. The question of supervision of the lawfulness of the Council's resolutions remains open then, with the International Court of Justice being probably the best placed candidate for the job.[41]

The Council has been forced to take steps to ensure greater 'accountability' of the sanctions committees whose decisions have been increasingly contested. It is the threat of paralysis of the sanctions system that has prompted the Council to act. First in the context of sanctions against Iraq, the Council was led to ask the committees to better evaluate the humanitarian and economic impact of their sanctions, which meant closer consultation especially with the countries most directly affected.[42] In the same spirit, the same provisions enable humanitarian organisations to apply directly to the committees for 'humanitarian exemptions' from the sanctions regime.[43] But it is primarily the procedure of inclusion on lists drawn up by the sanctions committees that has prompted most protest and contestation including in terms of litigation in national and European courts and tribunals.[44] The Council has responded by introducing two measures.

First, it has put in place a *focal point to receive de-listing requests* as part of the Secretariat, created by Resolution 1730 (2006): any individuals or entities whose names are included on lists established by application of several resolutions relating to terrorism may apply for them to be de-listed either

[41] See esp M Bedjaoui, 'Du contrôle de légalité des actes du Conseil de sécurité' in *Nouveaux itinéraires en droit. Hommage à François Rigaux* (Brussels, Bruylant, 1993) 68–110; M Bedjaoui, *Nouvel ordre mondial et contrôle de légalité des actes du Conseil de sécurité* (Brussels, Bruylant, 1994); G Guillaume, 'Quel contrôle sur les mesures de sécurité collective ?' in SFDI (Journée franco-tunisienne), *Les métamorphoses de la sécurité collective – droit, pratique et enjeux stratégiques* (Paris, Pédone, 2005) 241–52; V Bore Eveno, 'Le contrôle juridictionnel des résolutions du Conseil de sécurité: vers un constitutionnalisme international?' (2006) 4 *RGDIP* 827–60.

[42] S/1999/92, 29 January 1999.

[43] ibid para 14–15 and esp § 15.

[44] For an overview of the dispute from a comparative perspective see U Candas and A Miron, 'Assonances et dissonances dans la mise en œuvre des sanctions ciblées onusiennes par l'Union européenne et les ordres juridiques nationaux' (2011) 3 *JDI*, chron 8.

via the focal point process or via their state of residence or citizenship. Next, the Council resolved to implement a more robust mechanism with greater guarantees further to the *Kadi* case.[45] This took the form of the Office of the Ombudsperson tasked more specifically with including on the lists of Committee 1267 the names of anyone suspected of belonging to or being linked to Al-Qaida (Resolution 1904 of 17 December 2009).[46] Despite all its shortcomings, this is certainly the first institution actually subject to the rule of law in the Security Council's procedures. After collating the necessary information, the Ombudsperson presents a report to the Committee and may recommend the name be maintained on the list or de-listed. When the Ombudsperson recommends that the Committee contemplate de-listing, the individual or entity is de-listed unless the Committee decides by consensus within 60 days to maintain the listing.

While these are steps in the right direction, we are still a long way from any true accountability of the Council for its decisions. The shortcomings of the two mechanisms have been pointed out unanimously by the European Court of Justice,[47] by the UN Special Rapporteur on the promotion and protection of human rights while countering terrorism[48] and also by the Grand Chamber of the European Court of Human Rights in its judgment in *Al-Dulimi and Montana Management Inc v Switzerland*.[49] Commenting although exclusively on the *focal-point* mechanism under resolution 1730 (2006) – which was the only one the applicant could have access to – the Court found that '[a]ccess to these procedures could not therefore replace appropriate judicial scrutiny at the level of the respondent state or even partly compensate for the lack of such scrutiny'.[50] The three persons who successively served as Ombudsperson were to some extent critical of the procedure being implemented despite advances in recent years. Progress still needs to be made especially in terms of transparency and disclosure of the reasons

[45] On the case concerning *Kadi*, see esp D Simon and A Rigaux, 'Le jugement des pourvois dans les affaires Kadi et Al Barakaat: smart sanctions pour le Tribunal de première instance?', *Europe*, 2008, étude 9; J-P Jacqué, 'Primauté du droit international versus protection des droits fondamentaux' (2009) *RTDE* 161–79.

[46] See esp J Kokott and C Sobotta, 'The Kadi Case – Constitutional Core Values and International Law – Finding the Balance?' (2012) 23(4) *EJIL* 1015–24; GL Willis, 'Security Council Targeted Sanctions, Due Process and the 1267 Ombudsperson' (2011) 42 *Georgetown Journal of International Law* 673–745.

[47] Especially in judgments *Kadi I* and *Kadi II*: respectively Case C-402/05 P, *Kadi v Council and Commission* (ECJ, Grand Chamber, 3 September 2008); Joined cases C-584/10 P, C-593/10 P and C-595/10 P, *Commission and Others v Kadi* (ECJ, Grand Chamber, 18 July 2013).

[48] See the report of the Special Rapporteur A/67/396, 26 September 2012.

[49] Case of *Al-Dulimi and Montana Management Inc v Switzerland*, App no 5809/08 (ECtHR, Grand Chamber, 21 June 2016). See L-A Sicilianos, 'The European Court of Human Rights facing the Security Council: towards systemic harmonization' (2017) 66(4) *ICLQ* 783–804; A Orakhelashvili, 'Al-Dulimi v. Switzerland' (2016) 110(4) *American Journal of International Law* 767–74.

[50] *Al-Dulimi and Montana Management Inc v Switzerland* (n 50), para 153.

for decisions. In the ninth report of the Ombudsperson, Ms Kimberley Prost claimed that 'the Ombudsperson process remains one which is unnecessarily shrouded in mystery'.[51] Her successor, Catherine Marchi-Uhel, had to face the decision by the Committee to discontinue its practice of providing 'substantive reason letters' to petitioners, taking up excerpts of the Ombudsperson's analysis – that is some kind of quasi-judicial motivation.[52] The line of argument developed against such opacity is interesting because it leads us back to the question of legitimacy. Greater transparency – and therefore accountability – is what the procedure needs in order to safeguard the UN sanctions regime from criticism and from resorting to different courts of law that are led to challenge the primacy of United Nations law over states' other commitments. Again, it is a call for more democracy. To quote Kimberley Prost in the ninth report, failure to comply with the obligation to state reasons for decisions 'perpetuates an appearance of arbitrariness with respect to a process established by the Security Council which can otherwise be demonstrated to meet the requirement of fairness. As such, this lack of transparency jeopardises the overall fairness of the procedure and most significantly the perceptions as to its reasonableness'.[53]

IV. Conclusions

The measures presented here and the Security Council's efforts to introduce greater transparency in the organisation of its works and its decision making suggest that the Council can be reformed without amending the Charter. Such a reform essentially means making the Council more democratic. Perhaps such democratisation will bring about representative democracy, by enlargement of the Council. I have stated my doubts about this in terms of the actual feasibility of such enlargement and even more so of the relevance of the connection that is made between enlargement and democratisation. There remains, then, the other pathway, that of deliberative democracy. This involves greater transparency, greater participation by all concerned and greater accountability of the Council both prospectively and retrospectively.

Ultimately it is the question of the rule of law that is raised. Can and should the Security Council be subject to law? The question may seem complex but the answer is after all straightforward in legal terms. Article 24(2) of the UN Charter provides that '[i]n discharging these duties the Security Council shall act in accordance with the Purposes and Principles of the United Nations'.

[51] Ninth Report of the Ombudsperson: S/2015/80, 2 February 2015, para 41.

[52] Thirteenth Report of the Ombudsperson, S/2017/60, para 28; Fourteenth report of the Ombudsperson, S/2017/685, para 25; Fifteenth Report of the Ombudsperson, S/2018/120, para 25.

[53] Ninth Report of the Ombudsperson: S/2015/80, 2 February 2015, para 44.

The Charter includes among the purposes and principles of the United Nations to achieve international cooperation 'in promoting and encouraging respect for human rights and for fundamental freedoms for all without distinction as to race, sex, language, or religion'.

Yet all these reforms involving democratisation of the Council cannot overcome a fundamental problem not addressed here,[54] but that cannot be ignored. The Security Council will never be subject to the rule of law so long as five of its members enjoy the privilege of blocking at will any decision supported by a majority, and even a crushing majority, of the other permanent and non-permanent members. This outdated privilege of the right of veto is in its essence incompatible with any form of democracy, whether representative or deliberative, because it grants the one the right to have its interests prevail over the interests of the many and over the general interest. Until this matter is settled one way or another, the Security Council will remain an institution of limited effectiveness and dubious legitimacy at the beck and call of the great powers.

[54] See ch 14 in this volume.

14

The Right to Veto in the United Nations: Towards the Abolition of a Privilege

In his speech to the General Assembly of the United Nations on 24 September 2013, President of France François Hollande reiterated France's call for a 'code of conduct' whereby the five permanent member states of the Security Council would decide to collectively waive their right of veto in cases of mass crimes. Foreign affairs minister Mr Laurent Fabius expanded on this proposal in the newspaper *Le Monde*. The French proposal for Security Council members to waive their right of veto was not only warranted but it should serve as a basis for the reform of international relations.

Commenting on François Hollande's speech in an article in the online edition of *Le Monde*, my friends and colleagues Professors Anne-Thida Norodom and Pierre Bodeau doubted the proposal was feasible: 'No Security Council reform will end this privilege however anachronistic or anti-democratic it may seem.' They went on to ponder how to get around this difficulty but without really coming up with any tangible solution. The problem is that there is no other solution to the dilemma pointed to by former UN Secretary General Kofi Annan in 1999 shortly after NATO's unlawful intervention against Serbia: on the one side state sovereignty must be observed as a pillar of the international order; on the other side we cannot let any repeat Srebrenicas or Rwandas unfold before our eyes. The Syrian castastrophe by itself is evidence that states have failed to solve that dilemma, at the expense of thousands of murdered civilians victims, in total impunity.

Everyone agrees that the prohibition of the use of force in international relations and the collective security system established by the UN Charter at the end of World War II are values worth saving at any price. Admittedly the Security Council is far from perfect and thought needs to be given to how to make it more representative and improve its working methods by opening it more widely, in particular to input from civil society and other actors with something to say on questions of international peace and security. But that is not the essential point. Who can fail to see that the Security Council loses credibility – and consequently the whole of the collective security system loses its value – whenever one of its permanent members prevents it from reacting in situations which, through their human consequences, endanger international peace and security.

Defenders of the veto claim that its use justifies maintaining it. But scrutiny of its use since the beginning of the 2000s demonstrates on the contrary that such a privilege is illegitimate. Each time a member uses the veto it is fundamentally for the wrong reasons.[1] The United States has used it 14 times, almost all of them to block any initiative in the Israeli–Palestinian conflict. Russia has used it 25 times. Mostly to protect its own direct interests or those of its allies, whether in the Georgian conflict, the conflict in Syria or the situations in Myanmar or Zimbabwe. As for China, it totals 13, taking under its wing the junta in Myanmar, Robert Mugabe in Zimbabwe and Bashar al Assad in Syria.

It comes down in the end either to protecting allied rulers accused of violating the rights of their nationals or to safeguarding its most direct interests in its neck of the woods. France has not used its veto since 1989. It is not free from criticism, for all that, because until 2012 it threatened to use its privilege to prevent the setting up of a 'human rights' component in the United Nations Mission for the Referendum in Western Sahara (MINURSO). In this France yielded to the demands of its long-standing friend and ally Morocco, whose motives are hard to fathom seeing how it prides itself on wanting to introduce the rule of law and democracy into this disputed territory.

The veto is useless, except for preventing the Security Council from discussing and deciding on matters that fall fully within its jurisdiction and warrant its intervention. Far from ensuring international peace and security, the veto endangers them because Security Council inertia intensifies crises and instability. There is a need now to think up a more sophisticated system for the balance of power which, without sacrificing states' interests – and not just the interests of permanent members – safeguards the effectiveness of UN action for peace.

Pending the complete abolition of the veto, the French proposal for a code of conduct therefore seems welcome. The permanent members of the Security Council would waive beforehand any use of their veto on the basis of the crime being characterised by an independent body by a procedure to be defined. It is difficult, though, to understand how the 'realist' exception proposed by Laurent Fabius might work, namely that 'the code would exclude cases where the vital national interests of a permanent member of the Security Council were at stake'. Short of specifying what these 'vital interests' refer to and the procedure by which it could be decided impartially whether these vital interests were effectively at issue, this would be letting the veto in by the back door. Would the vital interests of the state have to be weighed

[1] For the list of vetoed resolutions, see research.un.org/en/docs/sc/quick/veto. Figures updated at July 2021.

against those of populations who were victims of mass crimes? In point of fact, the Syrian case prompts us to ponder this. Should one even wait for 'mass crimes' to be committed? From the moment a government fires on peaceful demonstrators and quells any expression of dissent, the Security Council must be in a position to react to effectively prevent any deterioration of the situation.

Abolishing or restricting the use of the right of veto is part of a broader agenda for UN reform. The Charter belongs to all citizens of all countries whether or not they see themselves as citizens of the world. An effective UN is nowadays a *sine qua non* condition for maintaining international peace, whether it be preventing genocides or combatting climate change and its disastrous consequences. Today more than ever, civil society must take up the question of UN reform, advertise the issues involved, organise public information campaigns and put pressure on rulers to come up with solutions. The age of privileges is over. It can now no longer be accepted that the interests of one, no matter how powerful or rich, should prevail over the interests of all. International society, too, must move into the democratic era.

Index

www.ingramcontent.com/pod-product-compliance
Ingram Content Group UK Ltd.
Pitfield, Milton Keynes, MK11 3LW, UK
UKHW020246290926
15470UKWH00002B/765

9 781509 938520